Ames Public Library
Ames, Iowa 50010

KIMMIE66

Published by DC Comics,

1700 Broadway,

New York, NY 10019.

Printed in Canada.

DC Comics, a Warner Bros.

Entertainment Company.

ISBN: 1-4012-0373-6

ISBN: 978-1-4012-0373-3

COVER BY AARON ALEXOVICH

kimmie66

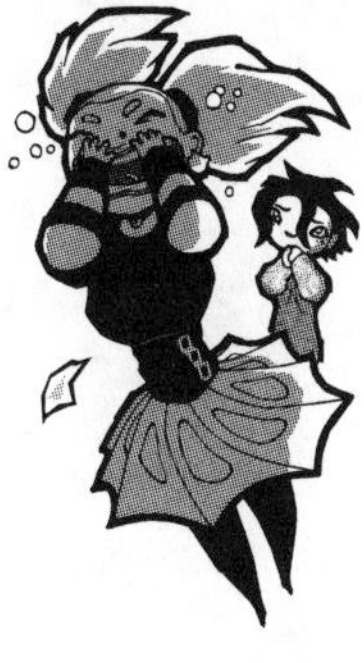

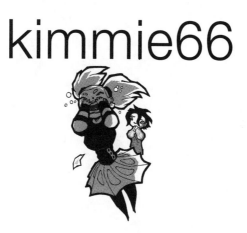

Written & Illustrated by Aaron Alexovich

Lettering by Robert Clark

minx

CHAPTER
ONE

"But.. is it *real*, Telly?"

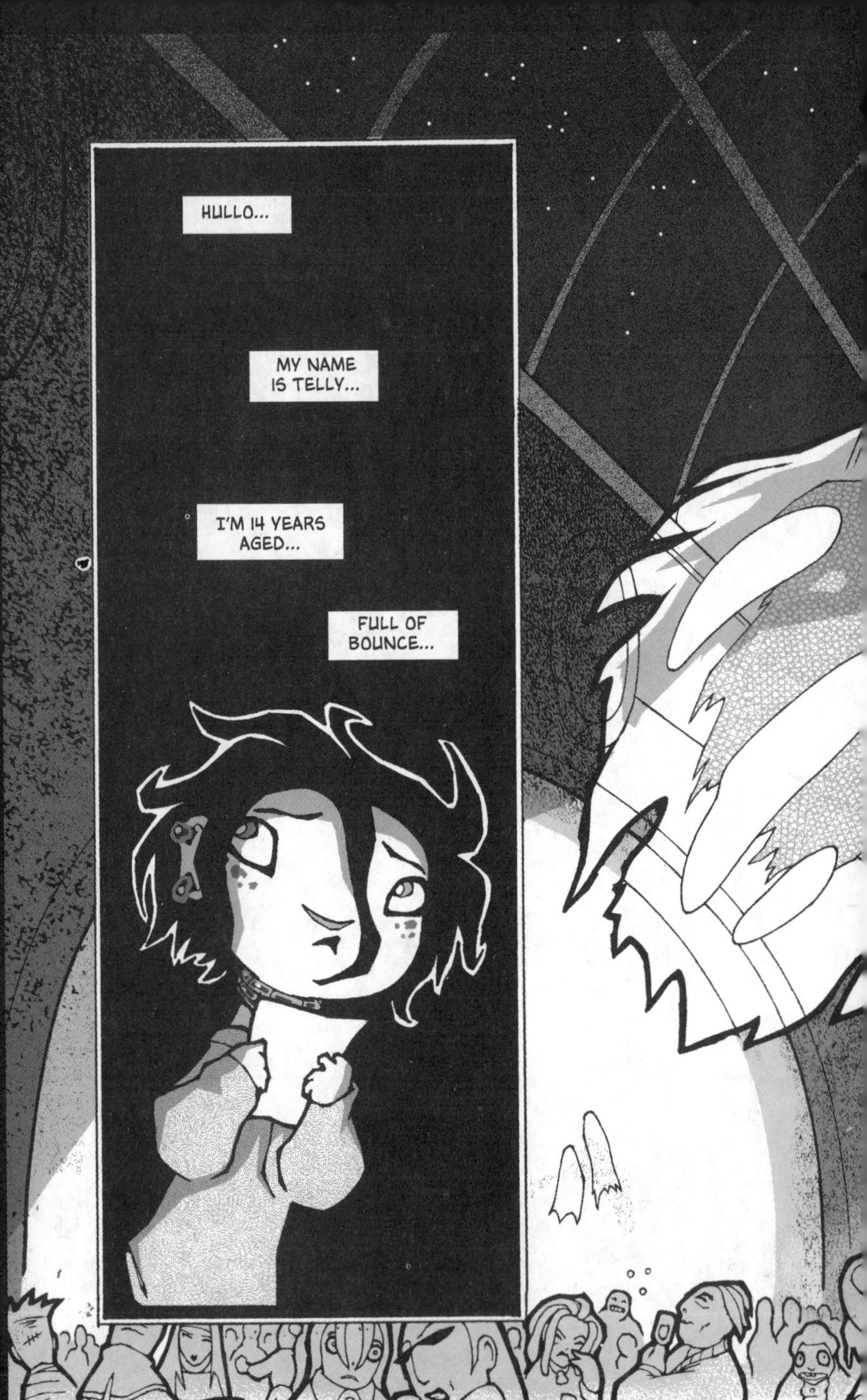
HULLO...
MY NAME IS TELLY...
I'M 14 YEARS AGED...
FULL OF BOUNCE...

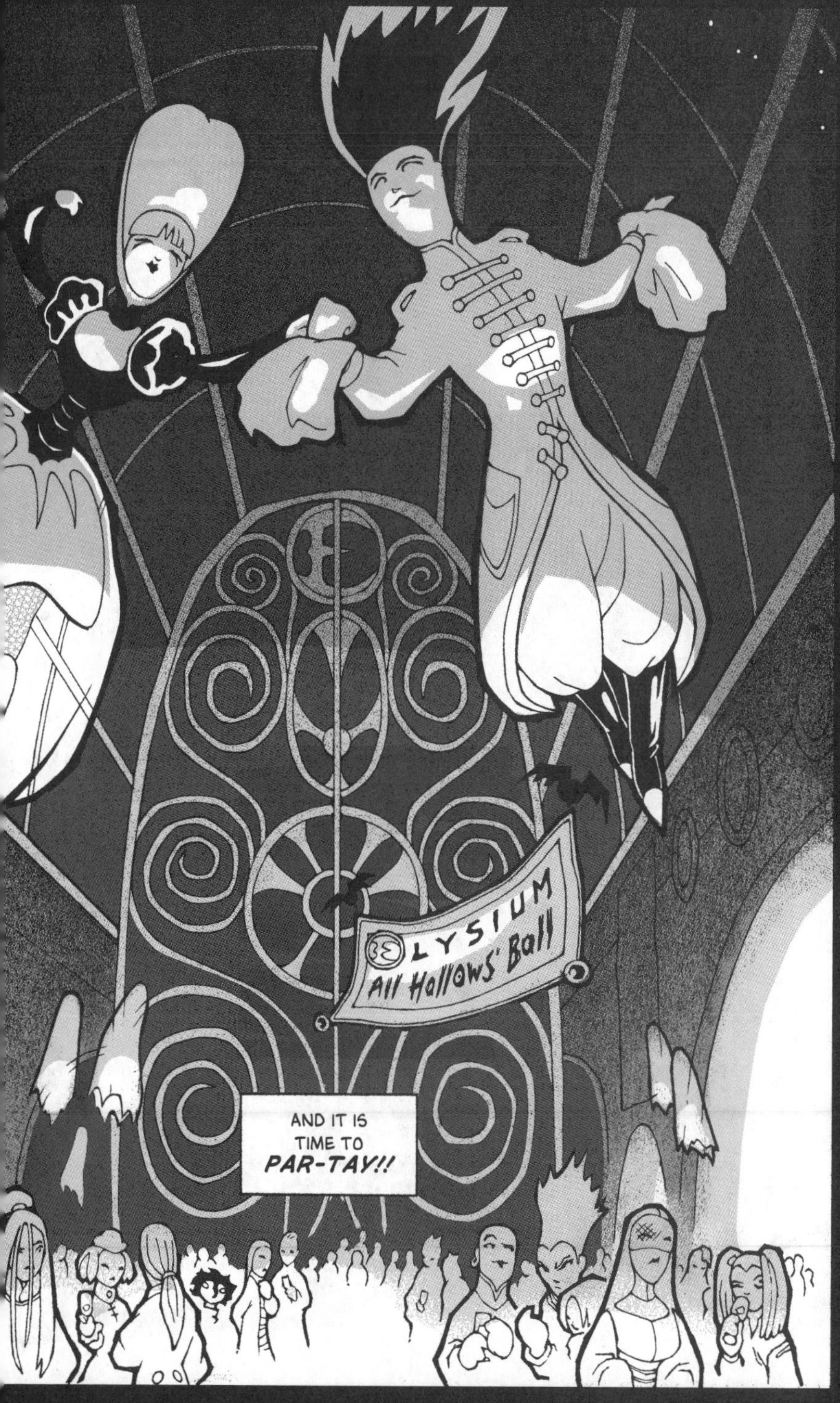
ELYSIUM
All Hallows' Ball
AND IT IS TIME TO PAR-TAY!!

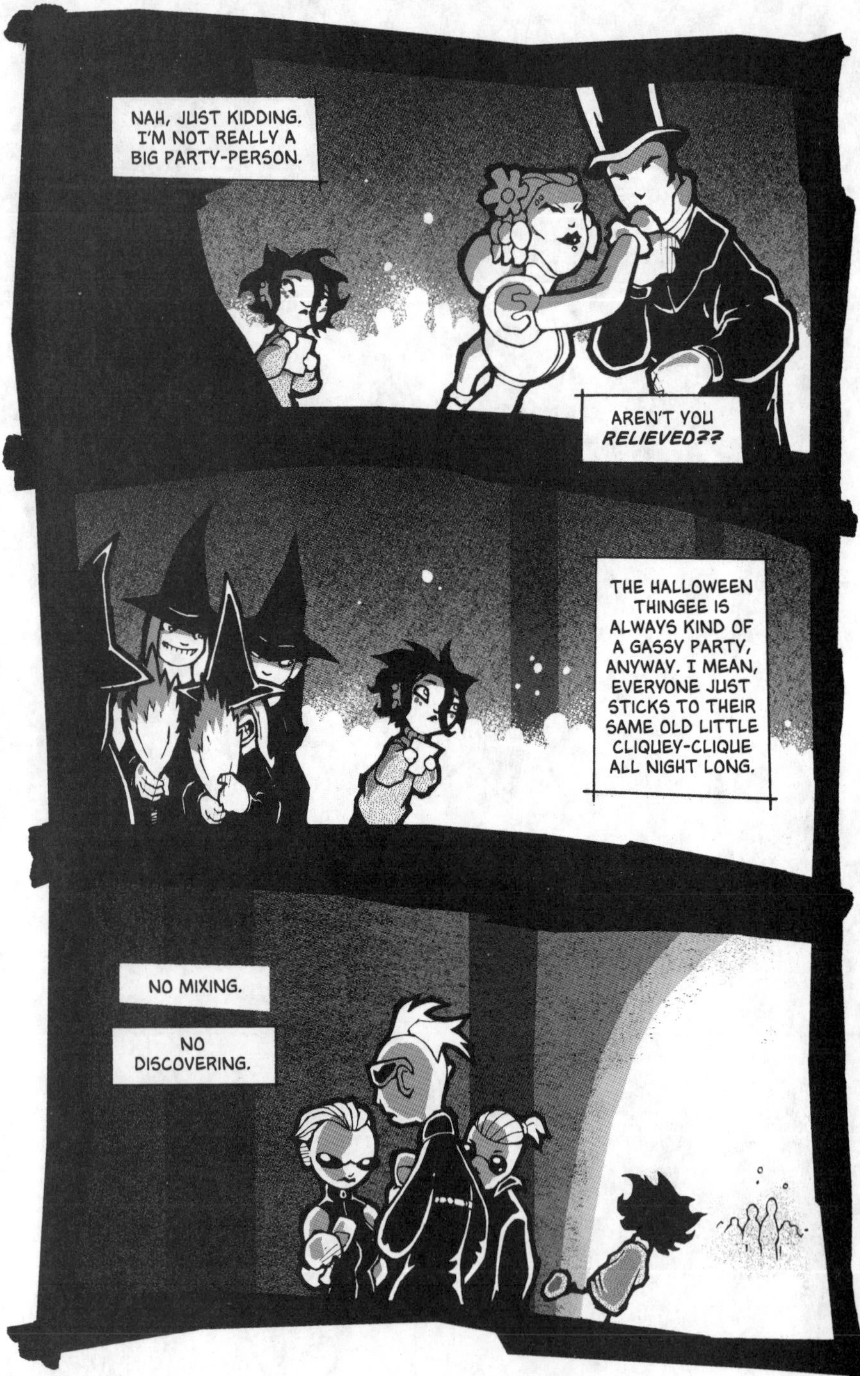
NAH, JUST KIDDING. I'M NOT REALLY A BIG PARTY-PERSON.
AREN'T YOU RELIEVED??
THE HALLOWEEN THINGEE IS ALWAYS KIND OF A GASSY PARTY, ANYWAY. I MEAN, EVERYONE JUST STICKS TO THEIR SAME OLD LITTLE CLIQUEY-CLIQUE ALL NIGHT LONG.
NO MIXING.
NO DISCOVERING.

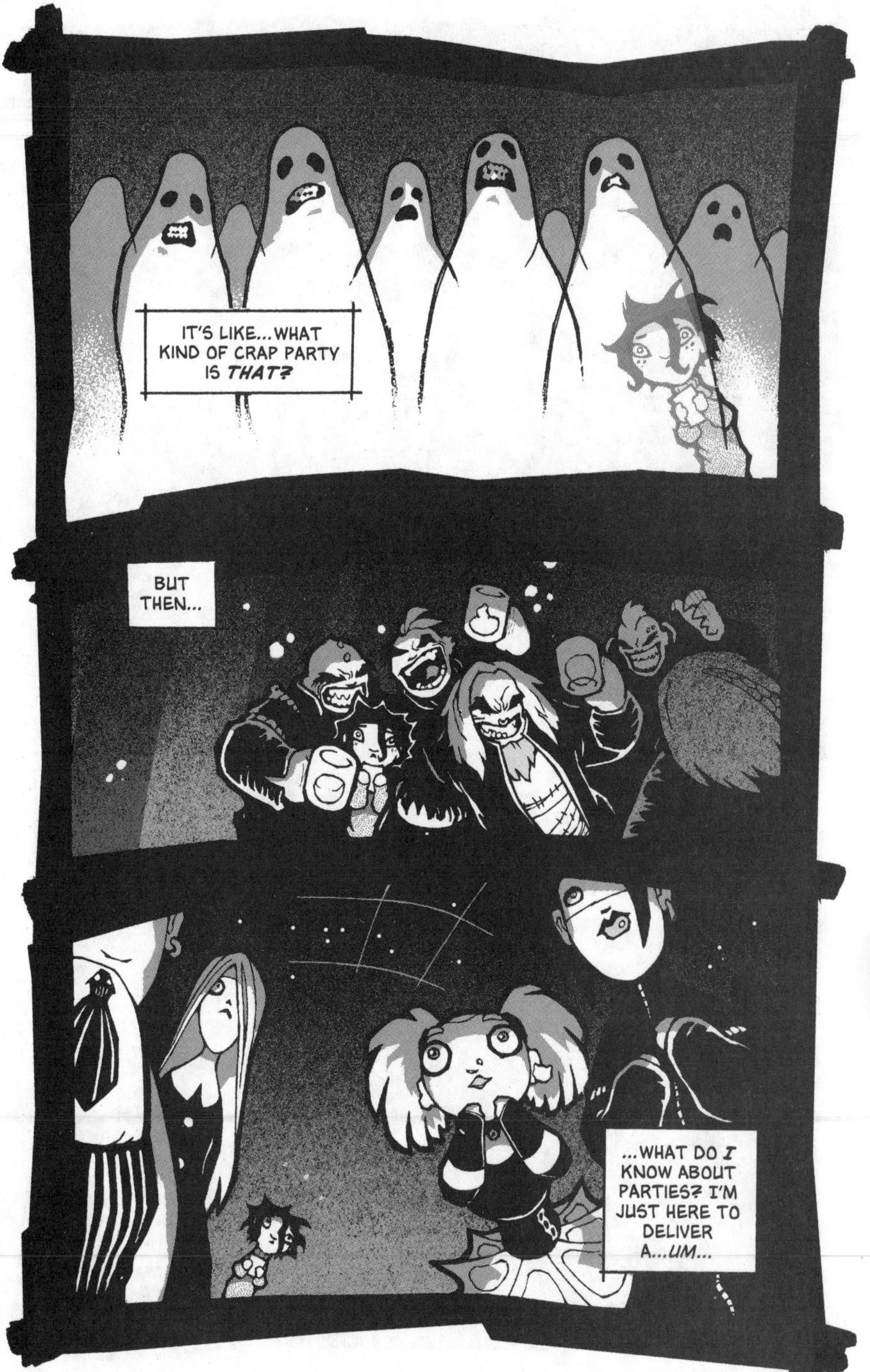
IT'S LIKE...WHAT KIND OF CRAP PARTY IS *THAT?*
BUT THEN...
...WHAT DO *I* KNOW ABOUT PARTIES? I'M JUST HERE TO DELIVER A...*UM*...

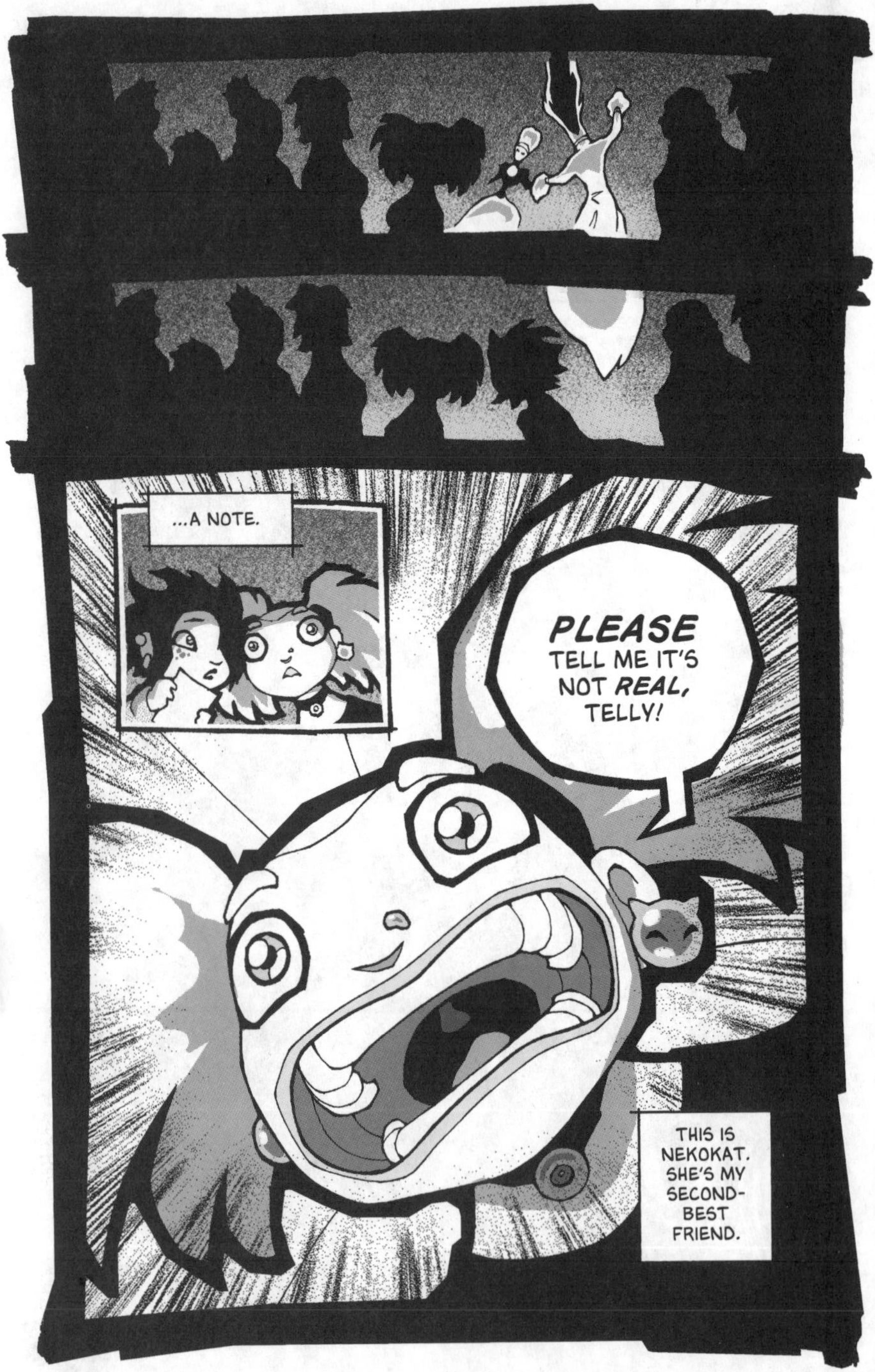
...A NOTE.
PLEASE TELL ME IT'S NOT REAL, TELLY!
THIS IS NEKOKAT. SHE'S MY SECOND-BEST FRIEND.

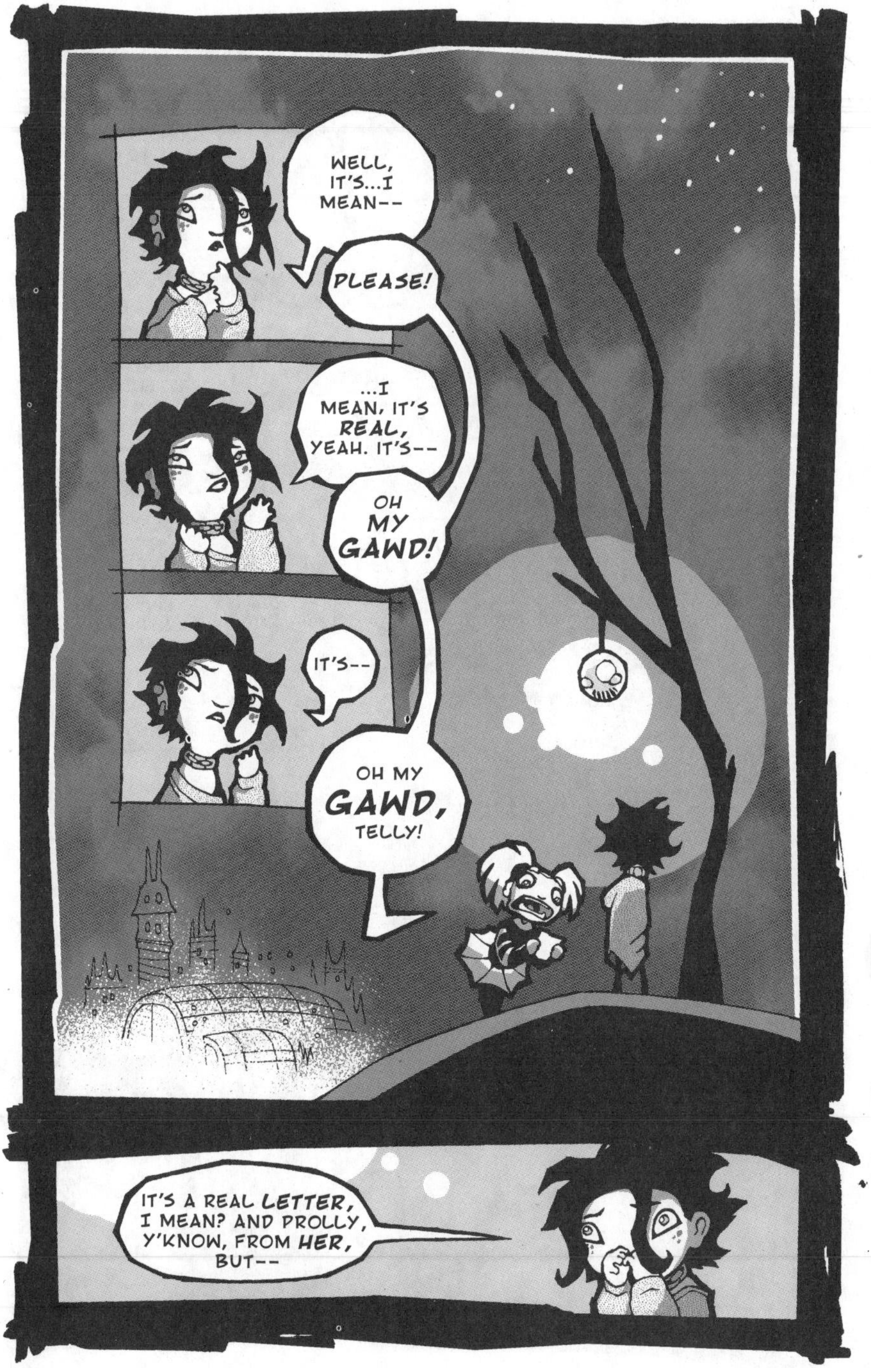
WELL, IT'S...I MEAN--
PLEASE!
...I MEAN, IT'S REAL, YEAH. IT'S--
OH MY GAWD!
IT'S--
OH MY GAWD, TELLY!
IT'S A REAL LETTER, I MEAN? AND PROLLY, Y'KNOW, FROM HER, BUT--

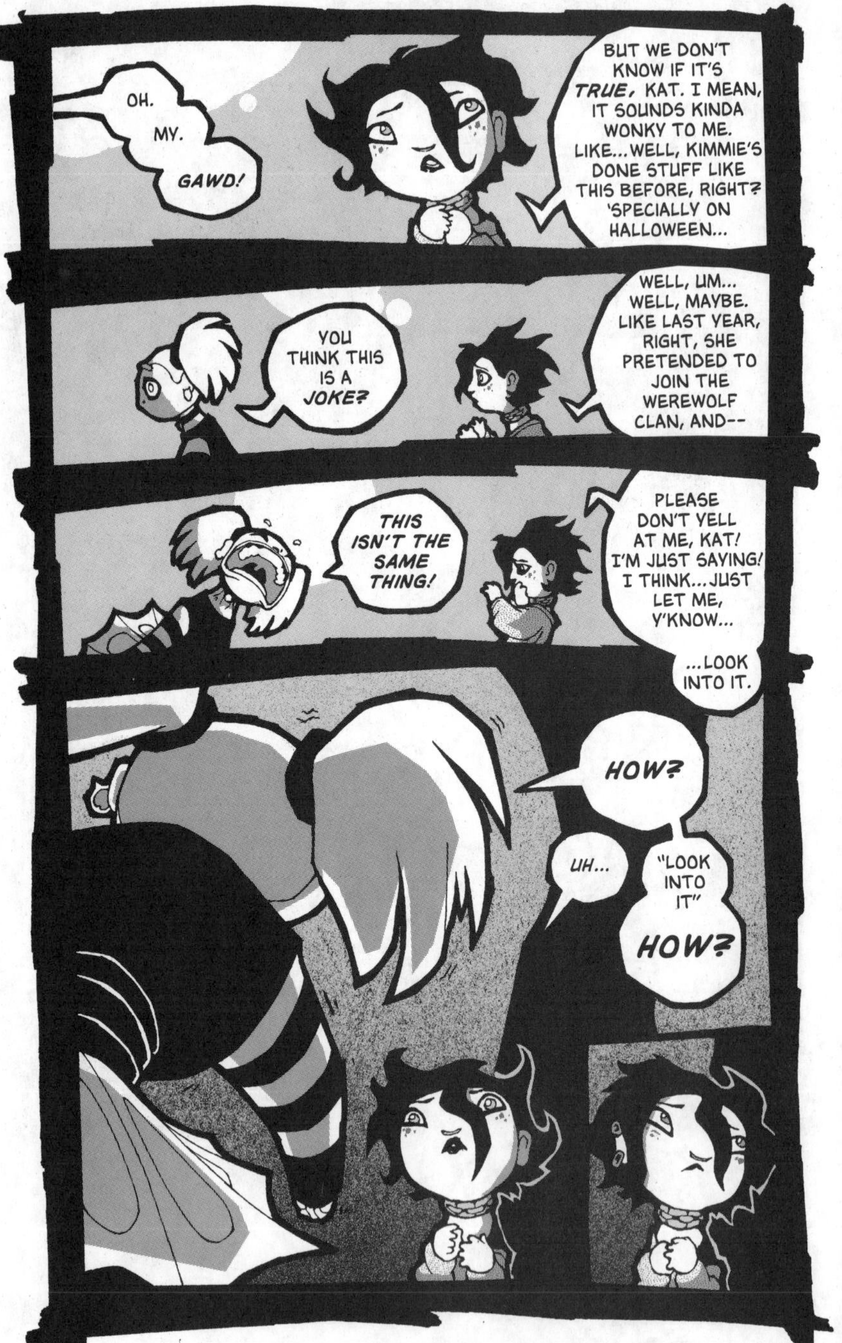

OH. MY. GAWD!
BUT WE DON'T KNOW IF IT'S TRUE, KAT. I MEAN, IT SOUNDS KINDA WONKY TO ME. LIKE... WELL, KIMMIE'S DONE STUFF LIKE THIS BEFORE, RIGHT? 'SPECIALLY ON HALLOWEEN...
YOU THINK THIS IS A JOKE?
WELL, UM... WELL, MAYBE. LIKE LAST YEAR, RIGHT, SHE PRETENDED TO JOIN THE WEREWOLF CLAN, AND--
THIS ISN'T THE SAME THING!
PLEASE DON'T YELL AT ME, KAT! I'M JUST SAYING! I THINK... JUST LET ME, Y'KNOW...
...LOOK INTO IT.
HOW?
UH...
"LOOK INTO IT" HOW?

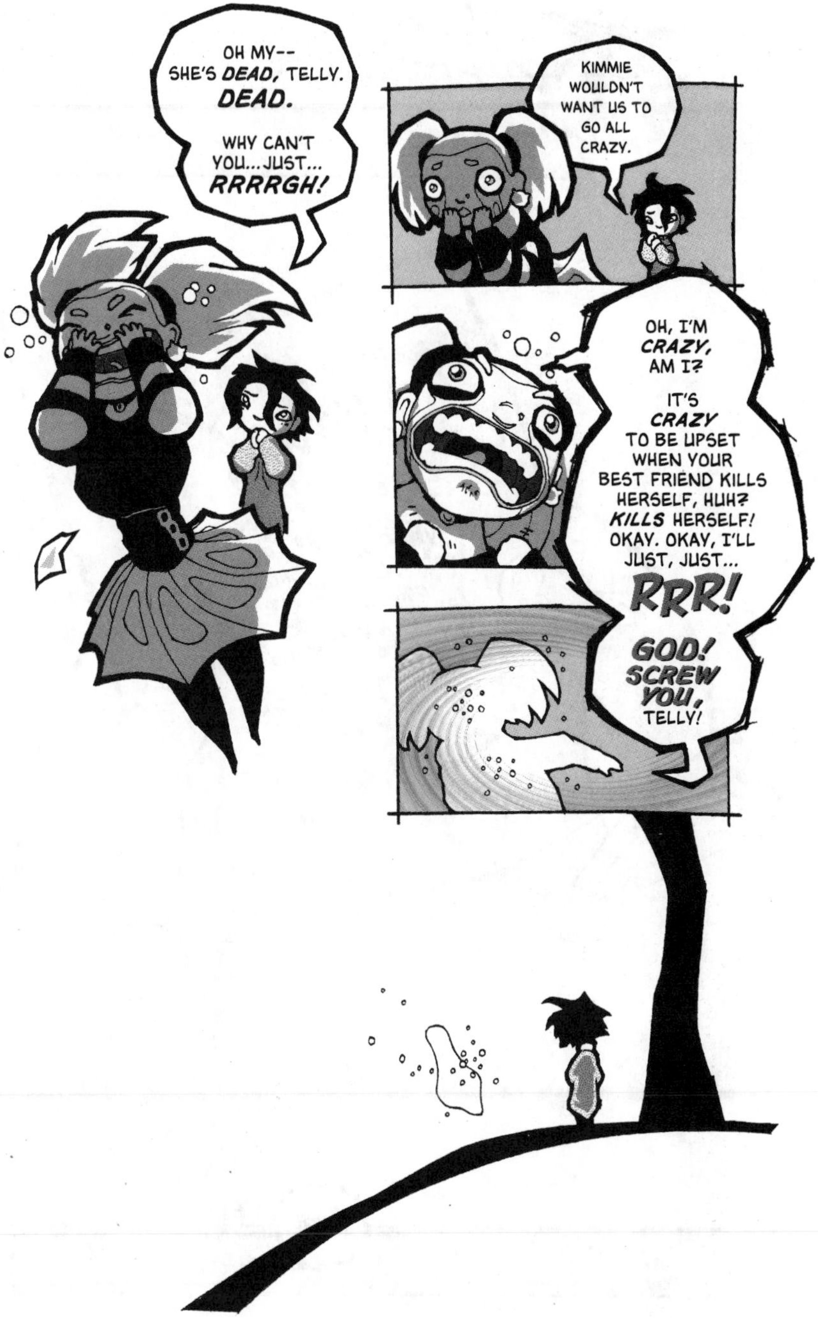

OH MY-- SHE'S DEAD, TELLY. DEAD.
WHY CAN'T YOU...JUST... RRRRGH!
KIMMIE WOULDN'T WANT US TO GO ALL CRAZY.
OH, I'M CRAZY, AM I?
IT'S CRAZY TO BE UPSET WHEN YOUR BEST FRIEND KILLS HERSELF, HUH? KILLS HERSELF! OKAY. OKAY, I'LL JUST, JUST...
RRR!
GOD! SCREW YOU, TELLY!

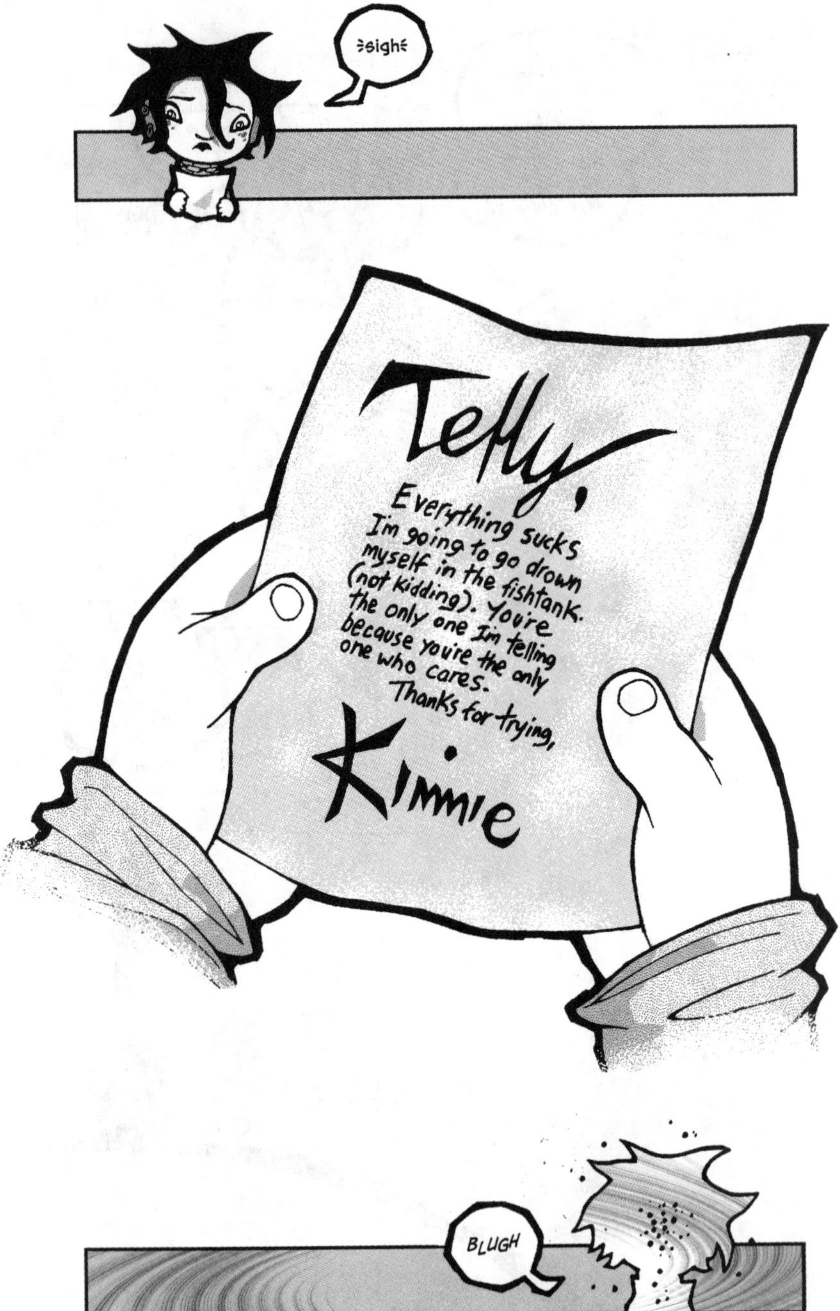

sigh
Telly,
Everything sucks
I'm going to go drown
myself in the fishtank.
(not kidding). You're
the only one I'm telling
because you're the only
one who cares.
Thanks for trying,
Kimmie
BLUGH

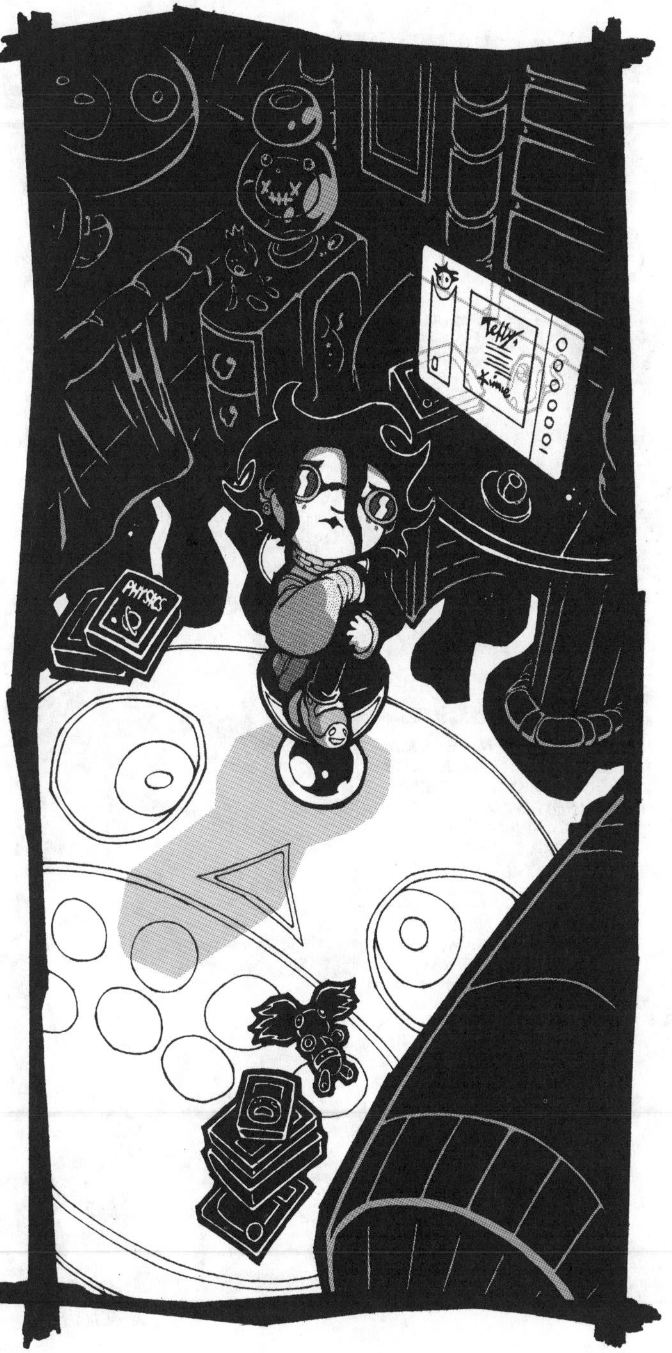

HOO.

BOY.

IT'S SUCH A PAIN IN THE BUTT WHEN YOU DON'T KNOW YOUR FRIENDS' REAL NAMES. I MEAN, PEOPLE WHO LIVE OUTSIDE THE LAIRS JUST DON'T HAVE PROBLEMS LIKE THIS, DO THEY?

IT'S LIKE... *UM*...

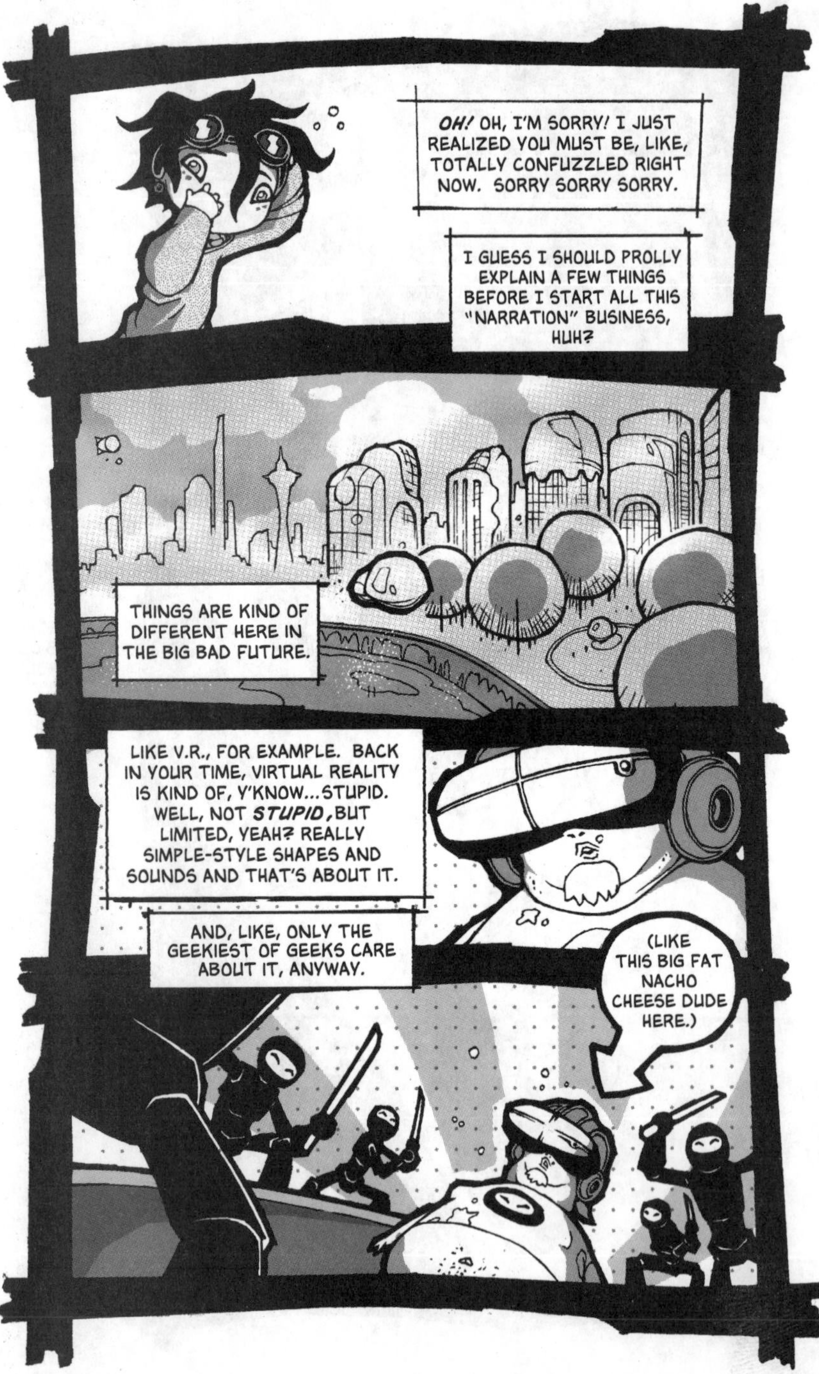
OH! OH, I'M SORRY! I JUST REALIZED YOU MUST BE, LIKE, TOTALLY CONFUZZLED RIGHT NOW. SORRY SORRY SORRY.
I GUESS I SHOULD PROLLY EXPLAIN A FEW THINGS BEFORE I START ALL THIS "NARRATION" BUSINESS, HUH?
THINGS ARE KIND OF DIFFERENT HERE IN THE BIG BAD FUTURE.
LIKE V.R., FOR EXAMPLE. BACK IN YOUR TIME, VIRTUAL REALITY IS KIND OF, Y'KNOW... STUPID. WELL, NOT STUPID, BUT LIMITED, YEAH? REALLY SIMPLE-STYLE SHAPES AND SOUNDS AND THAT'S ABOUT IT.
AND, LIKE, ONLY THE GEEKIEST OF GEEKS CARE ABOUT IT, ANYWAY.
(LIKE THIS BIG FAT NACHO CHEESE DUDE HERE.)

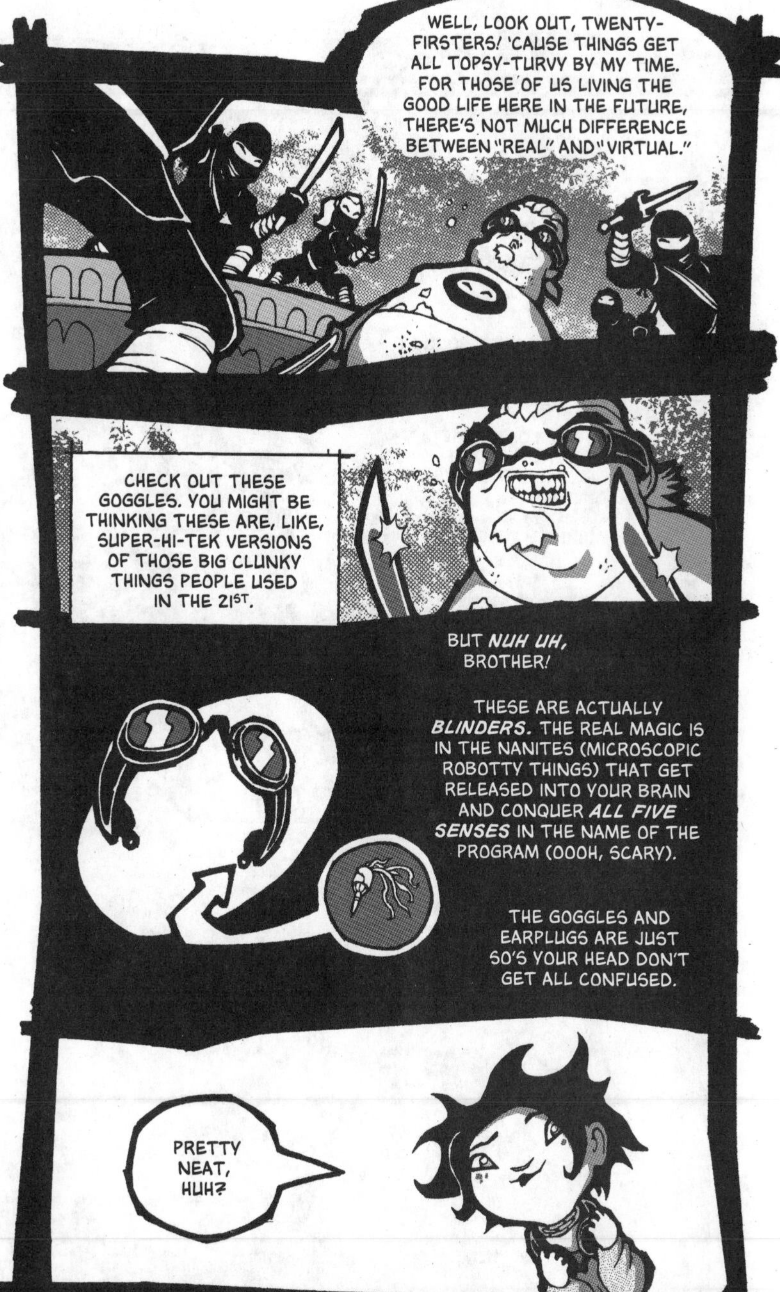
WELL, LOOK OUT, TWENTY-FIRSTERS! 'CAUSE THINGS GET ALL TOPSY-TURVY BY MY TIME. FOR THOSE OF US LIVING THE GOOD LIFE HERE IN THE FUTURE, THERE'S NOT MUCH DIFFERENCE BETWEEN "REAL" AND "VIRTUAL."
CHECK OUT THESE GOGGLES. YOU MIGHT BE THINKING THESE ARE, LIKE, SUPER-HI-TEK VERSIONS OF THOSE BIG CLUNKY THINGS PEOPLE USED IN THE 21ST.
BUT NUH UH, BROTHER!
THESE ARE ACTUALLY BLINDERS. THE REAL MAGIC IS IN THE NANITES (MICROSCOPIC ROBOTTY THINGS) THAT GET RELEASED INTO YOUR BRAIN AND CONQUER ALL FIVE SENSES IN THE NAME OF THE PROGRAM (OOOH, SCARY).
THE GOGGLES AND EARPLUGS ARE JUST SO'S YOUR HEAD DON'T GET ALL CONFUSED.
PRETTY NEAT, HUH?

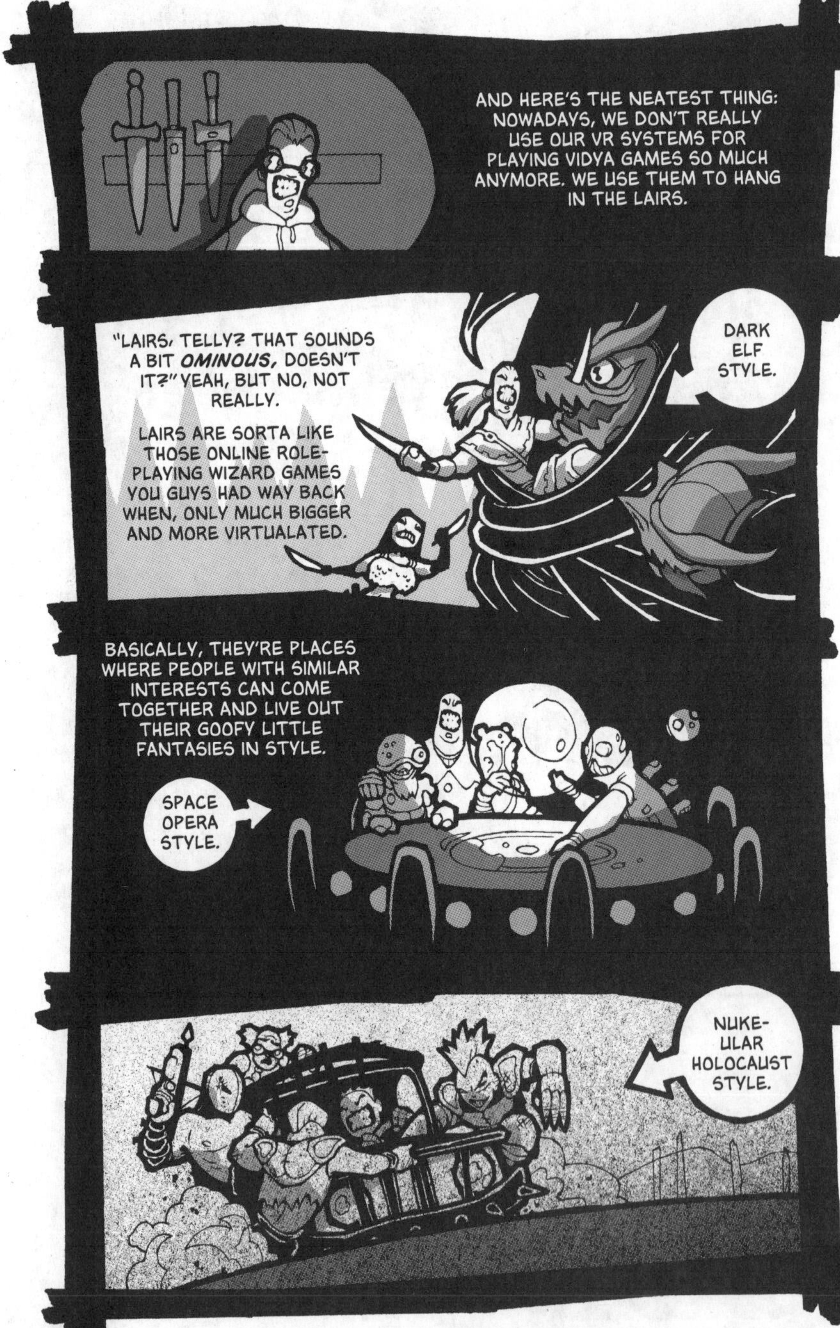

AND HERE'S THE NEATEST THING: NOWADAYS, WE DON'T REALLY USE OUR VR SYSTEMS FOR PLAYING VIDYA GAMES SO MUCH ANYMORE. WE USE THEM TO HANG IN THE LAIRS.
"LAIRS, TELLY? THAT SOUNDS A BIT *OMINOUS,* DOESN'T IT?" YEAH, BUT NO, NOT REALLY.
LAIRS ARE SORTA LIKE THOSE ONLINE ROLE-PLAYING WIZARD GAMES YOU GUYS HAD WAY BACK WHEN, ONLY MUCH BIGGER AND MORE VIRTUALATED.
DARK ELF STYLE.
BASICALLY, THEY'RE PLACES WHERE PEOPLE WITH SIMILAR INTERESTS CAN COME TOGETHER AND LIVE OUT THEIR GOOFY LITTLE FANTASIES IN STYLE.
SPACE OPERA STYLE.
NUKE-ULAR HOLOCAUST STYLE.

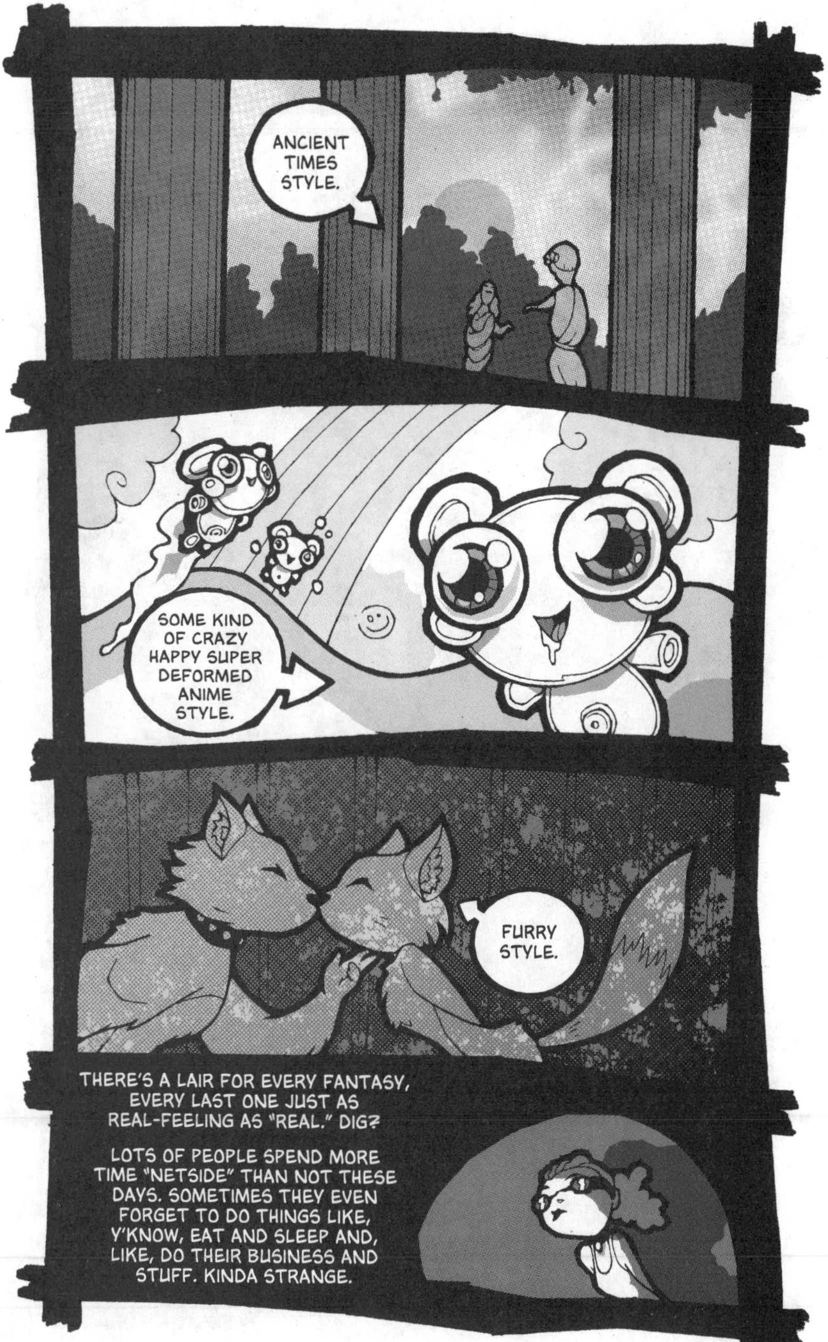
ANCIENT TIMES STYLE.
SOME KIND OF CRAZY HAPPY SUPER DEFORMED ANIME STYLE.
FURRY STYLE.
THERE'S A LAIR FOR EVERY FANTASY, EVERY LAST ONE JUST AS REAL-FEELING AS "REAL." DIG?
LOTS OF PEOPLE SPEND MORE TIME "NETSIDE" THAN NOT THESE DAYS. SOMETIMES THEY EVEN FORGET TO DO THINGS LIKE, Y'KNOW, EAT AND SLEEP AND, LIKE, DO THEIR BUSINESS AND STUFF. KINDA STRANGE.

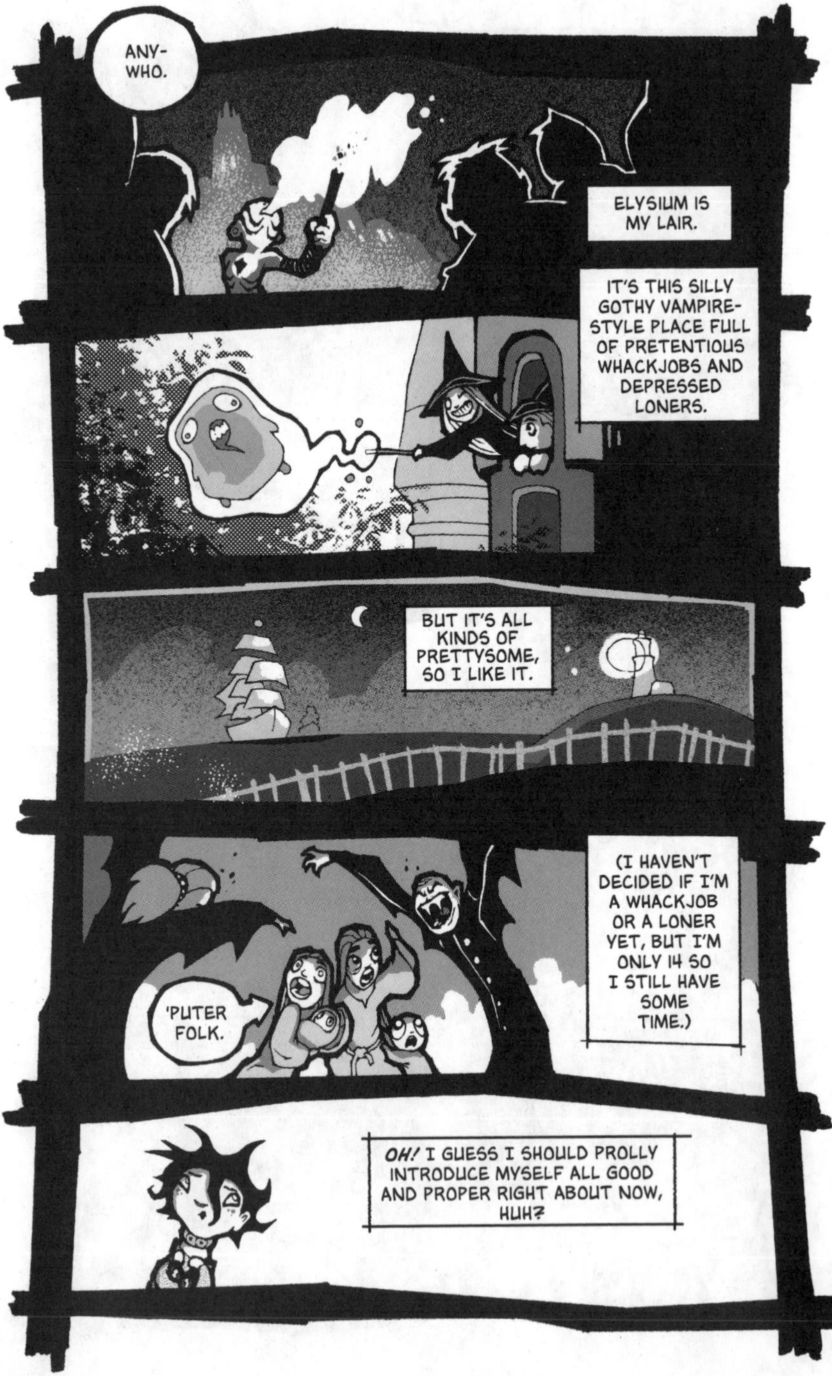
ANY-
WHO.
ELYSIUM IS
MY LAIR.
IT'S THIS SILLY
GOTHY VAMPIRE-
STYLE PLACE FULL
OF PRETENTIOUS
WHACKJOBS AND
DEPRESSED
LONERS.
BUT IT'S ALL
KINDS OF
PRETTYSOME,
SO I LIKE IT.
'PUTER
FOLK.
(I HAVEN'T
DECIDED IF I'M
A WHACKJOB
OR A LONER
YET, BUT I'M
ONLY 14 SO
I STILL HAVE
SOME
TIME.)
OH! I GUESS I SHOULD PROLLY
INTRODUCE MYSELF ALL GOOD
AND PROPER RIGHT ABOUT NOW,
HUH?

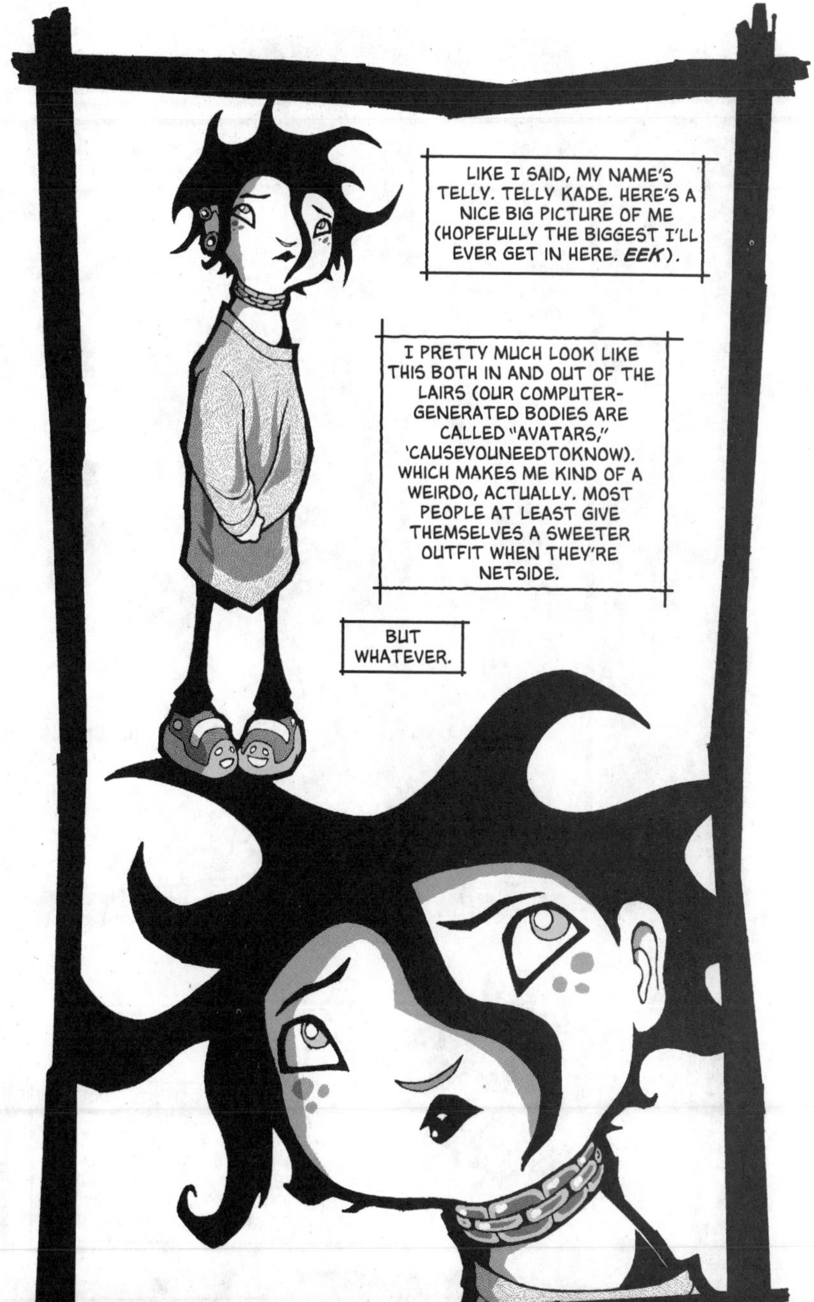

LIKE I SAID, MY NAME'S TELLY. TELLY KADE. HERE'S A NICE BIG PICTURE OF ME (HOPEFULLY THE BIGGEST I'LL EVER GET IN HERE. EEK).
I PRETTY MUCH LOOK LIKE THIS BOTH IN AND OUT OF THE LAIRS (OUR COMPUTER-GENERATED BODIES ARE CALLED "AVATARS," 'CAUSEYOUNEEDTOKNOW). WHICH MAKES ME KIND OF A WEIRDO, ACTUALLY. MOST PEOPLE AT LEAST GIVE THEMSELVES A SWEETER OUTFIT WHEN THEY'RE NETSIDE.
BUT WHATEVER.

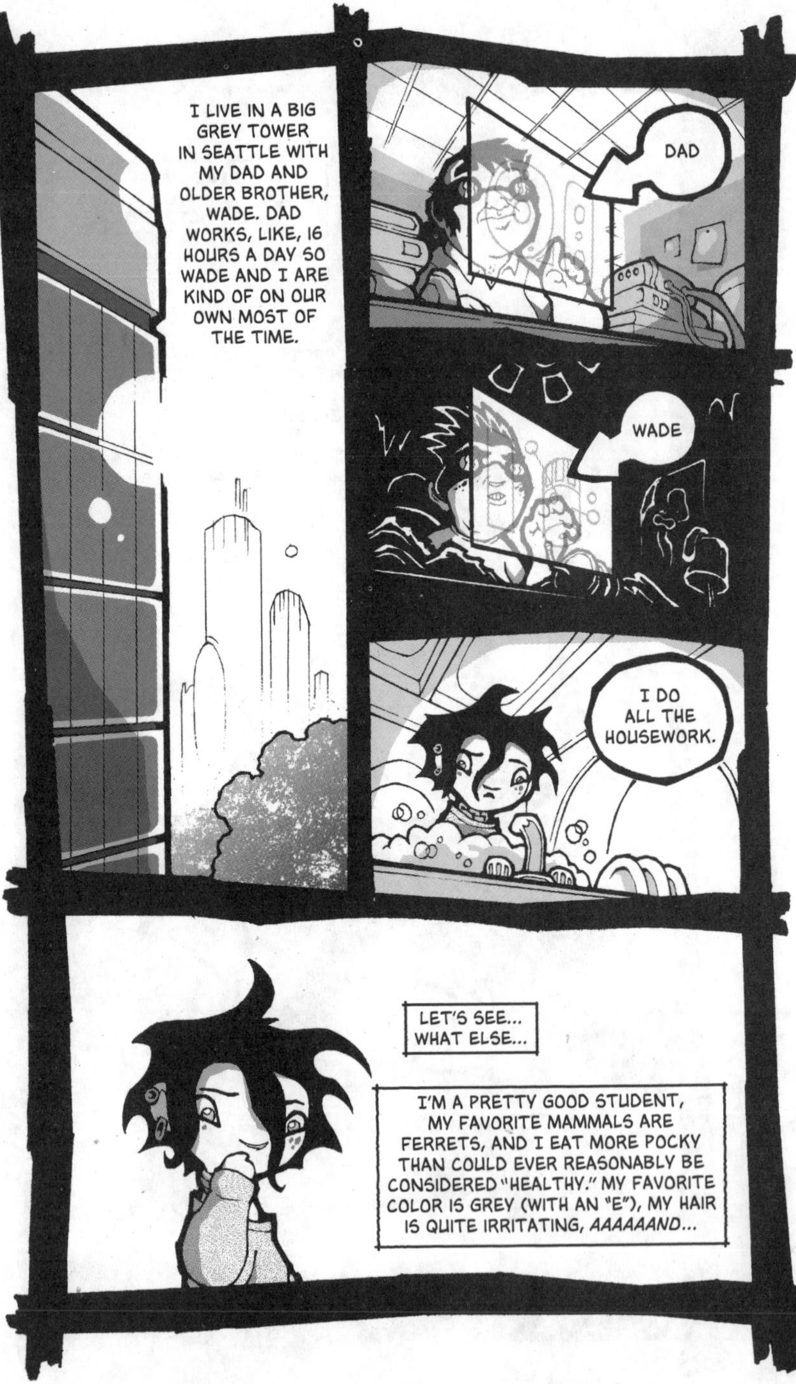
I LIVE IN A BIG GREY TOWER IN SEATTLE WITH MY DAD AND OLDER BROTHER, WADE. DAD WORKS, LIKE, 16 HOURS A DAY SO WADE AND I ARE KIND OF ON OUR OWN MOST OF THE TIME.
DAD
WADE
I DO ALL THE HOUSEWORK.
LET'S SEE... WHAT ELSE...
I'M A PRETTY GOOD STUDENT, MY FAVORITE MAMMALS ARE FERRETS, AND I EAT MORE POCKY THAN COULD EVER REASONABLY BE CONSIDERED "HEALTHY." MY FAVORITE COLOR IS GREY (WITH AN "E"), MY HAIR IS QUITE IRRITATING, *AAAAAAND...*

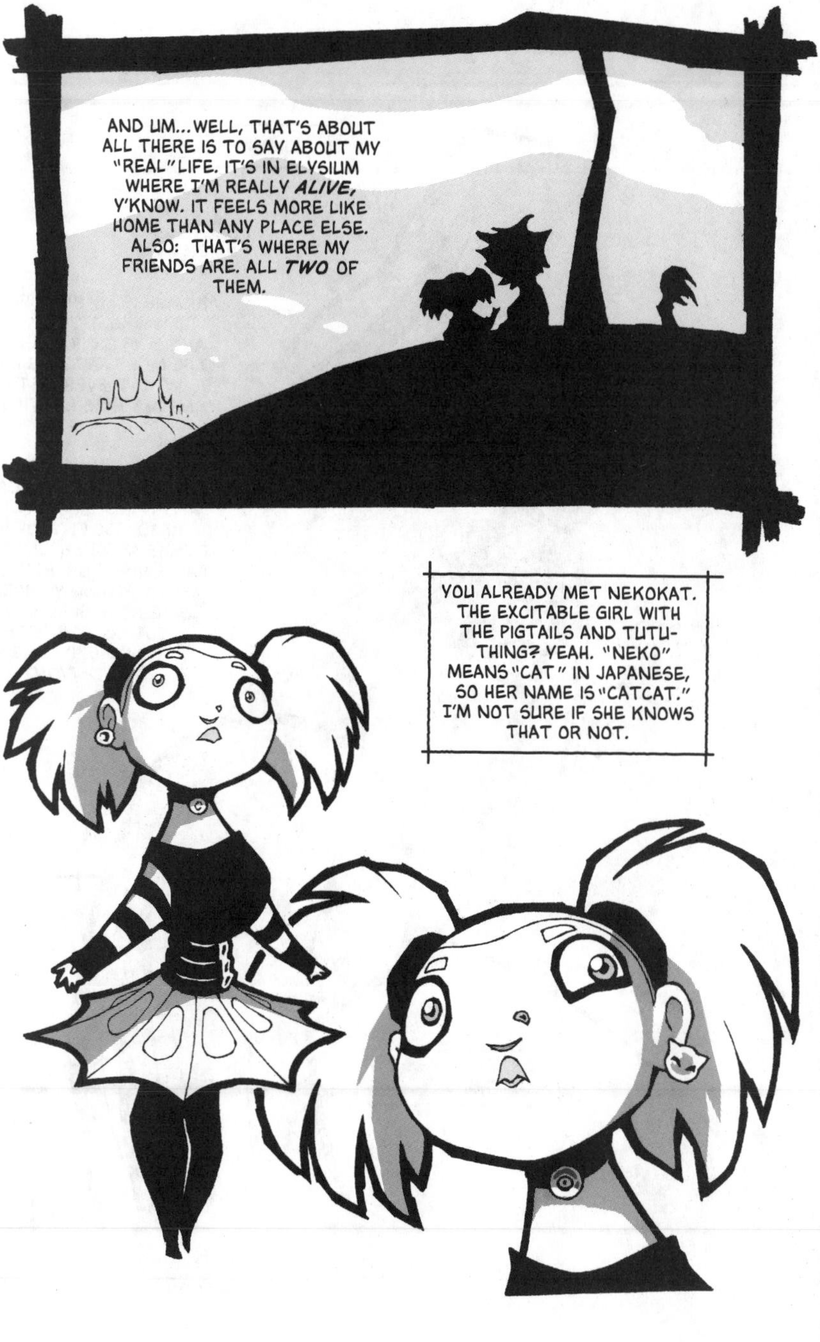
AND UM...WELL, THAT'S ABOUT ALL THERE IS TO SAY ABOUT MY "REAL" LIFE. IT'S IN ELYSIUM WHERE I'M REALLY *ALIVE,* Y'KNOW. IT FEELS MORE LIKE HOME THAN ANY PLACE ELSE. ALSO: THAT'S WHERE MY FRIENDS ARE. ALL *TWO* OF THEM.
YOU ALREADY MET NEKOKAT. THE EXCITABLE GIRL WITH THE PIGTAILS AND TUTU-THING? YEAH. "NEKO" MEANS "CAT" IN JAPANESE, SO HER NAME IS "CATCAT." I'M NOT SURE IF SHE KNOWS THAT OR NOT.

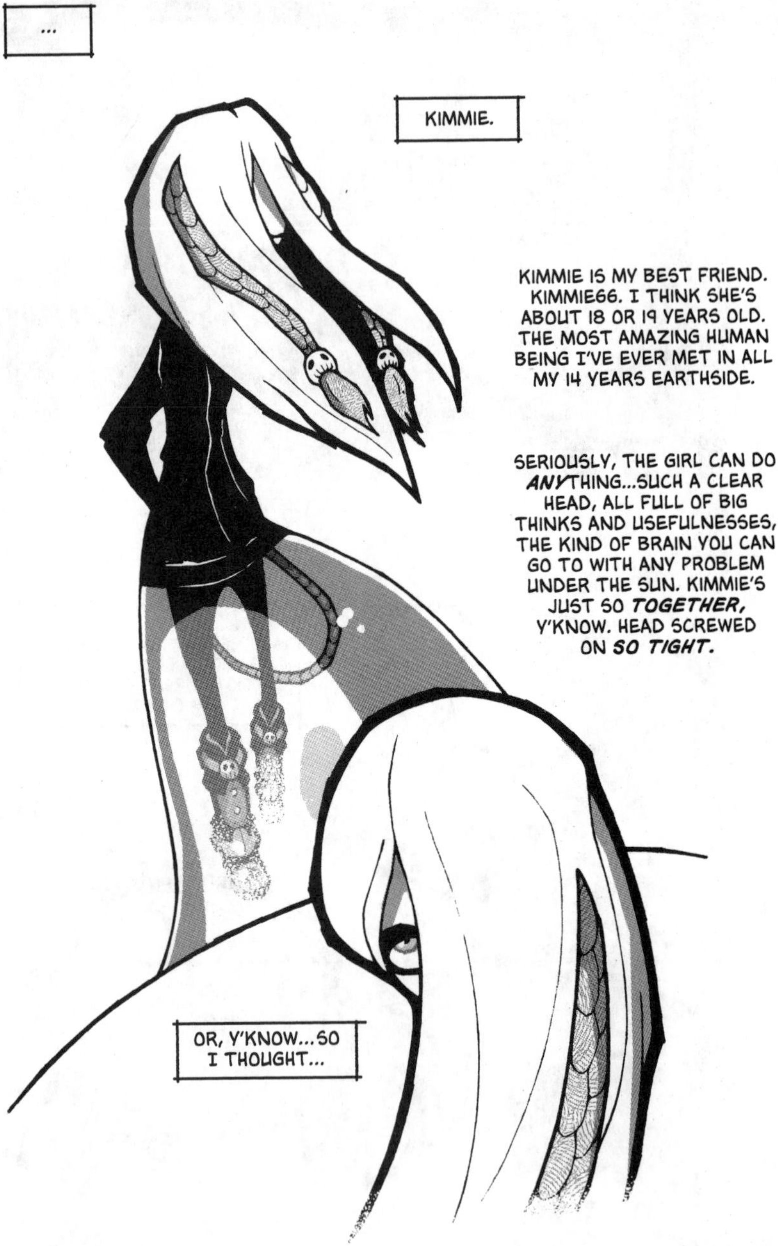
...
KIMMIE.
KIMMIE IS MY BEST FRIEND. KIMMIE66. I THINK SHE'S ABOUT 18 OR 19 YEARS OLD. THE MOST AMAZING HUMAN BEING I'VE EVER MET IN ALL MY 14 YEARS EARTHSIDE.
SERIOUSLY, THE GIRL CAN DO *ANY*THING...SUCH A CLEAR HEAD, ALL FULL OF BIG THINKS AND USEFULNESSES, THE KIND OF BRAIN YOU CAN GO TO WITH ANY PROBLEM UNDER THE SUN. KIMMIE'S JUST SO *TOGETHER,* Y'KNOW. HEAD SCREWED ON *SO TIGHT.*
OR, Y'KNOW...SO I THOUGHT...

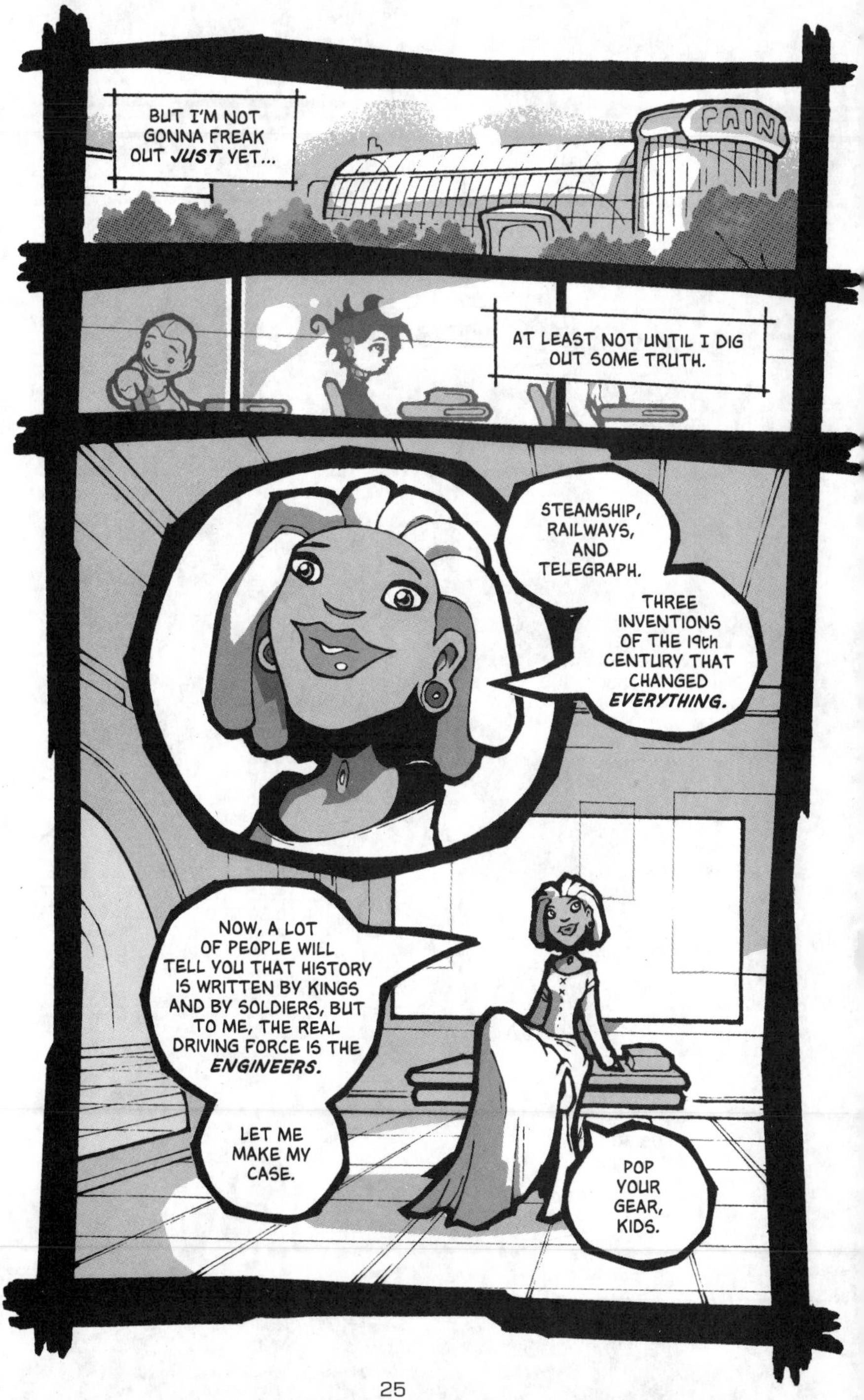
BUT I'M NOT GONNA FREAK OUT *JUST* YET...
PAIN
AT LEAST NOT UNTIL I DIG OUT SOME TRUTH.
STEAMSHIP, RAILWAYS, AND TELEGRAPH.
THREE INVENTIONS OF THE 19th CENTURY THAT CHANGED *EVERYTHING.*
NOW, A LOT OF PEOPLE WILL TELL YOU THAT HISTORY IS WRITTEN BY KINGS AND BY SOLDIERS, BUT TO ME, THE REAL DRIVING FORCE IS THE *ENGINEERS.*
LET ME MAKE MY CASE.
POP YOUR GEAR, KIDS.

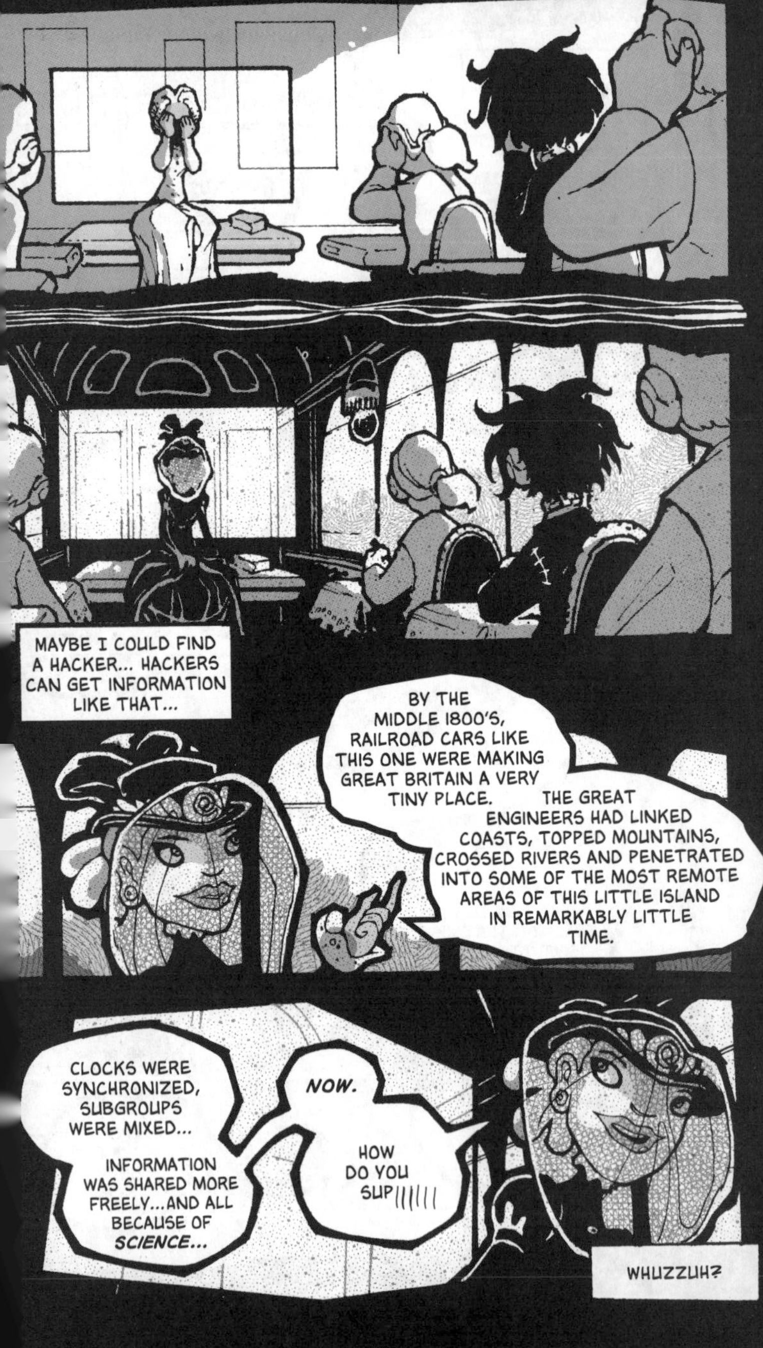

MAYBE I COULD FIND A HACKER... HACKERS CAN GET INFORMATION LIKE THAT...
BY THE MIDDLE 1800'S, RAILROAD CARS LIKE THIS ONE WERE MAKING GREAT BRITAIN A VERY TINY PLACE. THE GREAT ENGINEERS HAD LINKED COASTS, TOPPED MOUNTAINS, CROSSED RIVERS AND PENETRATED INTO SOME OF THE MOST REMOTE AREAS OF THIS LITTLE ISLAND IN REMARKABLY LITTLE TIME.
CLOCKS WERE SYNCHRONIZED, SUBGROUPS WERE MIXED... INFORMATION WAS SHARED MORE FREELY...AND ALL BECAUSE OF *SCIENCE...*
NOW. HOW DO YOU SUP
WHUZZUH?

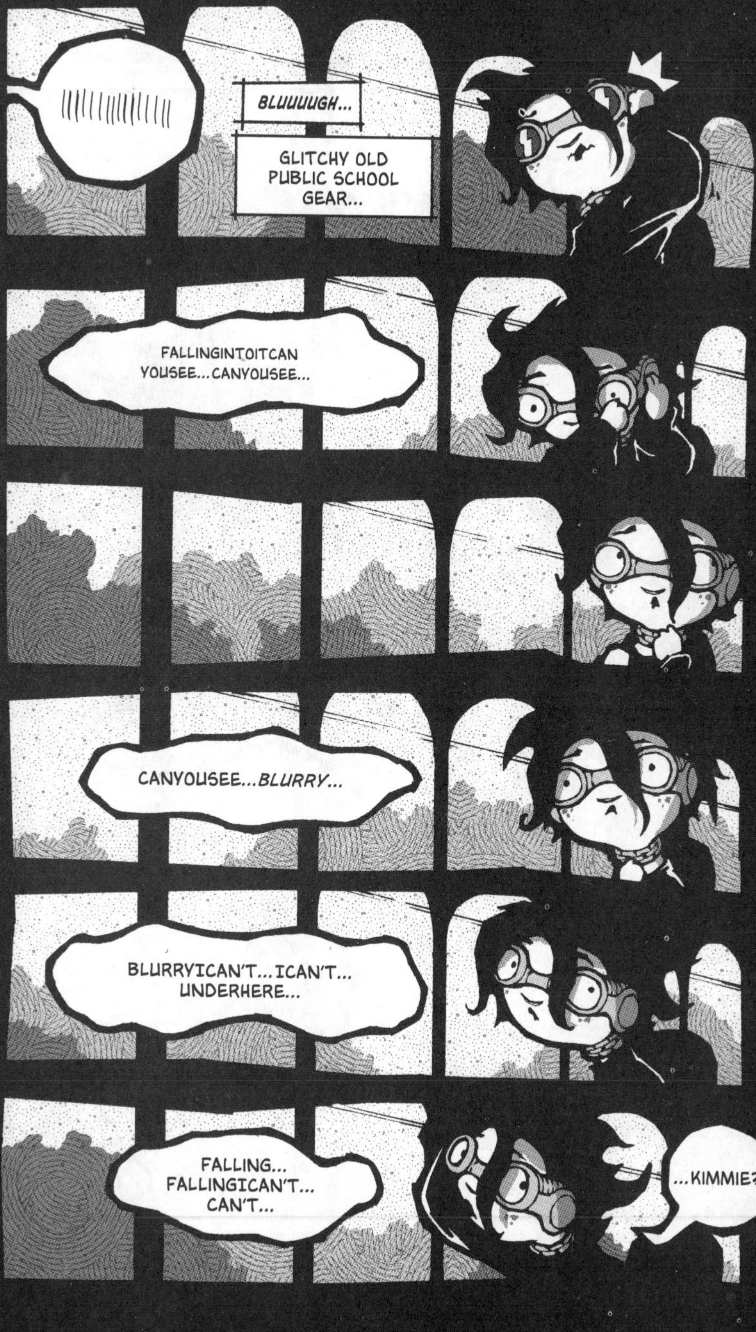

BLUUUUGH...
GLITCHY OLD PUBLIC SCHOOL GEAR...
FALLINGINTOITCAN YOUSEE...CANYOUSEE...
CANYOUSEE...BLURRY...
BLURRYICAN'T...ICAN'T... UNDERHERE...
FALLING... FALLINGICAN'T... CAN'T...
...KIMMIE?

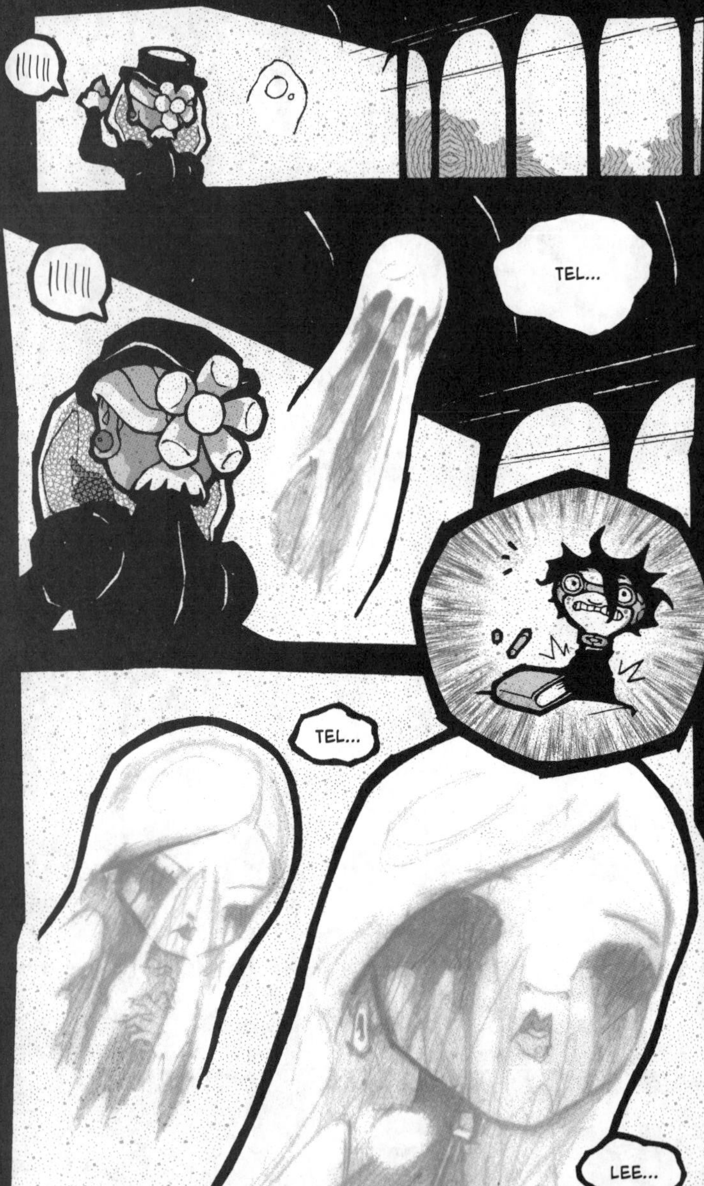
TEL...
TEL...
LEE...

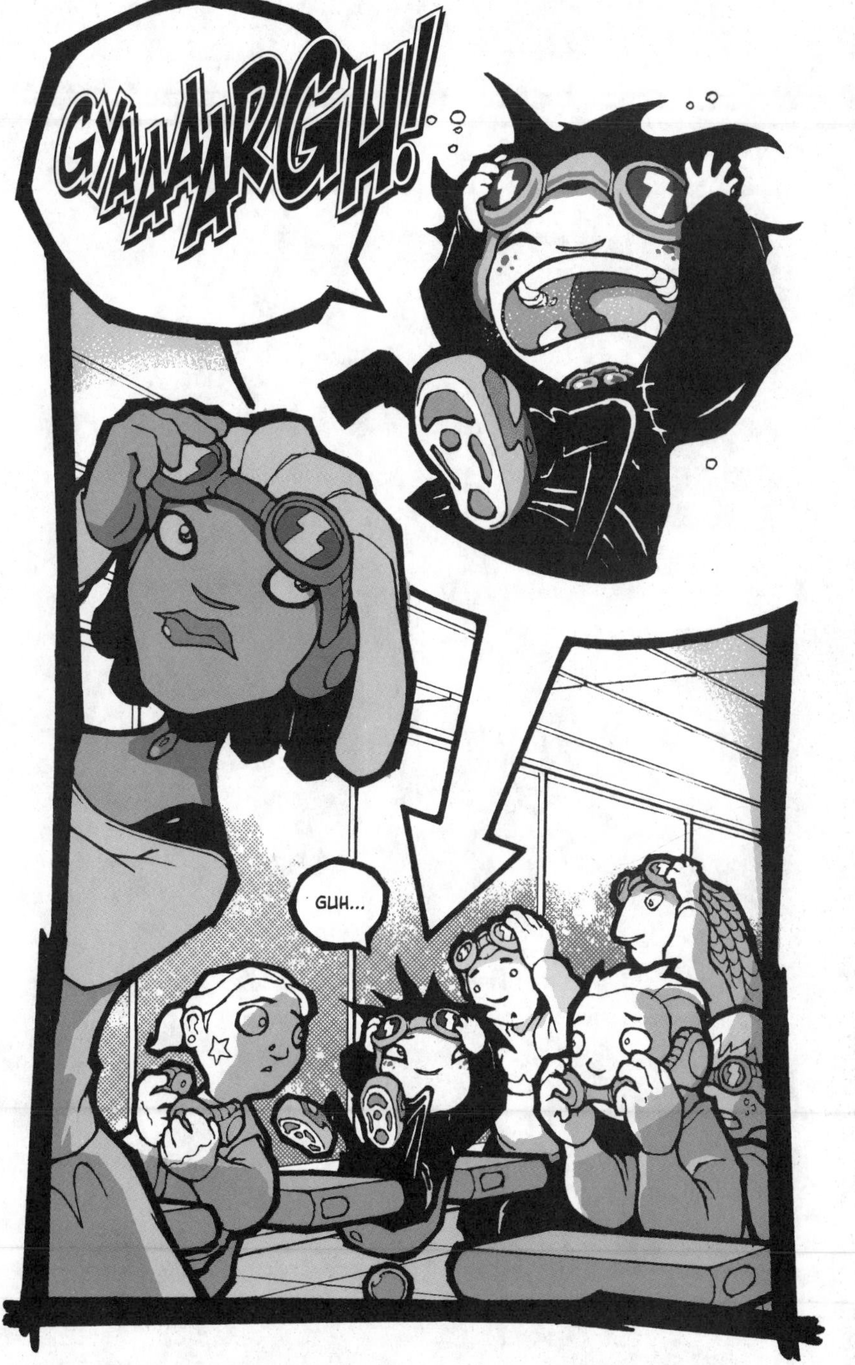
GYAAARGH!
GUH...

CHAPTER TWO

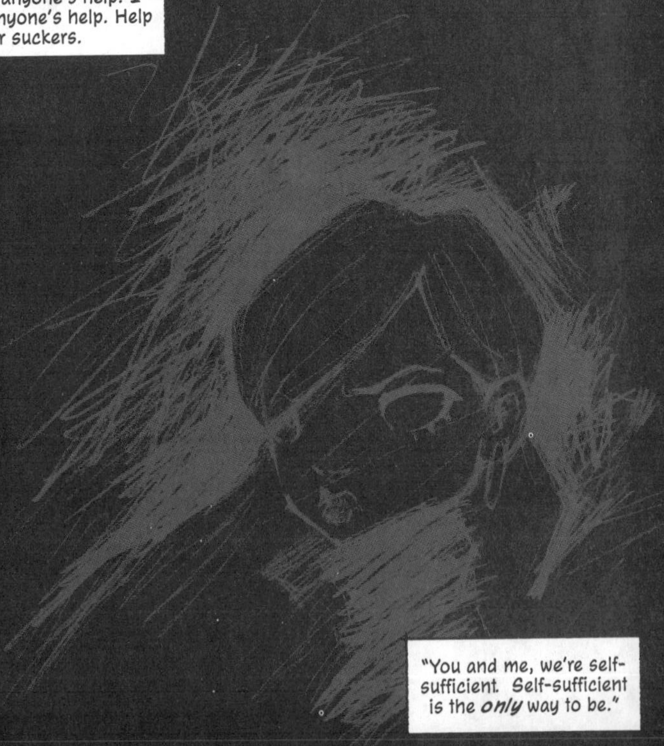
"Don't you see, Telly? You don't *need* anyone's help. I don't need anyone's help. Help is for suckers.
"You and me, we're self-sufficient. Self-sufficient is the *only* way to be."

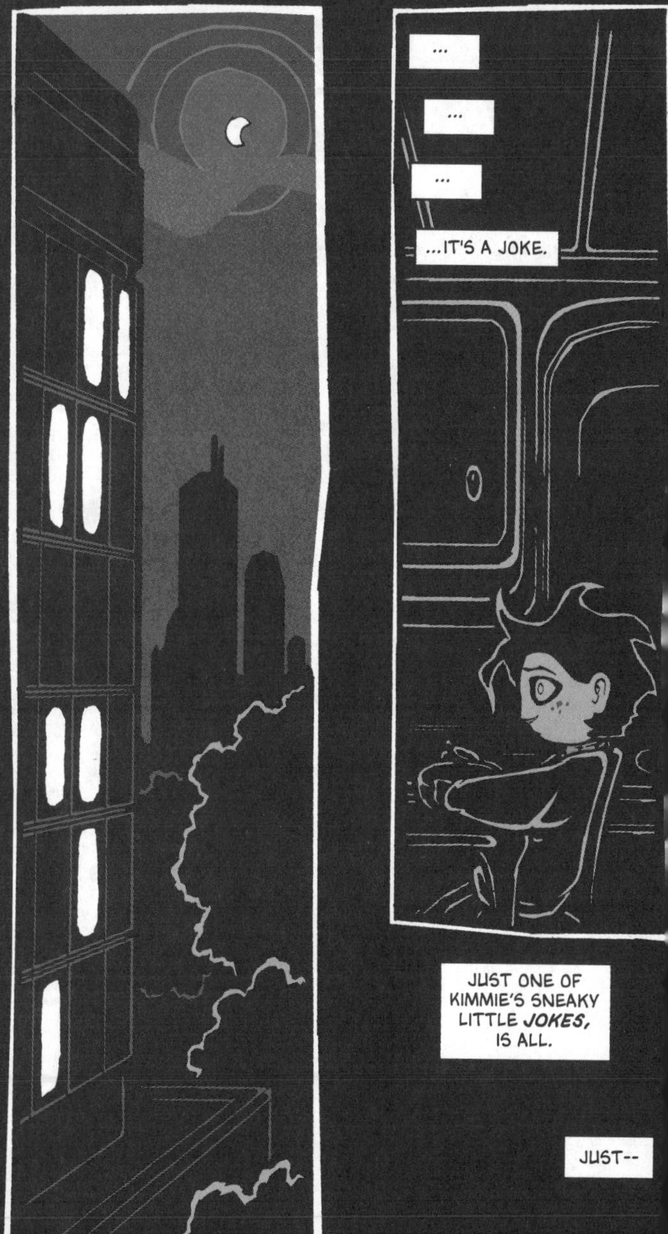
...
...
...
...IT'S A JOKE.
JUST ONE OF KIMMIE'S SNEAKY LITTLE *JOKES,* IS ALL.
JUST--

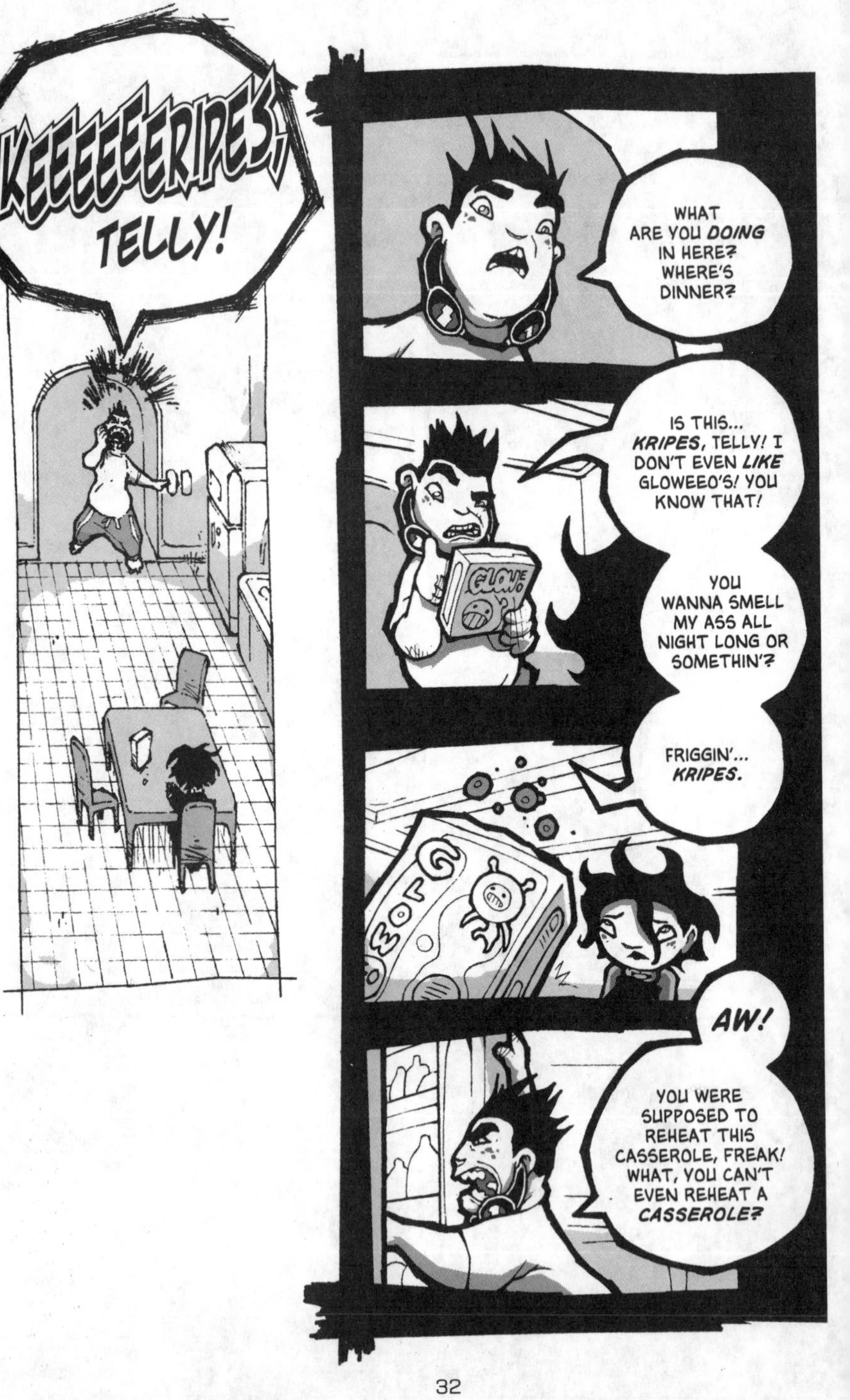
KEEEEEERIPES, TELLY!
WHAT ARE YOU DOING IN HERE? WHERE'S DINNER?
IS THIS... KRIPES, TELLY! I DON'T EVEN LIKE GLOWEEO'S! YOU KNOW THAT!
YOU WANNA SMELL MY ASS ALL NIGHT LONG OR SOMETHIN'?
FRIGGIN'... KRIPES.
AW!
YOU WERE SUPPOSED TO REHEAT THIS CASSEROLE, FREAK! WHAT, YOU CAN'T EVEN REHEAT A CASSEROLE?

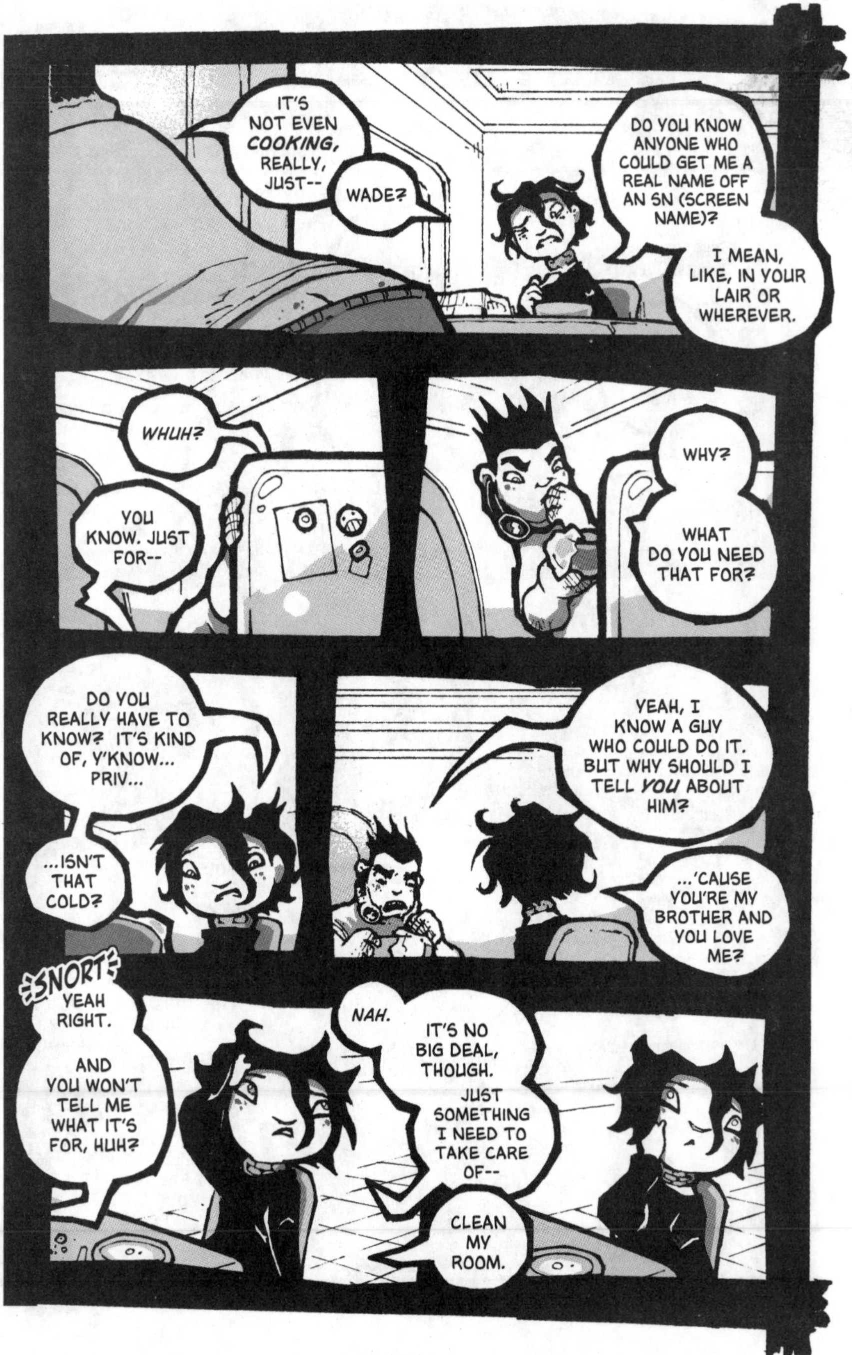
IT'S NOT EVEN *COOKING,* REALLY, JUST--
WADE?
DO YOU KNOW ANYONE WHO COULD GET ME A REAL NAME OFF AN SN (SCREEN NAME)?
I MEAN, LIKE, IN YOUR LAIR OR WHEREVER.
WHUH?
YOU KNOW. JUST FOR--
WHY?
WHAT DO YOU NEED THAT FOR?
DO YOU REALLY HAVE TO KNOW? IT'S KIND OF, Y'KNOW... PRIV...
...ISN'T THAT COLD?
YEAH, I KNOW A GUY WHO COULD DO IT. BUT WHY SHOULD I TELL *YOU* ABOUT HIM?
...'CAUSE YOU'RE MY BROTHER AND YOU LOVE ME?
SNORT
YEAH RIGHT.
AND YOU WON'T TELL ME WHAT IT'S FOR, HUH?
NAH.
IT'S NO BIG DEAL, THOUGH.
JUST SOMETHING I NEED TO TAKE CARE OF--
CLEAN MY ROOM.

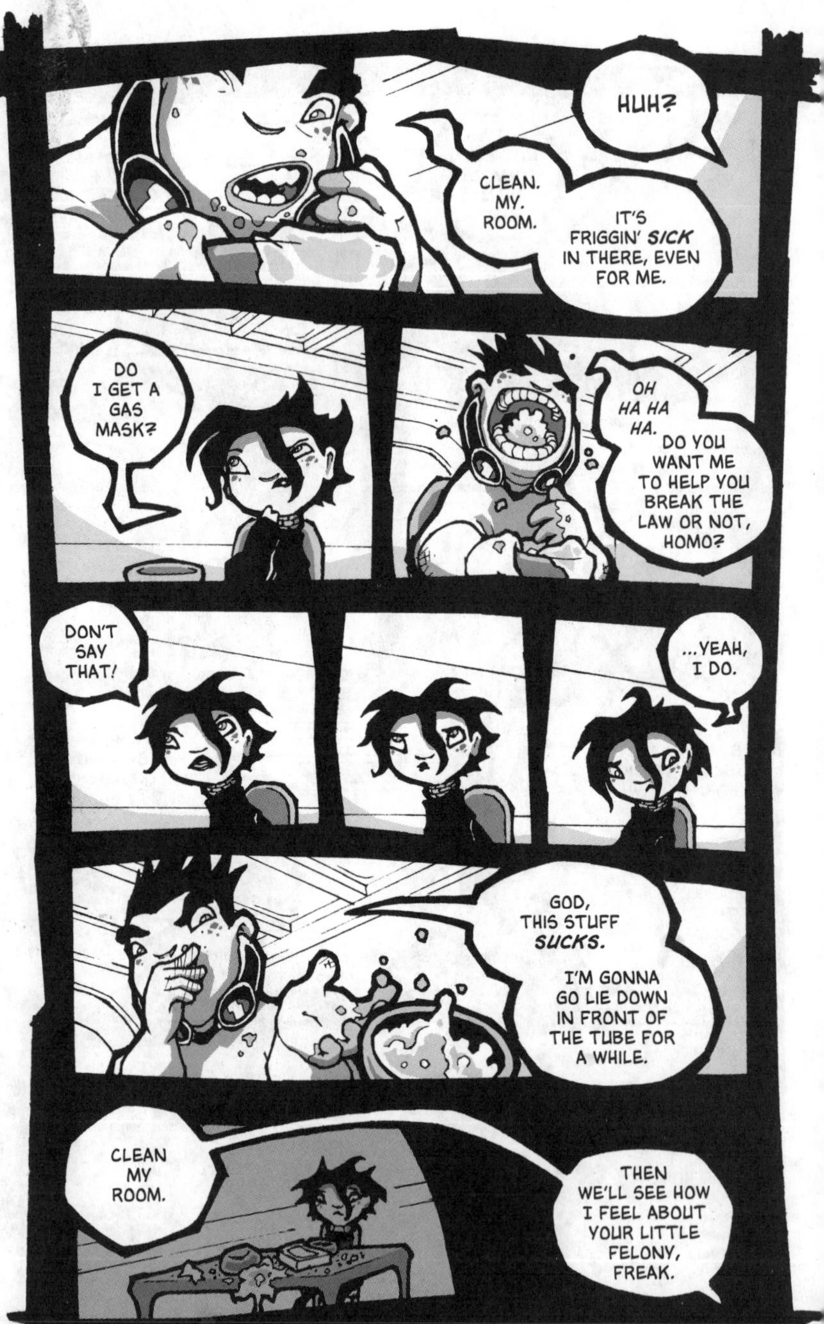
HUH?
CLEAN. MY. ROOM.
IT'S FRIGGIN' *SICK* IN THERE, EVEN FOR ME.
DO I GET A GAS MASK?
OH HA HA HA.
DO YOU WANT ME TO HELP YOU BREAK THE LAW OR NOT, HOMO?
DON'T SAY THAT!
...YEAH, I DO.
GOD, THIS STUFF ***SUCKS.***
I'M GONNA GO LIE DOWN IN FRONT OF THE TUBE FOR A WHILE.
CLEAN MY ROOM.
THEN WE'LL SEE HOW I FEEL ABOUT YOUR LITTLE FELONY, FREAK.

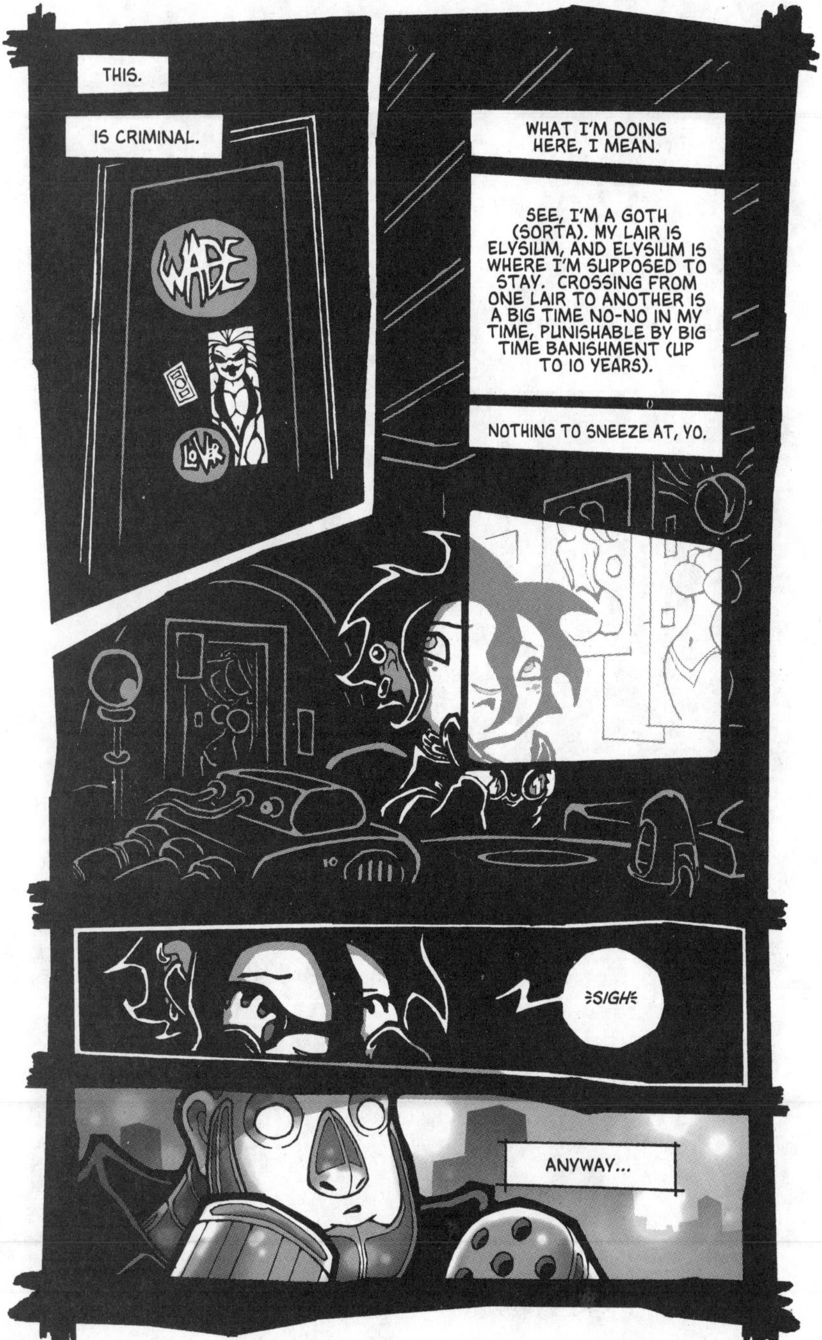
THIS.
IS CRIMINAL.
WADE
LOVER
WHAT I'M DOING HERE, I MEAN.
SEE, I'M A GOTH (SORTA). MY LAIR IS ELYSIUM, AND ELYSIUM IS WHERE I'M SUPPOSED TO STAY. CROSSING FROM ONE LAIR TO ANOTHER IS A BIG TIME NO-NO IN MY TIME, PUNISHABLE BY BIG TIME BANISHMENT (UP TO 10 YEARS).
NOTHING TO SNEEZE AT, YO.
SIGH
ANYWAY...

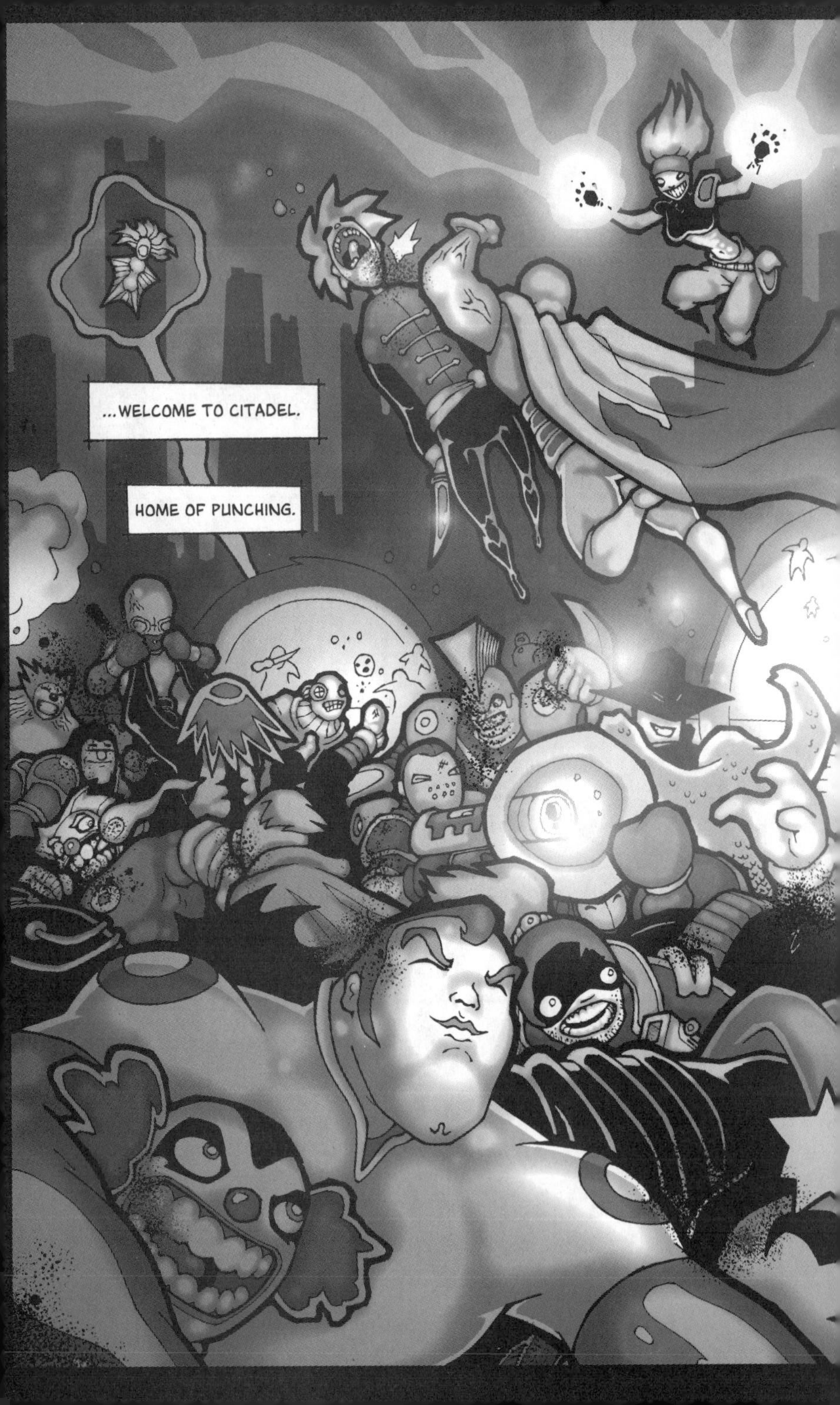
...WELCOME TO CITADEL.
HOME OF PUNCHING.

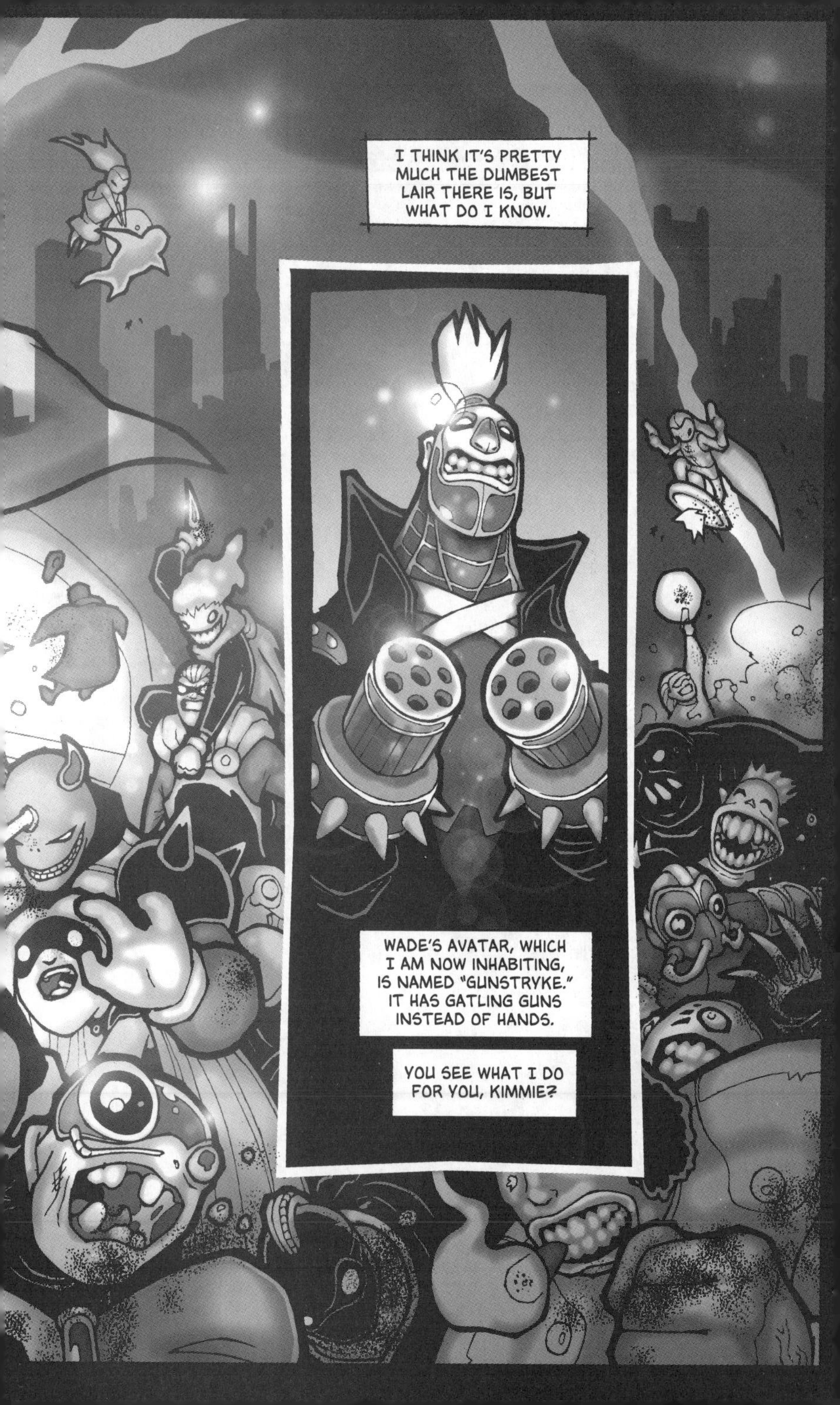
I THINK IT'S PRETTY MUCH THE DUMBEST LAIR THERE IS, BUT WHAT DO I KNOW.
WADE'S AVATAR, WHICH I AM NOW INHABITING, IS NAMED "GUNSTRYKE." IT HAS GATLING GUNS INSTEAD OF HANDS.
YOU SEE WHAT I DO FOR YOU, KIMMIE?

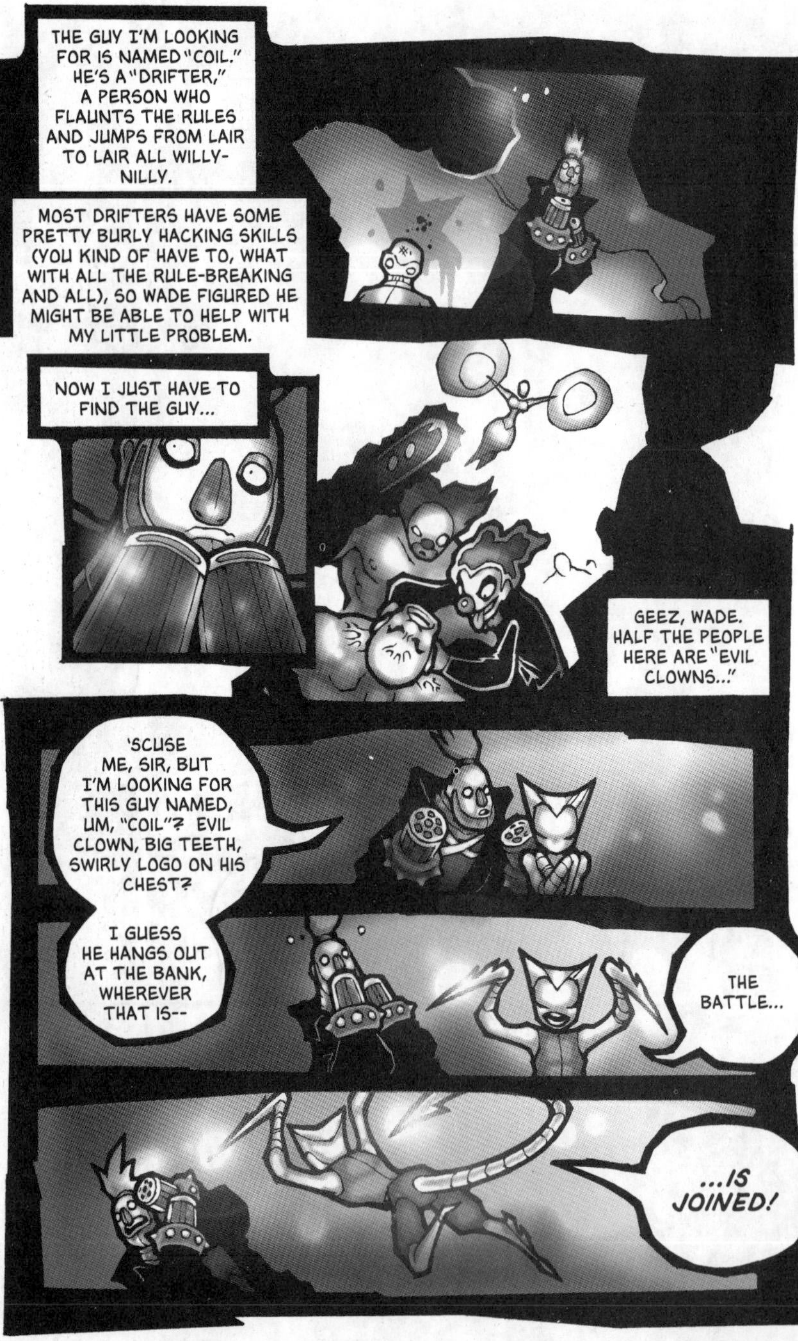
THE GUY I'M LOOKING FOR IS NAMED "COIL." HE'S A "DRIFTER," A PERSON WHO FLAUNTS THE RULES AND JUMPS FROM LAIR TO LAIR ALL WILLY-NILLY.
MOST DRIFTERS HAVE SOME PRETTY BURLY HACKING SKILLS (YOU KIND OF HAVE TO, WHAT WITH ALL THE RULE-BREAKING AND ALL), SO WADE FIGURED HE MIGHT BE ABLE TO HELP WITH MY LITTLE PROBLEM.
NOW I JUST HAVE TO FIND THE GUY...
GEEZ, WADE. HALF THE PEOPLE HERE ARE "EVIL CLOWNS..."
'SCUSE ME, SIR, BUT I'M LOOKING FOR THIS GUY NAMED, UM, "COIL"? EVIL CLOWN, BIG TEETH, SWIRLY LOGO ON HIS CHEST?
I GUESS HE HANGS OUT AT THE BANK, WHEREVER THAT IS--
THE BATTLE...
...IS JOINED!

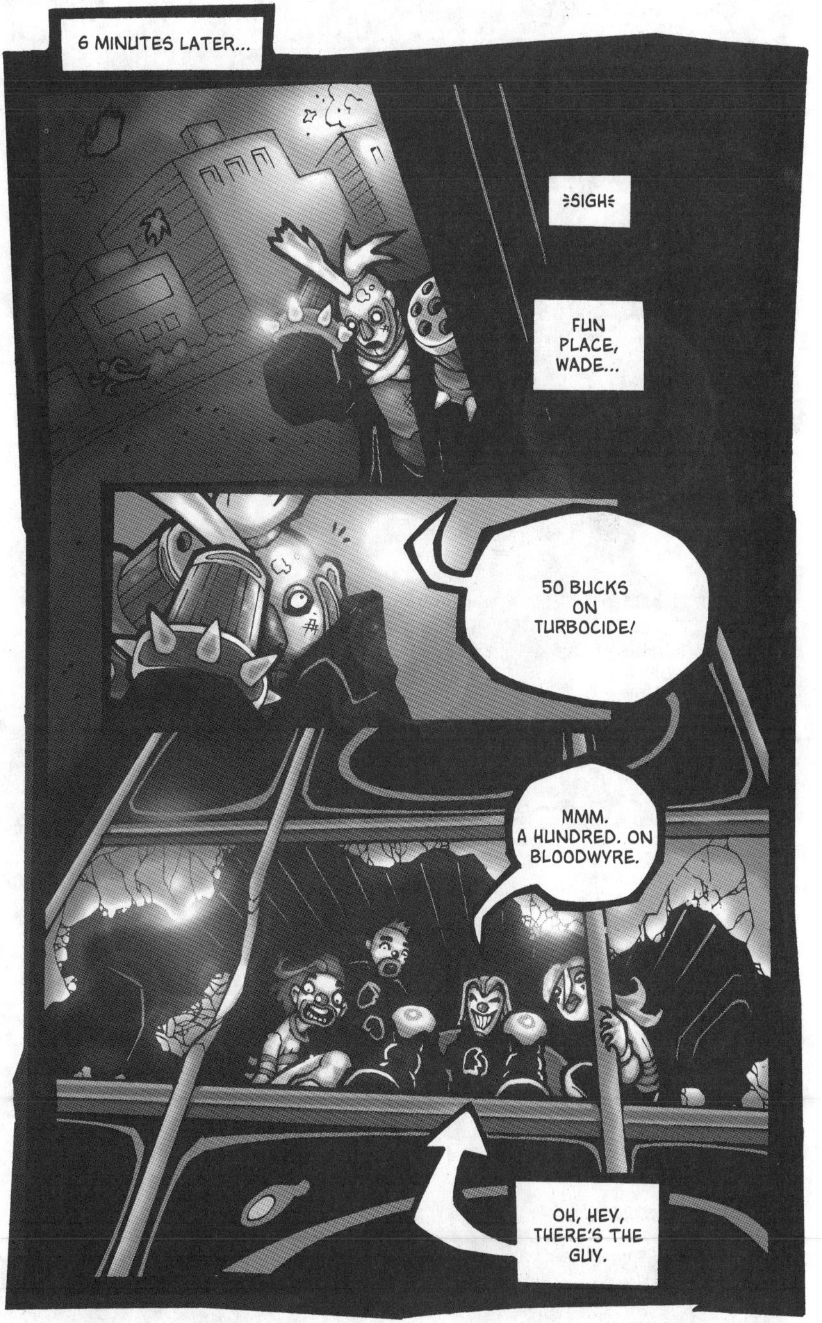
6 MINUTES LATER...
SIGH
FUN PLACE, WADE...
50 BUCKS ON TURBOCIDE!
MMM. A HUNDRED. ON BLOODWYRE.
OH, HEY, THERE'S THE GUY.

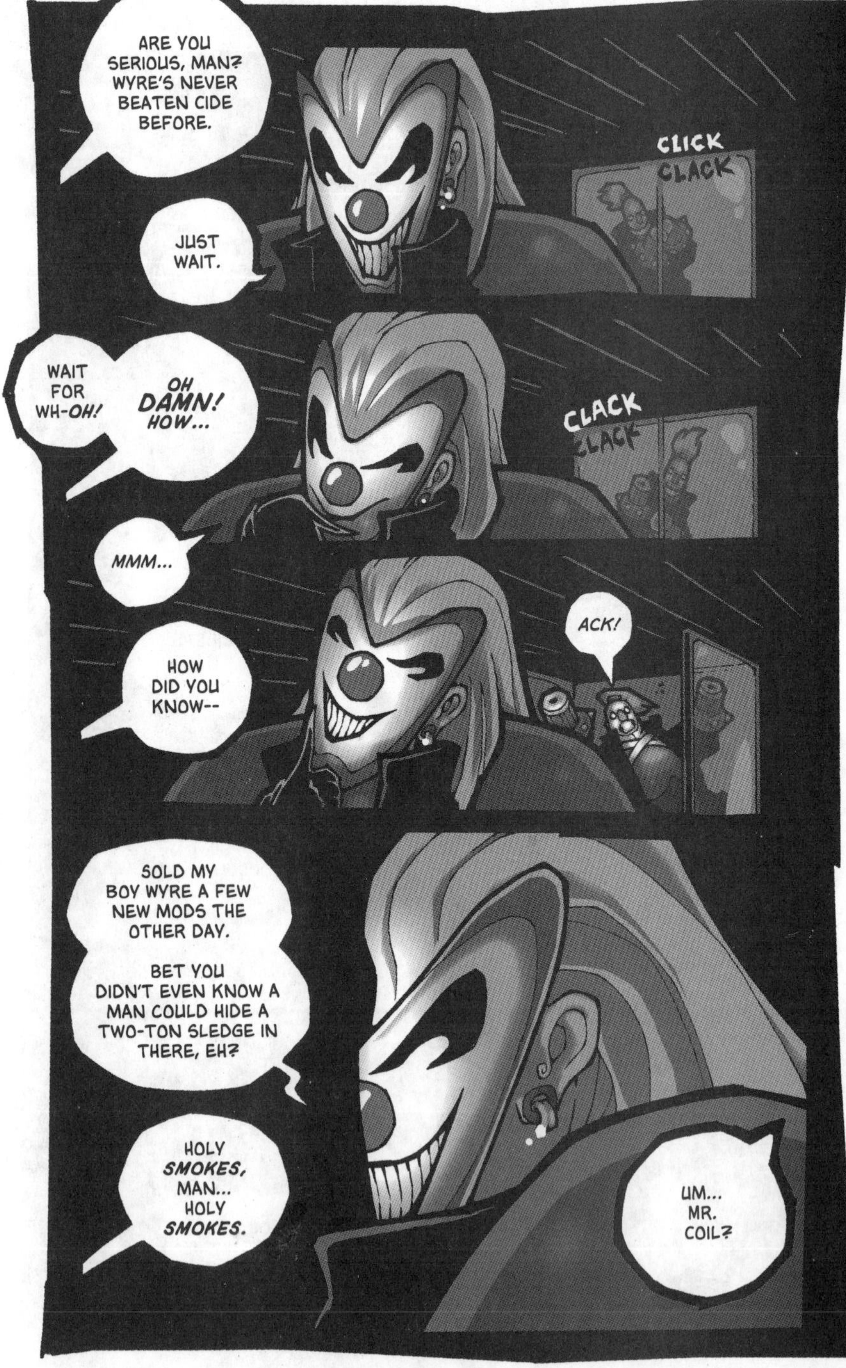

ARE YOU SERIOUS, MAN? WYRE'S NEVER BEATEN CIDE BEFORE.
CLICK CLACK
JUST WAIT.
WAIT FOR WH-*OH!*
OH DAMN! HOW...
CLACK CLACK
MMM...
HOW DID YOU KNOW--
ACK!
SOLD MY BOY WYRE A FEW NEW MODS THE OTHER DAY.
BET YOU DIDN'T EVEN KNOW A MAN COULD HIDE A TWO-TON SLEDGE IN THERE, EH?
HOLY *SMOKES,* MAN... HOLY *SMOKES.*
UM... MR. COIL?

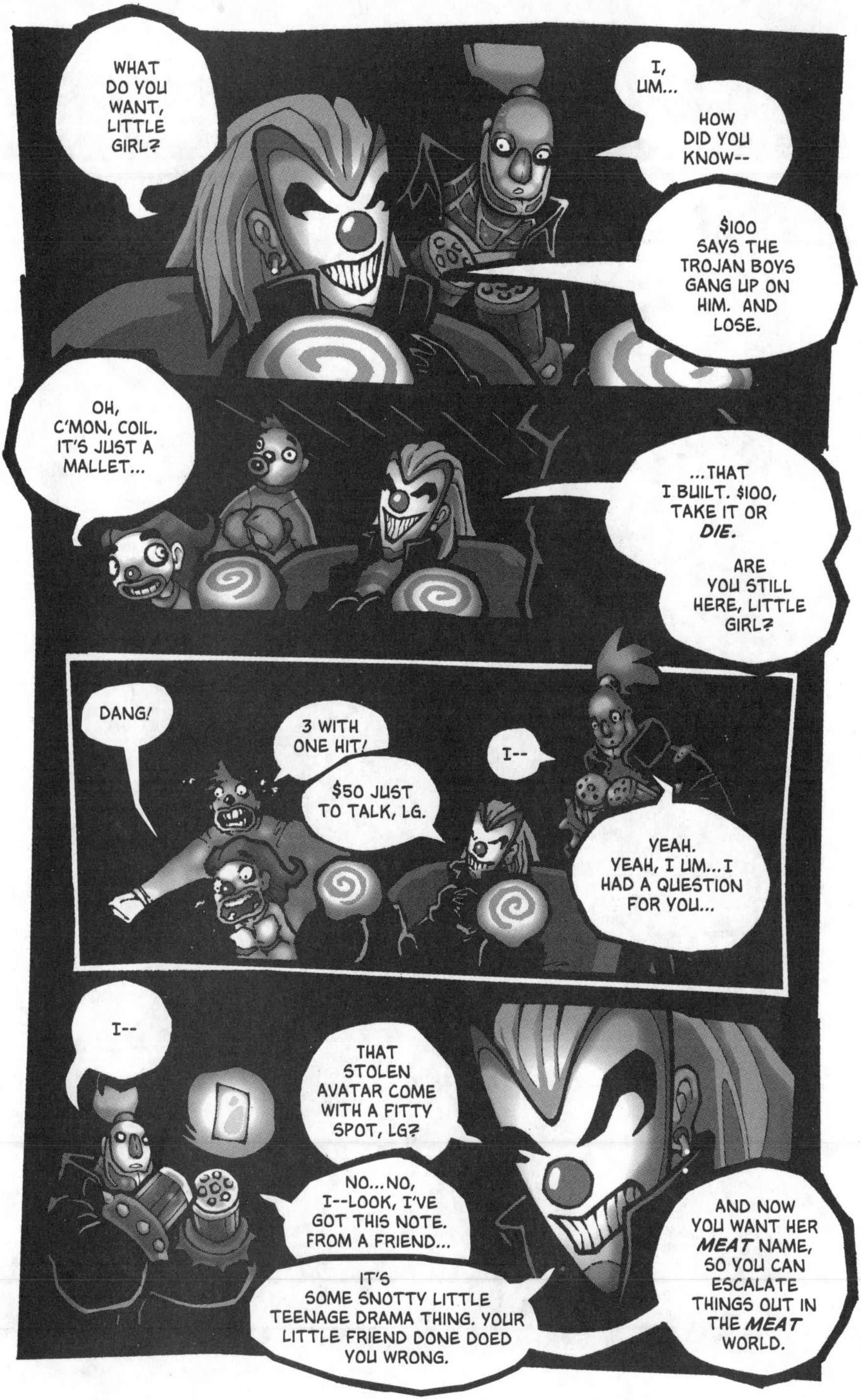
WHAT DO YOU WANT, LITTLE GIRL?
I, UM...
HOW DID YOU KNOW--
$100 SAYS THE TROJAN BOYS GANG UP ON HIM. AND LOSE.
OH, C'MON, COIL. IT'S JUST A MALLET...
...THAT I BUILT. $100, TAKE IT OR *DIE.*
ARE YOU STILL HERE, LITTLE GIRL?
DANG!
3 WITH ONE HIT!
$50 JUST TO TALK, LG.
I--
YEAH. YEAH, I UM... I HAD A QUESTION FOR YOU...
I--
THAT STOLEN AVATAR COME WITH A FITTY SPOT, LG?
NO... NO, I--LOOK, I'VE GOT THIS NOTE. FROM A FRIEND...
IT'S SOME SNOTTY LITTLE TEENAGE DRAMA THING. YOUR LITTLE FRIEND DONE DOED YOU WRONG.
AND NOW YOU WANT HER *MEAT* NAME, SO YOU CAN ESCALATE THINGS OUT IN THE *MEAT* WORLD.

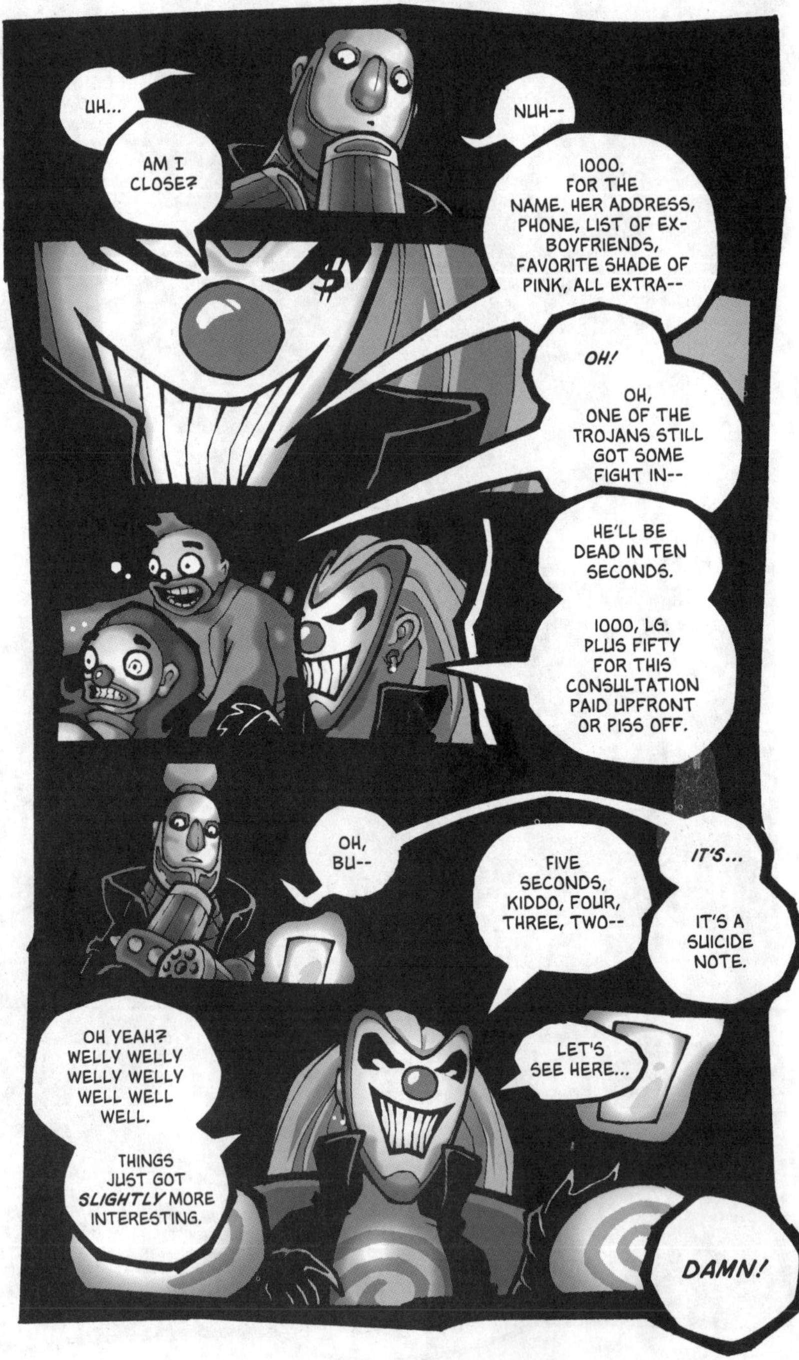
UH...
AM I CLOSE?
NUH--
1000. FOR THE NAME. HER ADDRESS, PHONE, LIST OF EX-BOYFRIENDS, FAVORITE SHADE OF PINK, ALL EXTRA--
OH!
OH, ONE OF THE TROJANS STILL GOT SOME FIGHT IN--
HE'LL BE DEAD IN TEN SECONDS.
1000, LG. PLUS FIFTY FOR THIS CONSULTATION PAID UPFRONT OR PISS OFF.
OH, BU--
FIVE SECONDS, KIDDO, FOUR, THREE, TWO--
IT'S...
IT'S A SUICIDE NOTE.
OH YEAH? WELLY WELLY WELLY WELLY WELL WELL WELL.
THINGS JUST GOT SLIGHTLY MORE INTERESTING.
LET'S SEE HERE...
DAMN!

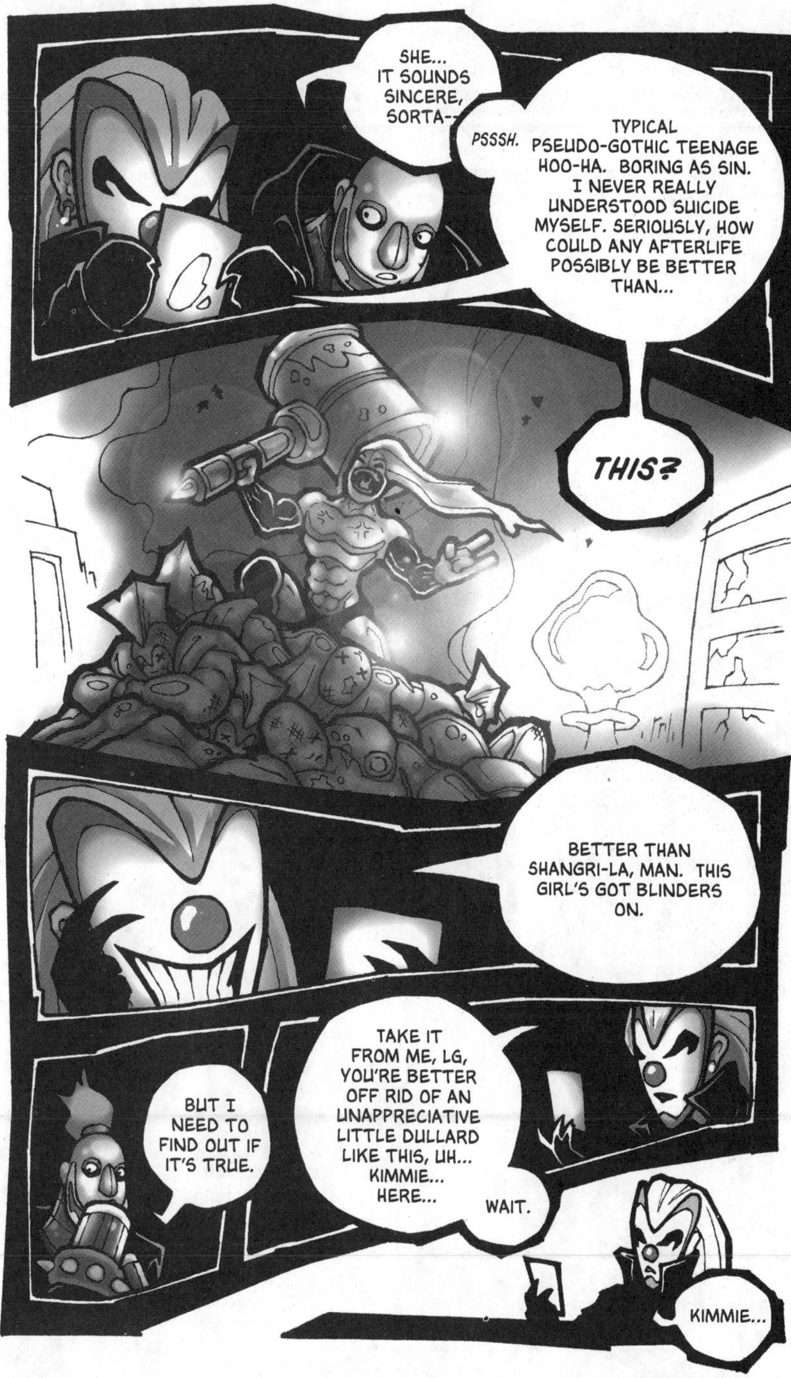
SHE...
IT SOUNDS SINCERE, SORTA--
PSSSH.
TYPICAL PSEUDO-GOTHIC TEENAGE HOO-HA. BORING AS SIN. I NEVER REALLY UNDERSTOOD SUICIDE MYSELF. SERIOUSLY, HOW COULD ANY AFTERLIFE POSSIBLY BE BETTER THAN...
THIS?
BETTER THAN SHANGRI-LA, MAN. THIS GIRL'S GOT BLINDERS ON.
BUT I NEED TO FIND OUT IF IT'S TRUE.
TAKE IT FROM ME, LG, YOU'RE BETTER OFF RID OF AN UNAPPRECIATIVE LITTLE DULLARD LIKE THIS, UH... KIMMIE... HERE...
WAIT.
KIMMIE...

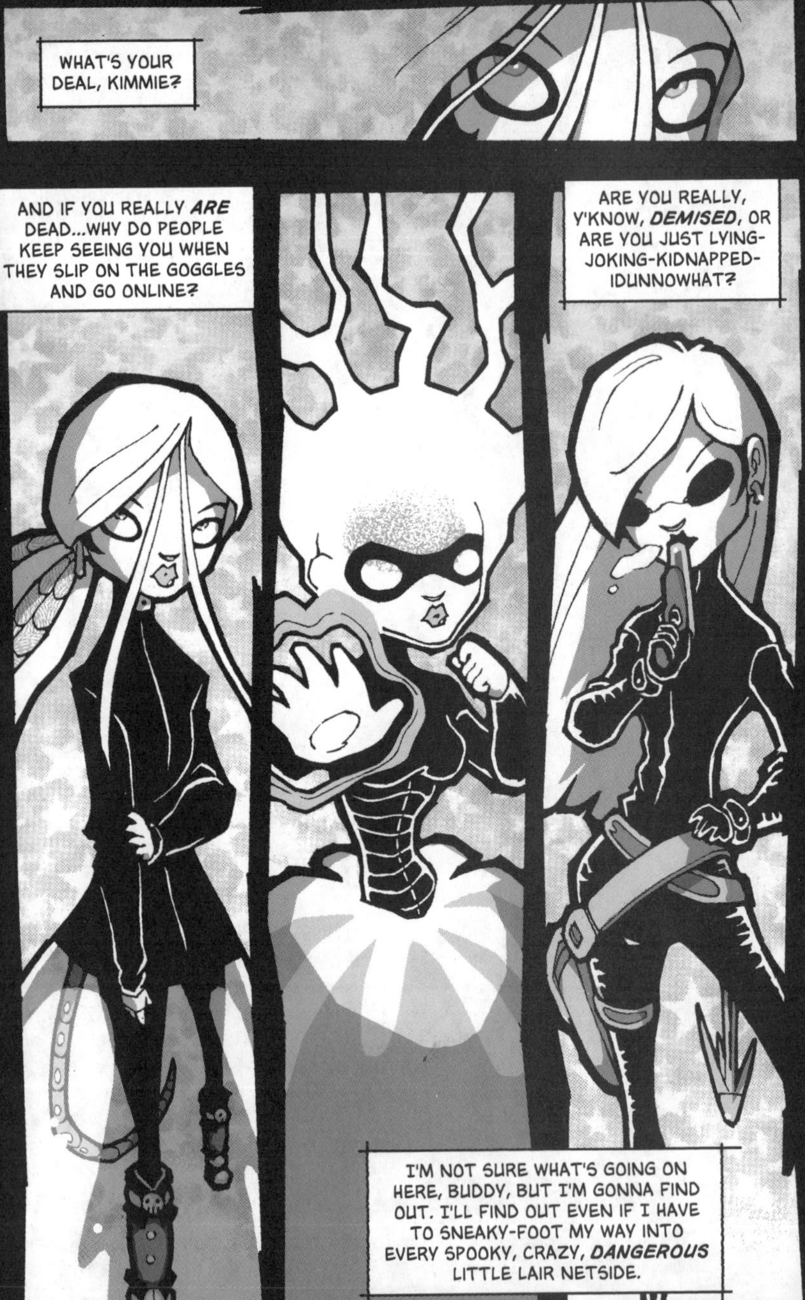
WHAT'S YOUR DEAL, KIMMIE?
AND IF YOU REALLY ARE DEAD...WHY DO PEOPLE KEEP SEEING YOU WHEN THEY SLIP ON THE GOGGLES AND GO ONLINE?
ARE YOU REALLY, Y'KNOW, DEMISED, OR ARE YOU JUST LYING-JOKING-KIDNAPPED-IDUNNOWHAT?
I'M NOT SURE WHAT'S GOING ON HERE, BUDDY, BUT I'M GONNA FIND OUT. I'LL FIND OUT EVEN IF I HAVE TO SNEAKY-FOOT MY WAY INTO EVERY SPOOKY, CRAZY, DANGEROUS LITTLE LAIR NETSIDE.

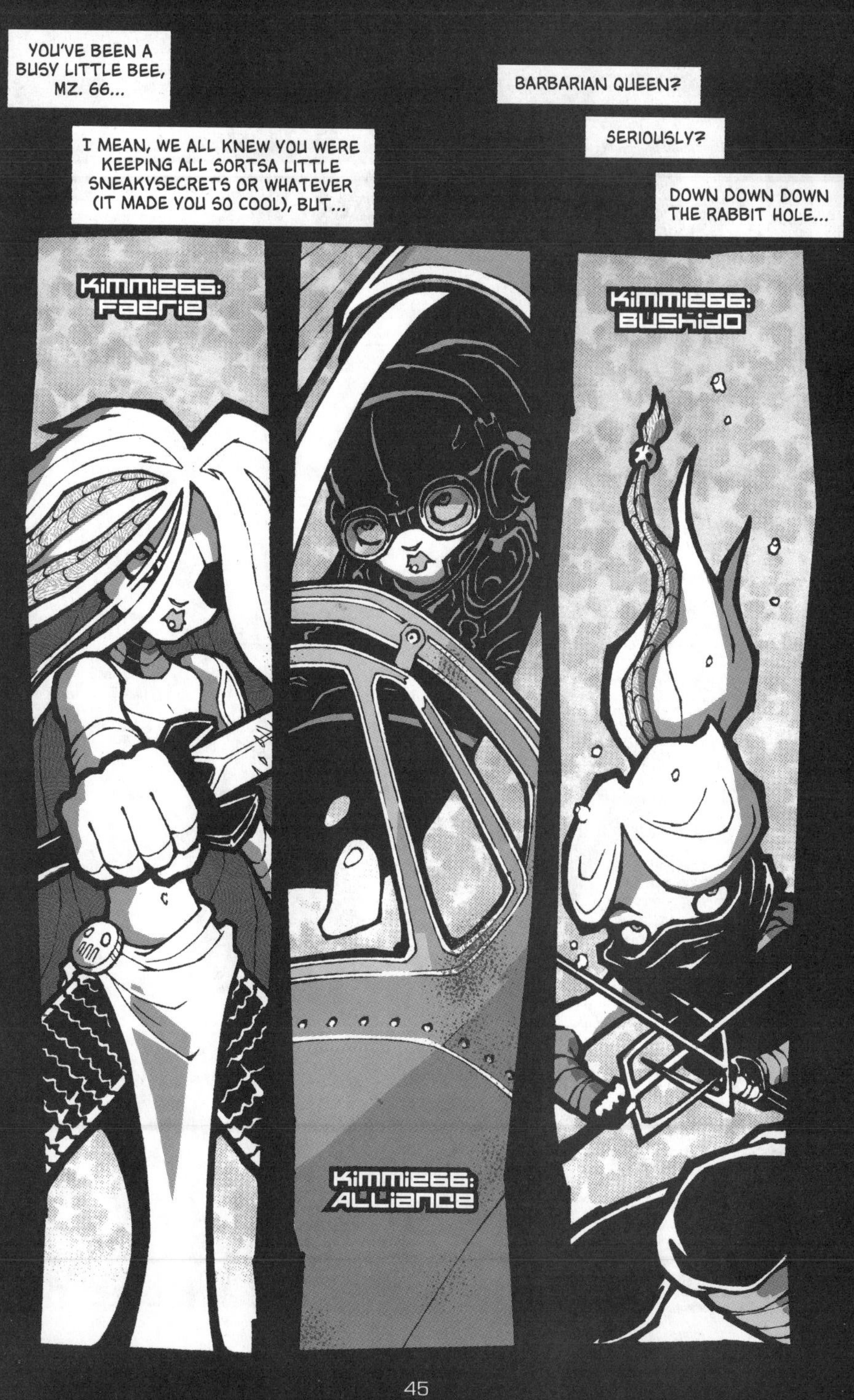
YOU'VE BEEN A BUSY LITTLE BEE, MZ. 66...
I MEAN, WE ALL KNEW YOU WERE KEEPING ALL SORTSA LITTLE SNEAKYSECRETS OR WHATEVER (IT MADE YOU SO COOL), BUT...
BARBARIAN QUEEN?
SERIOUSLY?
DOWN DOWN DOWN THE RABBIT HOLE...
KIMMIE66: FAERIE
KIMMIE66: ALLIANCE
KIMMIE66: BUSHIDO

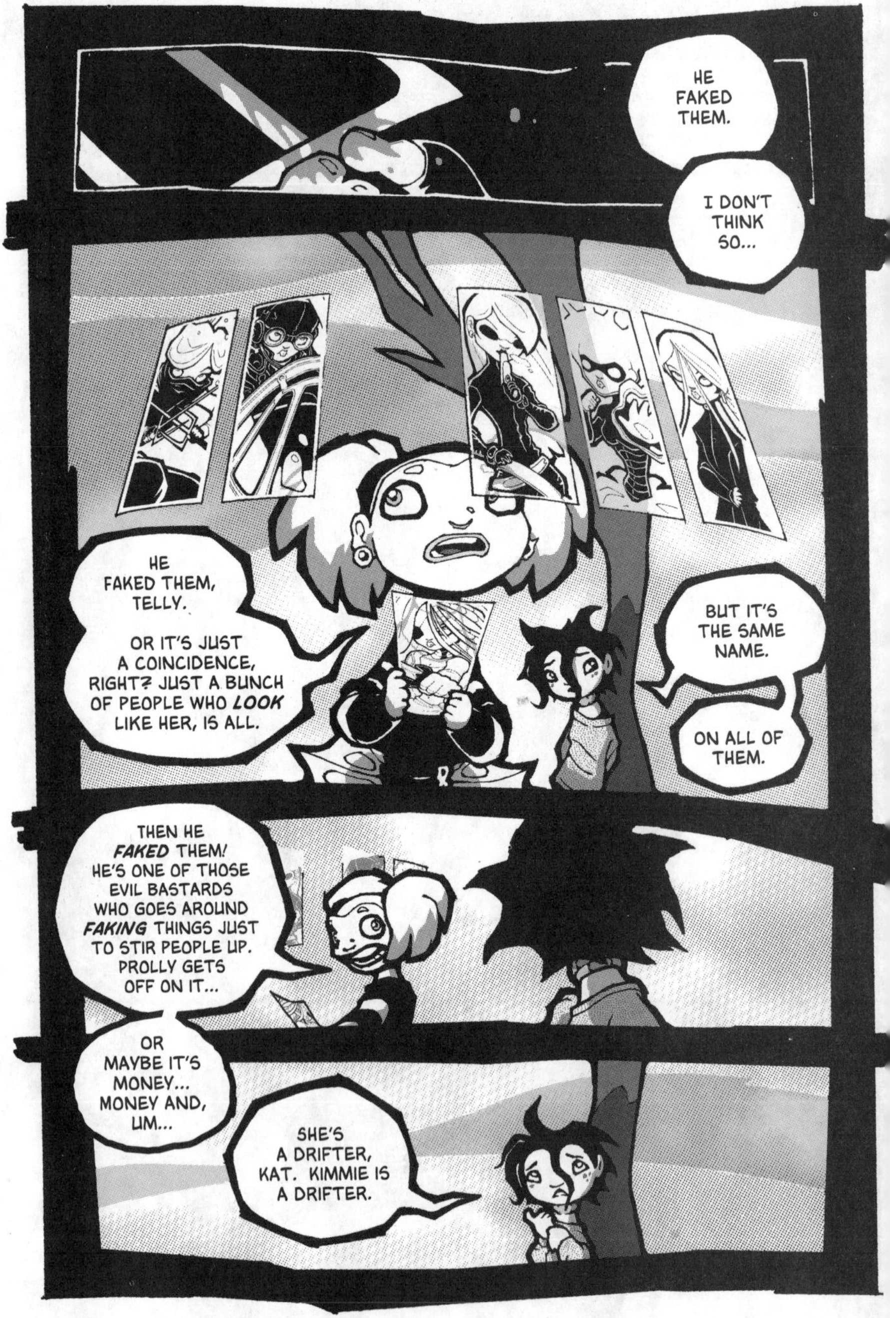

HE FAKED THEM.
I DON'T THINK SO...
HE FAKED THEM, TELLY.
OR IT'S JUST A COINCIDENCE, RIGHT? JUST A BUNCH OF PEOPLE WHO *LOOK* LIKE HER, IS ALL.
BUT IT'S THE SAME NAME.
ON ALL OF THEM.
THEN HE *FAKED* THEM! HE'S ONE OF THOSE EVIL BASTARDS WHO GOES AROUND *FAKING* THINGS JUST TO STIR PEOPLE UP. PROLLY GETS OFF ON IT...
OR MAYBE IT'S MONEY... MONEY AND, UM...
SHE'S A DRIFTER, KAT. KIMMIE IS A DRIFTER.

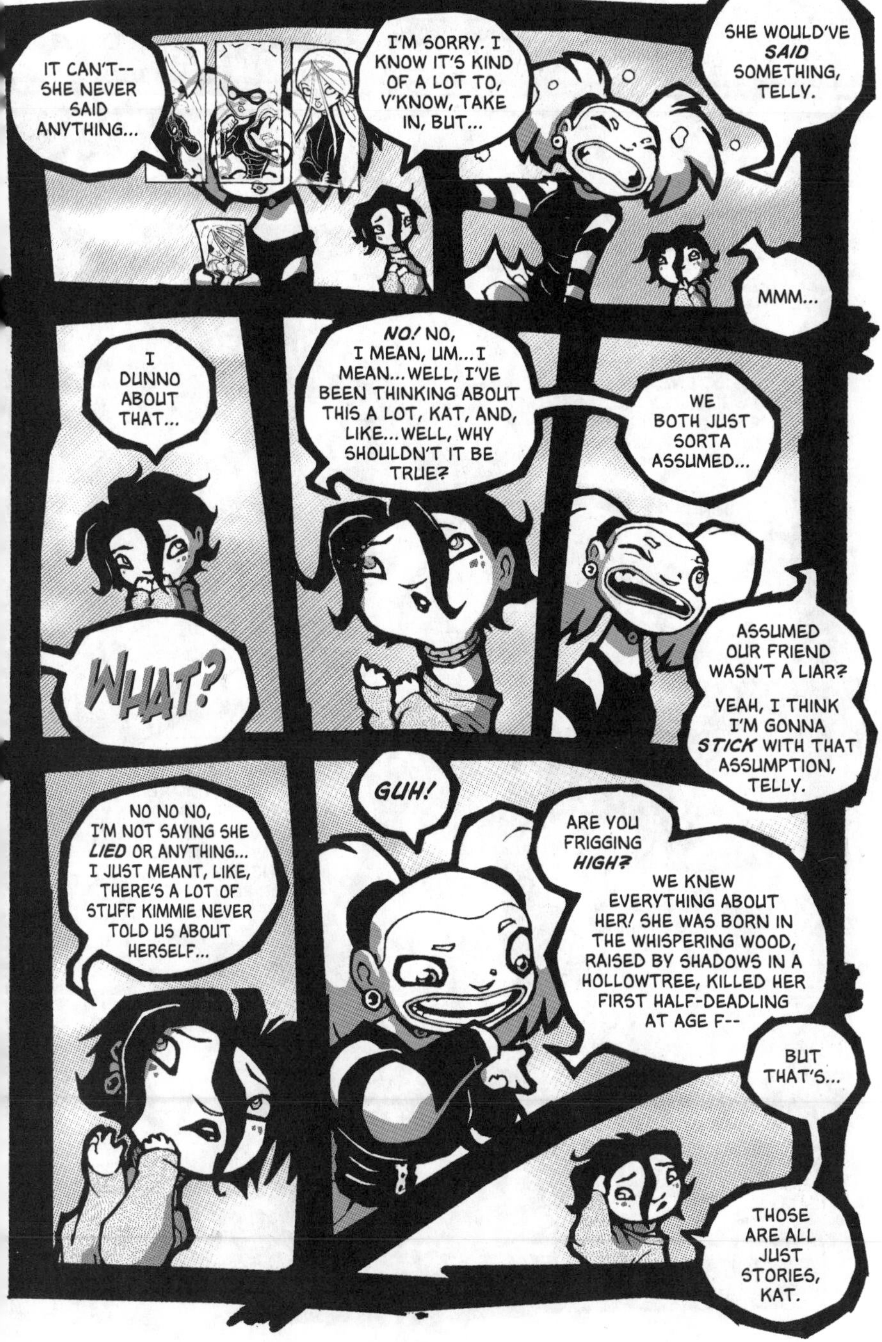
IT CAN'T-- SHE NEVER SAID ANYTHING...
I'M SORRY. I KNOW IT'S KIND OF A LOT TO, Y'KNOW, TAKE IN, BUT...
SHE WOULD'VE *SAID* SOMETHING, TELLY.
MMM...
I DUNNO ABOUT THAT...
WHAT?
NO! NO, I MEAN, UM...I MEAN...WELL, I'VE BEEN THINKING ABOUT THIS A LOT, KAT, AND, LIKE...WELL, WHY SHOULDN'T IT BE TRUE?
WE BOTH JUST SORTA ASSUMED...
ASSUMED OUR FRIEND WASN'T A LIAR?
YEAH, I THINK I'M GONNA *STICK* WITH THAT ASSUMPTION, TELLY.
NO NO NO, I'M NOT SAYING SHE *LIED* OR ANYTHING... I JUST MEANT, LIKE, THERE'S A LOT OF STUFF KIMMIE NEVER TOLD US ABOUT HERSELF...
GUH!
ARE YOU FRIGGING *HIGH?*
WE KNEW EVERYTHING ABOUT HER! SHE WAS BORN IN THE WHISPERING WOOD, RAISED BY SHADOWS IN A HOLLOWTREE, KILLED HER FIRST HALF-DEADLING AT AGE F--
BUT THAT'S...
THOSE ARE ALL JUST STORIES, KAT.

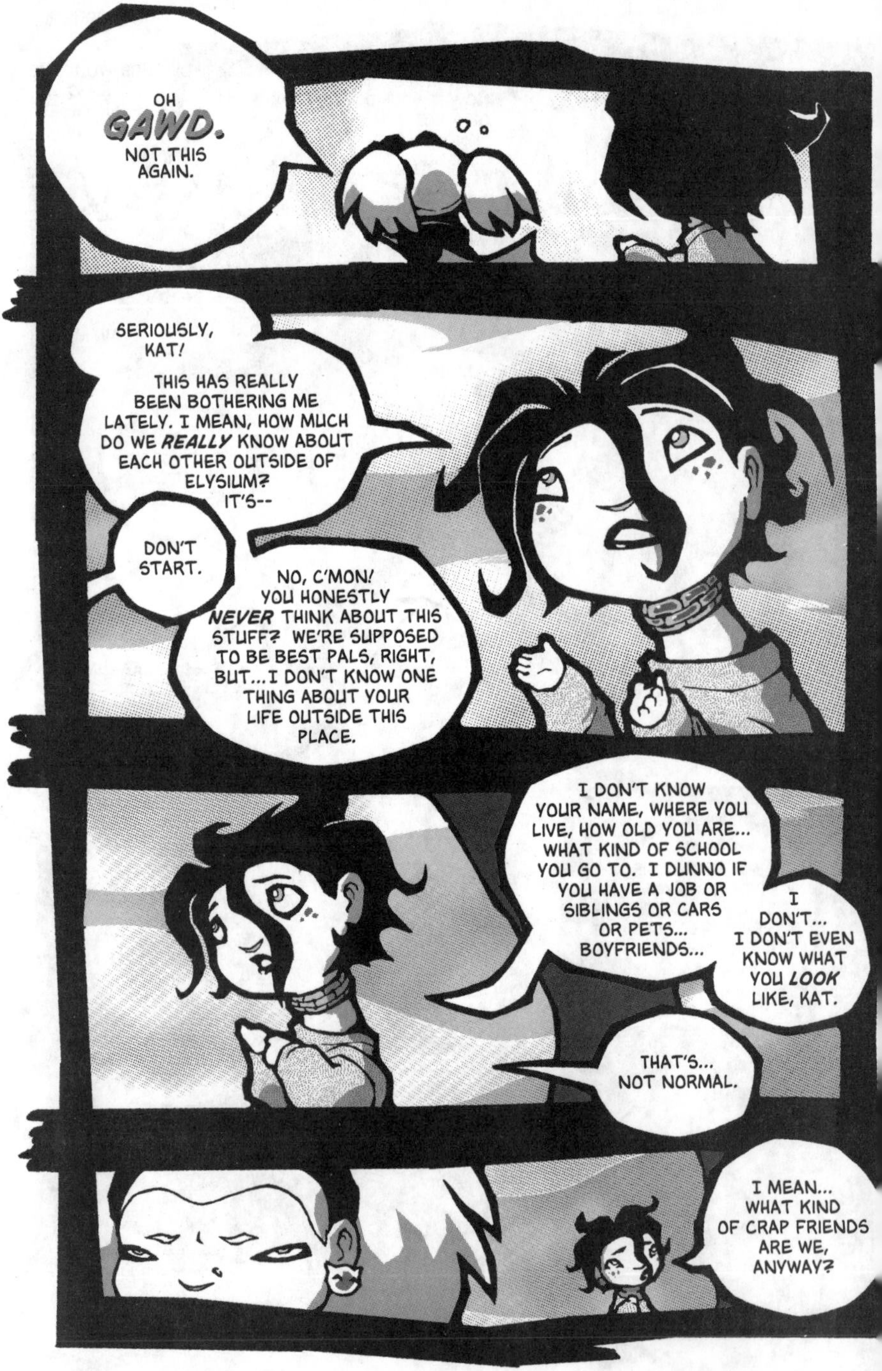

OH GAWD. NOT THIS AGAIN.
SERIOUSLY, KAT!
THIS HAS REALLY BEEN BOTHERING ME LATELY. I MEAN, HOW MUCH DO WE REALLY KNOW ABOUT EACH OTHER OUTSIDE OF ELYSIUM? IT'S--
DON'T START.
NO, C'MON! YOU HONESTLY NEVER THINK ABOUT THIS STUFF? WE'RE SUPPOSED TO BE BEST PALS, RIGHT, BUT...I DON'T KNOW ONE THING ABOUT YOUR LIFE OUTSIDE THIS PLACE.
I DON'T KNOW YOUR NAME, WHERE YOU LIVE, HOW OLD YOU ARE... WHAT KIND OF SCHOOL YOU GO TO. I DUNNO IF YOU HAVE A JOB OR SIBLINGS OR CARS OR PETS... BOYFRIENDS...
I DON'T... I DON'T EVEN KNOW WHAT YOU LOOK LIKE, KAT.
THAT'S... NOT NORMAL.
I MEAN... WHAT KIND OF CRAP FRIENDS ARE WE, ANYWAY?

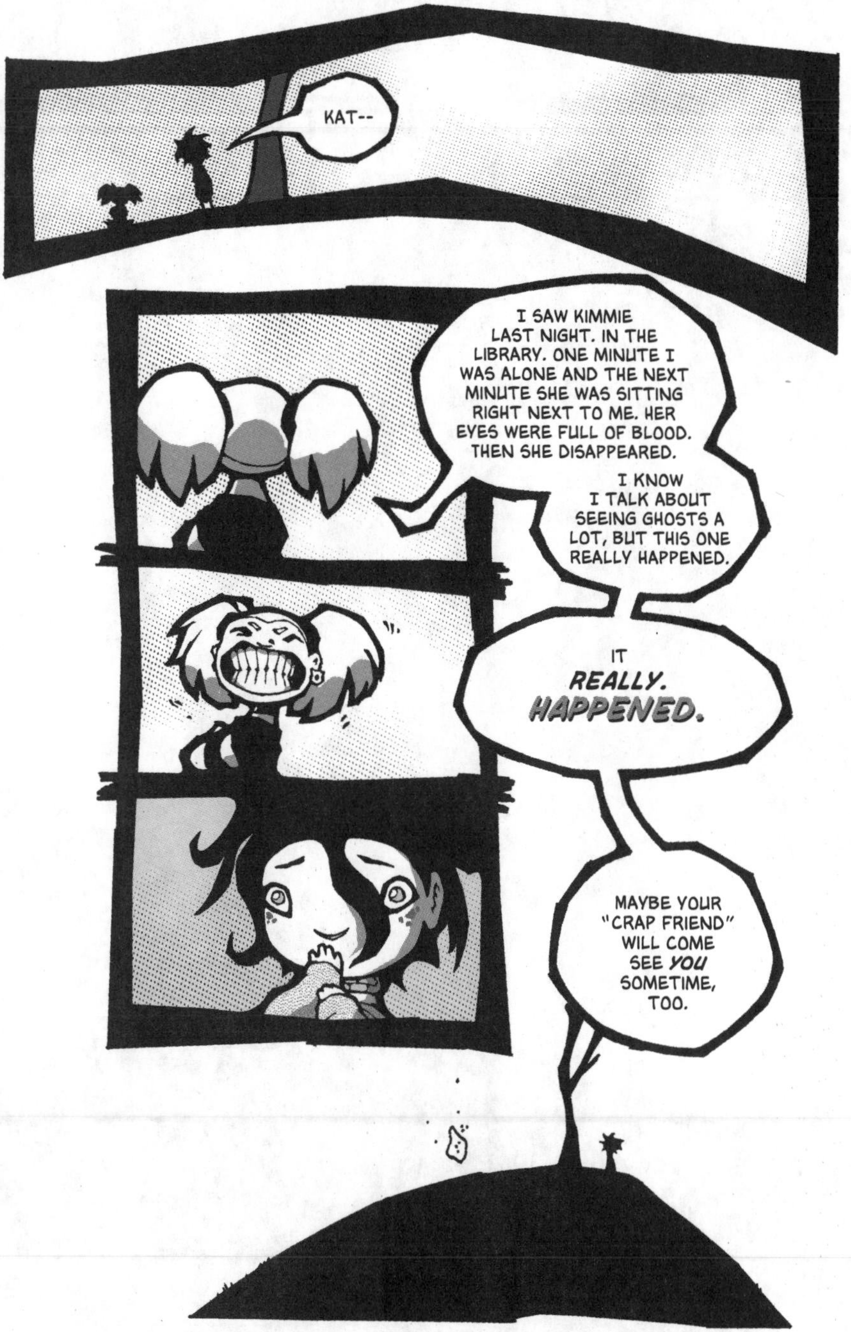
KAT--
I SAW KIMMIE LAST NIGHT. IN THE LIBRARY. ONE MINUTE I WAS ALONE AND THE NEXT MINUTE SHE WAS SITTING RIGHT NEXT TO ME. HER EYES WERE FULL OF BLOOD. THEN SHE DISAPPEARED.
I KNOW I TALK ABOUT SEEING GHOSTS A LOT, BUT THIS ONE REALLY HAPPENED.
IT *REALLY.* ***HAPPENED.***
MAYBE YOUR "CRAP FRIEND" WILL COME SEE *YOU* SOMETIME, TOO.

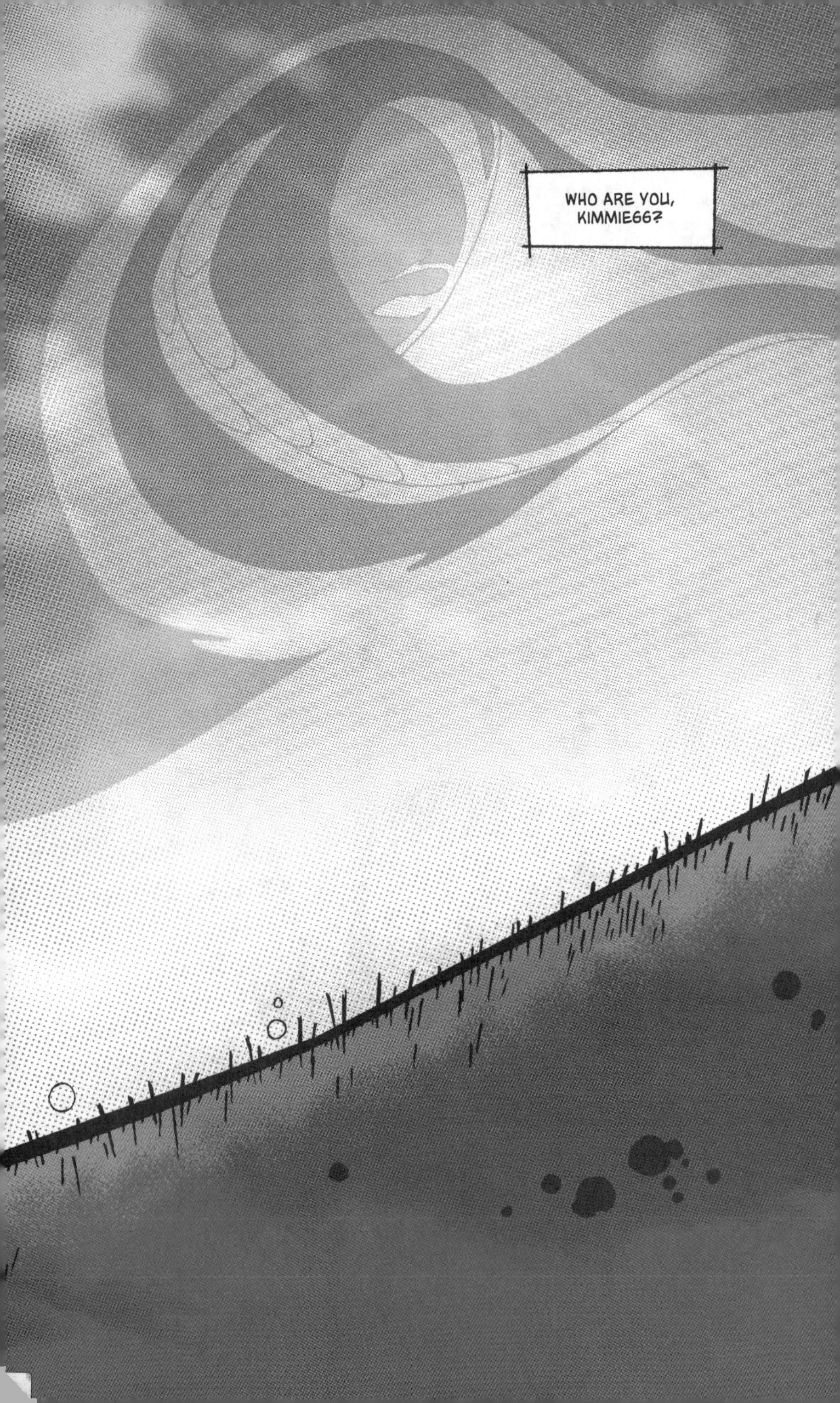
WHO ARE YOU, KIMMIE66?

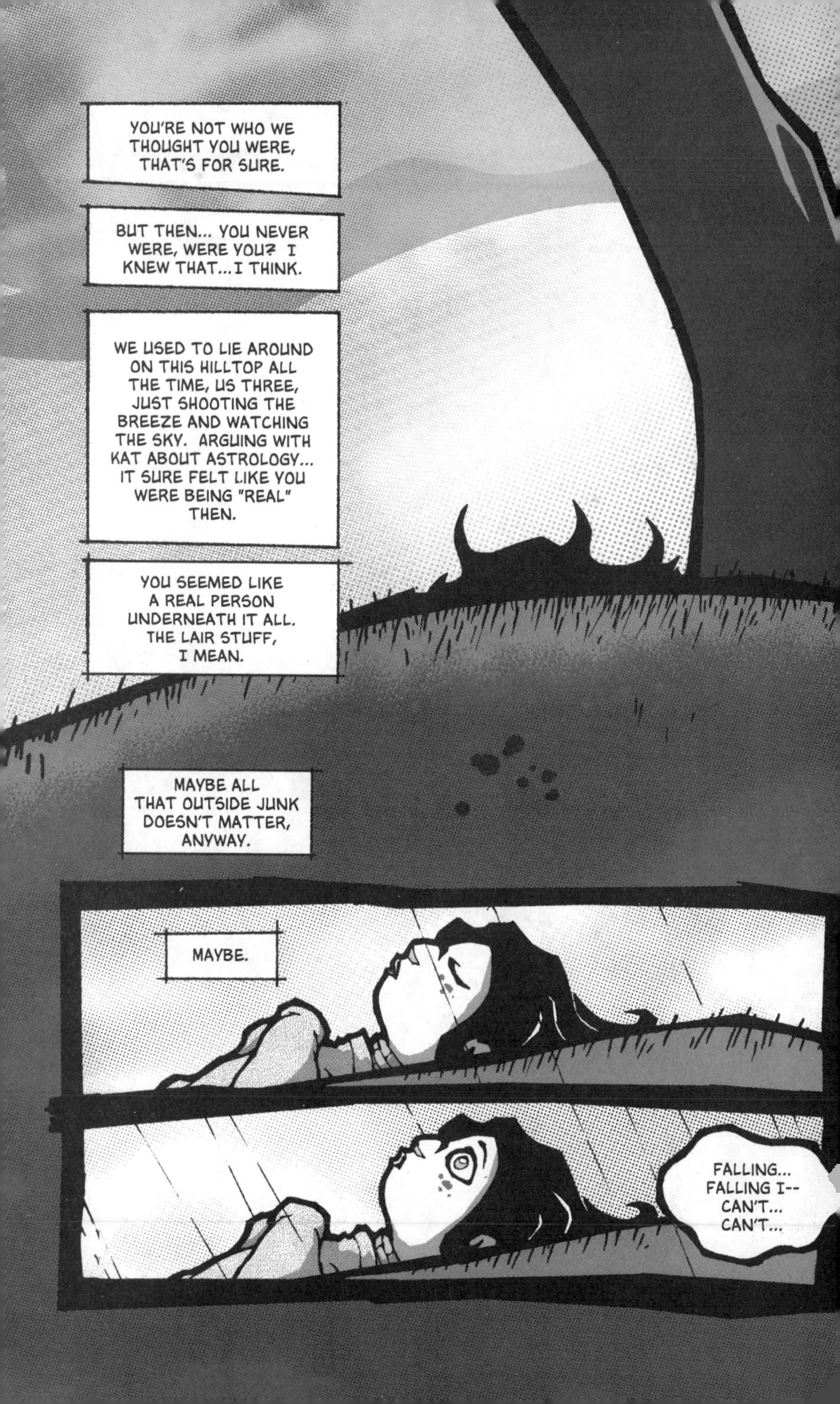
YOU'RE NOT WHO WE THOUGHT YOU WERE, THAT'S FOR SURE.
BUT THEN... YOU NEVER WERE, WERE YOU? I KNEW THAT...I THINK.
WE USED TO LIE AROUND ON THIS HILLTOP ALL THE TIME, US THREE, JUST SHOOTING THE BREEZE AND WATCHING THE SKY. ARGUING WITH KAT ABOUT ASTROLOGY... IT SURE FELT LIKE YOU WERE BEING "REAL" THEN.
YOU SEEMED LIKE A REAL PERSON UNDERNEATH IT ALL. THE LAIR STUFF, I MEAN.
MAYBE ALL THAT OUTSIDE JUNK DOESN'T MATTER, ANYWAY.
MAYBE.
FALLING... FALLING I-- CAN'T... CAN'T...

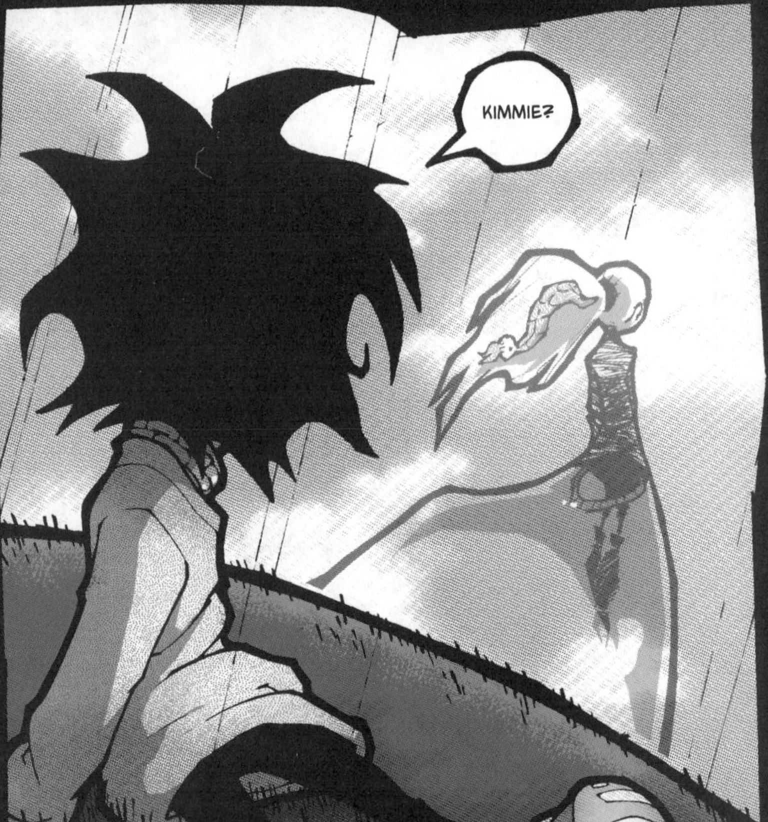
KIMMIE?

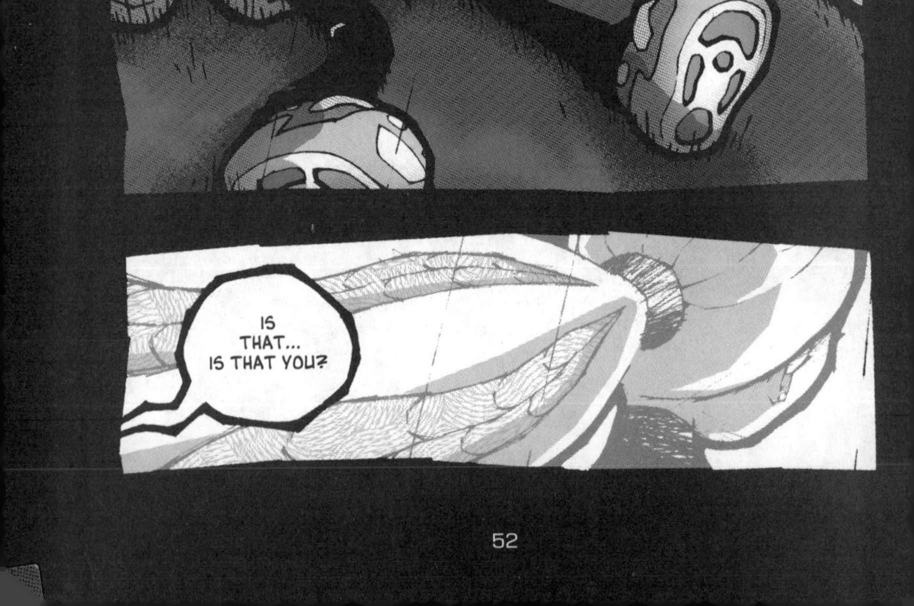
IS THAT... IS THAT YOU?

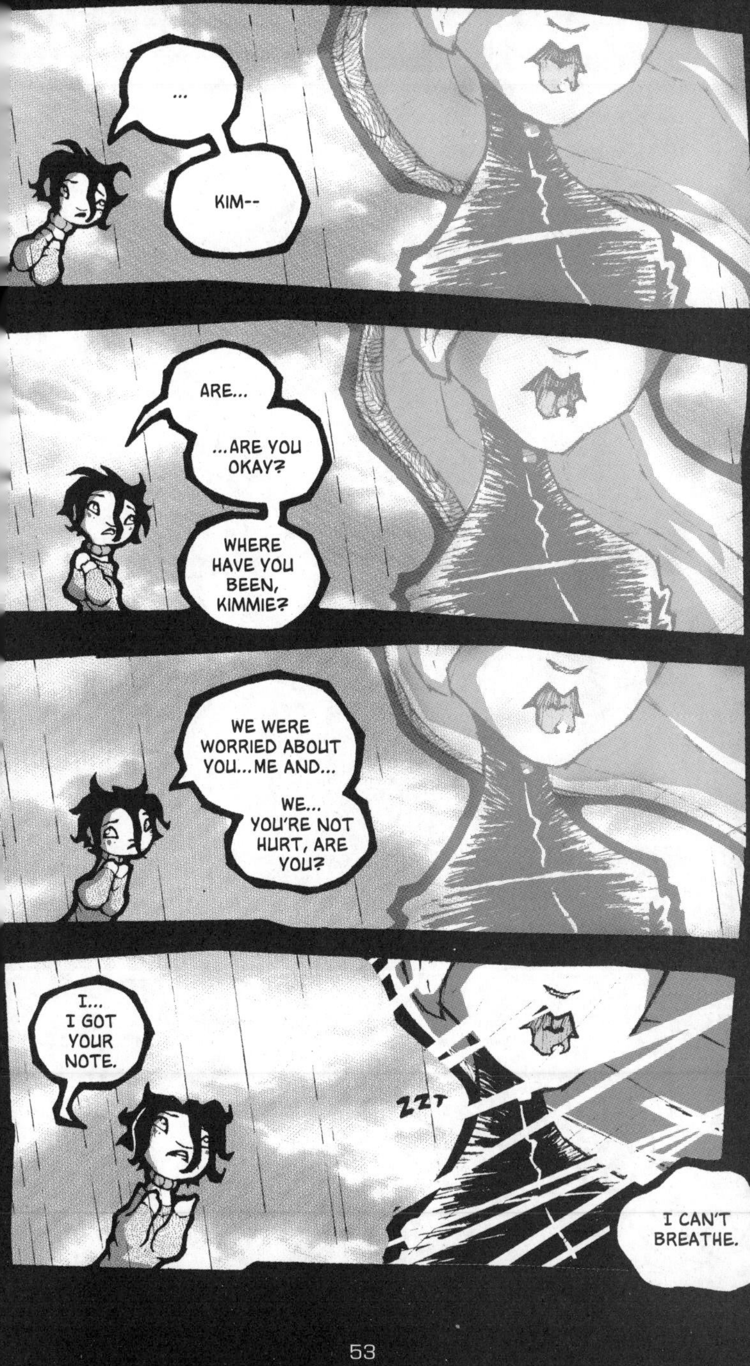
...
KIM--
ARE...
...ARE YOU OKAY?
WHERE HAVE YOU BEEN, KIMMIE?
WE WERE WORRIED ABOUT YOU...ME AND...
WE... YOU'RE NOT HURT, ARE YOU?
I... I GOT YOUR NOTE.
ZZT
I CAN'T BREATHE.

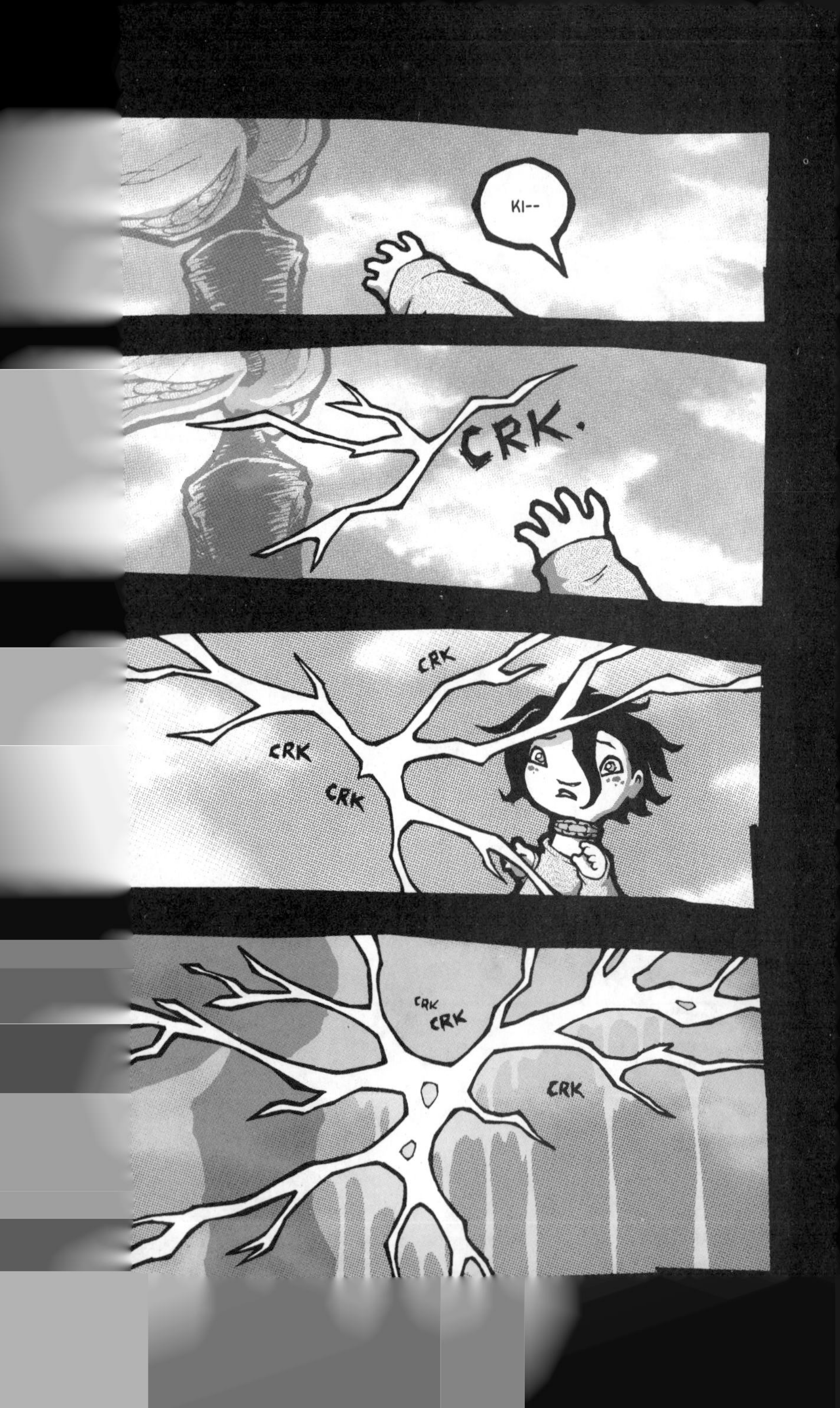
KI--
CRK.
CRK
CRK
CRK
CRK
CRK
CRK

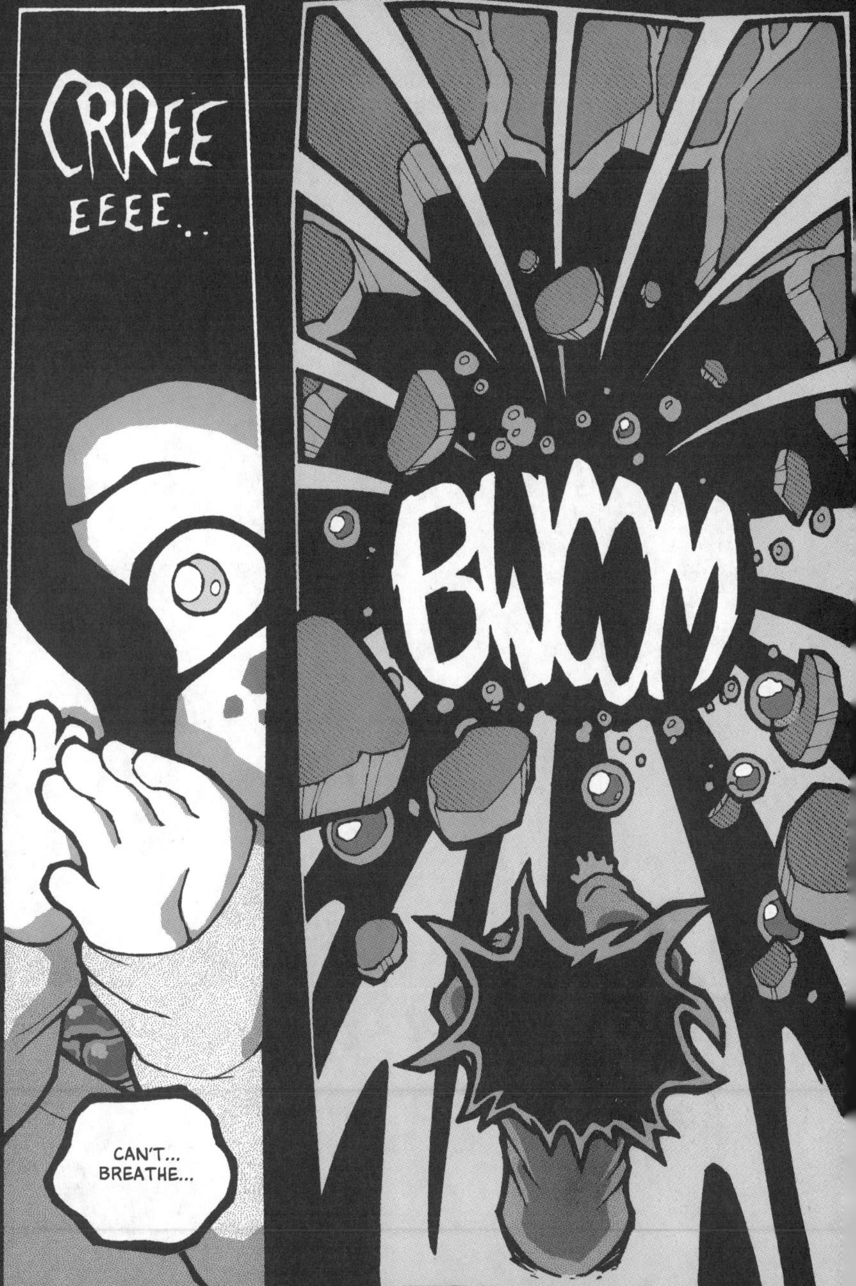
CRREE
EEEE...
CAN'T... BREATHE...
BWOOM

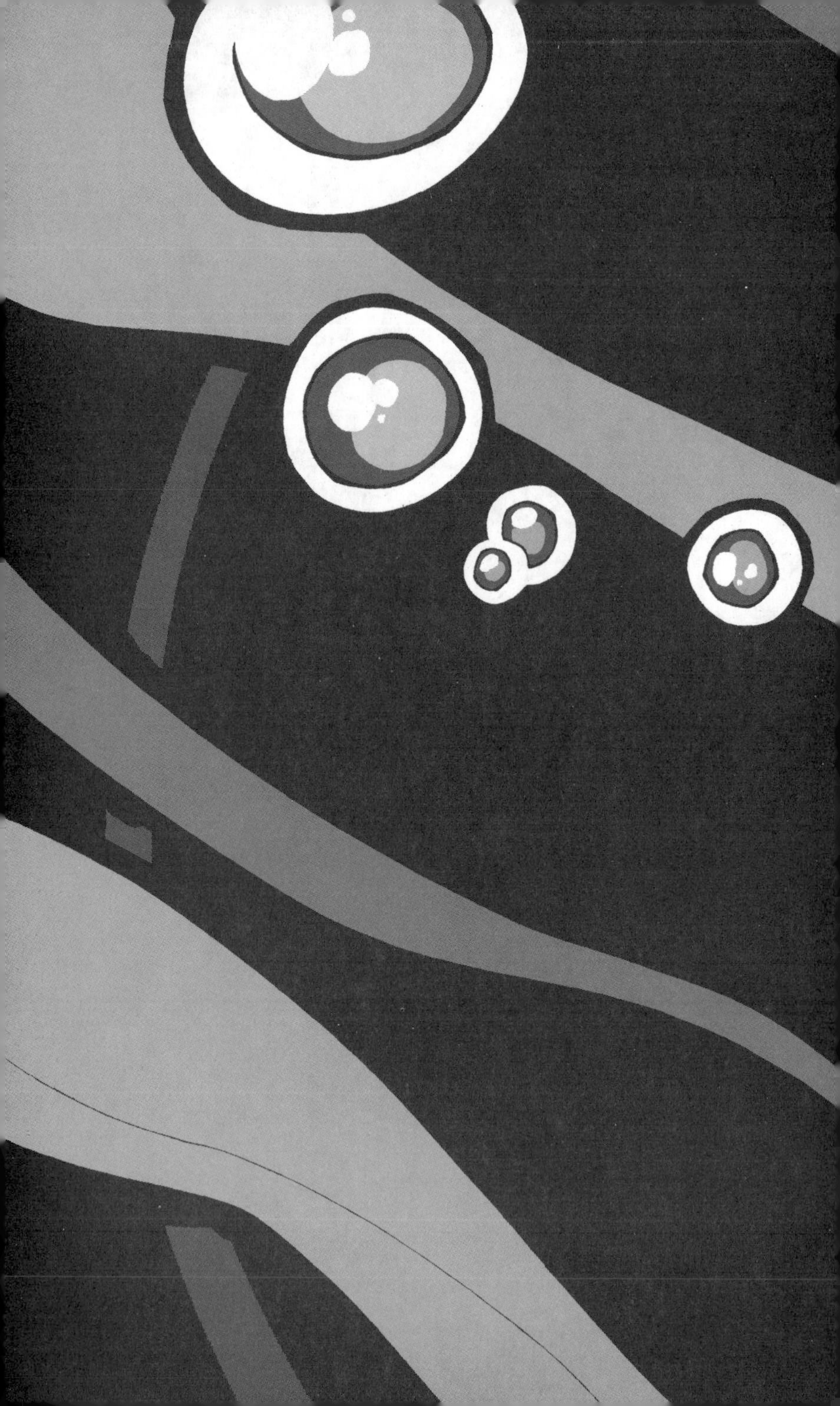

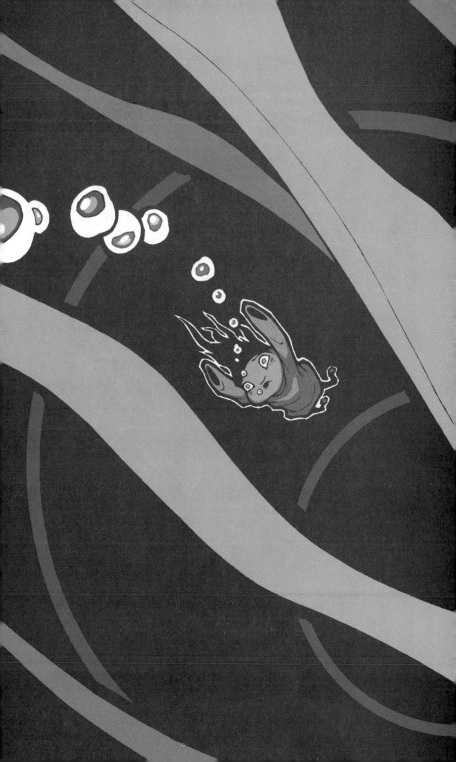

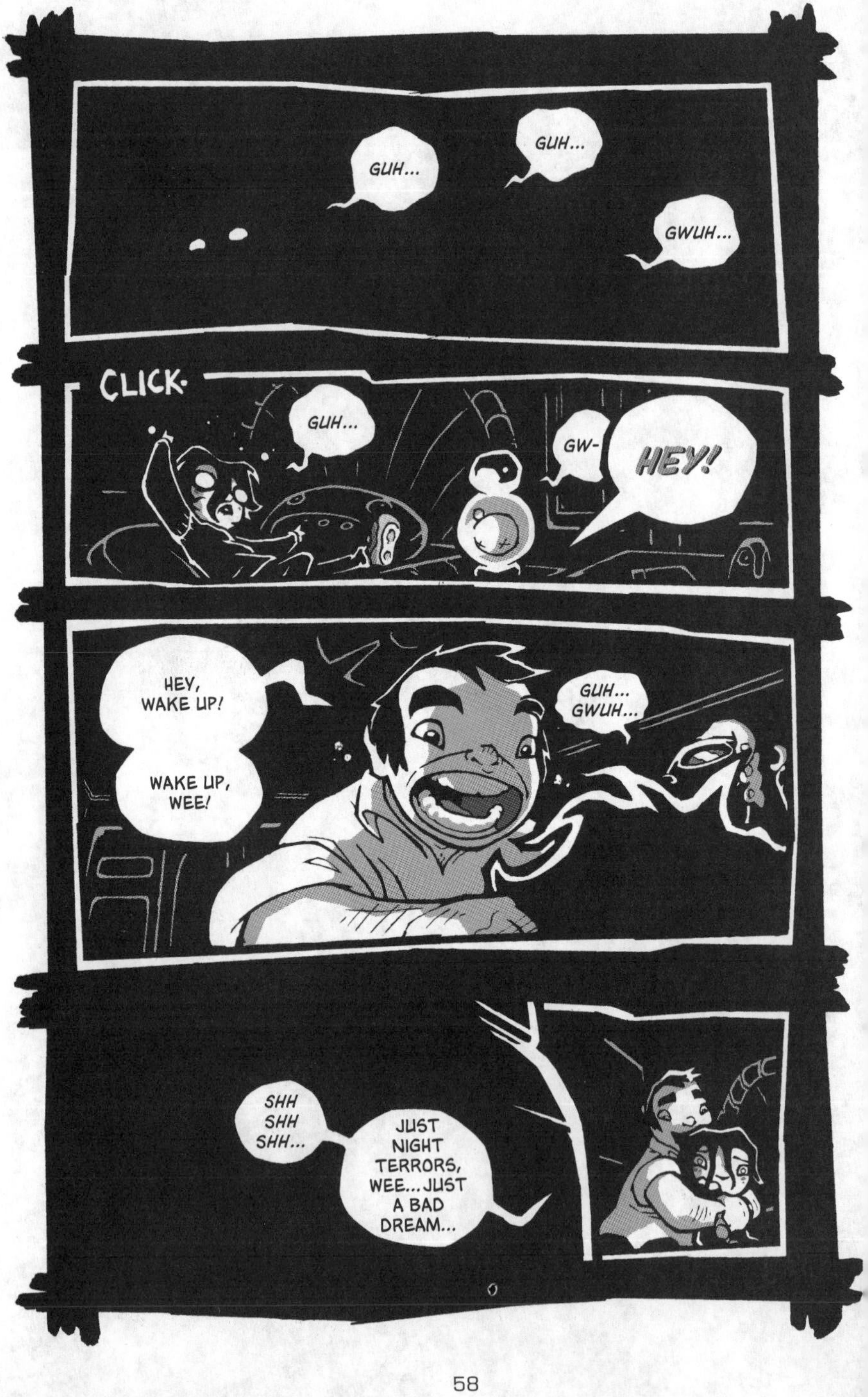
GUH...
GUH...
GWUH...
CLICK.
GUH...
GW-
HEY!
HEY, WAKE UP!
WAKE UP, WEE!
GUH... GWUH...
SHH SHH SHH...
JUST NIGHT TERRORS, WEE... JUST A BAD DREAM...

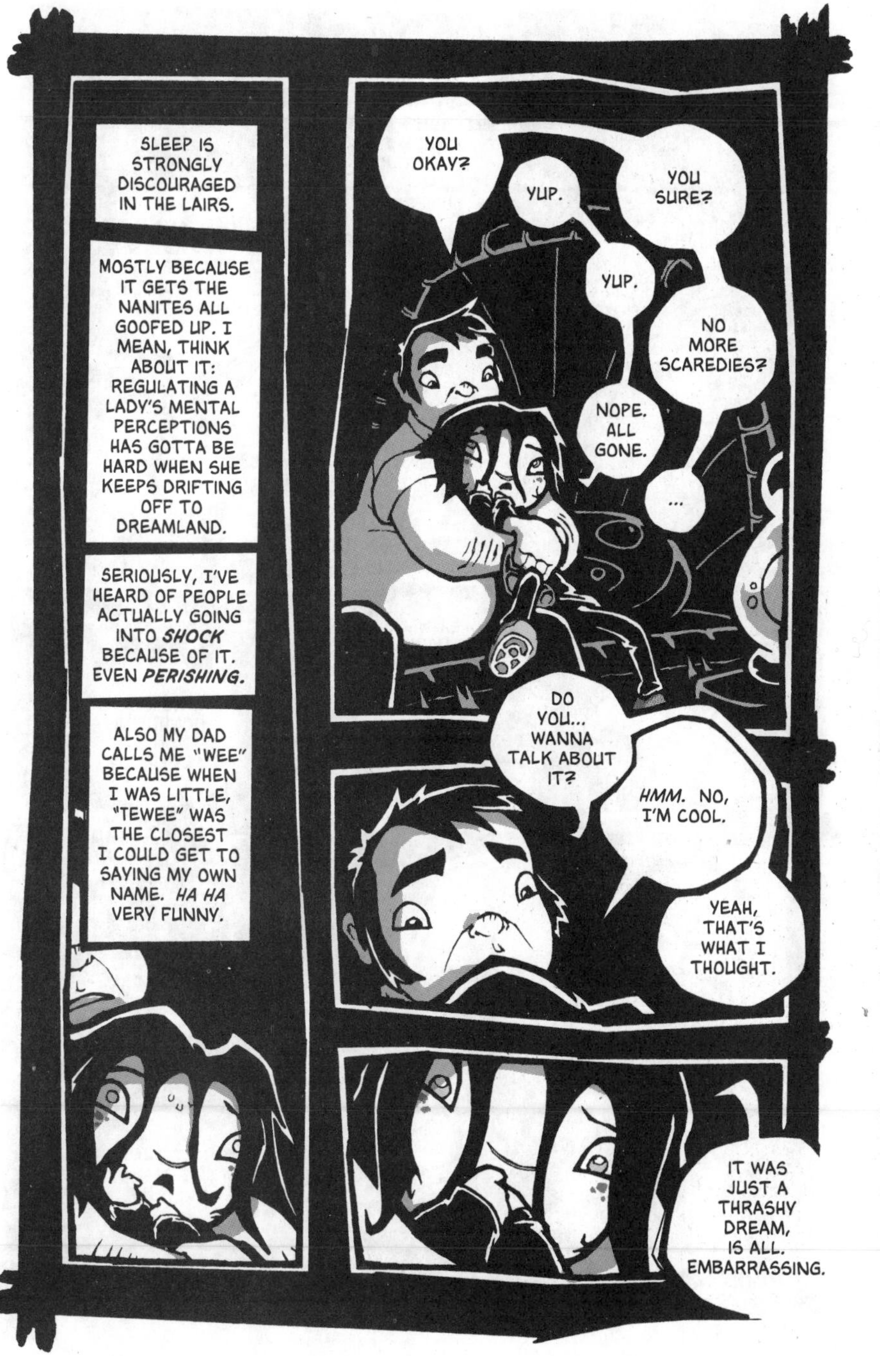
SLEEP IS STRONGLY DISCOURAGED IN THE LAIRS.
MOSTLY BECAUSE IT GETS THE NANITES ALL GOOFED UP. I MEAN, THINK ABOUT IT: REGULATING A LADY'S MENTAL PERCEPTIONS HAS GOTTA BE HARD WHEN SHE KEEPS DRIFTING OFF TO DREAMLAND.
SERIOUSLY, I'VE HEARD OF PEOPLE ACTUALLY GOING INTO *SHOCK* BECAUSE OF IT. EVEN *PERISHING.*
ALSO MY DAD CALLS ME "WEE" BECAUSE WHEN I WAS LITTLE, "TEWEE" WAS THE CLOSEST I COULD GET TO SAYING MY OWN NAME. *HA HA* VERY FUNNY.
YOU OKAY?
YUP.
YOU SURE?
YUP.
NO MORE SCAREDIES?
NOPE. ALL GONE.
...
DO YOU... WANNA TALK ABOUT IT?
HMM. NO, I'M COOL.
YEAH, THAT'S WHAT I THOUGHT.
IT WAS JUST A THRASHY DREAM, IS ALL. EMBARRASSING.

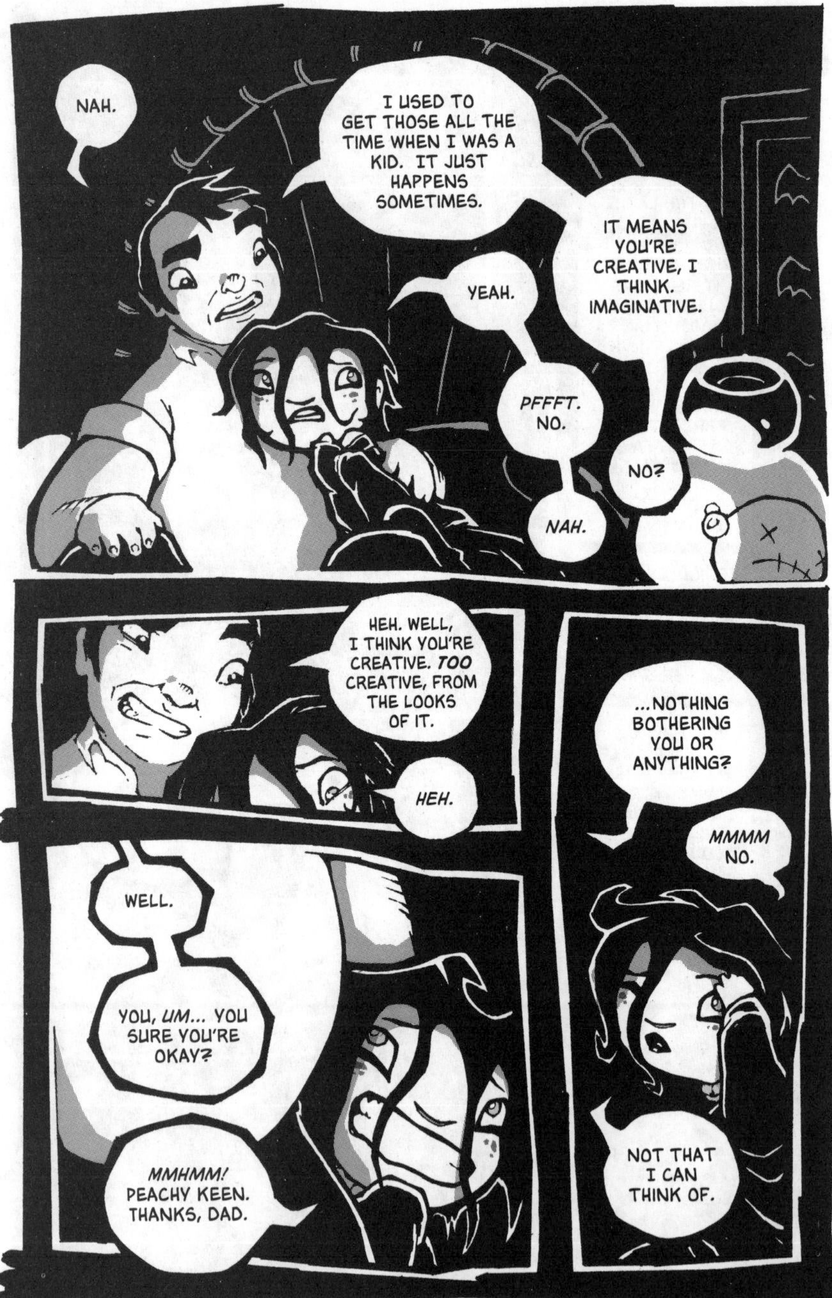
NAH.
I USED TO GET THOSE ALL THE TIME WHEN I WAS A KID. IT JUST HAPPENS SOMETIMES.
YEAH.
IT MEANS YOU'RE CREATIVE, I THINK. IMAGINATIVE.
PFFFT. NO.
NO?
NAH.
HEH. WELL, I THINK YOU'RE CREATIVE. *TOO* CREATIVE, FROM THE LOOKS OF IT.
HEH.
...NOTHING BOTHERING YOU OR ANYTHING?
MMMM NO.
NOT THAT I CAN THINK OF.
WELL.
YOU, *UM*... YOU SURE YOU'RE OKAY?
MMHMM! PEACHY KEEN. THANKS, DAD.

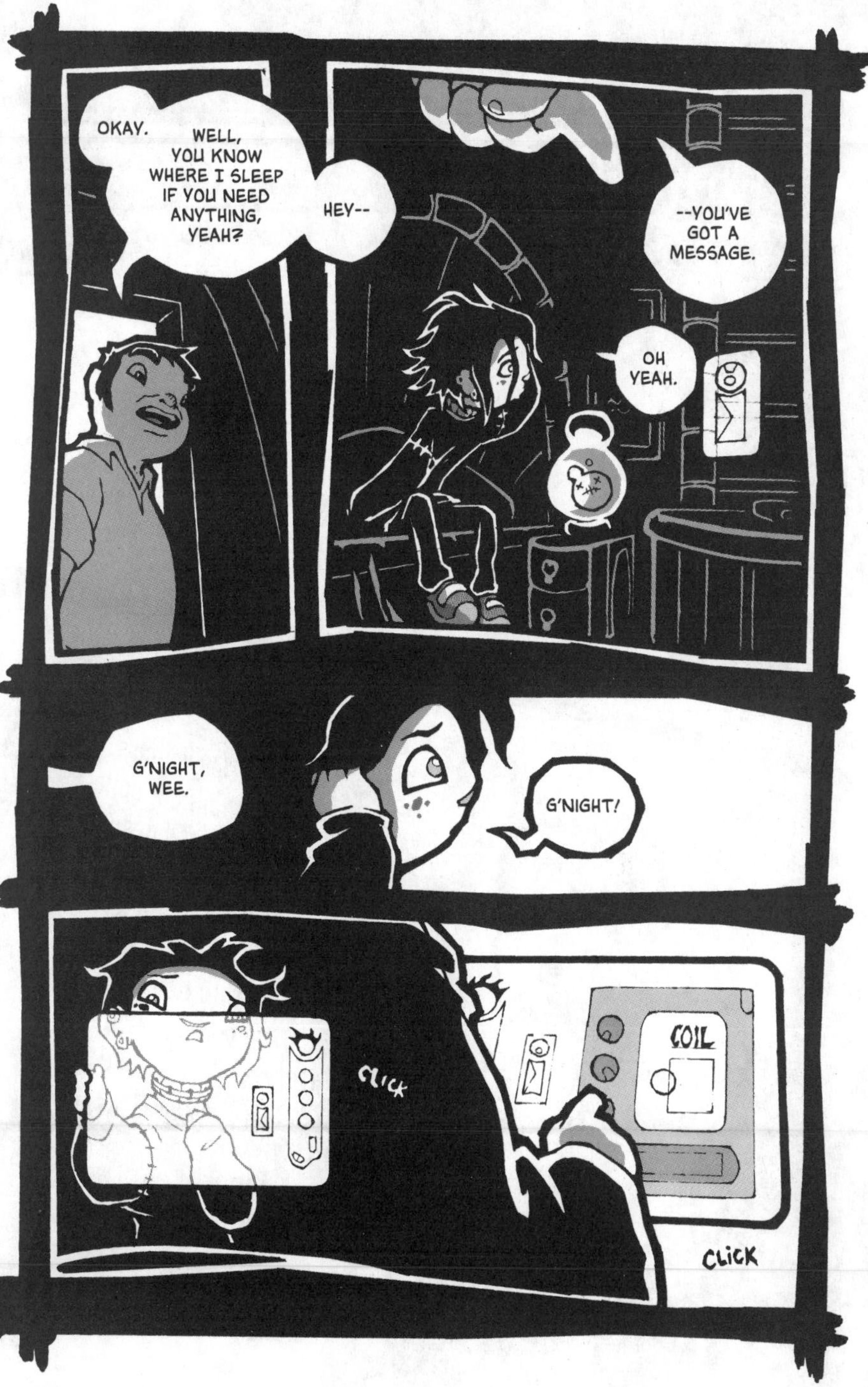
OKAY. WELL, YOU KNOW WHERE I SLEEP IF YOU NEED ANYTHING, YEAH?
HEY--
--YOU'VE GOT A MESSAGE.
OH YEAH.
G'NIGHT, WEE.
G'NIGHT!
CLICK
COIL
CLICK

<_TennSYS Heir Found Dead>

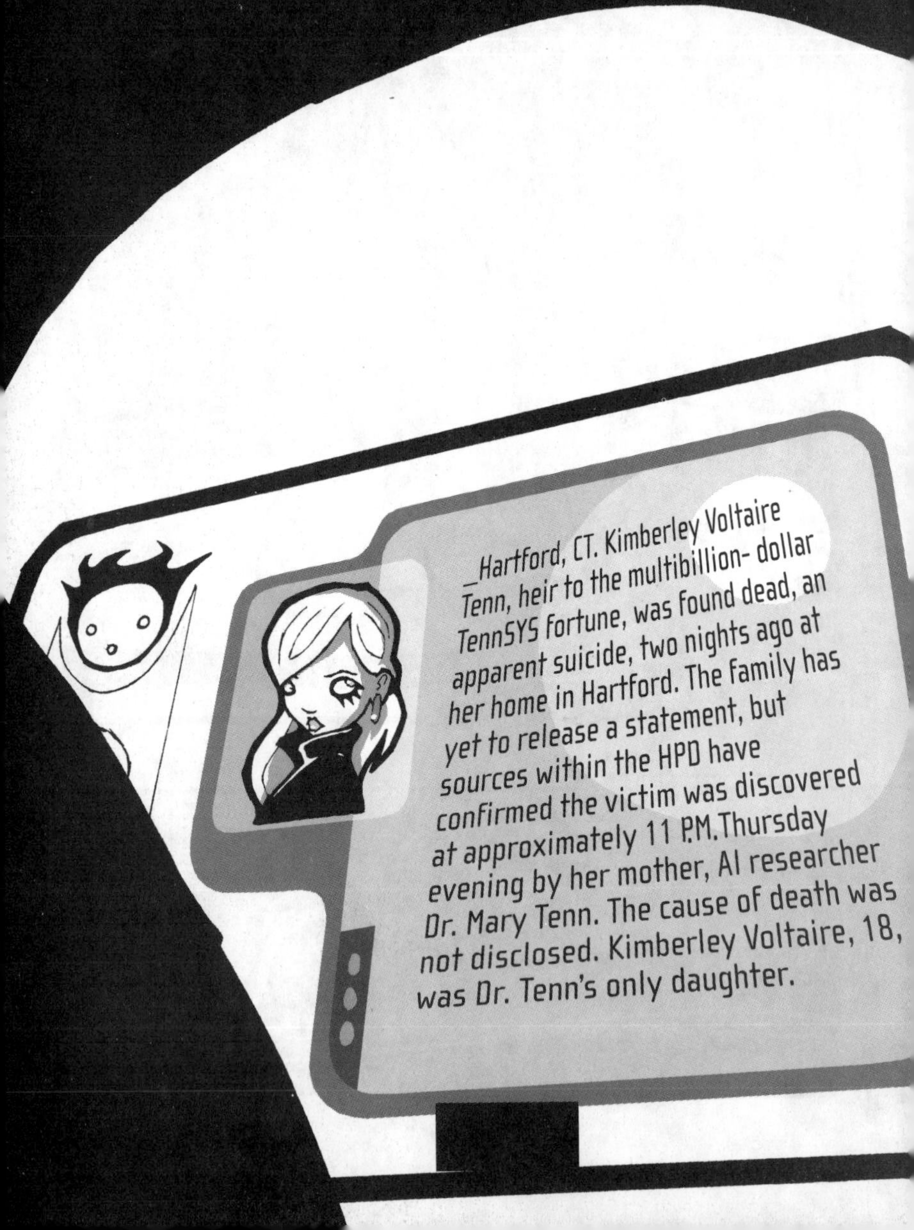
_Hartford, CT. Kimberley Voltaire Tenn, heir to the multibillion- dollar TennSYS fortune, was found dead, an apparent suicide, two nights ago at her home in Hartford. The family has yet to release a statement, but sources within the HPD have confirmed the victim was discovered at approximately 11 P.M.Thursday evening by her mother, AI researcher Dr. Mary Tenn. The cause of death was not disclosed. Kimberley Voltaire, 18, was Dr. Tenn's only daughter.

CHAPTER THREE

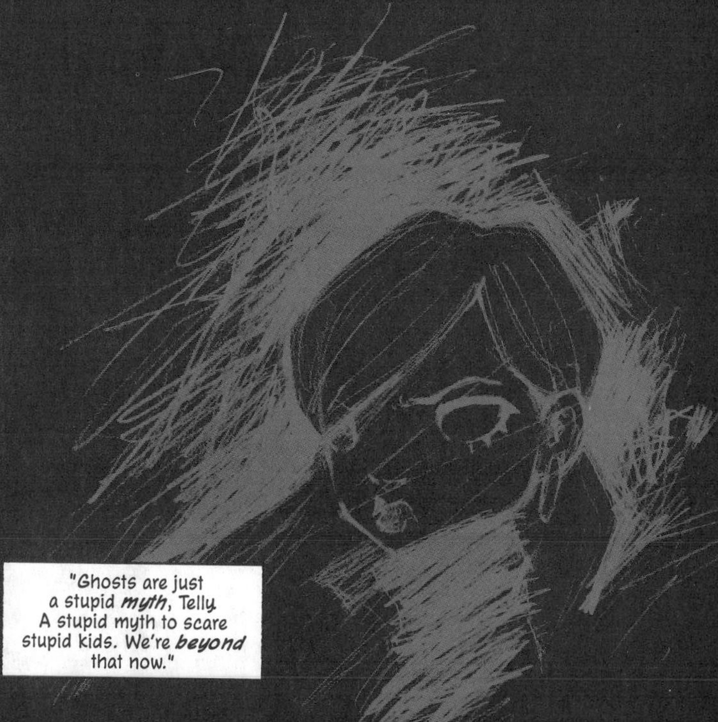
"Ghosts are just a stupid *myth*, Telly. A stupid myth to scare stupid kids. We're *beyond* that now."

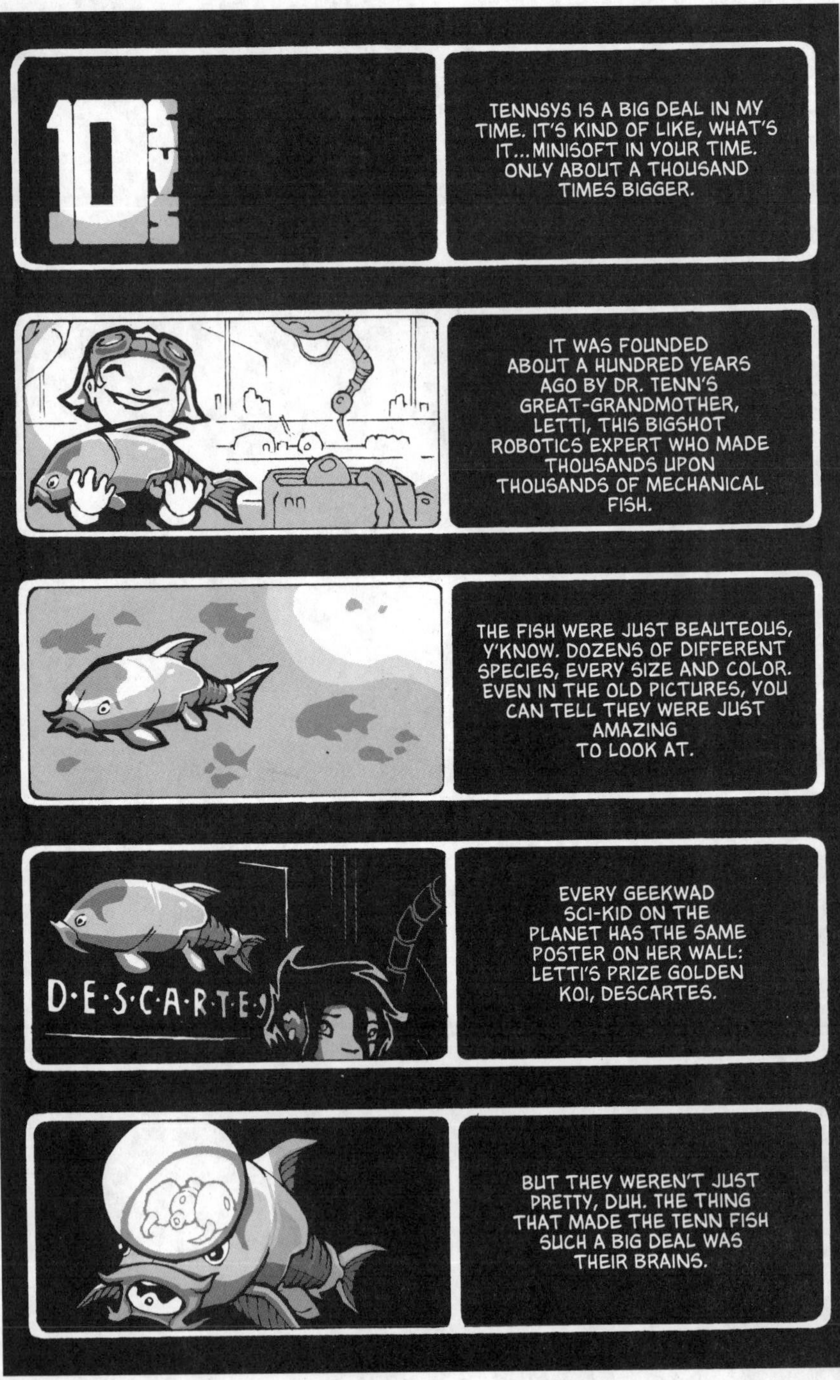
TENNSYS IS A BIG DEAL IN MY TIME. IT'S KIND OF LIKE, WHAT'S IT...MINISOFT IN YOUR TIME. ONLY ABOUT A THOUSAND TIMES BIGGER.
IT WAS FOUNDED ABOUT A HUNDRED YEARS AGO BY DR. TENN'S GREAT-GRANDMOTHER, LETTI, THIS BIGSHOT ROBOTICS EXPERT WHO MADE THOUSANDS UPON THOUSANDS OF MECHANICAL FISH.
THE FISH WERE JUST BEAUTEOUS, Y'KNOW. DOZENS OF DIFFERENT SPECIES, EVERY SIZE AND COLOR. EVEN IN THE OLD PICTURES, YOU CAN TELL THEY WERE JUST AMAZING TO LOOK AT.
D·E·S·C·A·R·T·E·S
EVERY GEEKWAD SCI-KID ON THE PLANET HAS THE SAME POSTER ON HER WALL: LETTI'S PRIZE GOLDEN KOI, DESCARTES.
BUT THEY WEREN'T JUST PRETTY, DUH. THE THING THAT MADE THE TENN FISH SUCH A BIG DEAL WAS THEIR BRAINS.

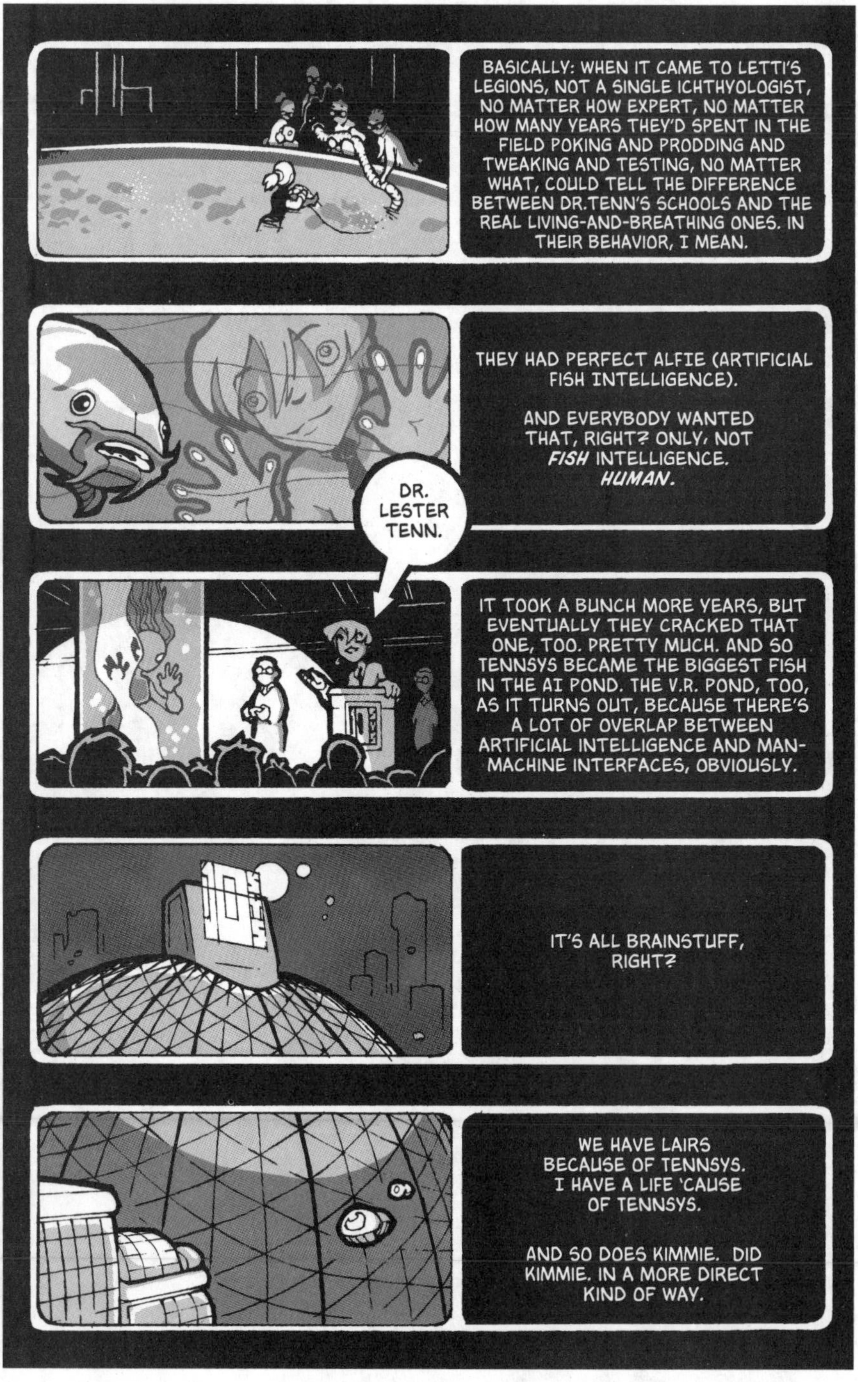

BASICALLY: WHEN IT CAME TO LETTI'S LEGIONS, NOT A SINGLE ICHTHYOLOGIST, NO MATTER HOW EXPERT, NO MATTER HOW MANY YEARS THEY'D SPENT IN THE FIELD POKING AND PRODDING AND TWEAKING AND TESTING, NO MATTER WHAT, COULD TELL THE DIFFERENCE BETWEEN DR. TENN'S SCHOOLS AND THE REAL LIVING-AND-BREATHING ONES. IN THEIR BEHAVIOR, I MEAN.
THEY HAD PERFECT ALFIE (ARTIFICIAL FISH INTELLIGENCE).
AND EVERYBODY WANTED THAT, RIGHT? ONLY, NOT *FISH* INTELLIGENCE. ***HUMAN.***
DR. LESTER TENN.
IT TOOK A BUNCH MORE YEARS, BUT EVENTUALLY THEY CRACKED THAT ONE, TOO. PRETTY MUCH. AND SO TENNSYS BECAME THE BIGGEST FISH IN THE AI POND. THE V.R. POND, TOO, AS IT TURNS OUT, BECAUSE THERE'S A LOT OF OVERLAP BETWEEN ARTIFICIAL INTELLIGENCE AND MAN-MACHINE INTERFACES, OBVIOUSLY.
IT'S ALL BRAINSTUFF, RIGHT?
WE HAVE LAIRS BECAUSE OF TENNSYS. I HAVE A LIFE 'CAUSE OF TENNSYS.
AND SO DOES KIMMIE. DID KIMMIE. IN A MORE DIRECT KIND OF WAY.

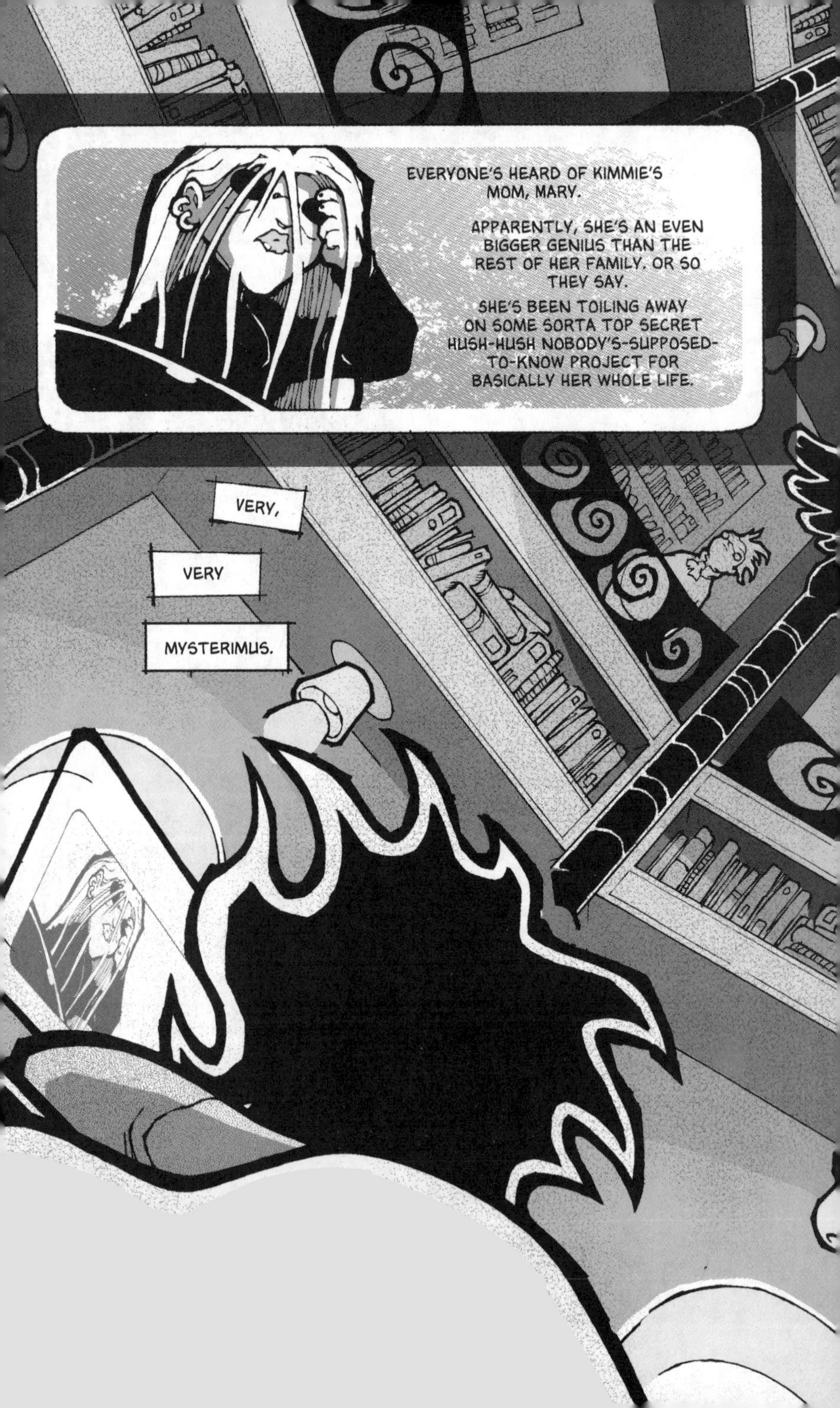
EVERYONE'S HEARD OF KIMMIE'S MOM, MARY.
APPARENTLY, SHE'S AN EVEN BIGGER GENIUS THAN THE REST OF HER FAMILY. OR SO THEY SAY.
SHE'S BEEN TOILING AWAY ON SOME SORTA TOP SECRET HUSH-HUSH NOBODY'S-SUPPOSED-TO-KNOW PROJECT FOR BASICALLY HER WHOLE LIFE.
VERY,
VERY
MYSTERIMUS.

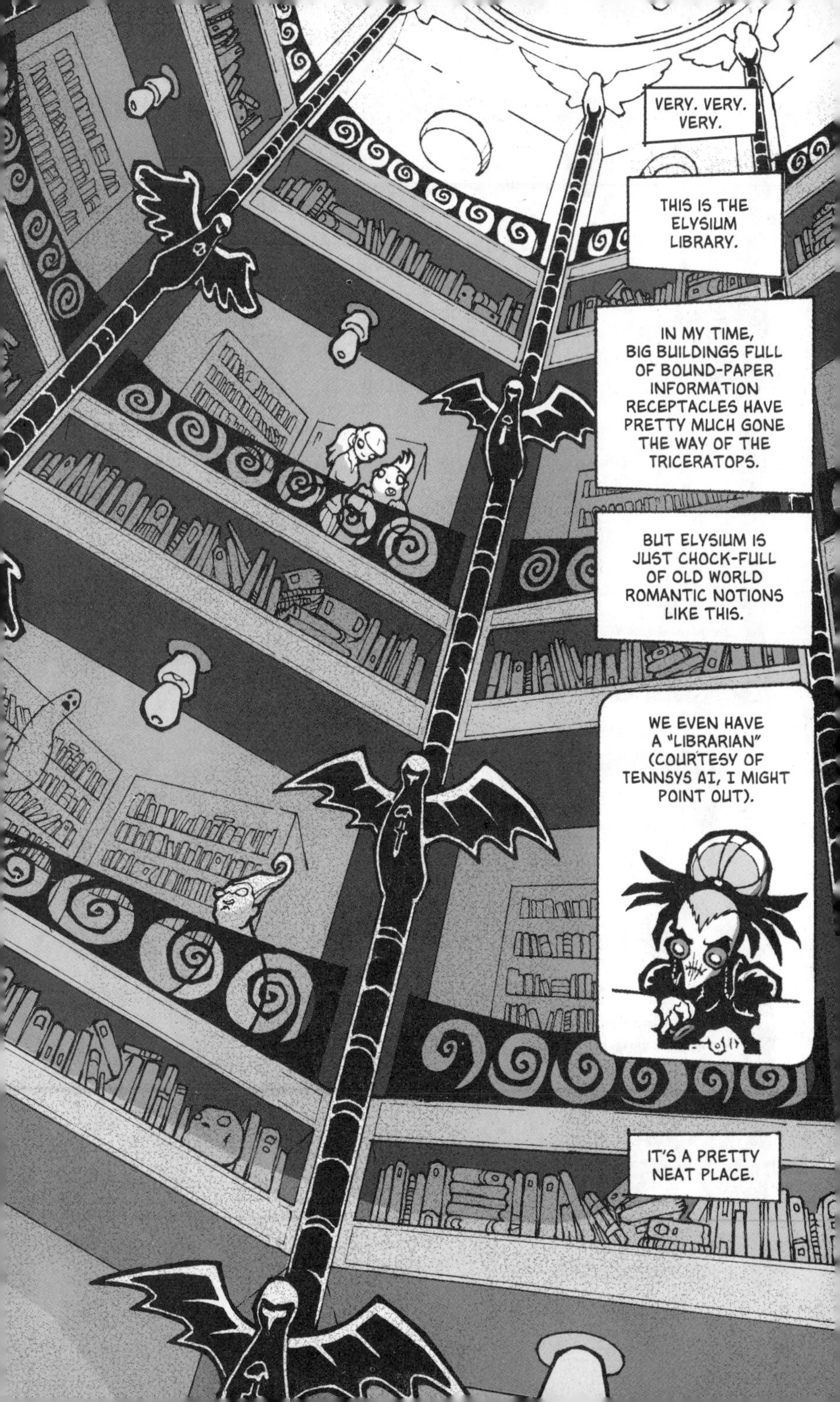
VERY. VERY. VERY.
THIS IS THE ELYSIUM LIBRARY.
IN MY TIME, BIG BUILDINGS FULL OF BOUND-PAPER INFORMATION RECEPTACLES HAVE PRETTY MUCH GONE THE WAY OF THE TRICERATOPS.
BUT ELYSIUM IS JUST CHOCK-FULL OF OLD WORLD ROMANTIC NOTIONS LIKE THIS.
WE EVEN HAVE A "LIBRARIAN" (COURTESY OF TENNSYS AI, I MIGHT POINT OUT).
IT'S A PRETTY NEAT PLACE.

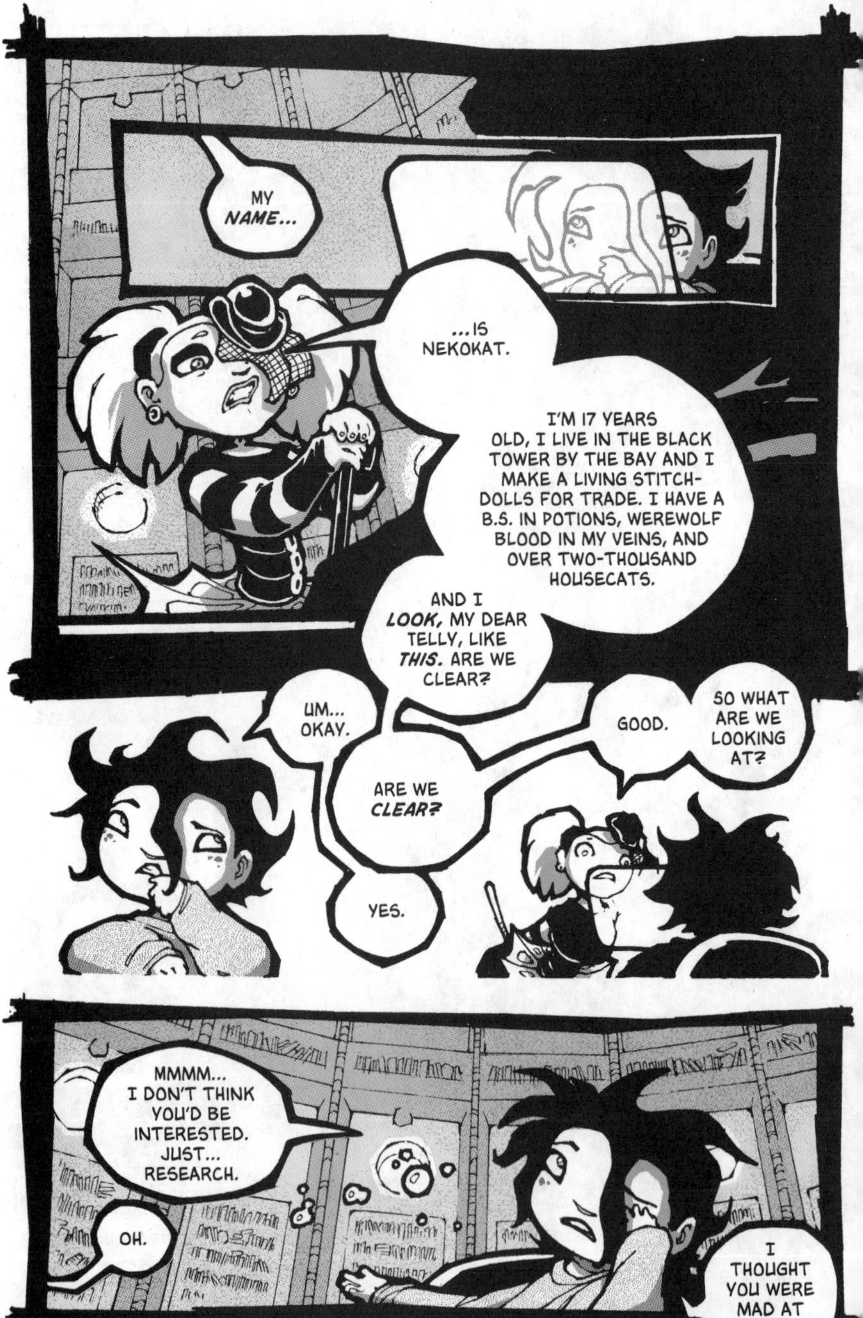
MY NAME...
...IS NEKOKAT.
I'M 17 YEARS OLD, I LIVE IN THE BLACK TOWER BY THE BAY AND I MAKE A LIVING STITCH-DOLLS FOR TRADE. I HAVE A B.S. IN POTIONS, WEREWOLF BLOOD IN MY VEINS, AND OVER TWO-THOUSAND HOUSECATS.
AND I LOOK, MY DEAR TELLY, LIKE THIS. ARE WE CLEAR?
UM... OKAY.
ARE WE CLEAR?
YES.
GOOD.
SO WHAT ARE WE LOOKING AT?
MMMM... I DON'T THINK YOU'D BE INTERESTED. JUST... RESEARCH.
OH.
I THOUGHT YOU WERE MAD AT ME.

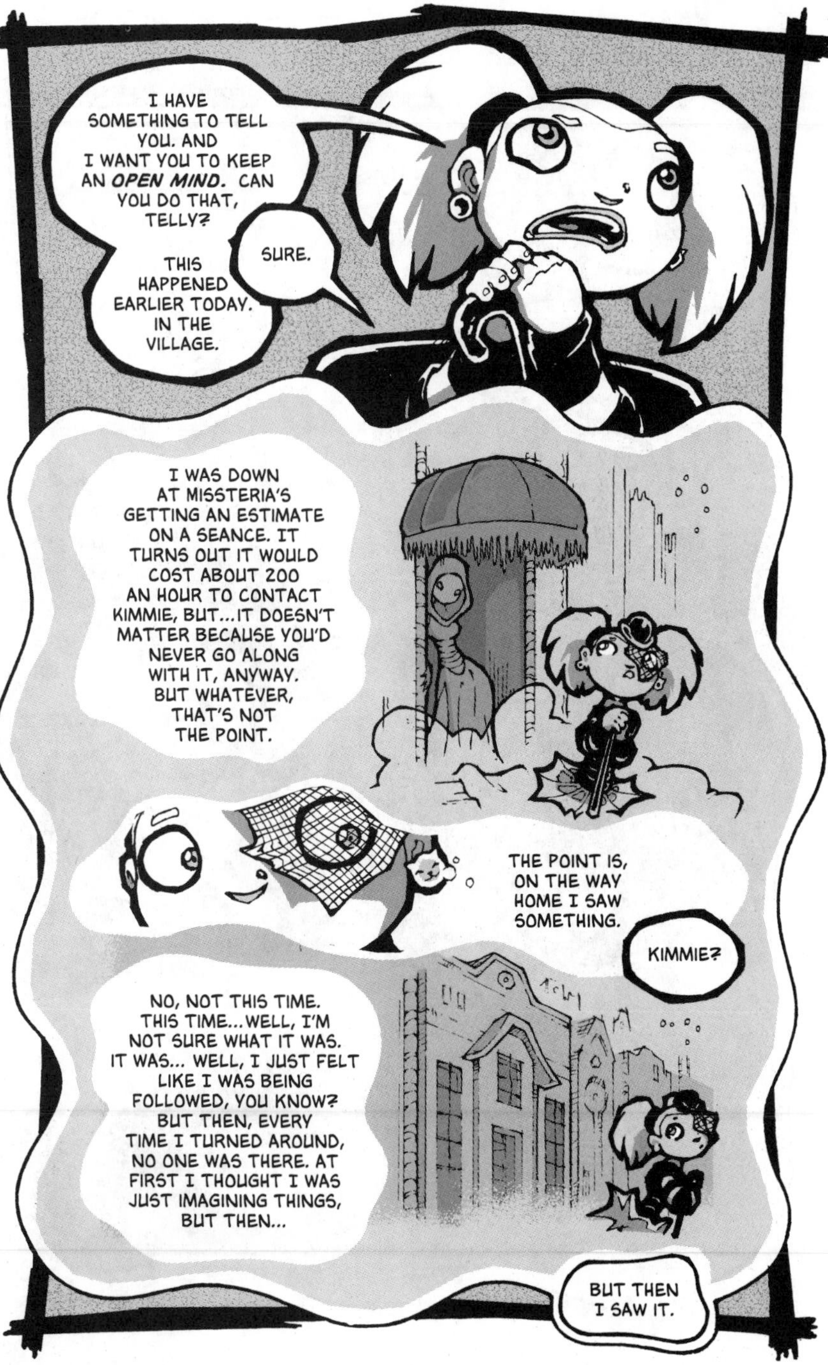
I HAVE SOMETHING TO TELL YOU. AND I WANT YOU TO KEEP AN *OPEN MIND.* CAN YOU DO THAT, TELLY?
SURE.
THIS HAPPENED EARLIER TODAY. IN THE VILLAGE.
I WAS DOWN AT MISSTERIA'S GETTING AN ESTIMATE ON A SEANCE. IT TURNS OUT IT WOULD COST ABOUT 200 AN HOUR TO CONTACT KIMMIE, BUT...IT DOESN'T MATTER BECAUSE YOU'D NEVER GO ALONG WITH IT, ANYWAY. BUT WHATEVER, THAT'S NOT THE POINT.
THE POINT IS, ON THE WAY HOME I SAW SOMETHING.
KIMMIE?
NO, NOT THIS TIME. THIS TIME...WELL, I'M NOT SURE WHAT IT WAS. IT WAS... WELL, I JUST FELT LIKE I WAS BEING FOLLOWED, YOU KNOW? BUT THEN, EVERY TIME I TURNED AROUND, NO ONE WAS THERE. AT FIRST I THOUGHT I WAS JUST IMAGINING THINGS, BUT THEN...
BUT THEN I SAW IT.

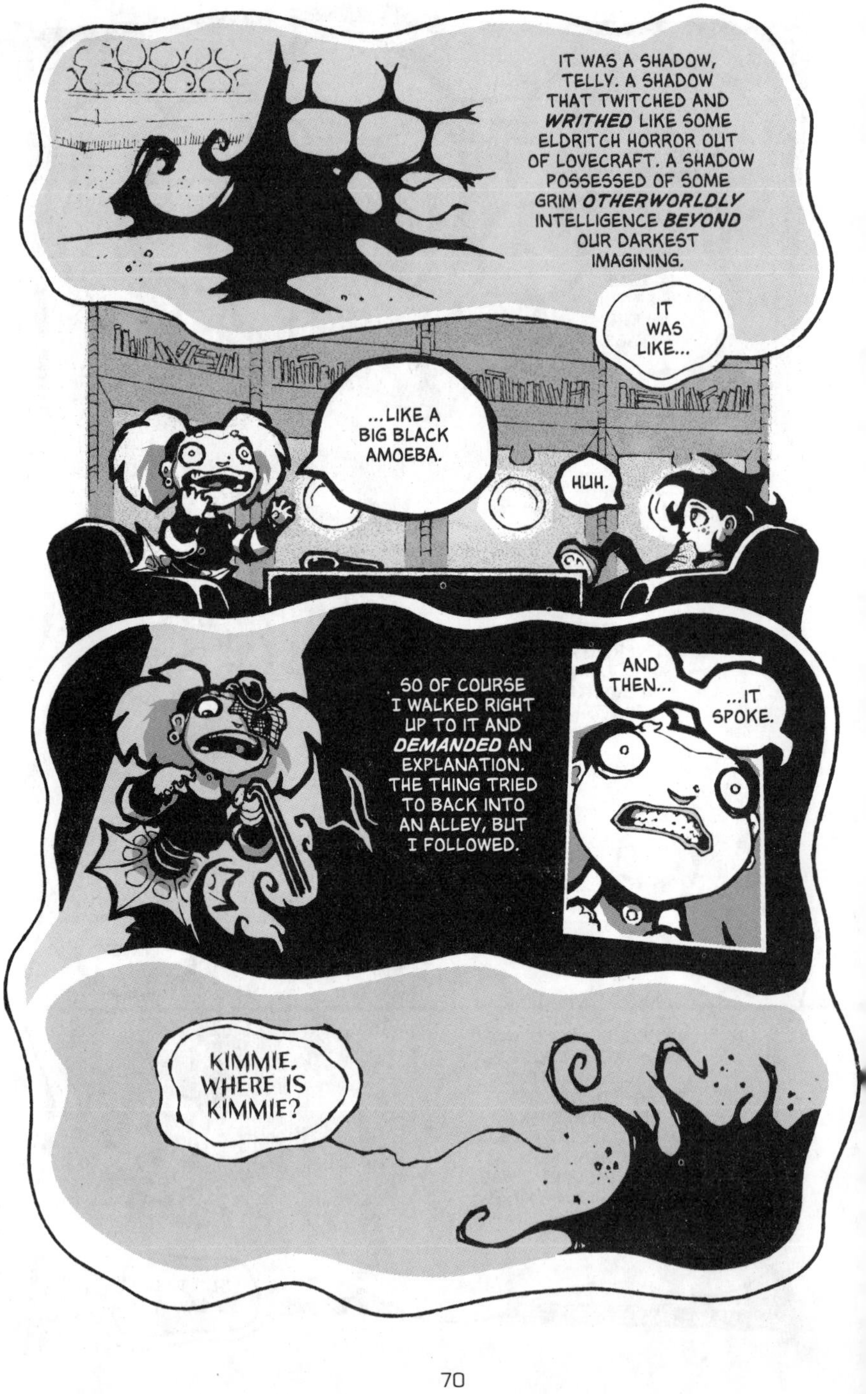
IT WAS A SHADOW, TELLY. A SHADOW THAT TWITCHED AND *WRITHED* LIKE SOME ELDRITCH HORROR OUT OF LOVECRAFT. A SHADOW POSSESSED OF SOME GRIM *OTHERWORLDLY* INTELLIGENCE *BEYOND* OUR DARKEST IMAGINING.
IT WAS LIKE...
...LIKE A BIG BLACK AMOEBA.
HUH.
SO OF COURSE I WALKED RIGHT UP TO IT AND *DEMANDED* AN EXPLANATION. THE THING TRIED TO BACK INTO AN ALLEY, BUT I FOLLOWED.
AND THEN...
...IT SPOKE.
KIMMIE. WHERE IS KIMMIE?

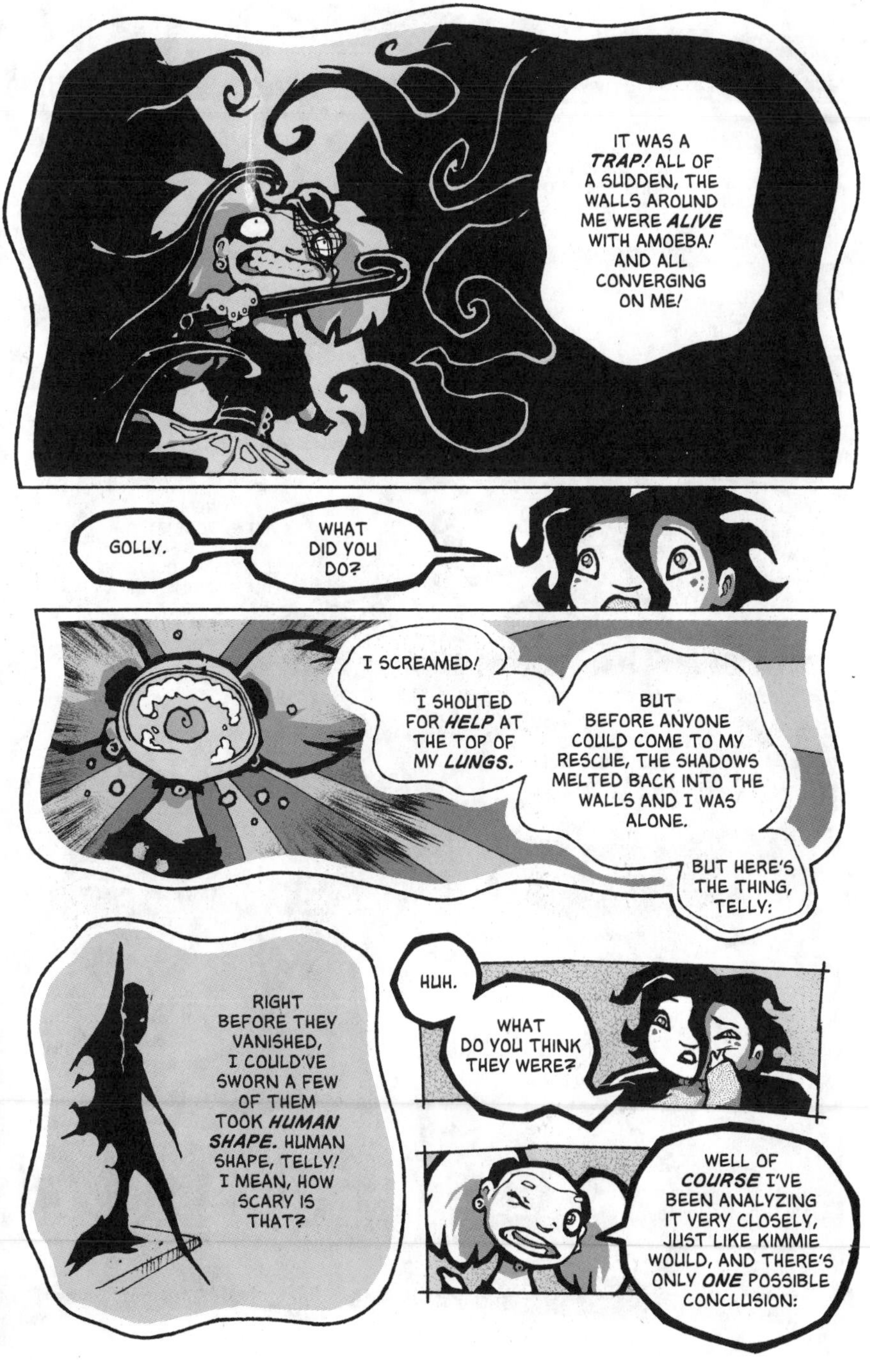
IT WAS A ***TRAP!*** ALL OF A SUDDEN, THE WALLS AROUND ME WERE ***ALIVE*** WITH AMOEBA! AND ALL CONVERGING ON ME!
GOLLY.
WHAT DID YOU DO?
I SCREAMED!
I SHOUTED FOR ***HELP*** AT THE TOP OF MY ***LUNGS.***
BUT BEFORE ANYONE COULD COME TO MY RESCUE, THE SHADOWS MELTED BACK INTO THE WALLS AND I WAS ALONE.
BUT HERE'S THE THING, TELLY:
RIGHT BEFORE THEY VANISHED, I COULD'VE SWORN A FEW OF THEM TOOK ***HUMAN SHAPE.*** HUMAN SHAPE, TELLY! I MEAN, HOW SCARY IS THAT?
HUH.
WHAT DO YOU THINK THEY WERE?
WELL OF ***COURSE*** I'VE BEEN ANALYZING IT VERY CLOSELY, JUST LIKE KIMMIE WOULD, AND THERE'S ONLY ***ONE*** POSSIBLE CONCLUSION:

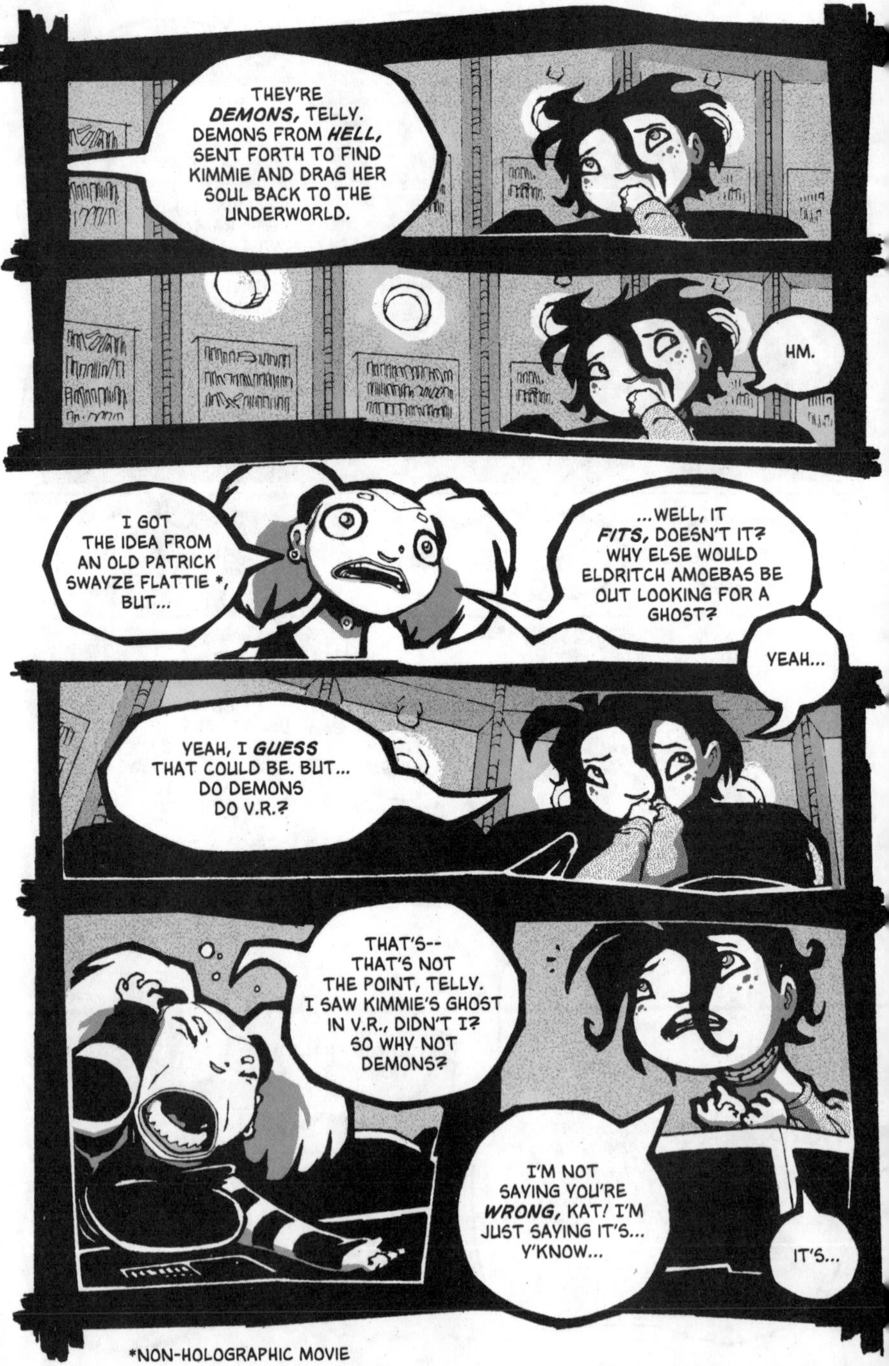
THEY'RE *DEMONS,* TELLY. DEMONS FROM *HELL,* SENT FORTH TO FIND KIMMIE AND DRAG HER SOUL BACK TO THE UNDERWORLD.
HM.
I GOT THE IDEA FROM AN OLD PATRICK SWAYZE FLATTIE *, BUT...
...WELL, IT *FITS,* DOESN'T IT? WHY ELSE WOULD ELDRITCH AMOEBAS BE OUT LOOKING FOR A GHOST?
YEAH...
YEAH, I *GUESS* THAT COULD BE. BUT... DO DEMONS DO V.R.?
THAT'S-- THAT'S NOT THE POINT, TELLY. I SAW KIMMIE'S GHOST IN V.R., DIDN'T I? SO WHY NOT DEMONS?
I'M NOT SAYING YOU'RE *WRONG,* KAT! I'M JUST SAYING IT'S... Y'KNOW...
IT'S...

*NON-HOLOGRAPHIC MOVIE

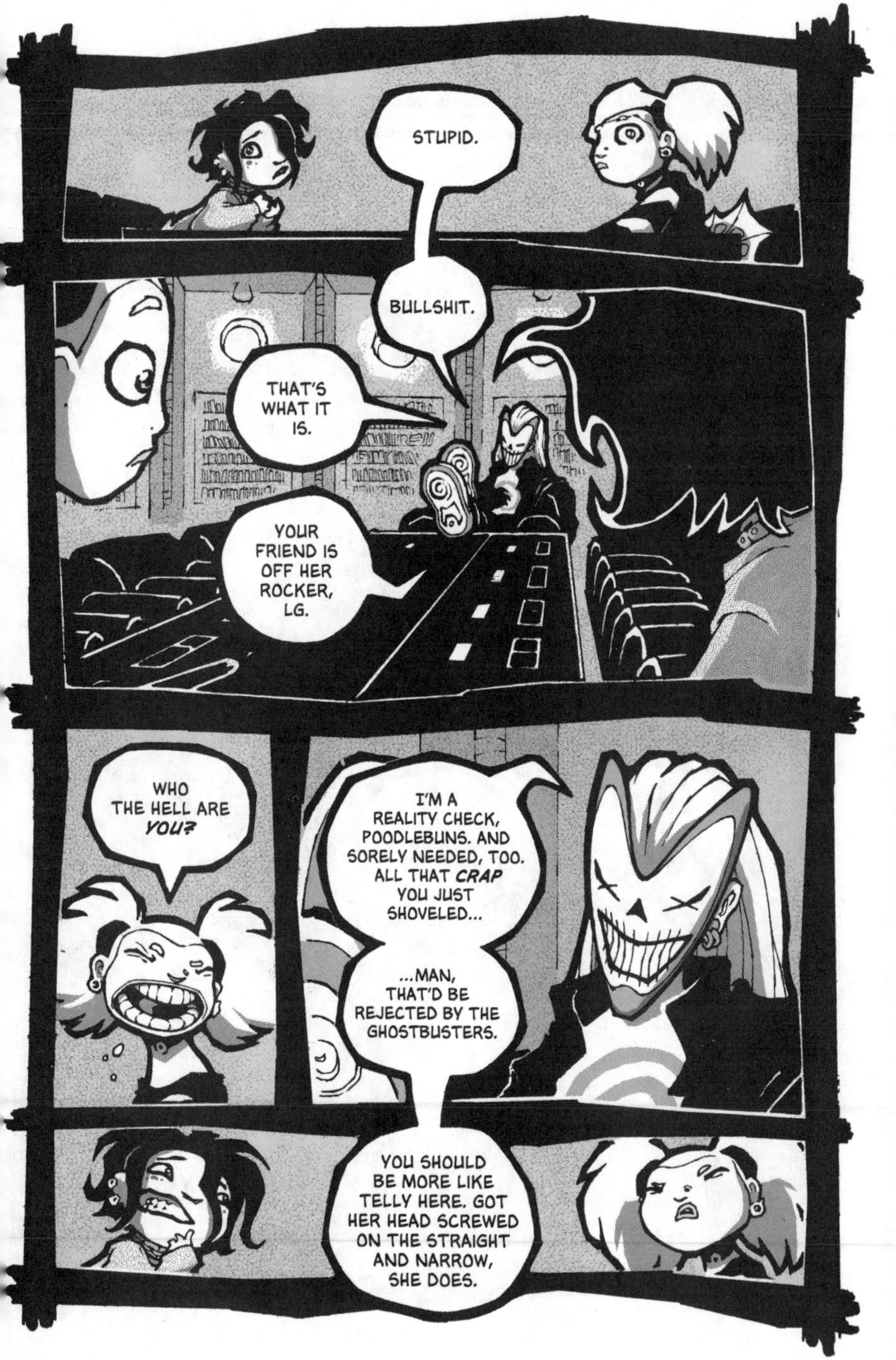
STUPID.
BULLSHIT.
THAT'S WHAT IT IS.
YOUR FRIEND IS OFF HER ROCKER, LG.
WHO THE HELL ARE *YOU?*
I'M A REALITY CHECK, POODLEBUNS. AND SORELY NEEDED, TOO. ALL THAT *CRAP* YOU JUST SHOVELED...
...MAN, THAT'D BE REJECTED BY THE GHOSTBUSTERS.
YOU SHOULD BE MORE LIKE TELLY HERE. GOT HER HEAD SCREWED ON THE STRAIGHT AND NARROW, SHE DOES.

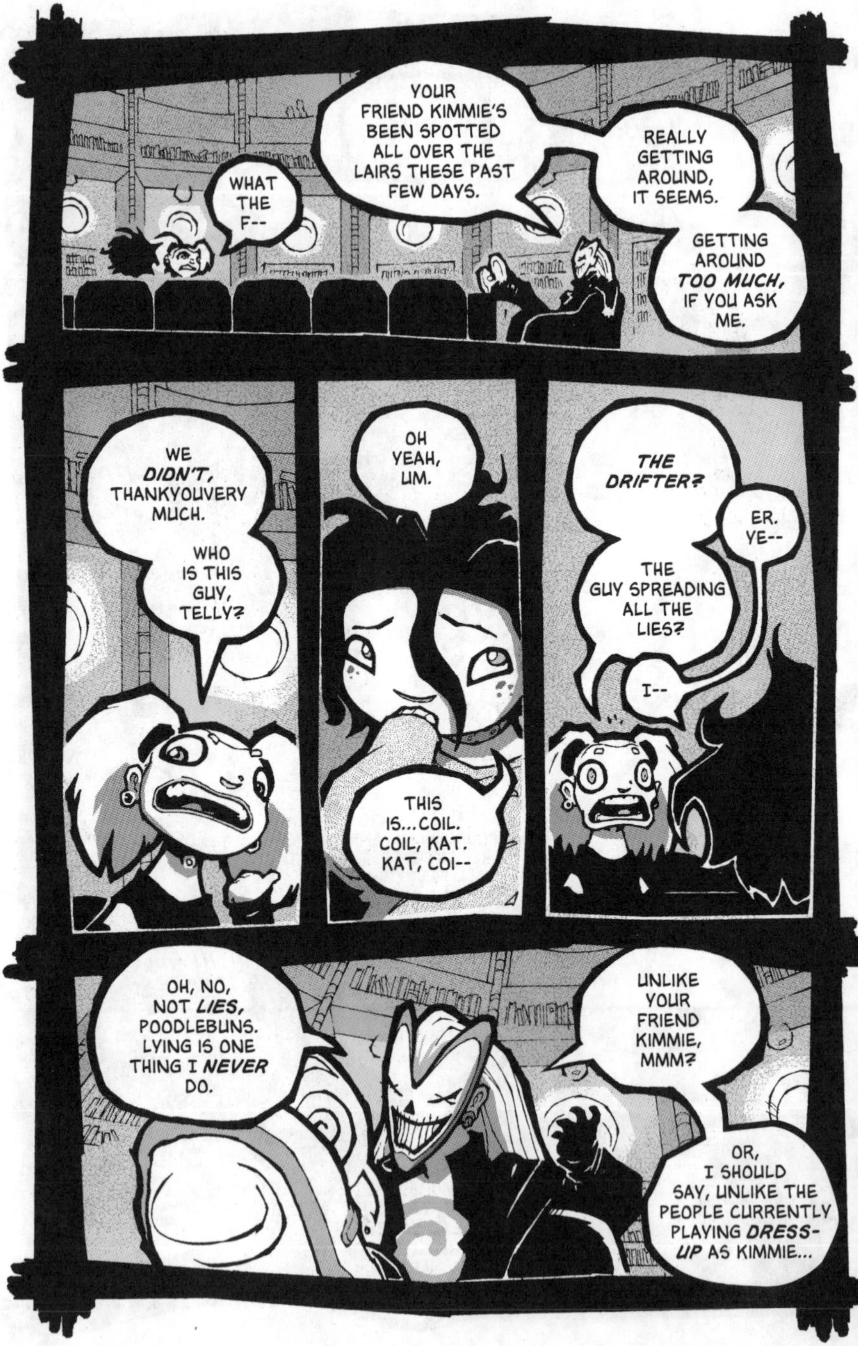
YOUR FRIEND KIMMIE'S BEEN SPOTTED ALL OVER THE LAIRS THESE PAST FEW DAYS.
WHAT THE F--
REALLY GETTING AROUND, IT SEEMS.
GETTING AROUND *TOO MUCH,* IF YOU ASK ME.
WE *DIDN'T,* THANKYOUVERY MUCH.
WHO IS THIS GUY, TELLY?
OH YEAH, UM.
THIS IS...COIL. COIL, KAT. KAT, COI--
THE DRIFTER?
ER. YE--
THE GUY SPREADING ALL THE LIES?
I--
OH, NO, NOT *LIES,* POODLEBUNS. LYING IS ONE THING I *NEVER* DO.
UNLIKE YOUR FRIEND KIMMIE, MMM?
OR, I SHOULD SAY, UNLIKE THE PEOPLE CURRENTLY PLAYING *DRESS-UP* AS KIMMIE...

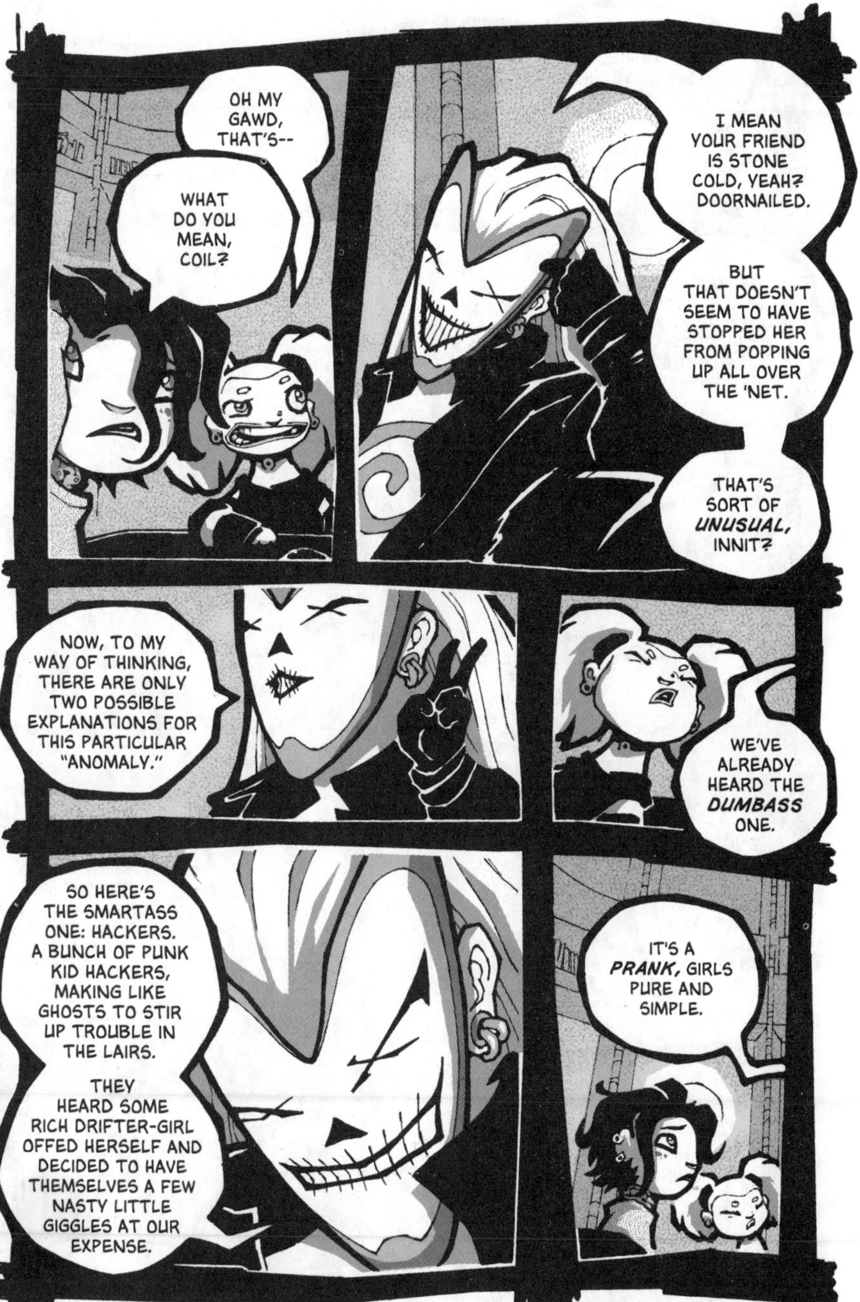
OH MY GAWD, THAT'S--
WHAT DO YOU MEAN, COIL?
I MEAN YOUR FRIEND IS STONE COLD, YEAH? DOORNAILED.
BUT THAT DOESN'T SEEM TO HAVE STOPPED HER FROM POPPING UP ALL OVER THE 'NET.
THAT'S SORT OF *UNUSUAL,* INNIT?
NOW, TO MY WAY OF THINKING, THERE ARE ONLY TWO POSSIBLE EXPLANATIONS FOR THIS PARTICULAR "ANOMALY."
WE'VE ALREADY HEARD THE *DUMBASS* ONE.
SO HERE'S THE SMARTASS ONE: HACKERS. A BUNCH OF PUNK KID HACKERS, MAKING LIKE GHOSTS TO STIR UP TROUBLE IN THE LAIRS.
THEY HEARD SOME RICH DRIFTER-GIRL OFFED HERSELF AND DECIDED TO HAVE THEMSELVES A FEW NASTY LITTLE GIGGLES AT OUR EXPENSE.
IT'S A *PRANK,* GIRLS PURE AND SIMPLE.

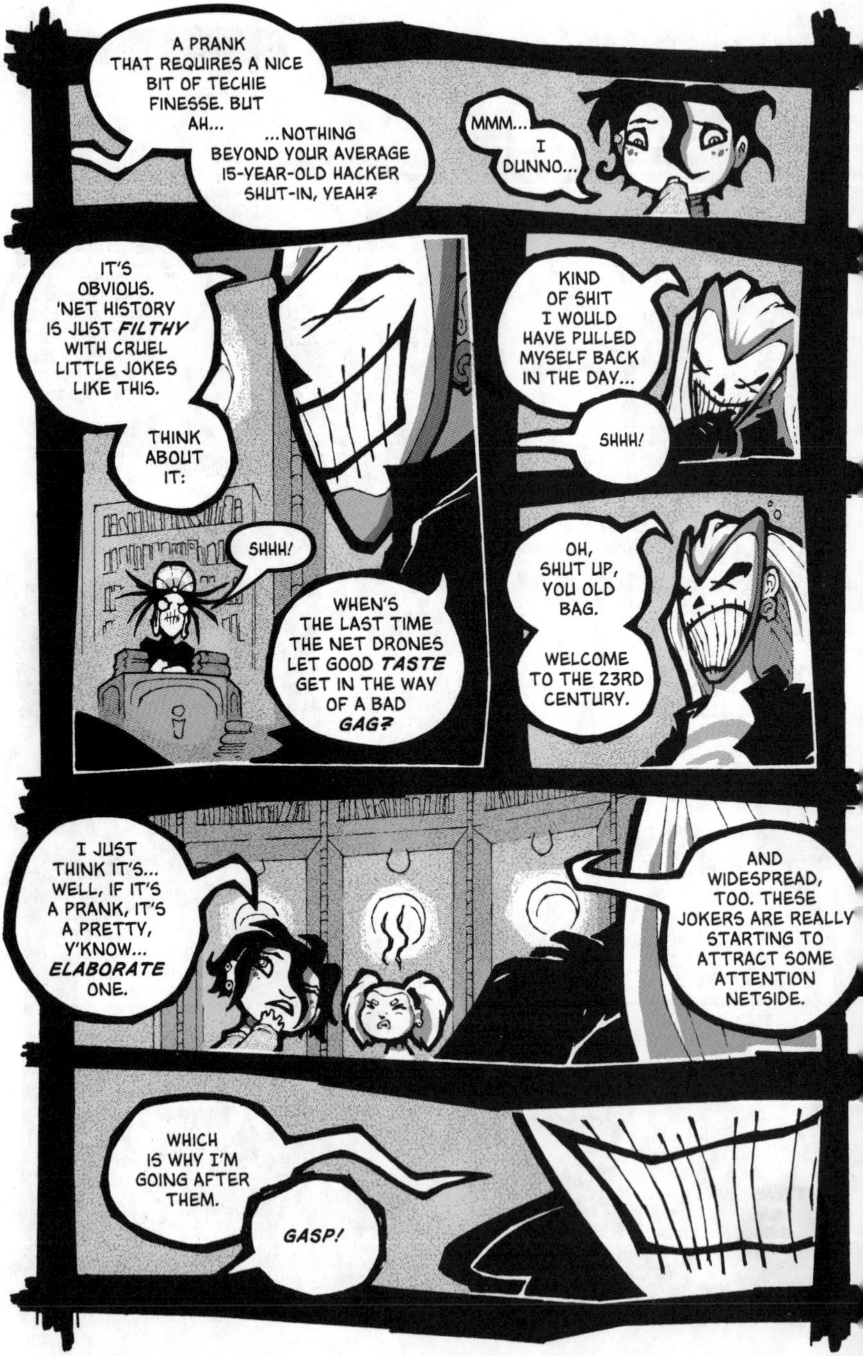

A PRANK THAT REQUIRES A NICE BIT OF TECHIE FINESSE. BUT AH...
...NOTHING BEYOND YOUR AVERAGE 15-YEAR-OLD HACKER SHUT-IN, YEAH?
MMM... I DUNNO...
IT'S OBVIOUS. 'NET HISTORY IS JUST *FILTHY* WITH CRUEL LITTLE JOKES LIKE THIS.
THINK ABOUT IT:
SHHH!
WHEN'S THE LAST TIME THE NET DRONES LET GOOD *TASTE* GET IN THE WAY OF A BAD *GAG?*
KIND OF SHIT I WOULD HAVE PULLED MYSELF BACK IN THE DAY...
SHHH!
OH, SHUT UP, YOU OLD BAG.
WELCOME TO THE 23RD CENTURY.
I JUST THINK IT'S... WELL, IF IT'S A PRANK, IT'S A PRETTY, Y'KNOW... *ELABORATE* ONE.
AND WIDESPREAD, TOO. THESE JOKERS ARE REALLY STARTING TO ATTRACT SOME ATTENTION NETSIDE.
WHICH IS WHY I'M GOING AFTER THEM.
GASP!

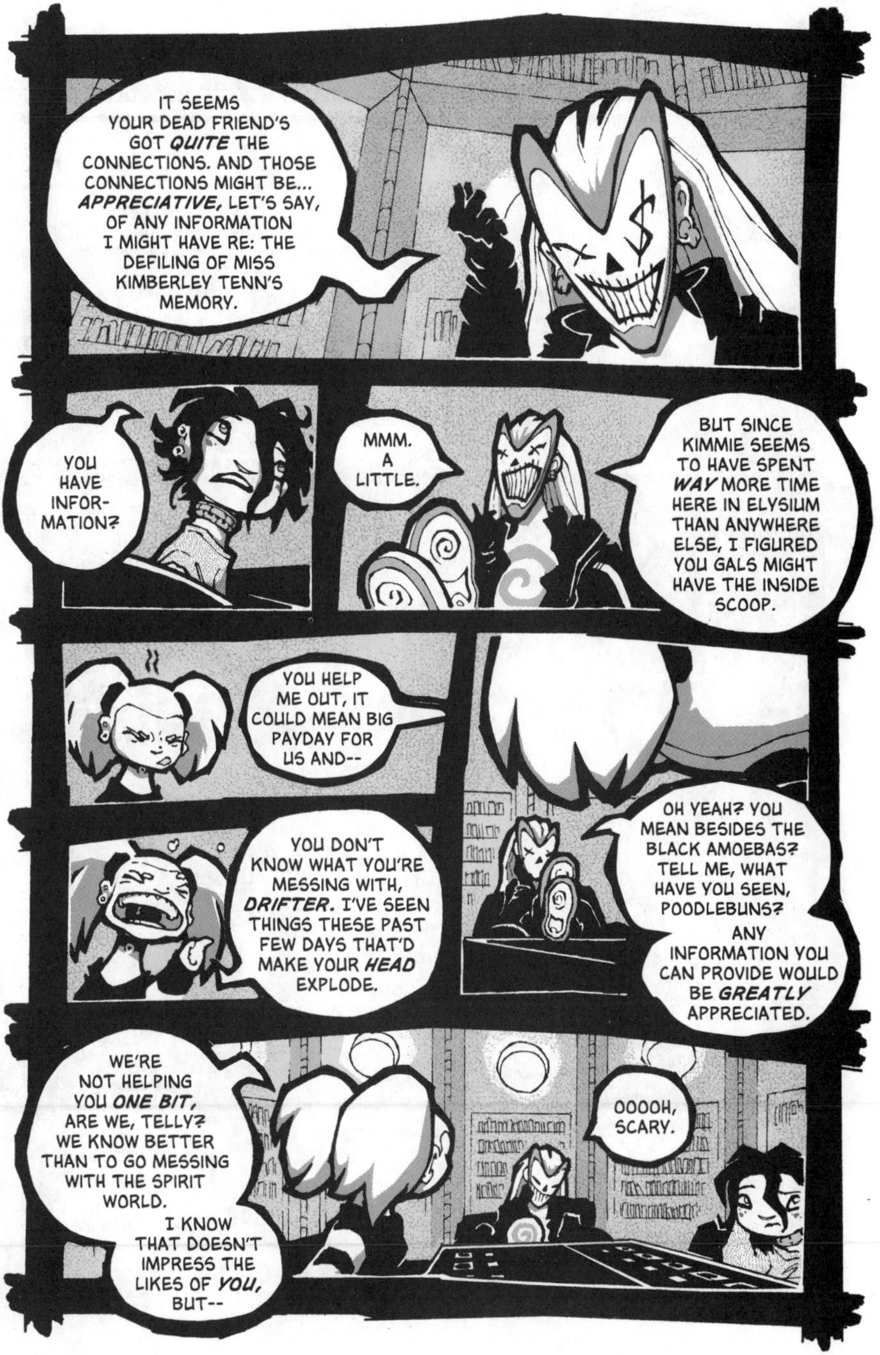
IT SEEMS YOUR DEAD FRIEND'S GOT QUITE THE CONNECTIONS. AND THOSE CONNECTIONS MIGHT BE... APPRECIATIVE, LET'S SAY, OF ANY INFORMATION I MIGHT HAVE RE: THE DEFILING OF MISS KIMBERLEY TENN'S MEMORY.
YOU HAVE INFOR-MATION?
MMM. A LITTLE.
BUT SINCE KIMMIE SEEMS TO HAVE SPENT WAY MORE TIME HERE IN ELYSIUM THAN ANYWHERE ELSE, I FIGURED YOU GALS MIGHT HAVE THE INSIDE SCOOP.
YOU HELP ME OUT, IT COULD MEAN BIG PAYDAY FOR US AND--
YOU DON'T KNOW WHAT YOU'RE MESSING WITH, DRIFTER. I'VE SEEN THINGS THESE PAST FEW DAYS THAT'D MAKE YOUR HEAD EXPLODE.
OH YEAH? YOU MEAN BESIDES THE BLACK AMOEBAS? TELL ME, WHAT HAVE YOU SEEN, POODLEBUNS?
ANY INFORMATION YOU CAN PROVIDE WOULD BE GREATLY APPRECIATED.
WE'RE NOT HELPING YOU ONE BIT, ARE WE, TELLY? WE KNOW BETTER THAN TO GO MESSING WITH THE SPIRIT WORLD.
I KNOW THAT DOESN'T IMPRESS THE LIKES OF YOU, BUT--
OOOOH, SCARY.

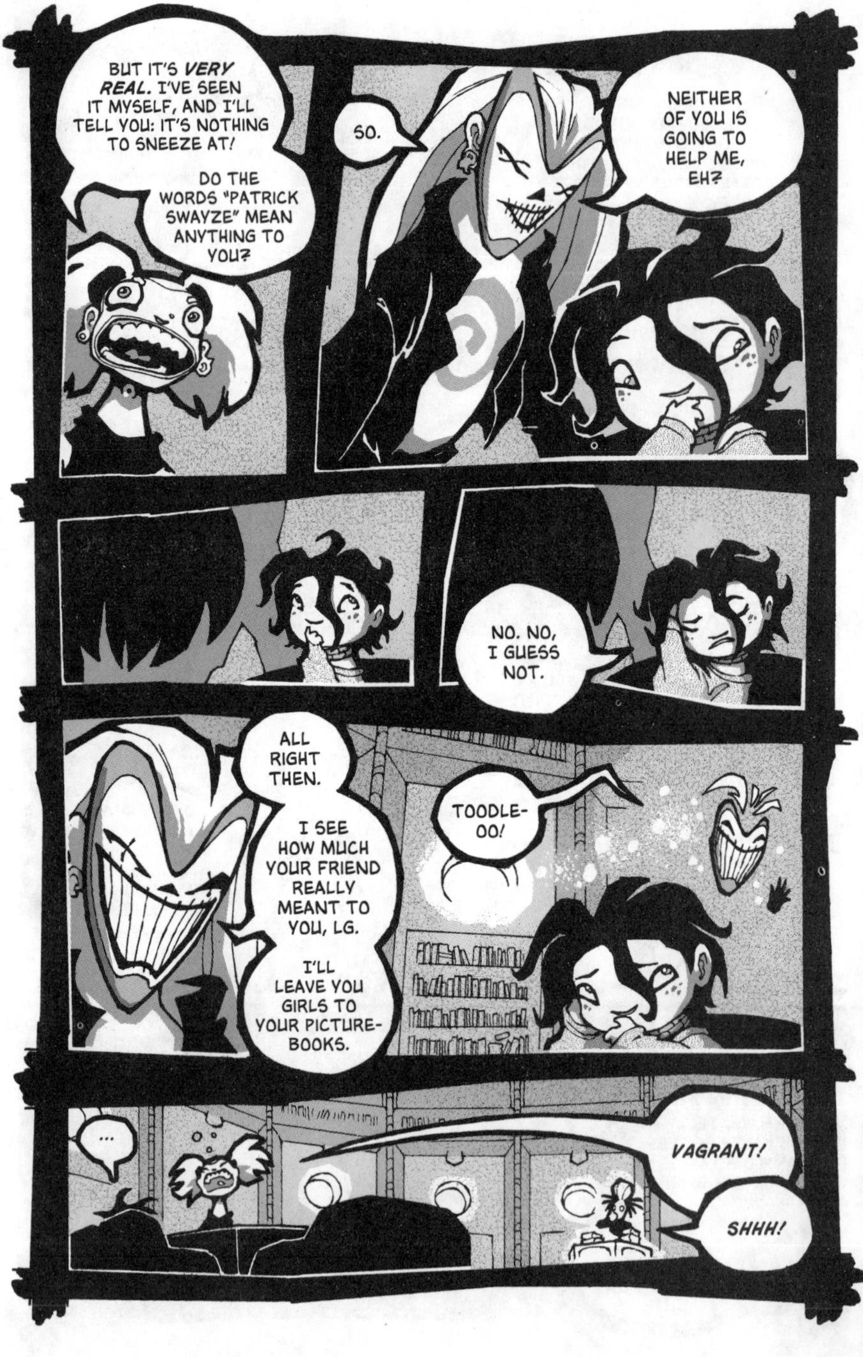
BUT IT'S VERY REAL. I'VE SEEN IT MYSELF, AND I'LL TELL YOU: IT'S NOTHING TO SNEEZE AT!
DO THE WORDS "PATRICK SWAYZE" MEAN ANYTHING TO YOU?
SO.
NEITHER OF YOU IS GOING TO HELP ME, EH?
NO. NO, I GUESS NOT.
ALL RIGHT THEN.
I SEE HOW MUCH YOUR FRIEND REALLY MEANT TO YOU, LG.
I'LL LEAVE YOU GIRLS TO YOUR PICTURE-BOOKS.
TOODLE-OO!
...
VAGRANT!
SHHH!

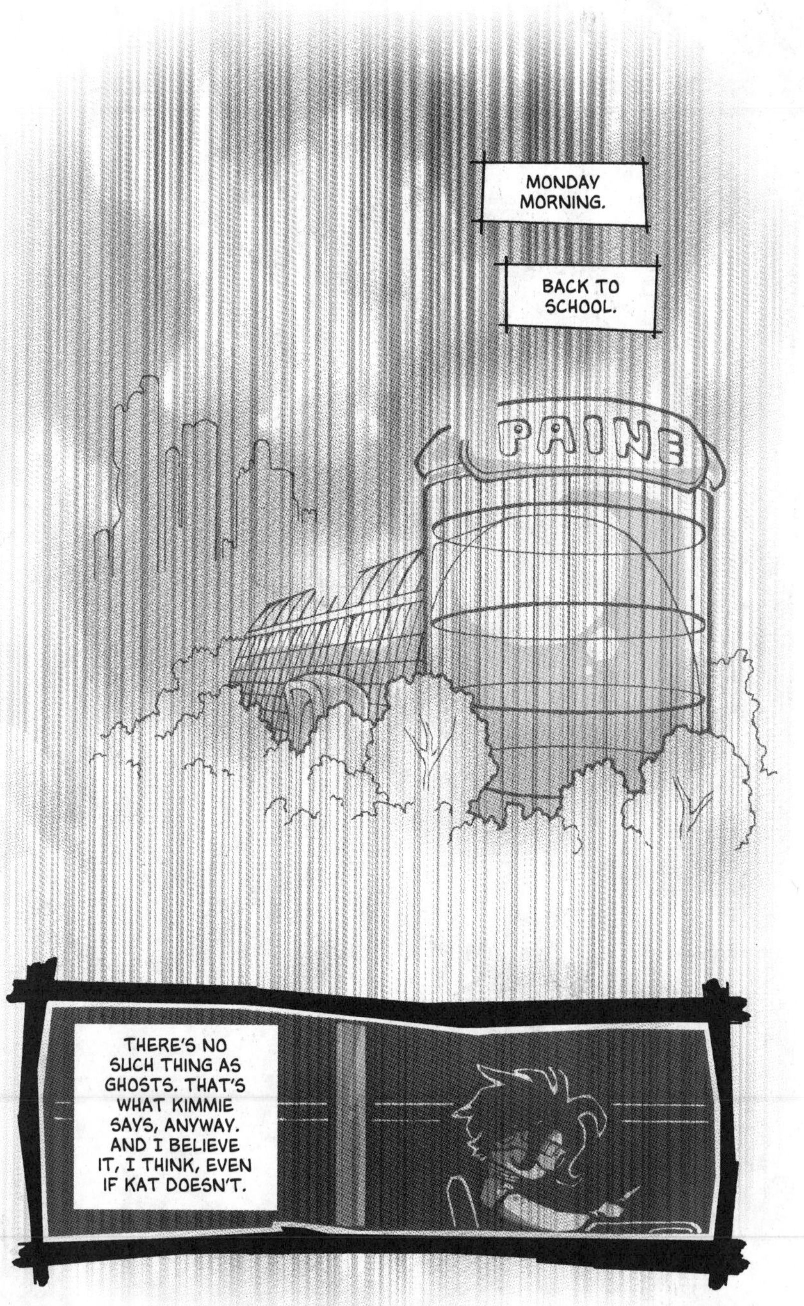
MONDAY MORNING.
BACK TO SCHOOL.
PAINE
THERE'S NO SUCH THING AS GHOSTS. THAT'S WHAT KIMMIE SAYS, ANYWAY. AND I BELIEVE IT, I THINK, EVEN IF KAT DOESN'T.

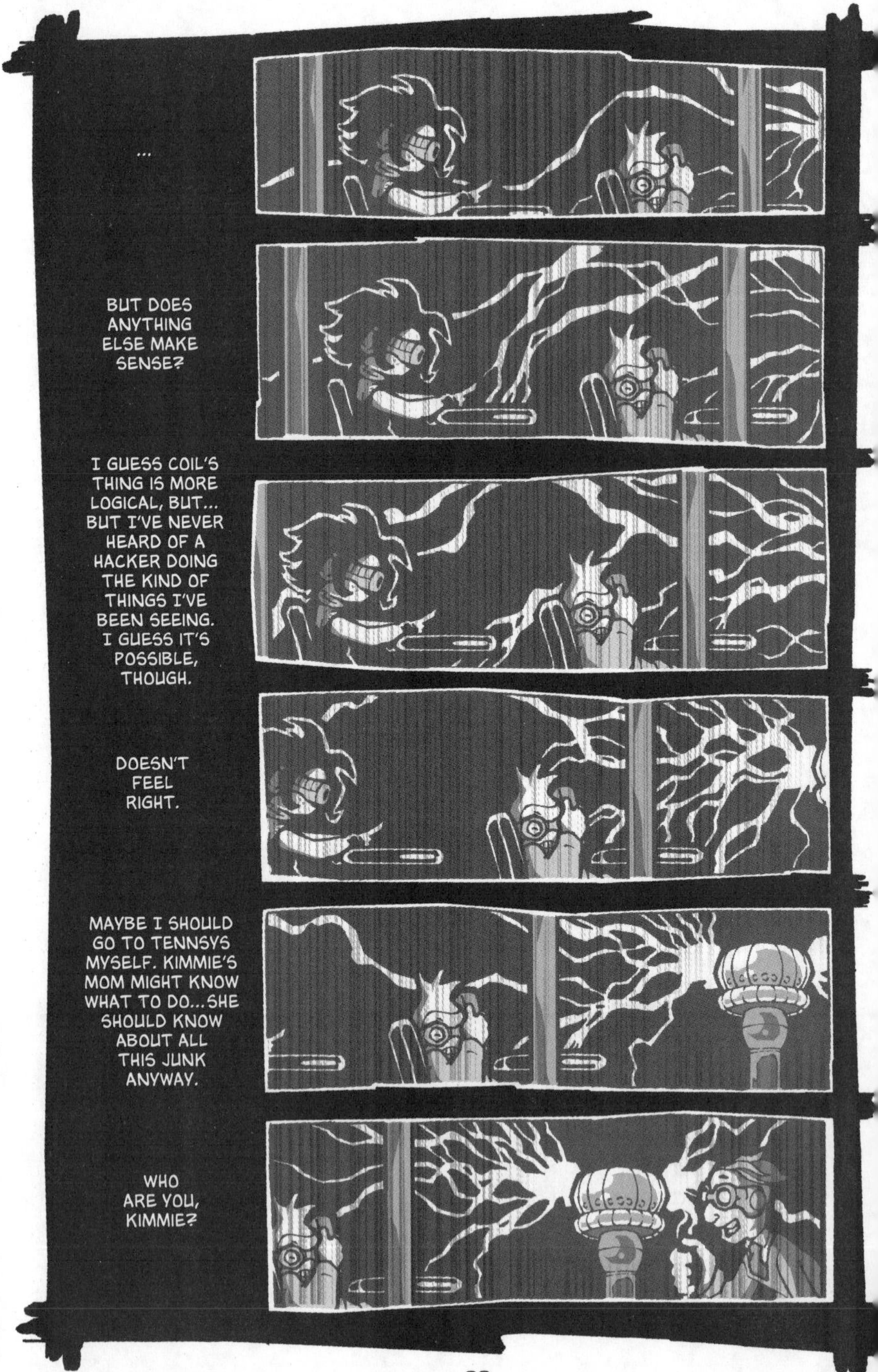
...
BUT DOES ANYTHING ELSE MAKE SENSE?
I GUESS COIL'S THING IS MORE LOGICAL, BUT... BUT I'VE NEVER HEARD OF A HACKER DOING THE KIND OF THINGS I'VE BEEN SEEING. I GUESS IT'S POSSIBLE, THOUGH.
DOESN'T FEEL RIGHT.
MAYBE I SHOULD GO TO TENNSYS MYSELF. KIMMIE'S MOM MIGHT KNOW WHAT TO DO...SHE SHOULD KNOW ABOUT ALL THIS JUNK ANYWAY.
WHO ARE YOU, KIMMIE?

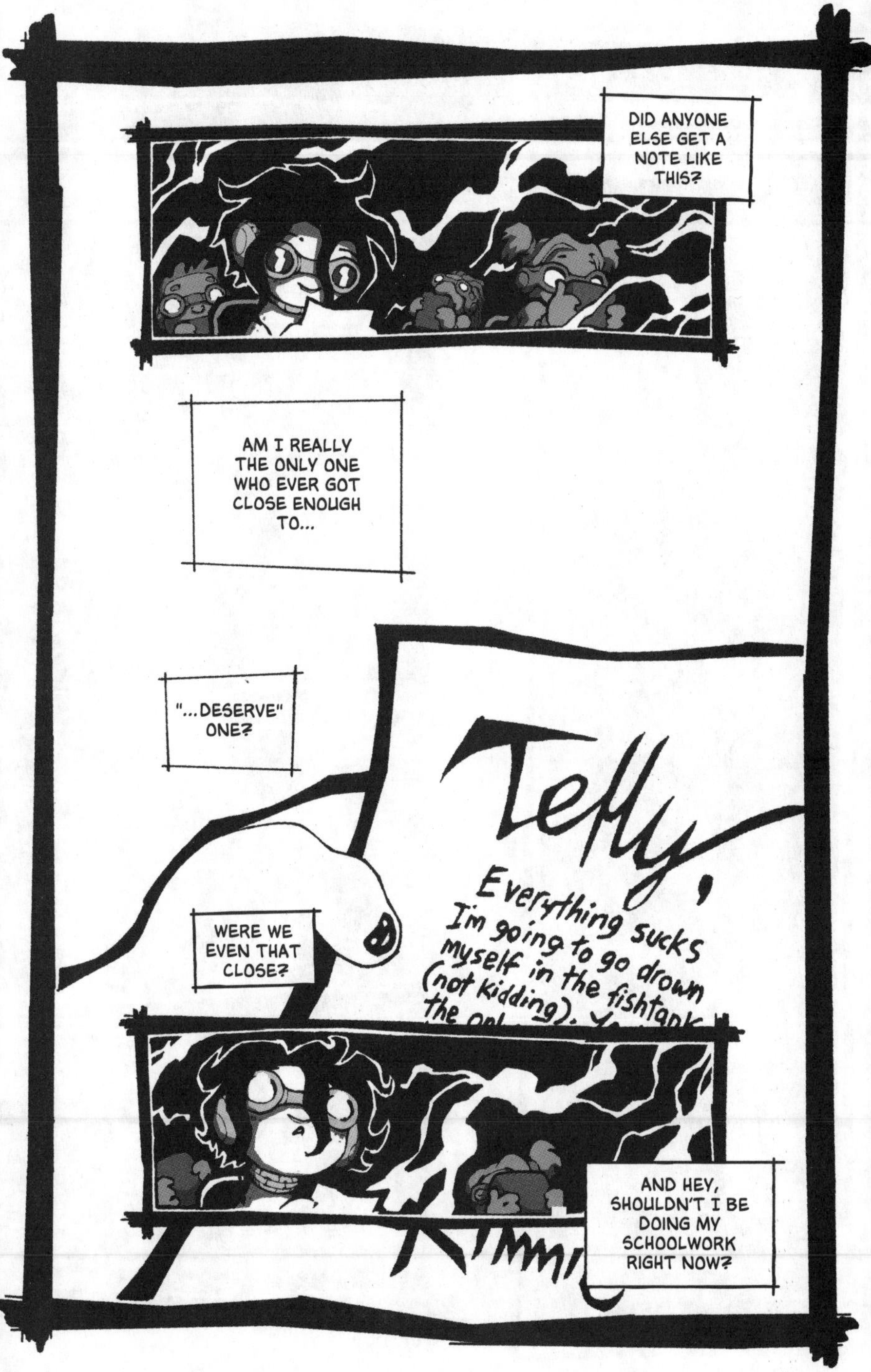
DID ANYONE ELSE GET A NOTE LIKE THIS?
AM I REALLY THE ONLY ONE WHO EVER GOT CLOSE ENOUGH TO...
"...DESERVE" ONE?
Telly,
Everything sucks
I'm going to go drown
myself in the fishtank
(not kidding).
WERE WE EVEN THAT CLOSE?
AND HEY, SHOULDN'T I BE DOING MY SCHOOLWORK RIGHT NOW?

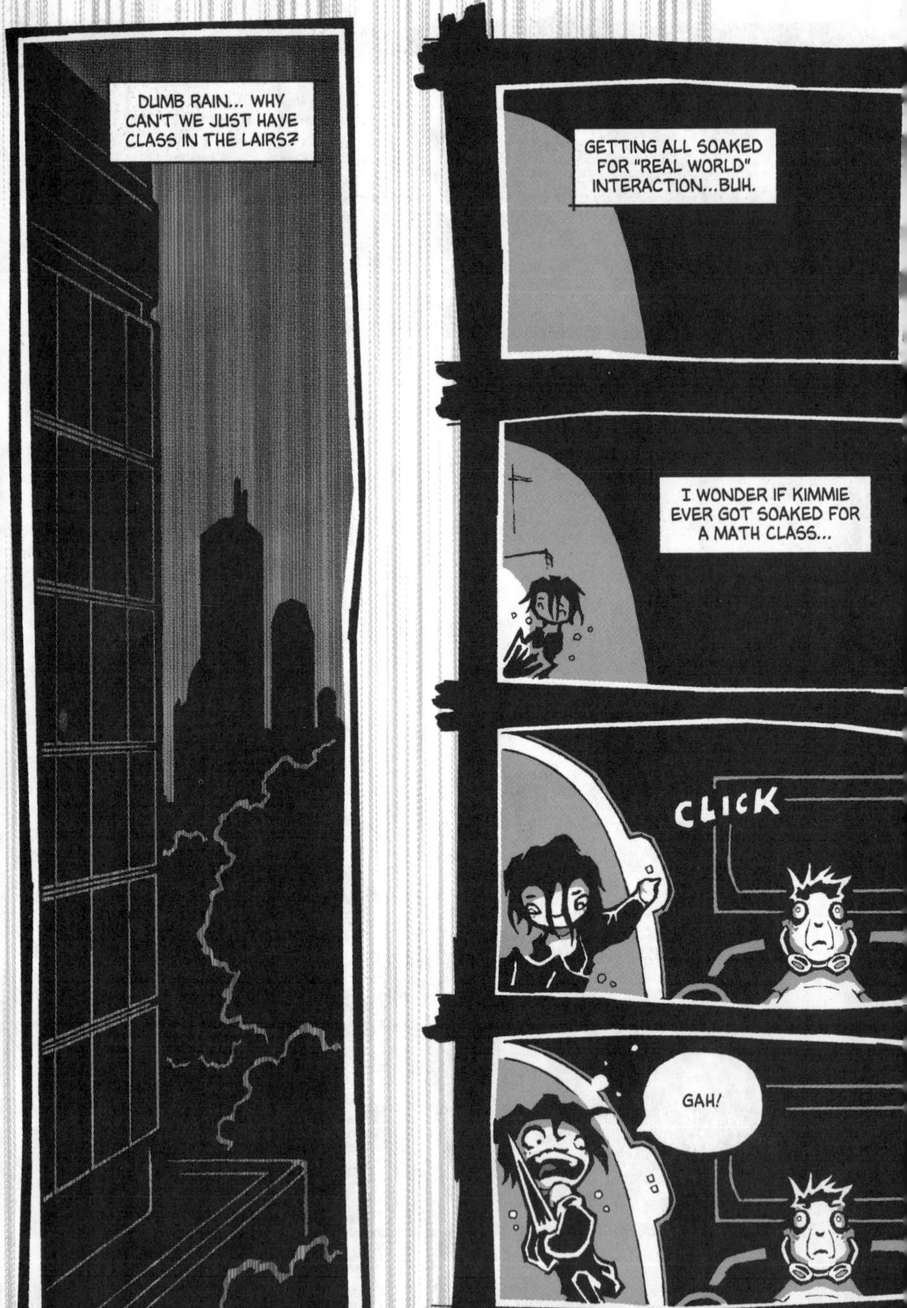
DUMB RAIN... WHY CAN'T WE JUST HAVE CLASS IN THE LAIRS?
GETTING ALL SOAKED FOR "REAL WORLD" INTERACTION...BUH.
I WONDER IF KIMMIE EVER GOT SOAKED FOR A MATH CLASS...
CLICK
GAH!

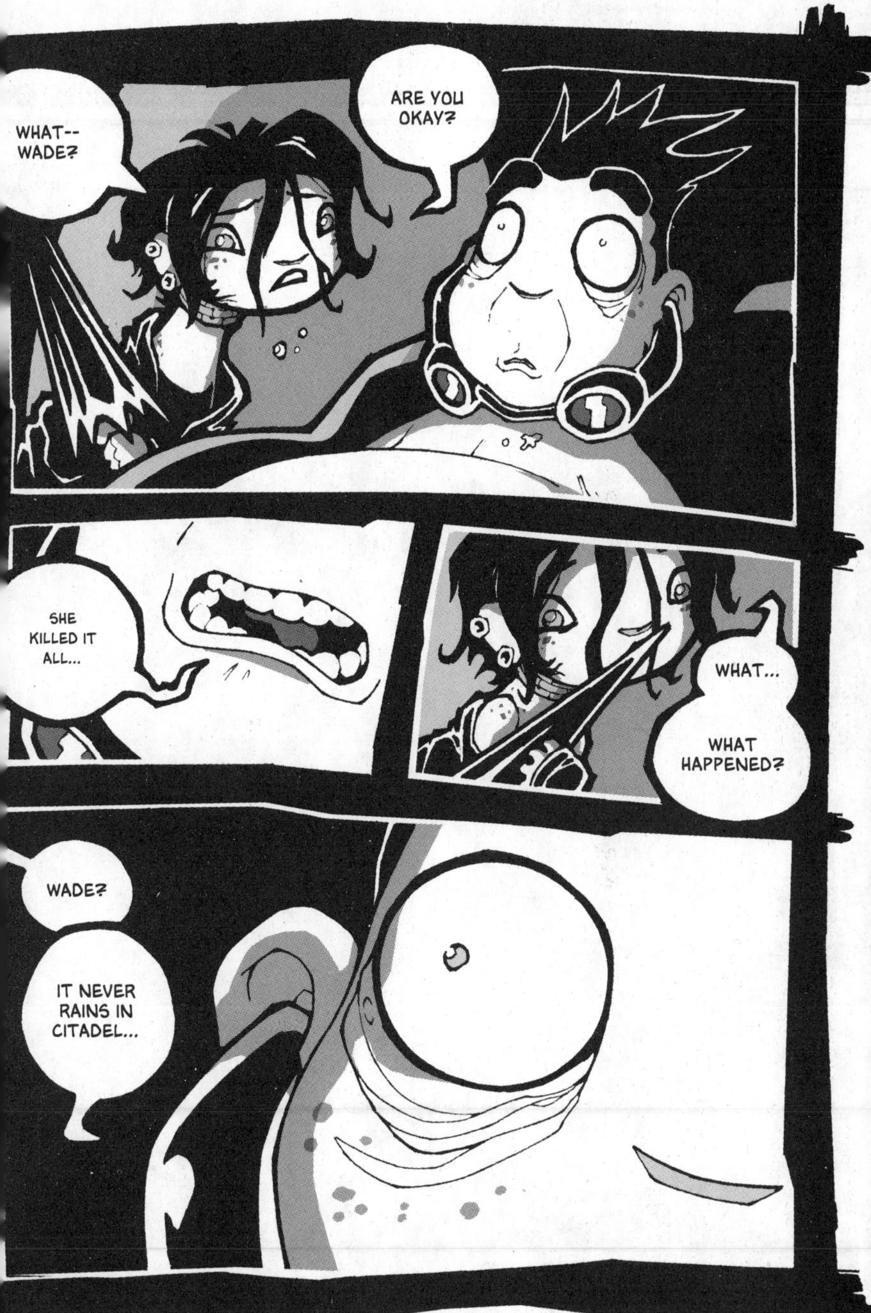
WHAT-- WADE?
ARE YOU OKAY?
SHE KILLED IT ALL...
WHAT...
WHAT HAPPENED?
WADE?
IT NEVER RAINS IN CITADEL...

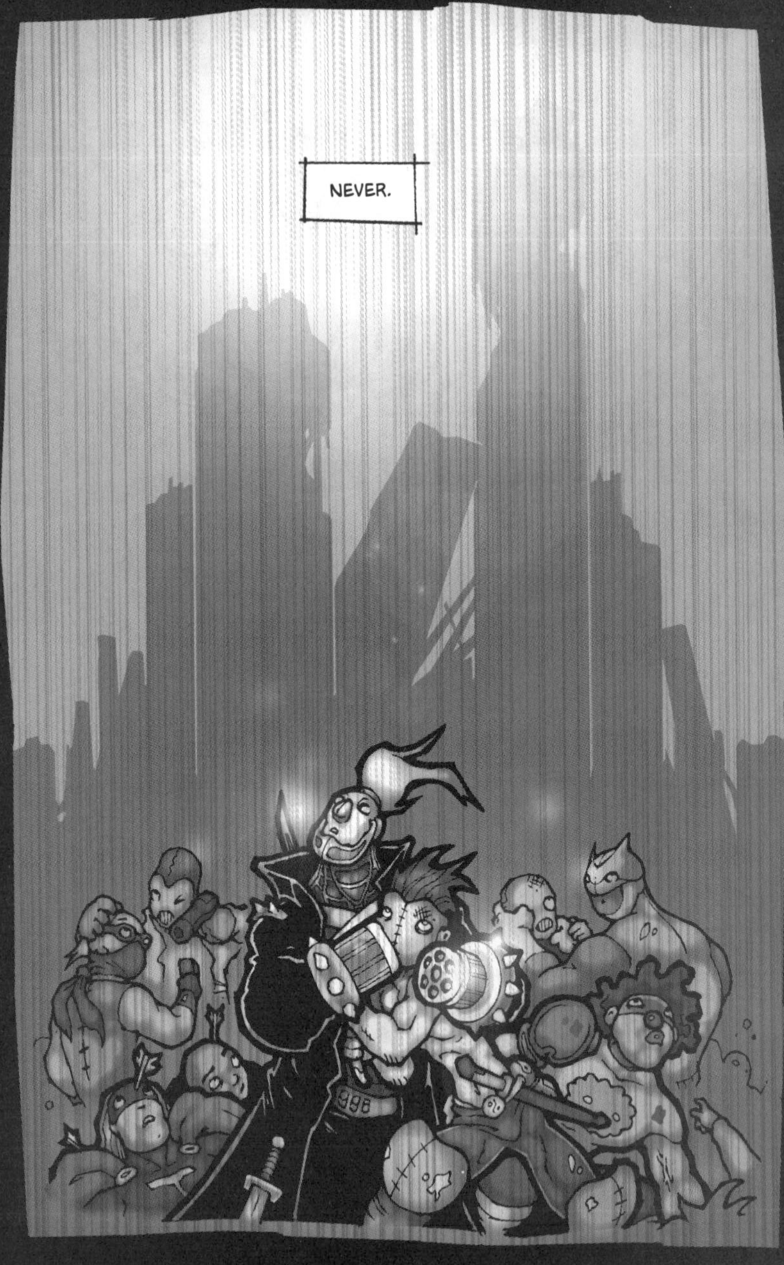
NEVER.

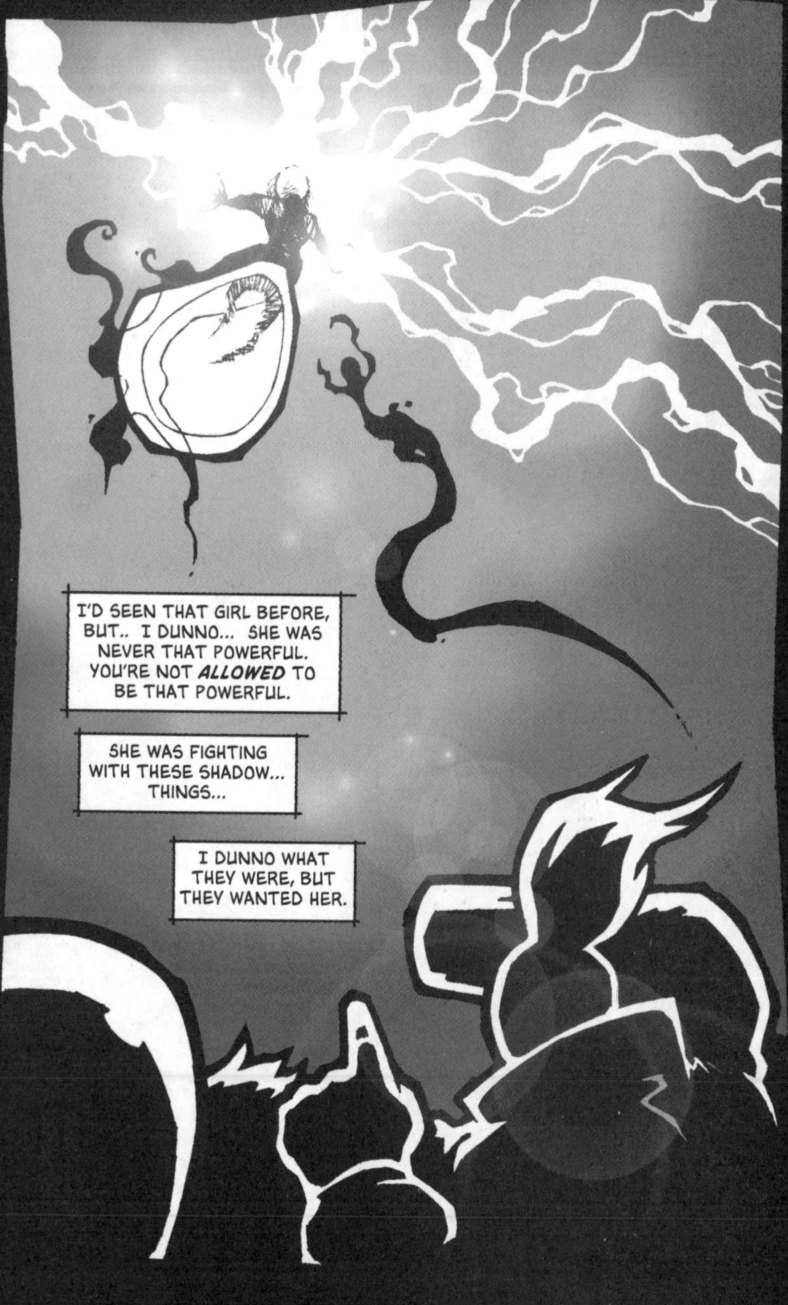
I'D SEEN THAT GIRL BEFORE, BUT.. I DUNNO... SHE WAS NEVER THAT POWERFUL. YOU'RE NOT ***ALLOWED*** TO BE THAT POWERFUL.
SHE WAS FIGHTING WITH THESE SHADOW... THINGS...
I DUNNO WHAT THEY WERE, BUT THEY WANTED HER.

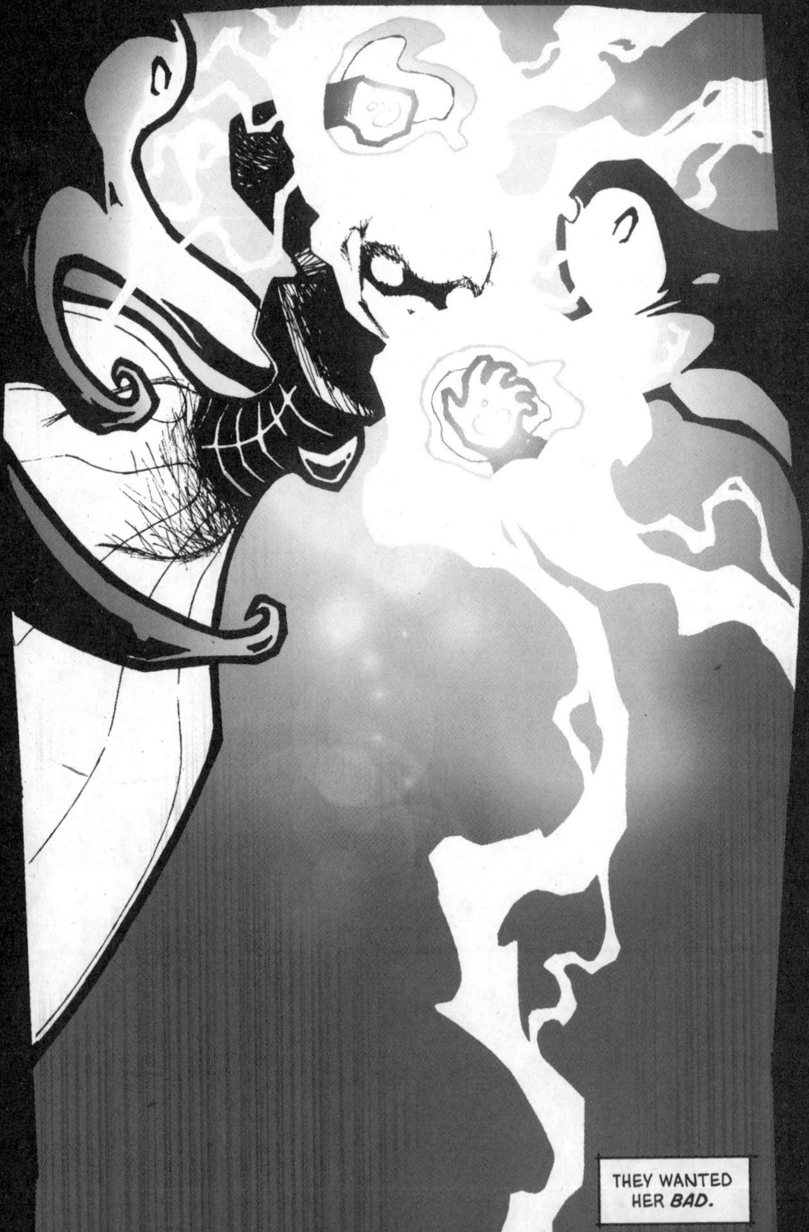
THEY WANTED HER *BAD.*

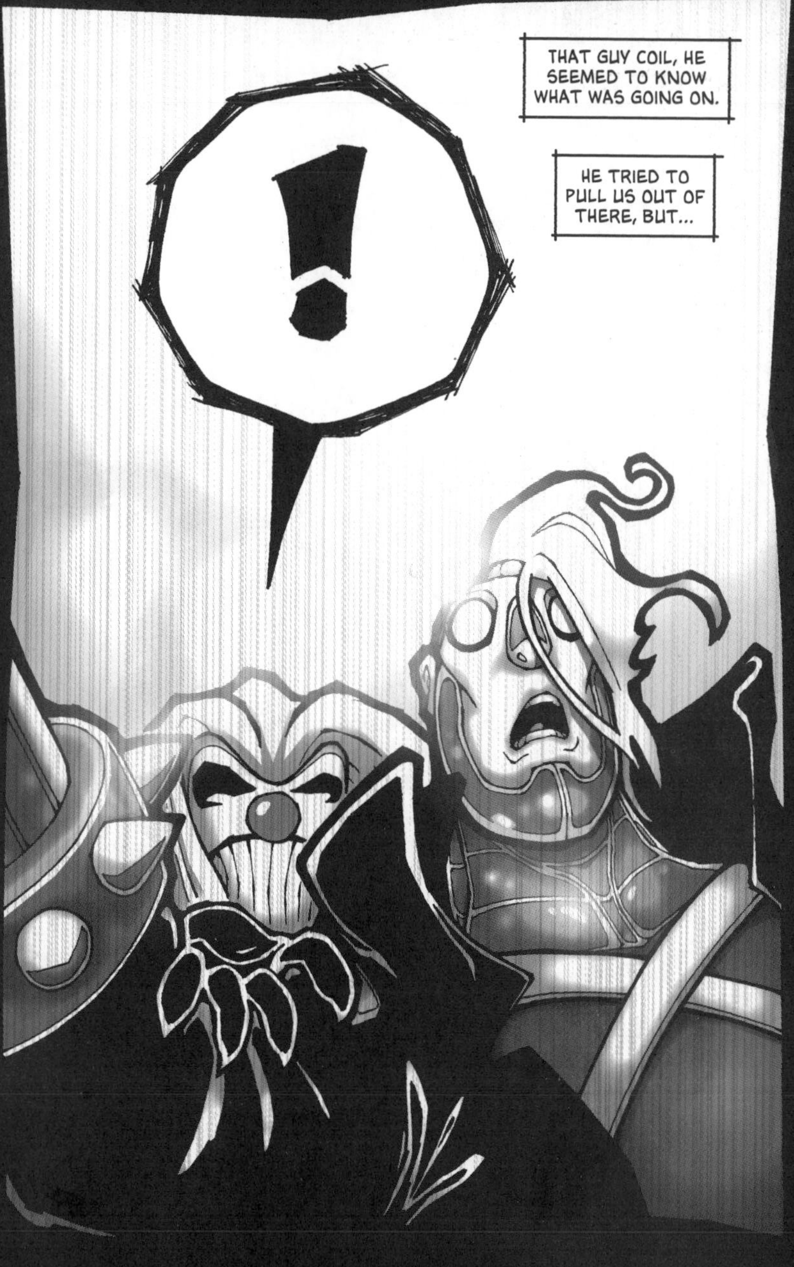
THAT GUY COIL, HE SEEMED TO KNOW WHAT WAS GOING ON.
HE TRIED TO PULL US OUT OF THERE, BUT...
!

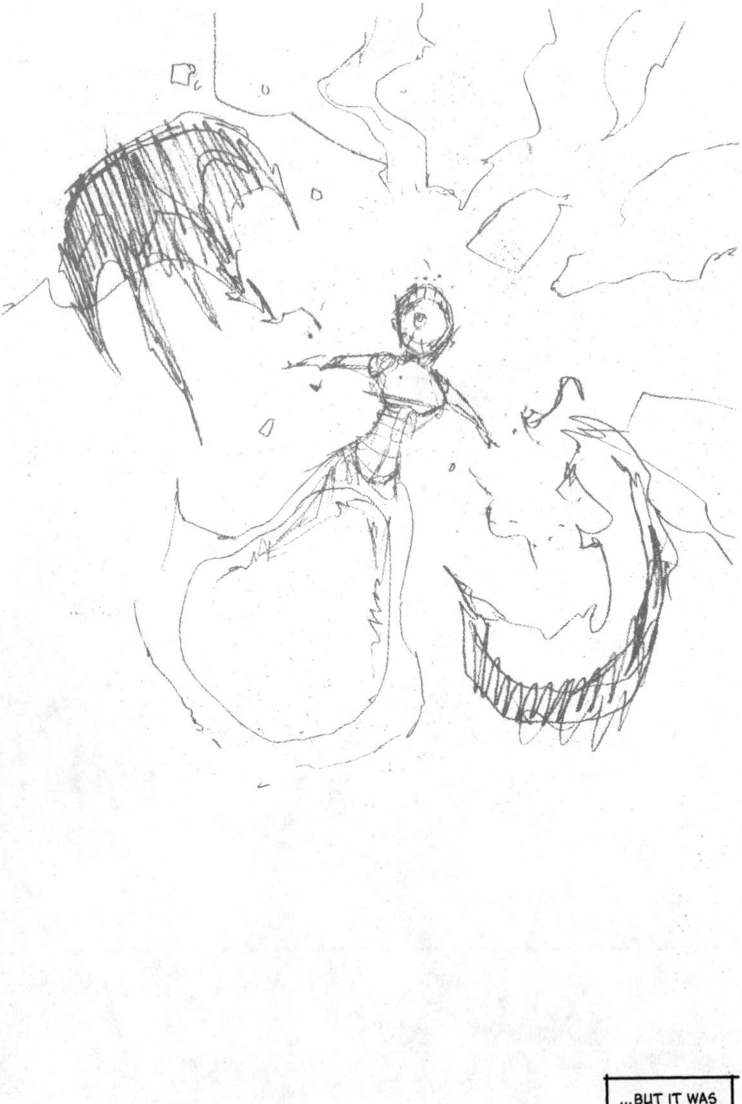
...BUT IT WAS TOO LATE.

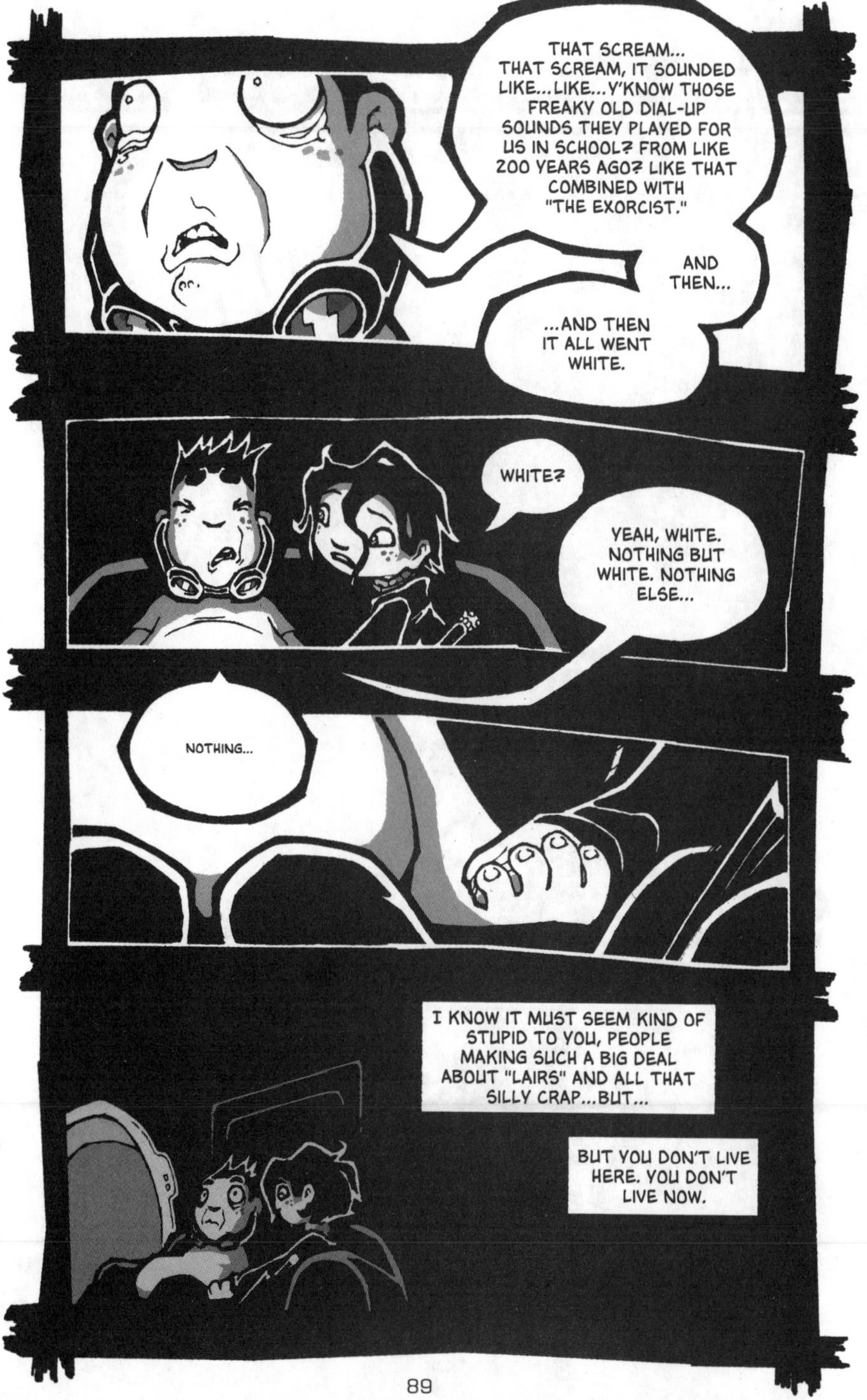
THAT SCREAM... THAT SCREAM, IT SOUNDED LIKE... LIKE... Y'KNOW THOSE FREAKY OLD DIAL-UP SOUNDS THEY PLAYED FOR US IN SCHOOL? FROM LIKE 200 YEARS AGO? LIKE THAT COMBINED WITH "THE EXORCIST."
AND THEN...
...AND THEN IT ALL WENT WHITE.
WHITE?
YEAH, WHITE. NOTHING BUT WHITE. NOTHING ELSE...
NOTHING...
I KNOW IT MUST SEEM KIND OF STUPID TO YOU, PEOPLE MAKING SUCH A BIG DEAL ABOUT "LAIRS" AND ALL THAT SILLY CRAP... BUT...
BUT YOU DON'T LIVE HERE. YOU DON'T LIVE NOW.

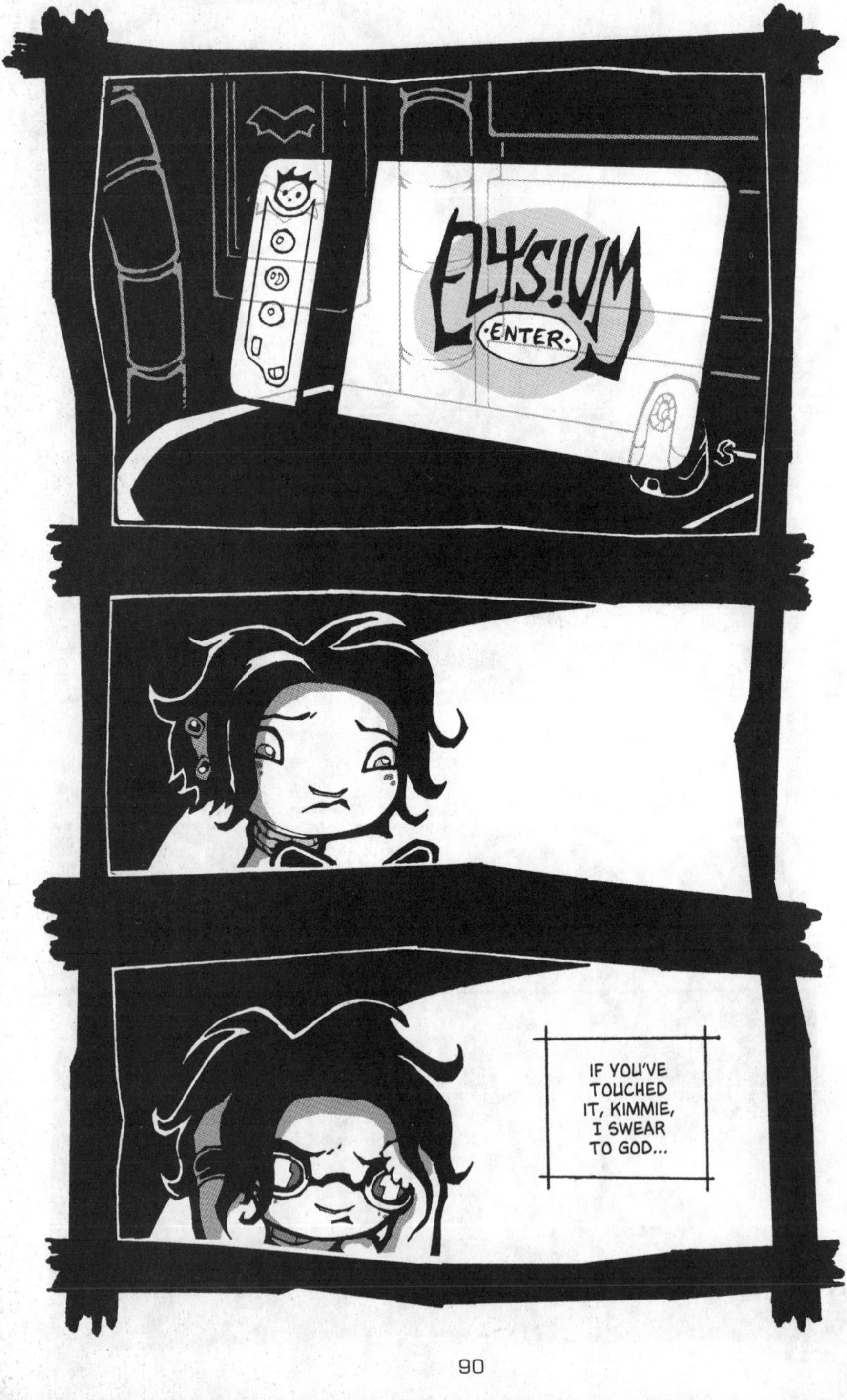

ELYSIUM
ENTER
IF YOU'VE TOUCHED IT, KIMMIE, I SWEAR TO GOD...

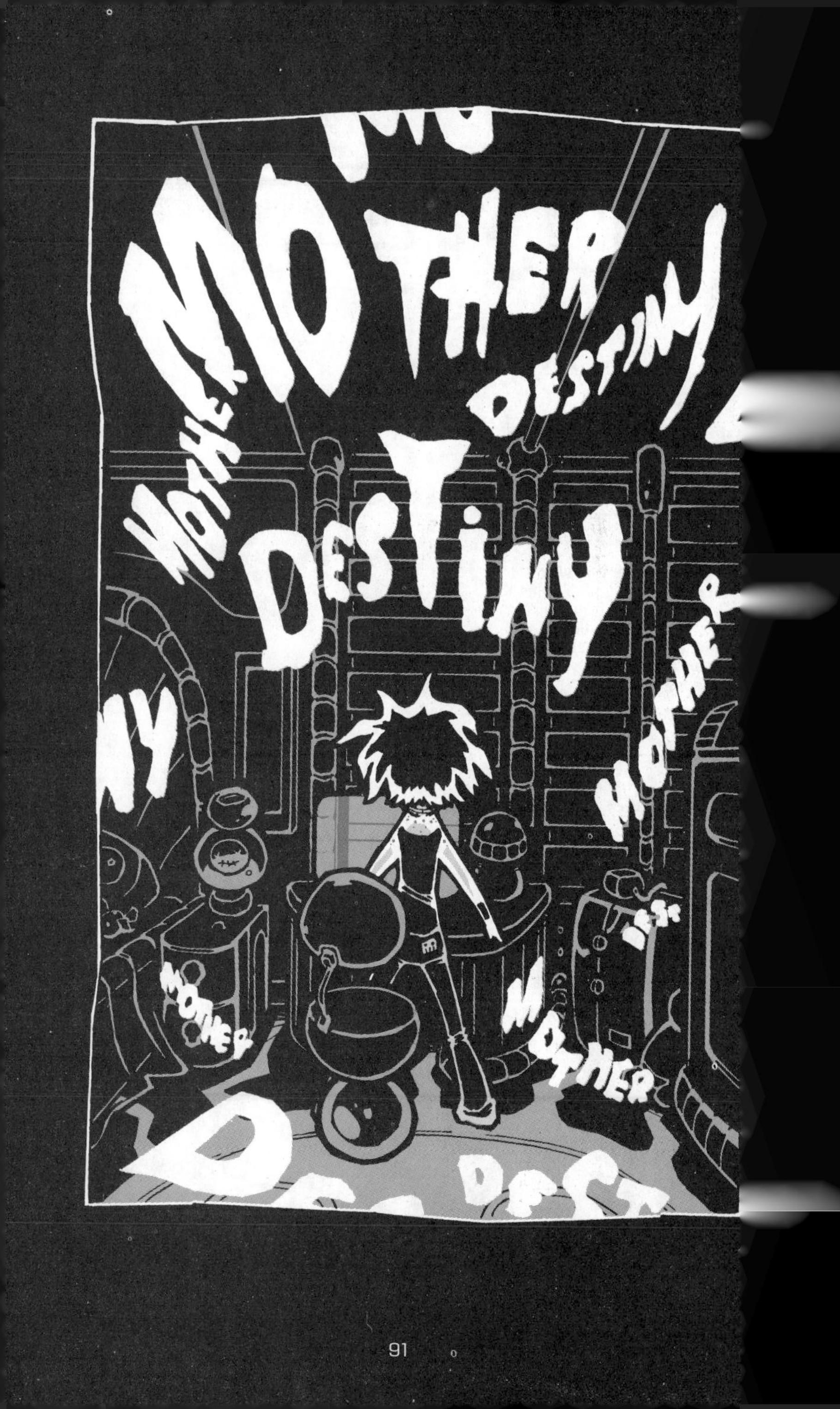
MOTHER
MOTHER
DESTINY
DESTINY
MOTHER
MOTHER
MOTHER

CHAPTER FOUR

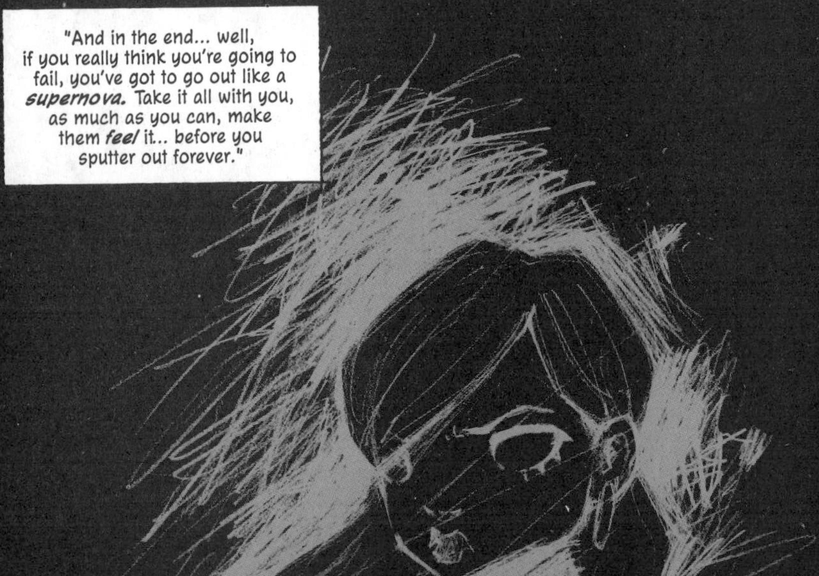
"And in the end... well, if you really think you're going to fail, you've got to go out like a *supernova.* Take it all with you, as much as you can, make them *feel* it... before you sputter out forever."
"So people don't forget."

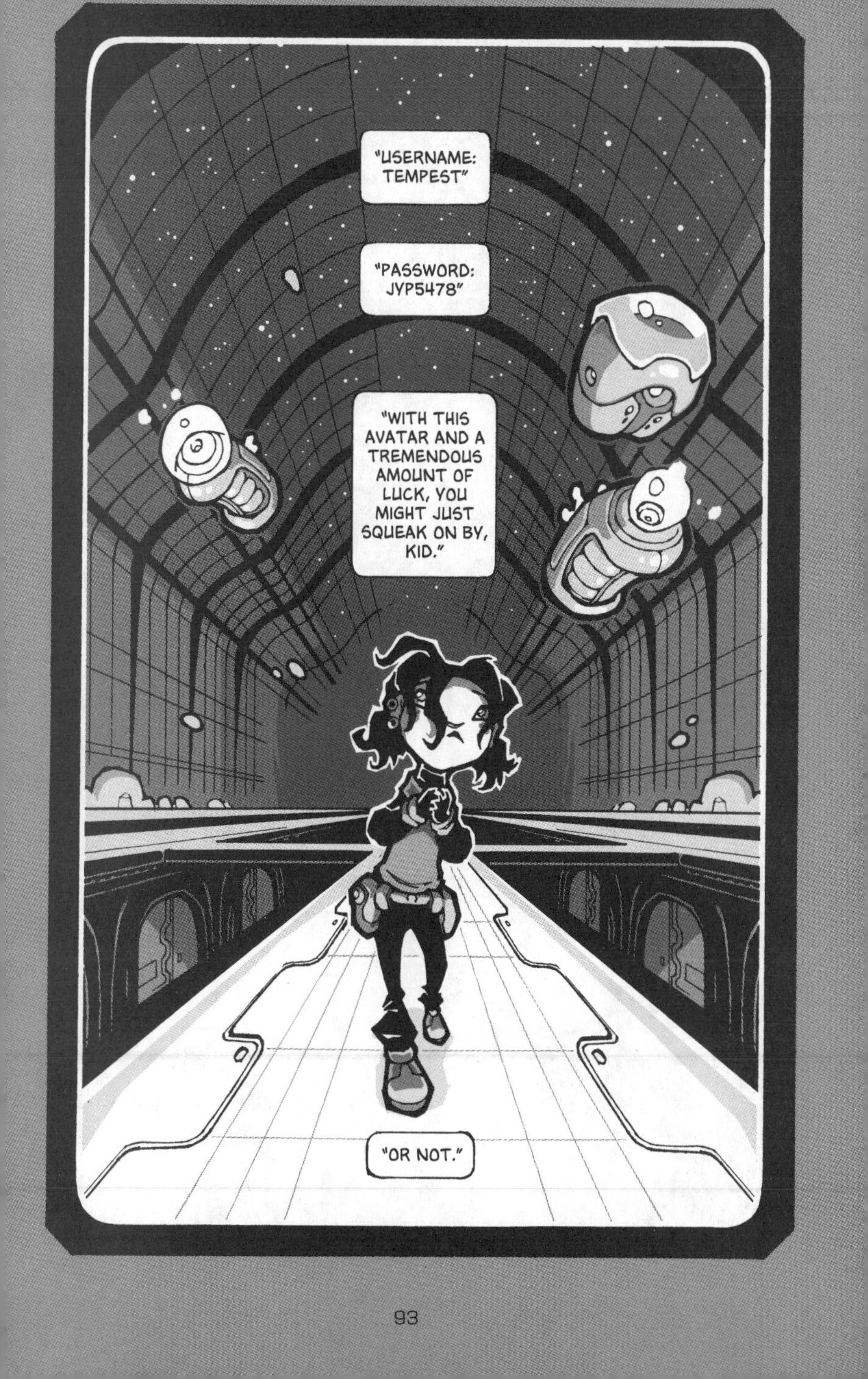
"USERNAME:
TEMPEST"
"PASSWORD:
JYP5478"
"WITH THIS AVATAR AND A TREMENDOUS AMOUNT OF LUCK, YOU MIGHT JUST SQUEAK ON BY, KID."
"OR NOT."

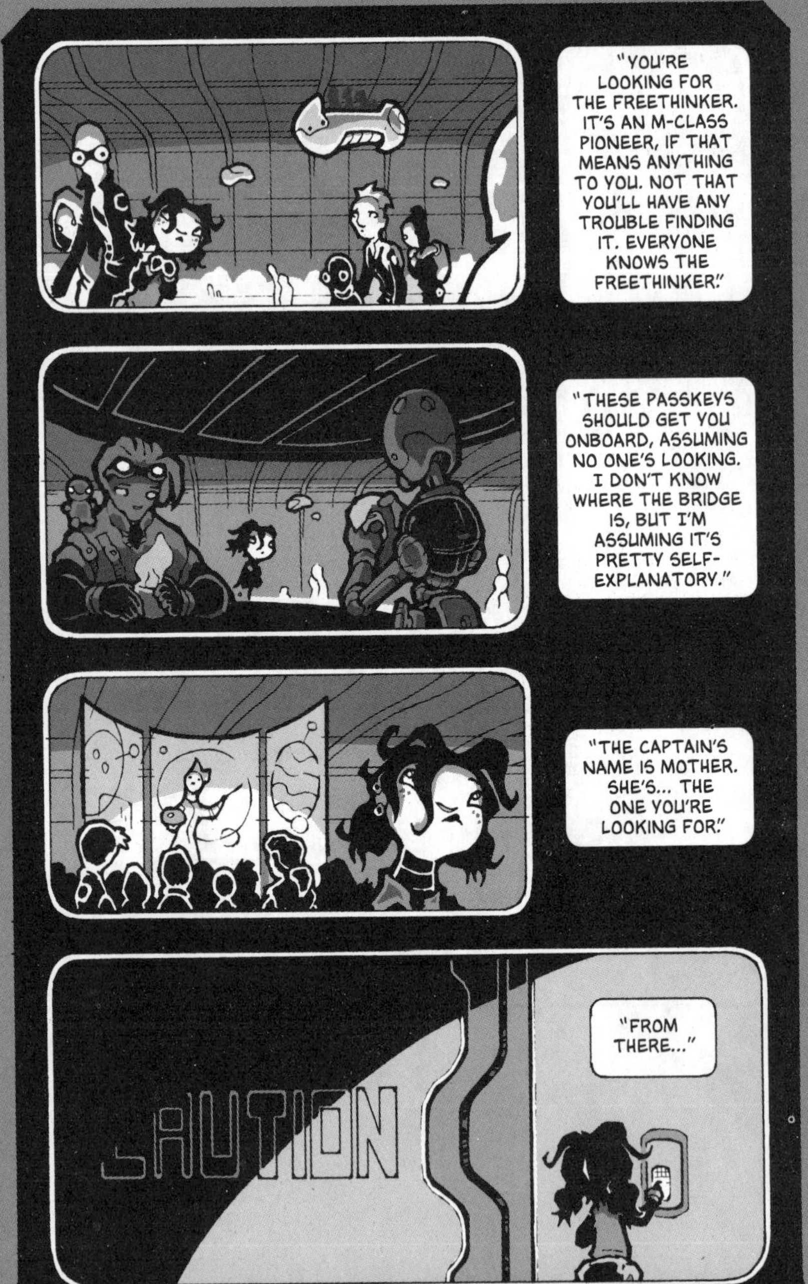
"YOU'RE LOOKING FOR THE FREETHINKER. IT'S AN M-CLASS PIONEER, IF THAT MEANS ANYTHING TO YOU. NOT THAT YOU'LL HAVE ANY TROUBLE FINDING IT. EVERYONE KNOWS THE FREETHINKER."
"THESE PASSKEYS SHOULD GET YOU ONBOARD, ASSUMING NO ONE'S LOOKING. I DON'T KNOW WHERE THE BRIDGE IS, BUT I'M ASSUMING IT'S PRETTY SELF-EXPLANATORY."
"THE CAPTAIN'S NAME IS MOTHER. SHE'S... THE ONE YOU'RE LOOKING FOR."
"FROM THERE..."
AUTION

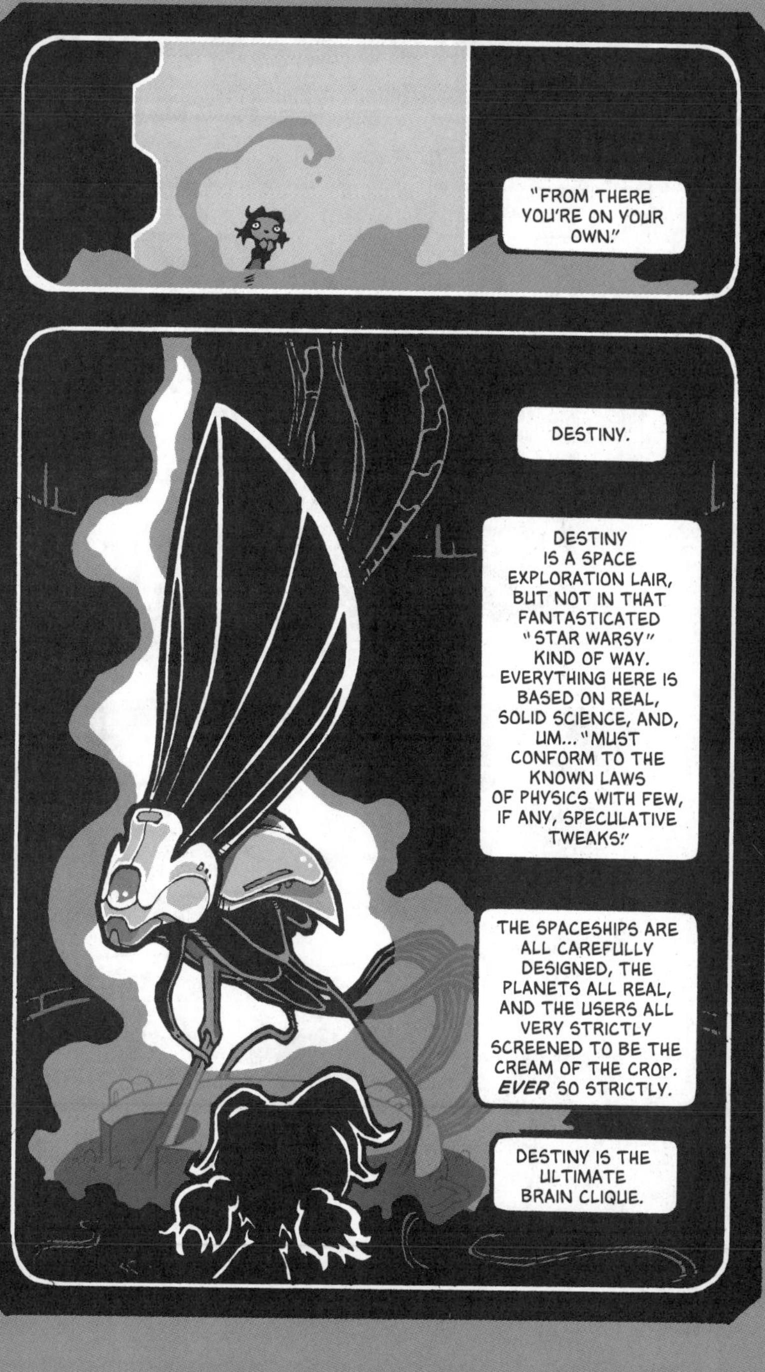
"FROM THERE YOU'RE ON YOUR OWN."
DESTINY.
DESTINY IS A SPACE EXPLORATION LAIR, BUT NOT IN THAT FANTASTICATED "STAR WARSY" KIND OF WAY. EVERYTHING HERE IS BASED ON REAL, SOLID SCIENCE, AND, UM... "MUST CONFORM TO THE KNOWN LAWS OF PHYSICS WITH FEW, IF ANY, SPECULATIVE TWEAKS!"
THE SPACESHIPS ARE ALL CAREFULLY DESIGNED, THE PLANETS ALL REAL, AND THE USERS ALL VERY STRICTLY SCREENED TO BE THE CREAM OF THE CROP. *EVER* SO STRICTLY.
DESTINY IS THE ULTIMATE BRAIN CLIQUE.

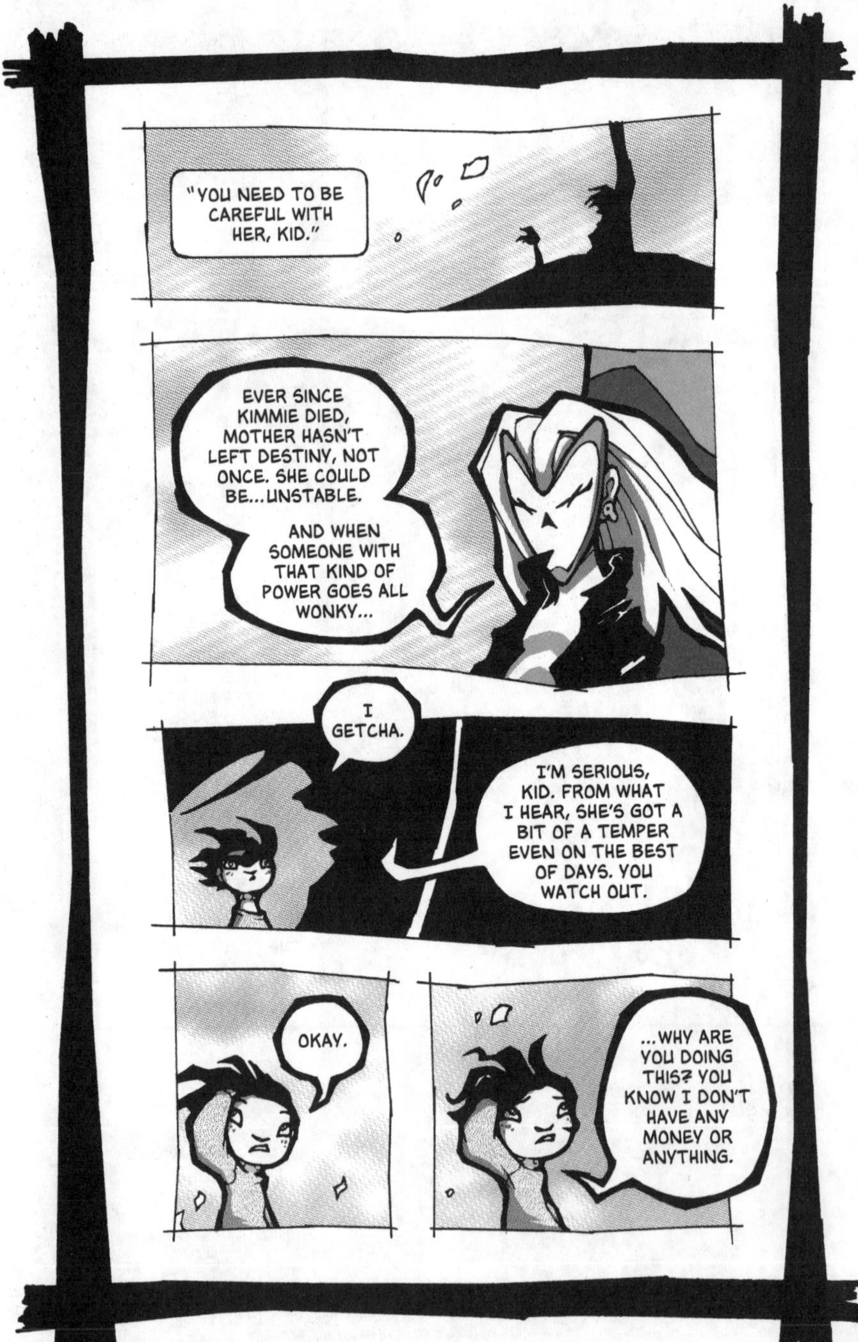
"YOU NEED TO BE CAREFUL WITH HER, KID."
EVER SINCE KIMMIE DIED, MOTHER HASN'T LEFT DESTINY, NOT ONCE. SHE COULD BE...UNSTABLE.
AND WHEN SOMEONE WITH THAT KIND OF POWER GOES ALL WONKY...
I GETCHA.
I'M SERIOUS, KID. FROM WHAT I HEAR, SHE'S GOT A BIT OF A TEMPER EVEN ON THE BEST OF DAYS. YOU WATCH OUT.
OKAY.
...WHY ARE YOU DOING THIS? YOU KNOW I DON'T HAVE ANY MONEY OR ANYTHING.

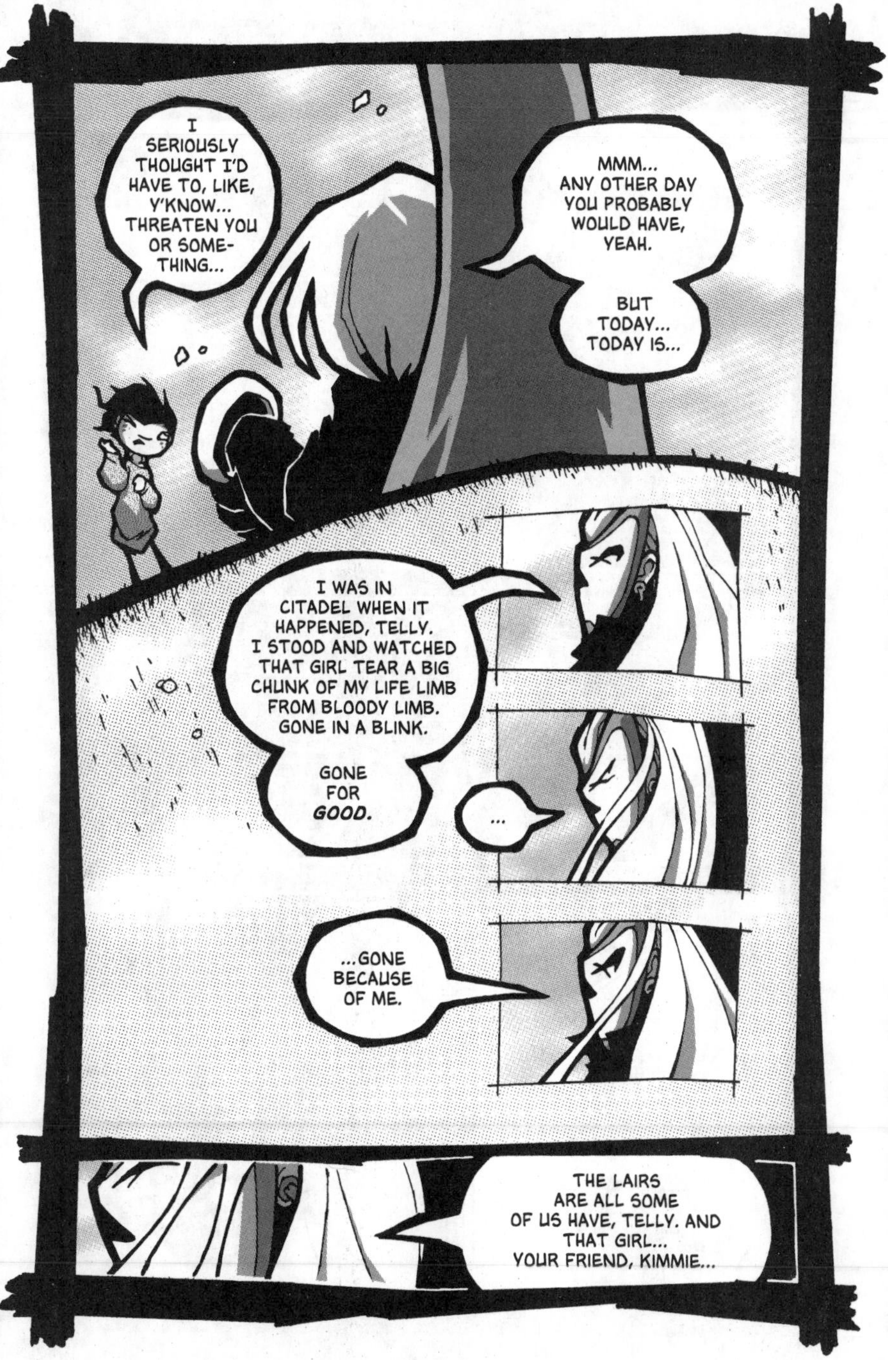
I SERIOUSLY THOUGHT I'D HAVE TO, LIKE, Y'KNOW... THREATEN YOU OR SOME-THING...
MMM... ANY OTHER DAY YOU PROBABLY WOULD HAVE, YEAH.
BUT TODAY... TODAY IS...
I WAS IN CITADEL WHEN IT HAPPENED, TELLY. I STOOD AND WATCHED THAT GIRL TEAR A BIG CHUNK OF MY LIFE LIMB FROM BLOODY LIMB. GONE IN A BLINK.
GONE FOR *GOOD.*
...
...GONE BECAUSE OF ME.
THE LAIRS ARE ALL SOME OF US HAVE, TELLY. AND THAT GIRL... YOUR FRIEND, KIMMIE...

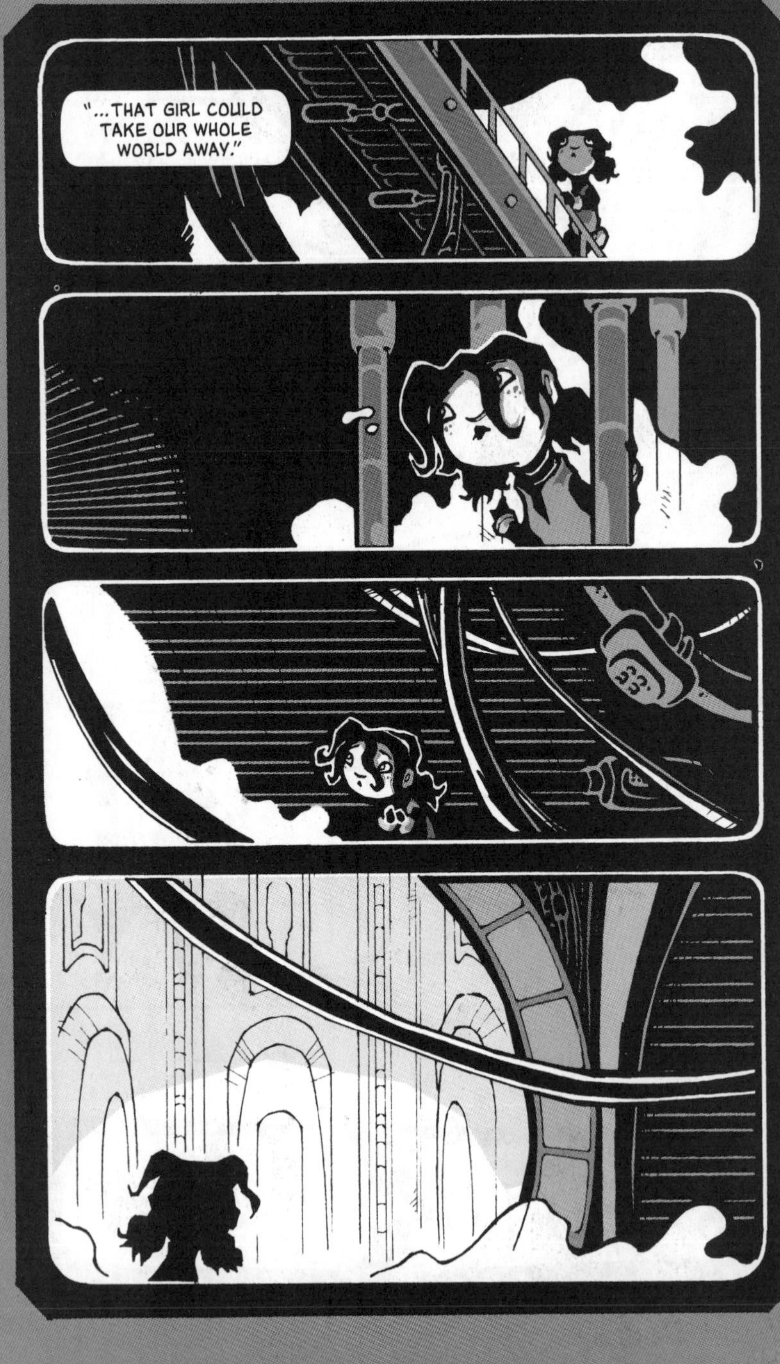
"...THAT GIRL COULD TAKE OUR WHOLE WORLD AWAY."

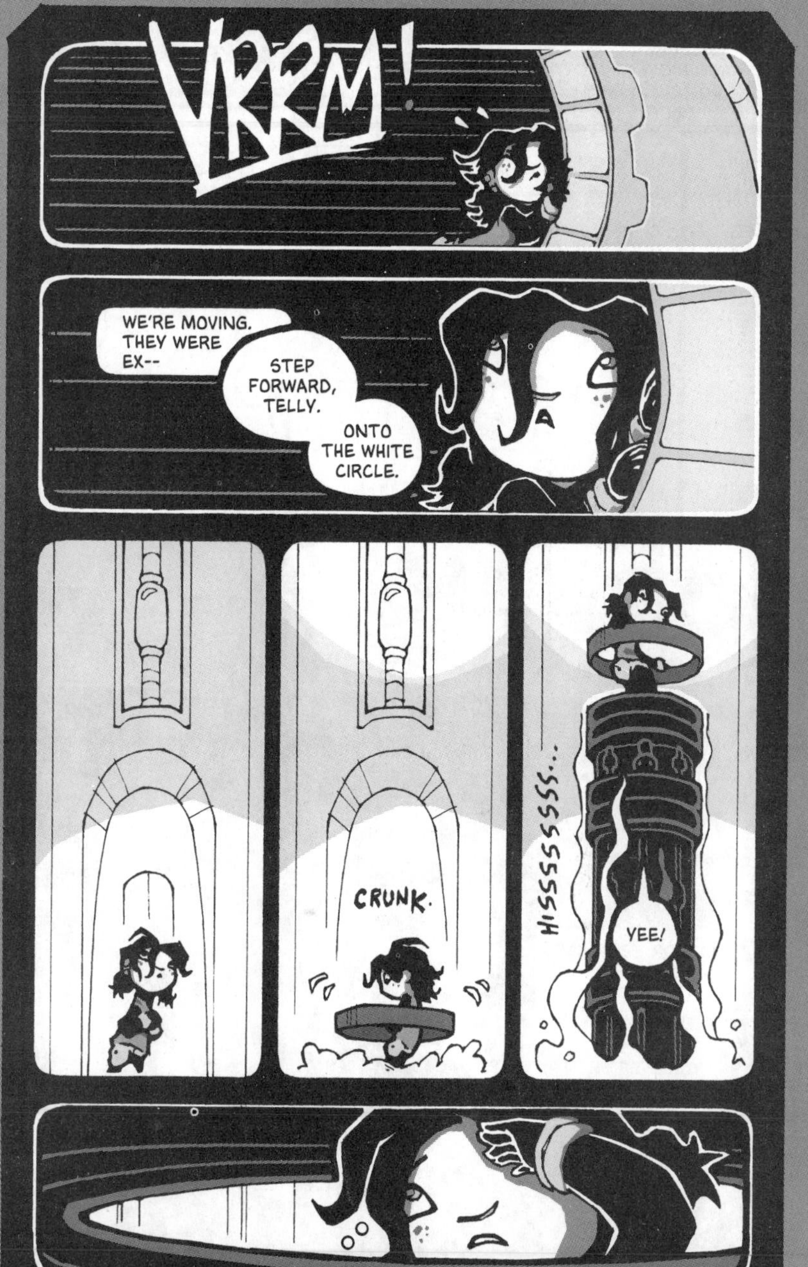
VRRM!
WE'RE MOVING. THEY WERE EX--
STEP FORWARD, TELLY.
ONTO THE WHITE CIRCLE.
CRUNK.
HISSSSSSSSS...
YEE!

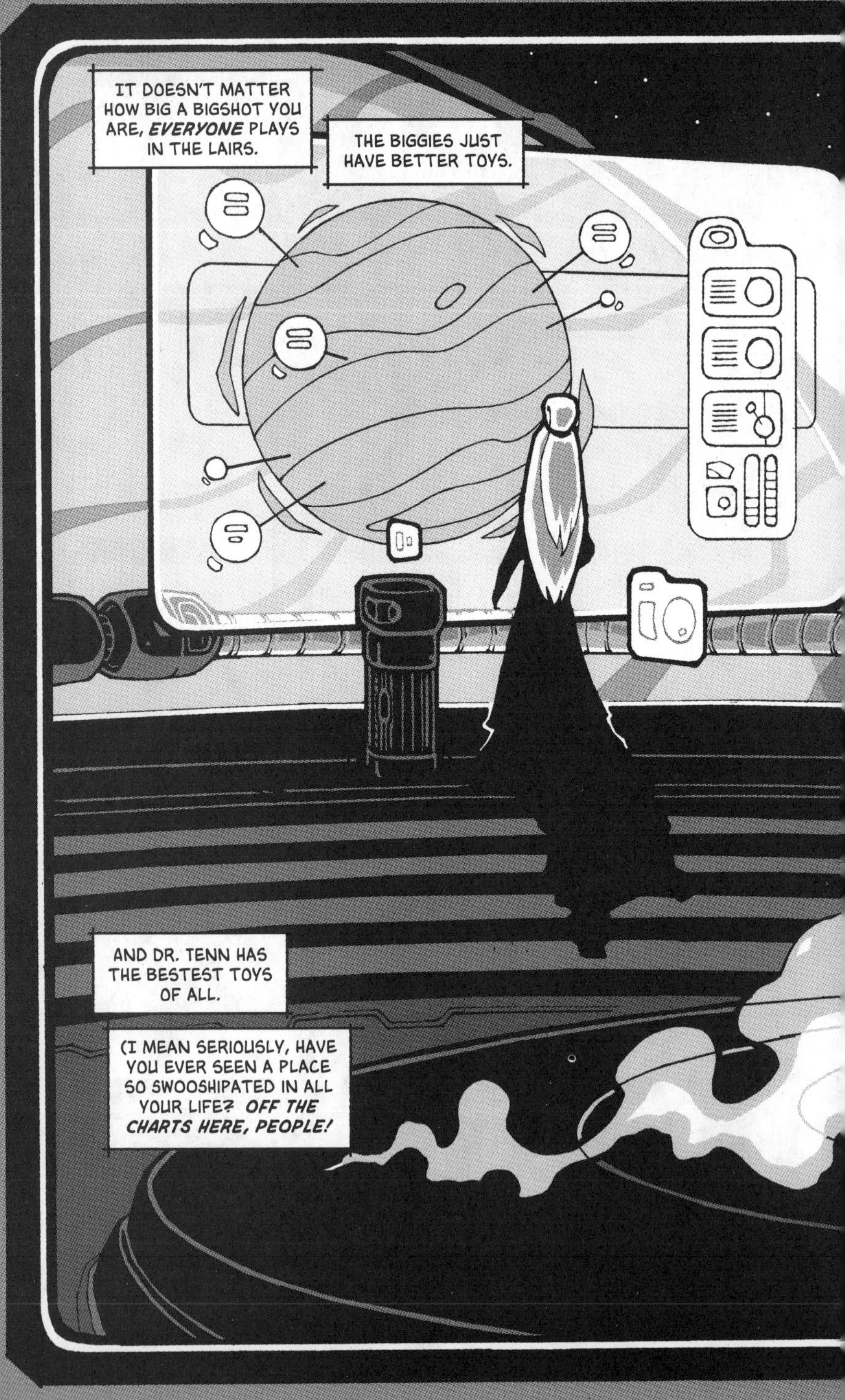
IT DOESN'T MATTER HOW BIG A BIGSHOT YOU ARE, *EVERYONE* PLAYS IN THE LAIRS.
THE BIGGIES JUST HAVE BETTER TOYS.
AND DR. TENN HAS THE BESTEST TOYS OF ALL.
(I MEAN SERIOUSLY, HAVE YOU EVER SEEN A PLACE SO SWOOSHIPATED IN ALL YOUR LIFE? *OFF THE CHARTS HERE, PEOPLE!*

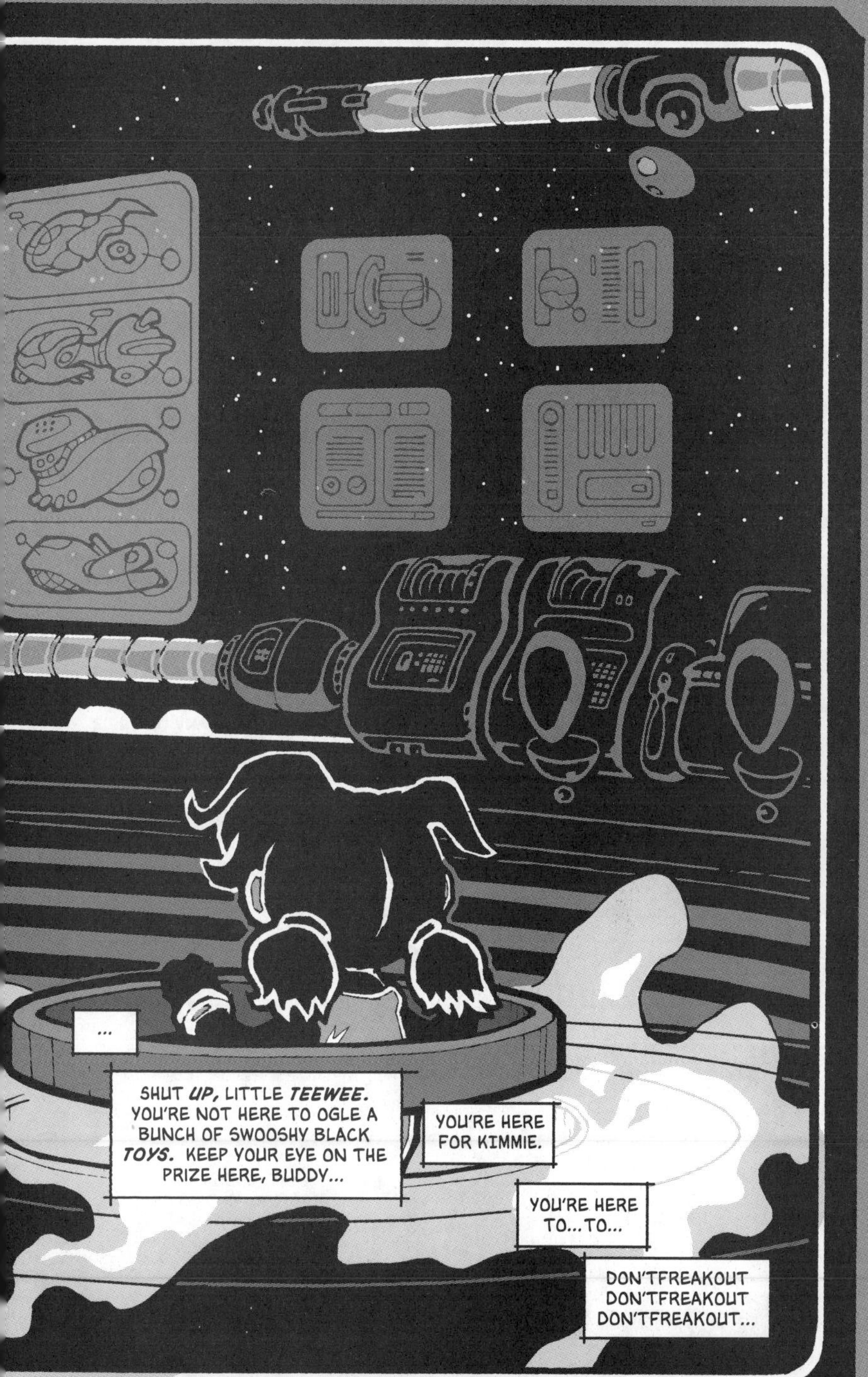
...
SHUT *UP,* LITTLE *TEEWEE.* YOU'RE NOT HERE TO OGLE A BUNCH OF SWOOSHY BLACK *TOYS.* KEEP YOUR EYE ON THE PRIZE HERE, BUDDY...
YOU'RE HERE FOR KIMMIE.
YOU'RE HERE TO...TO...
DON'TFREAKOUT DON'TFREAKOUT DON'TFREAKOUT...

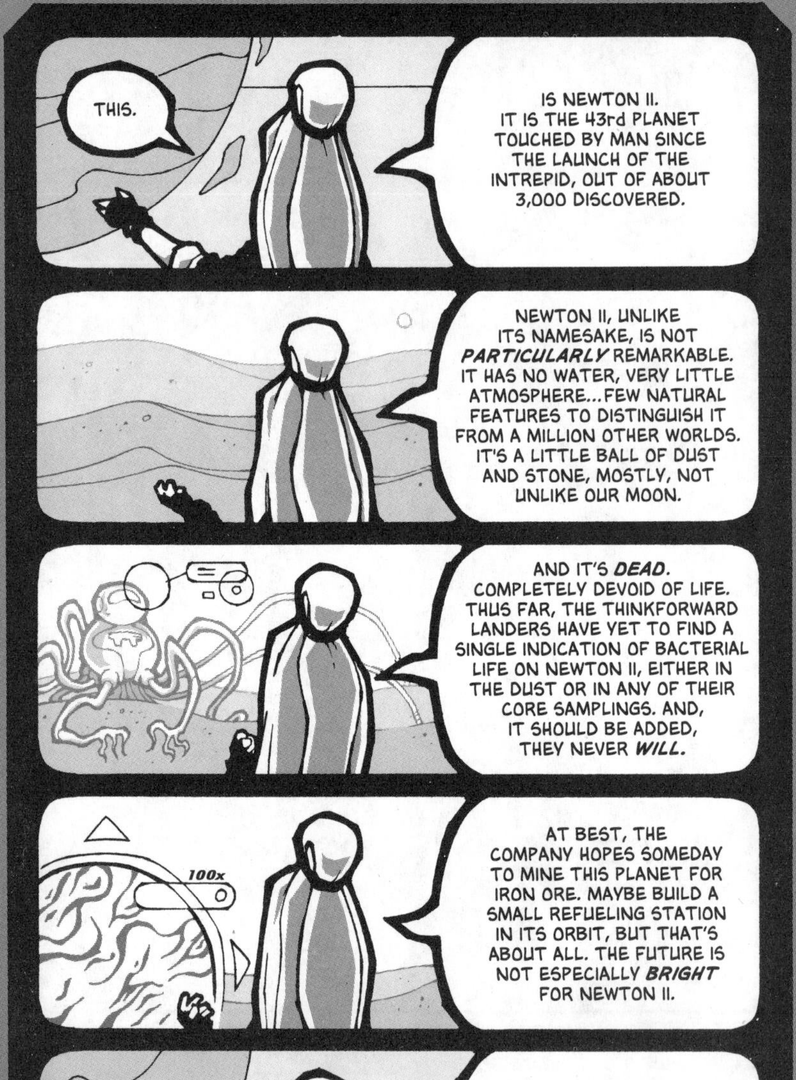

THIS.
IS NEWTON II. IT IS THE 43rd PLANET TOUCHED BY MAN SINCE THE LAUNCH OF THE INTREPID, OUT OF ABOUT 3,000 DISCOVERED.
NEWTON II, UNLIKE ITS NAMESAKE, IS NOT *PARTICULARLY* REMARKABLE. IT HAS NO WATER, VERY LITTLE ATMOSPHERE...FEW NATURAL FEATURES TO DISTINGUISH IT FROM A MILLION OTHER WORLDS. IT'S A LITTLE BALL OF DUST AND STONE, MOSTLY, NOT UNLIKE OUR MOON.
AND IT'S *DEAD.* COMPLETELY DEVOID OF LIFE. THUS FAR, THE THINKFORWARD LANDERS HAVE YET TO FIND A SINGLE INDICATION OF BACTERIAL LIFE ON NEWTON II, EITHER IN THE DUST OR IN ANY OF THEIR CORE SAMPLINGS. AND, IT SHOULD BE ADDED, THEY NEVER *WILL.*
100x
AT BEST, THE COMPANY HOPES SOMEDAY TO MINE THIS PLANET FOR IRON ORE. MAYBE BUILD A SMALL REFUELING STATION IN ITS ORBIT, BUT THAT'S ABOUT ALL. THE FUTURE IS NOT ESPECIALLY *BRIGHT* FOR NEWTON II.
IN THE REAL WORLD, THAT IS. HERE IN THE LAIRS, THINGS ARE *QUITE* DIFFERENT.

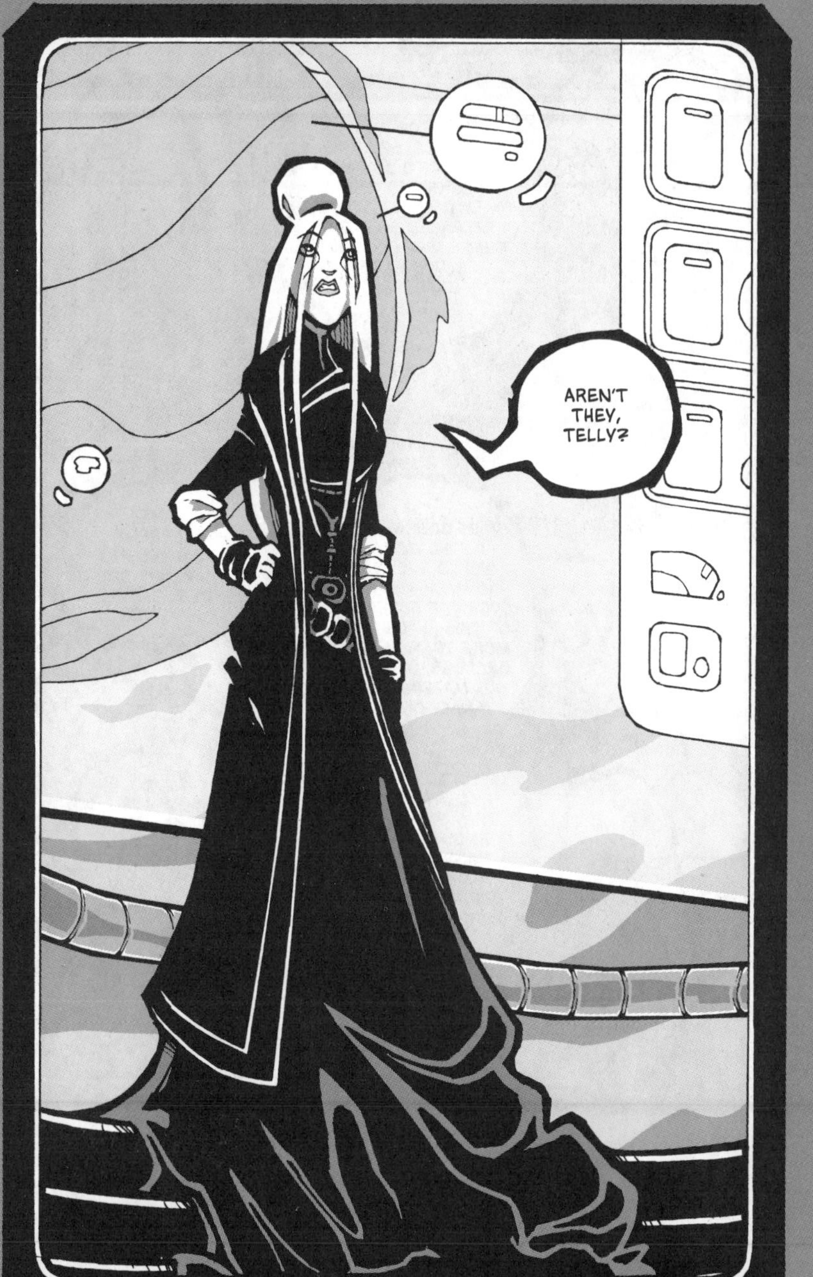
AREN'T THEY, TELLY?

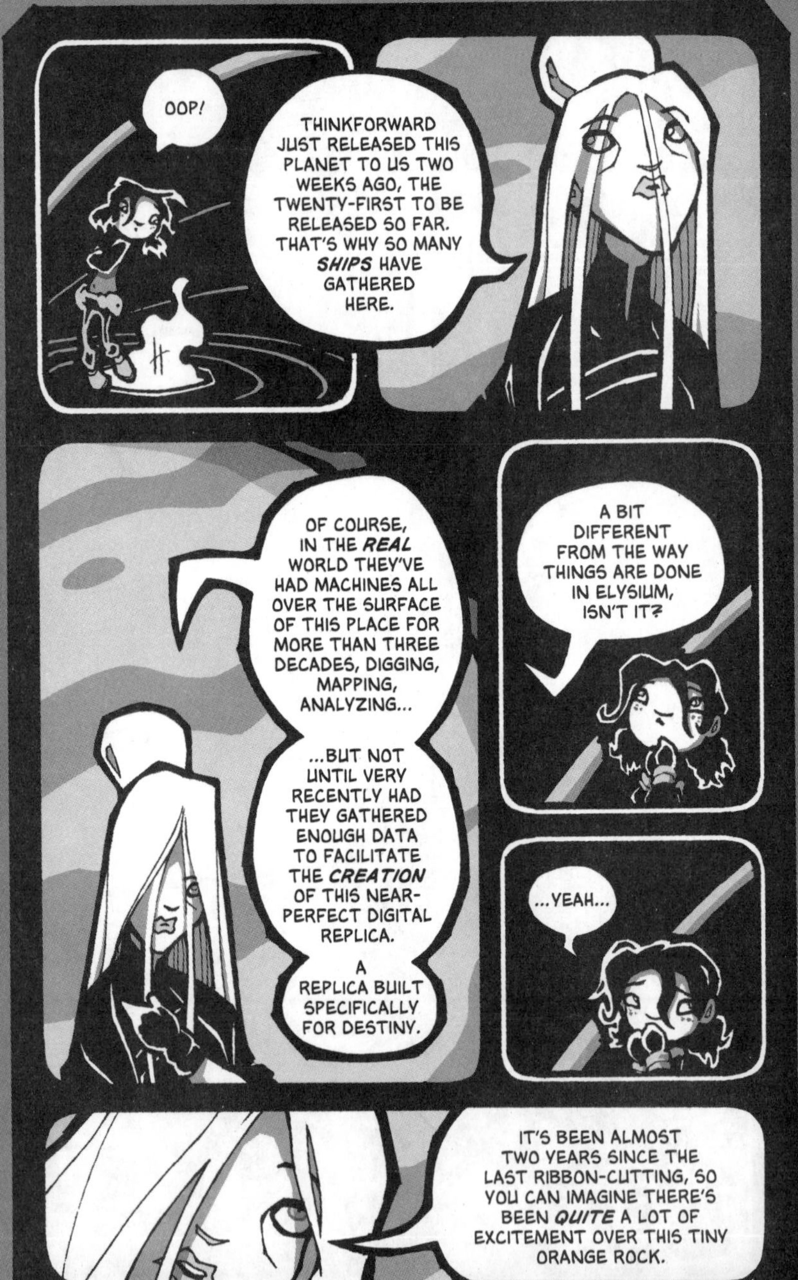
OOP!
THINKFORWARD JUST RELEASED THIS PLANET TO US TWO WEEKS AGO, THE TWENTY-FIRST TO BE RELEASED SO FAR. THAT'S WHY SO MANY *SHIPS* HAVE GATHERED HERE.
OF COURSE, IN THE *REAL* WORLD THEY'VE HAD MACHINES ALL OVER THE SURFACE OF THIS PLACE FOR MORE THAN THREE DECADES, DIGGING, MAPPING, ANALYZING...
...BUT NOT UNTIL VERY RECENTLY HAD THEY GATHERED ENOUGH DATA TO FACILITATE THE *CREATION* OF THIS NEAR-PERFECT DIGITAL REPLICA.
A REPLICA BUILT SPECIFICALLY FOR DESTINY.
A BIT DIFFERENT FROM THE WAY THINGS ARE DONE IN ELYSIUM, ISN'T IT?
...YEAH...
IT'S BEEN ALMOST TWO YEARS SINCE THE LAST RIBBON-CUTTING, SO YOU CAN IMAGINE THERE'S BEEN *QUITE* A LOT OF EXCITEMENT OVER THIS TINY ORANGE ROCK.

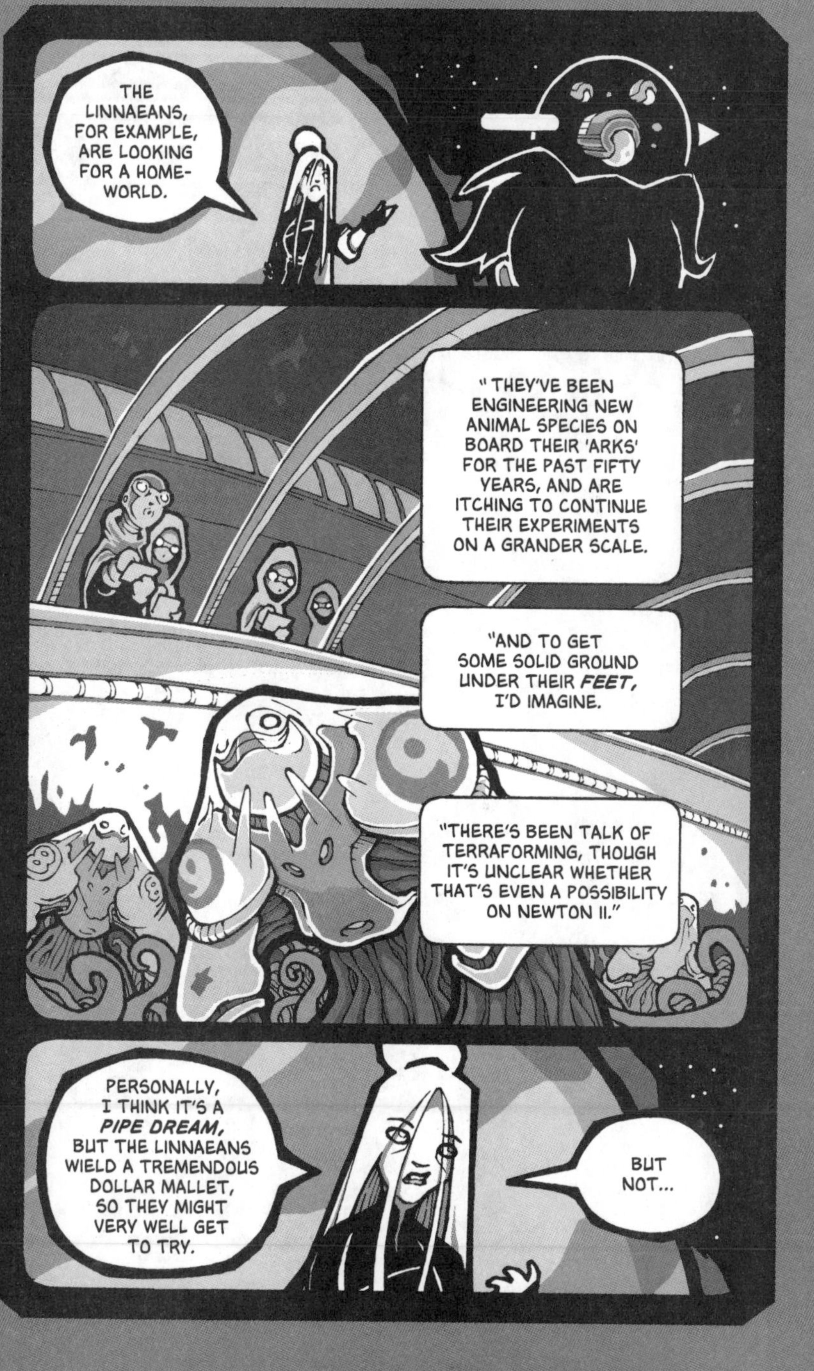
THE LINNAEANS, FOR EXAMPLE, ARE LOOKING FOR A HOME-WORLD.
"THEY'VE BEEN ENGINEERING NEW ANIMAL SPECIES ON BOARD THEIR 'ARKS' FOR THE PAST FIFTY YEARS, AND ARE ITCHING TO CONTINUE THEIR EXPERIMENTS ON A GRANDER SCALE.
"AND TO GET SOME SOLID GROUND UNDER THEIR *FEET,* I'D IMAGINE.
"THERE'S BEEN TALK OF TERRAFORMING, THOUGH IT'S UNCLEAR WHETHER THAT'S EVEN A POSSIBILITY ON NEWTON II."
PERSONALLY, I THINK IT'S A ***PIPE DREAM,*** BUT THE LINNAEANS WIELD A TREMENDOUS DOLLAR MALLET, SO THEY MIGHT VERY WELL GET TO TRY.
BUT NOT...

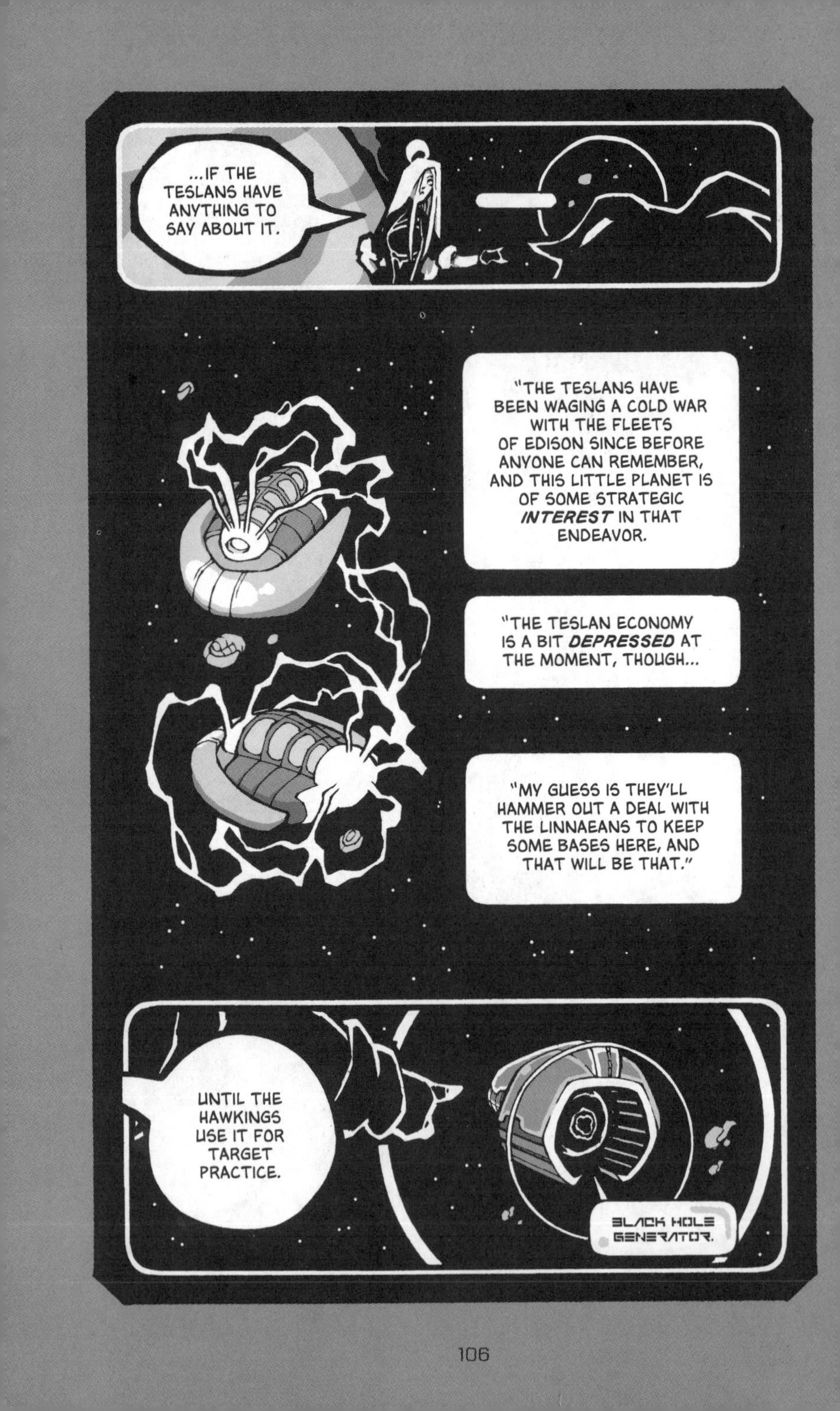
...IF THE TESLANS HAVE ANYTHING TO SAY ABOUT IT.
"THE TESLANS HAVE BEEN WAGING A COLD WAR WITH THE FLEETS OF EDISON SINCE BEFORE ANYONE CAN REMEMBER, AND THIS LITTLE PLANET IS OF SOME STRATEGIC *INTEREST* IN THAT ENDEAVOR.
"THE TESLAN ECONOMY IS A BIT *DEPRESSED* AT THE MOMENT, THOUGH...
"MY GUESS IS THEY'LL HAMMER OUT A DEAL WITH THE LINNAEANS TO KEEP SOME BASES HERE, AND THAT WILL BE THAT."
UNTIL THE HAWKINGS USE IT FOR TARGET PRACTICE.
BLACK HOLE GENERATOR.

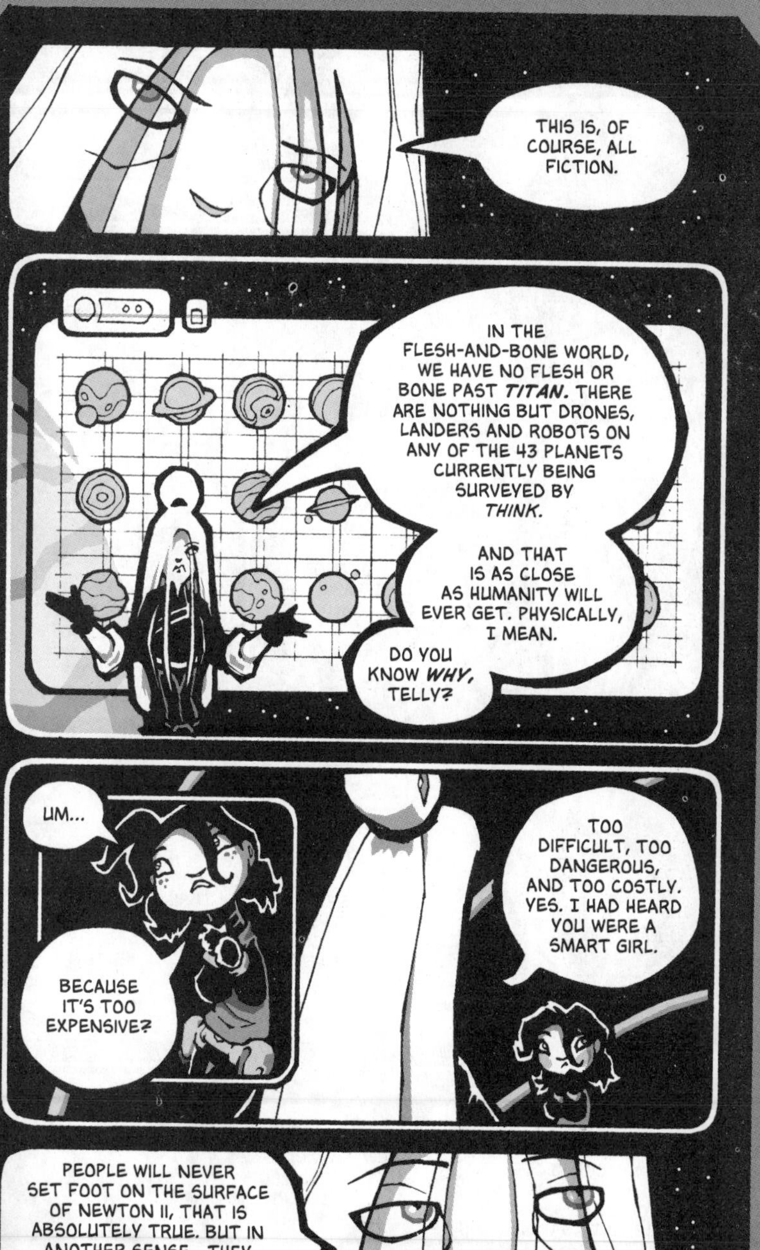
THIS IS, OF COURSE, ALL FICTION.
IN THE FLESH-AND-BONE WORLD, WE HAVE NO FLESH OR BONE PAST *TITAN.* THERE ARE NOTHING BUT DRONES, LANDERS AND ROBOTS ON ANY OF THE 43 PLANETS CURRENTLY BEING SURVEYED BY *THINK.*
AND THAT IS AS CLOSE AS HUMANITY WILL EVER GET. PHYSICALLY, I MEAN.
DO YOU KNOW ***WHY,*** TELLY?
UM...
BECAUSE IT'S TOO EXPENSIVE?
TOO DIFFICULT, TOO DANGEROUS, AND TOO COSTLY. YES. I HAD HEARD YOU WERE A SMART GIRL.
PEOPLE WILL NEVER SET FOOT ON THE SURFACE OF NEWTON II, THAT IS ABSOLUTELY TRUE. BUT IN ANOTHER SENSE... THEY ALREADY HAVE.

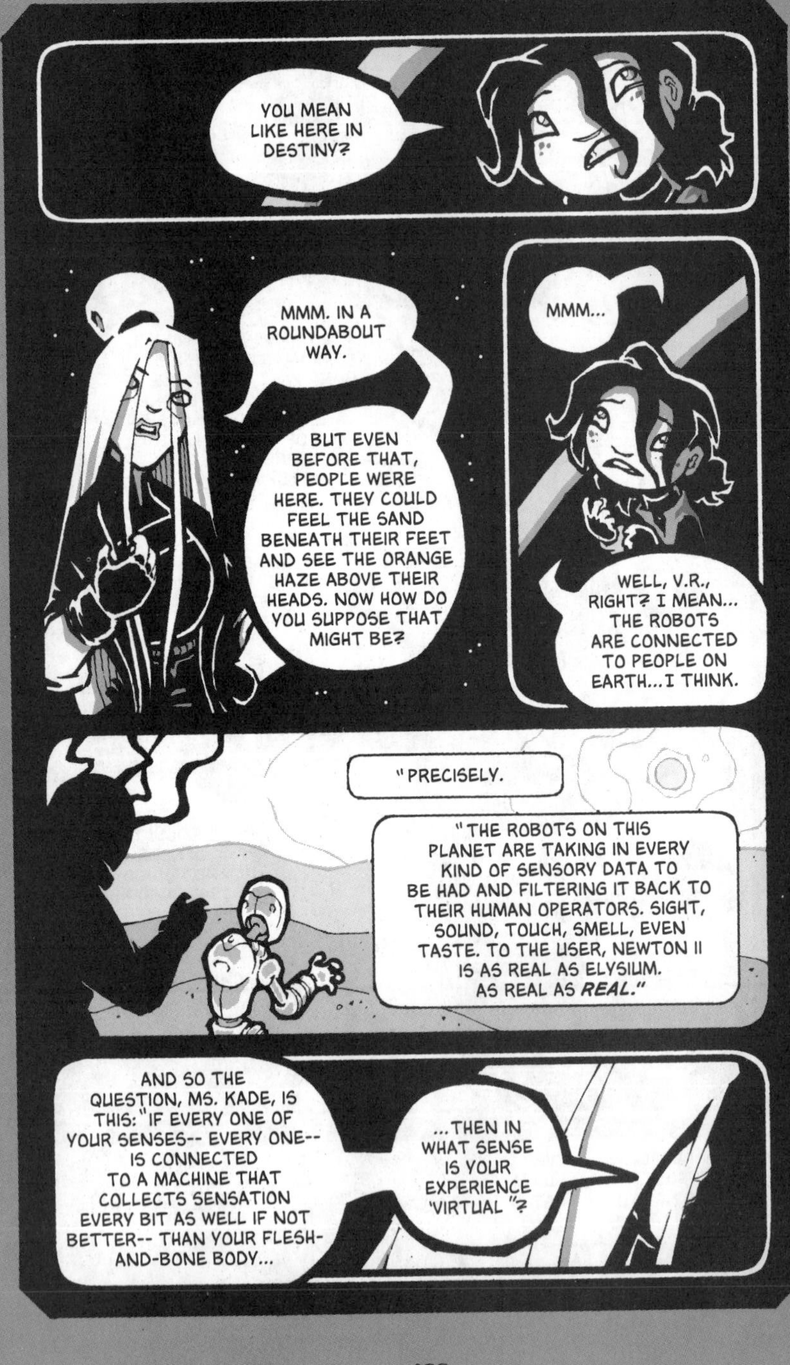
YOU MEAN LIKE HERE IN DESTINY?
MMM. IN A ROUNDABOUT WAY.
BUT EVEN BEFORE THAT, PEOPLE WERE HERE. THEY COULD FEEL THE SAND BENEATH THEIR FEET AND SEE THE ORANGE HAZE ABOVE THEIR HEADS. NOW HOW DO YOU SUPPOSE THAT MIGHT BE?
MMM...
WELL, V.R., RIGHT? I MEAN... THE ROBOTS ARE CONNECTED TO PEOPLE ON EARTH...I THINK.
"PRECISELY.
"THE ROBOTS ON THIS PLANET ARE TAKING IN EVERY KIND OF SENSORY DATA TO BE HAD AND FILTERING IT BACK TO THEIR HUMAN OPERATORS. SIGHT, SOUND, TOUCH, SMELL, EVEN TASTE. TO THE USER, NEWTON II IS AS REAL AS ELYSIUM. AS REAL AS *REAL*."
AND SO THE QUESTION, MS. KADE, IS THIS: "IF EVERY ONE OF YOUR SENSES-- EVERY ONE-- IS CONNECTED TO A MACHINE THAT COLLECTS SENSATION EVERY BIT AS WELL IF NOT BETTER-- THAN YOUR FLESH-AND-BONE BODY...
...THEN IN WHAT SENSE IS YOUR EXPERIENCE 'VIRTUAL'"?

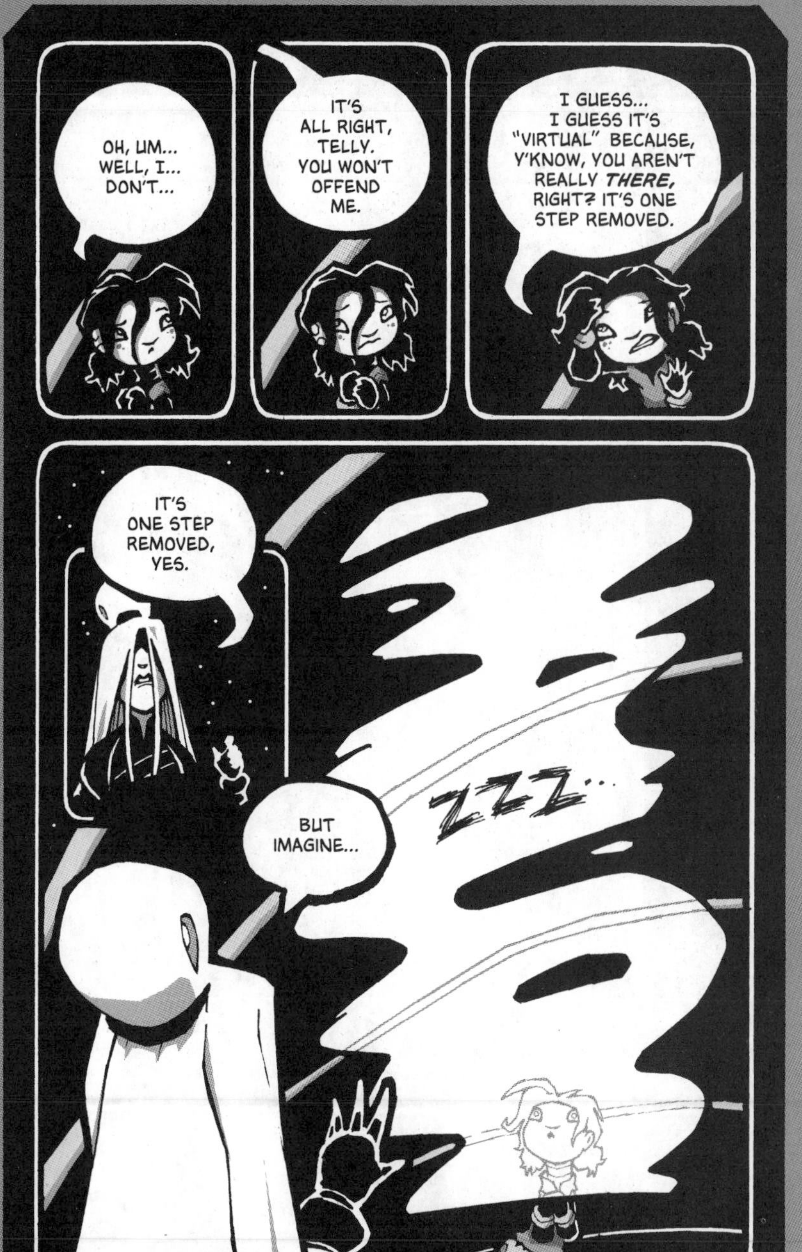
OH, UM... WELL, I... DON'T...
IT'S ALL RIGHT, TELLY. YOU WON'T OFFEND ME.
I GUESS... I GUESS IT'S "VIRTUAL" BECAUSE, Y'KNOW, YOU AREN'T REALLY *THERE,* RIGHT? IT'S ONE STEP REMOVED.
IT'S ONE STEP REMOVED, YES.
BUT IMAGINE...
ZZZ...

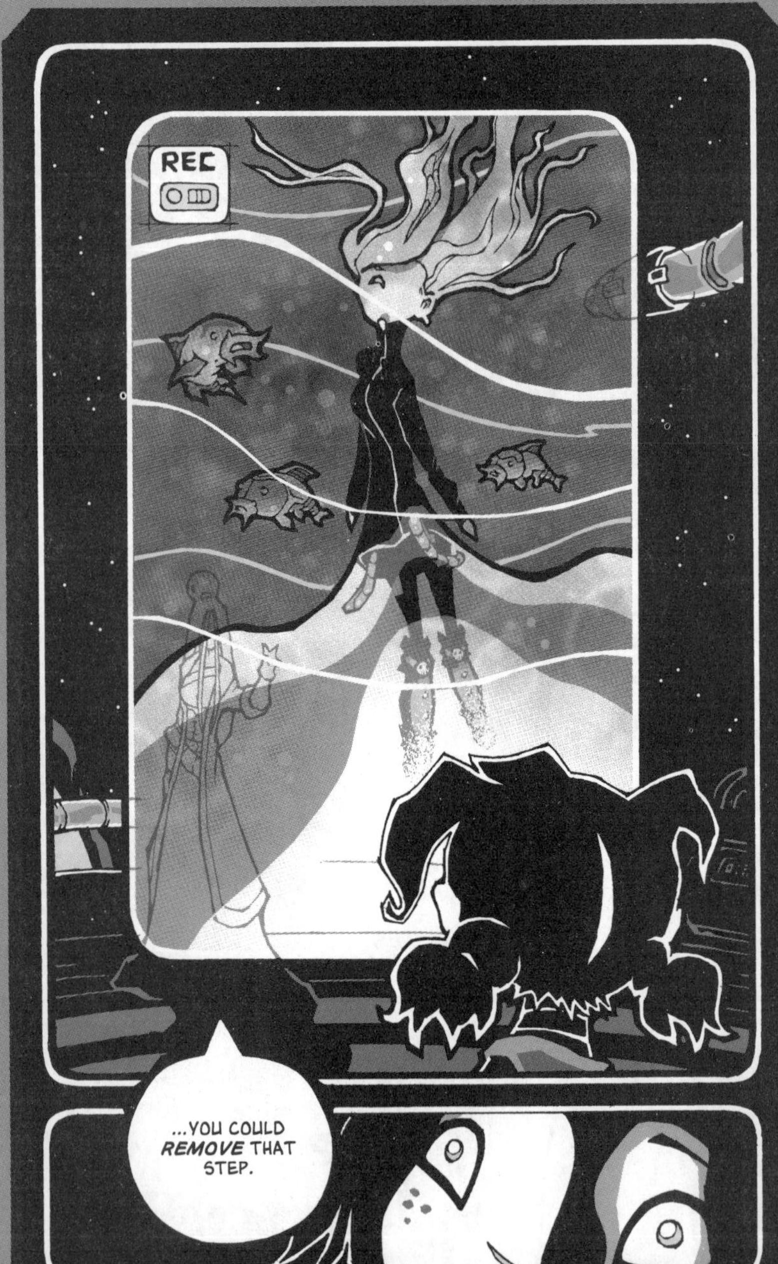
REC
...YOU COULD *REMOVE* THAT STEP.

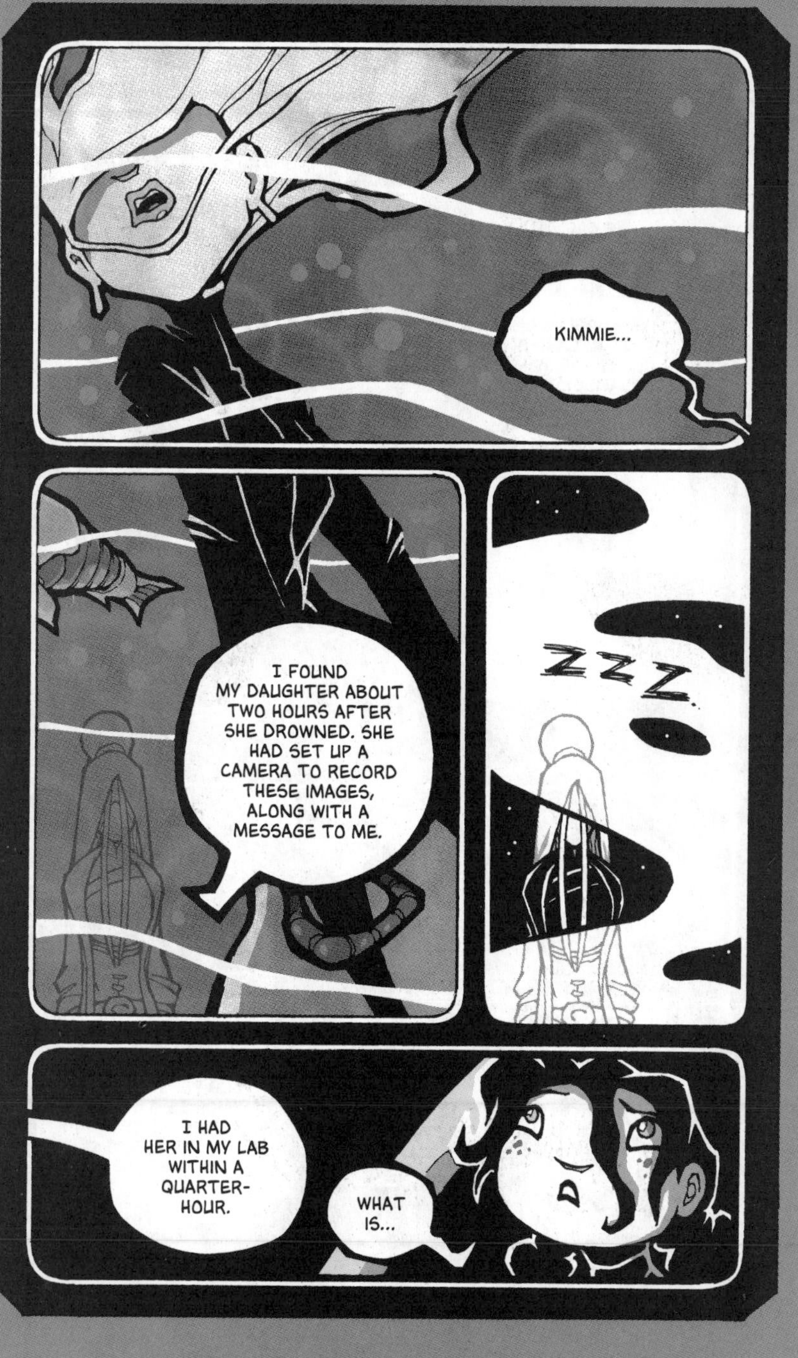
KIMMIE...
I FOUND MY DAUGHTER ABOUT TWO HOURS AFTER SHE DROWNED. SHE HAD SET UP A CAMERA TO RECORD THESE IMAGES, ALONG WITH A MESSAGE TO ME.
ZZZ.
I HAD HER IN MY LAB WITHIN A QUARTER-HOUR.
WHAT IS...

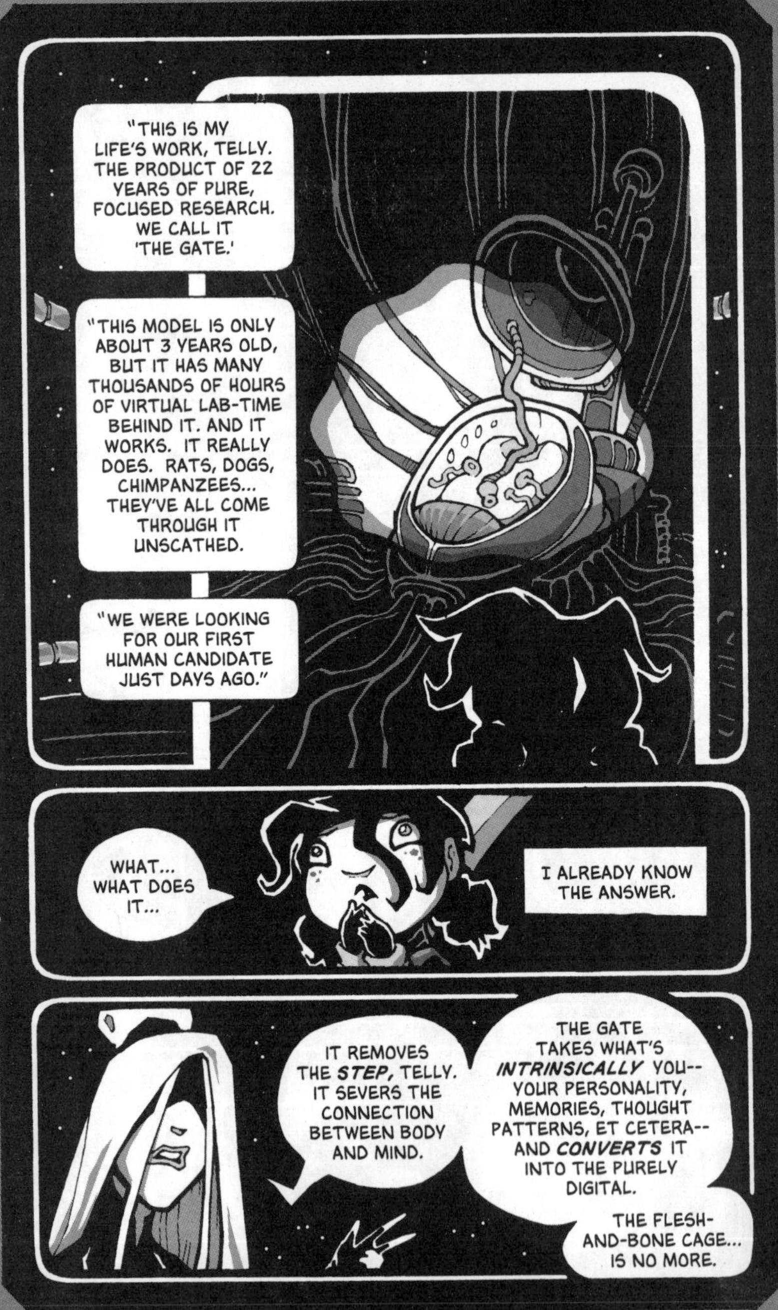
"THIS IS MY LIFE'S WORK, TELLY. THE PRODUCT OF 22 YEARS OF PURE, FOCUSED RESEARCH. WE CALL IT 'THE GATE.'
"THIS MODEL IS ONLY ABOUT 3 YEARS OLD, BUT IT HAS MANY THOUSANDS OF HOURS OF VIRTUAL LAB-TIME BEHIND IT. AND IT WORKS. IT REALLY DOES. RATS, DOGS, CHIMPANZEES... THEY'VE ALL COME THROUGH IT UNSCATHED.
"WE WERE LOOKING FOR OUR FIRST HUMAN CANDIDATE JUST DAYS AGO."
WHAT... WHAT DOES IT...
I ALREADY KNOW THE ANSWER.
IT REMOVES THE STEP, TELLY. IT SEVERS THE CONNECTION BETWEEN BODY AND MIND.
THE GATE TAKES WHAT'S INTRINSICALLY YOU-- YOUR PERSONALITY, MEMORIES, THOUGHT PATTERNS, ET CETERA-- AND CONVERTS IT INTO THE PURELY DIGITAL.
THE FLESH-AND-BONE CAGE... IS NO MORE.

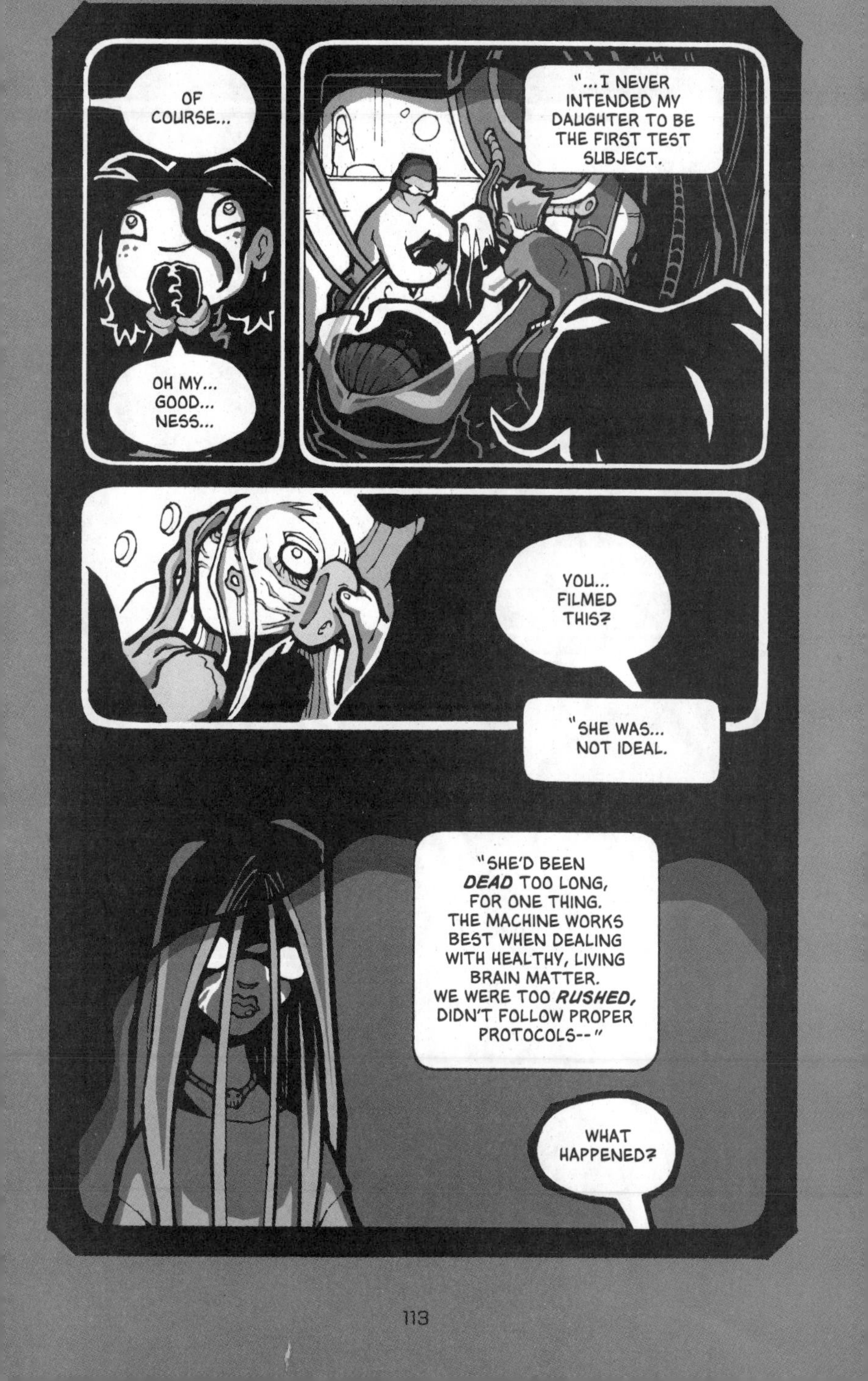
OF COURSE...
OH MY... GOOD... NESS...
"...I NEVER INTENDED MY DAUGHTER TO BE THE FIRST TEST SUBJECT.
YOU... FILMED THIS?
"SHE WAS... NOT IDEAL.
"SHE'D BEEN ***DEAD*** TOO LONG, FOR ONE THING. THE MACHINE WORKS BEST WHEN DEALING WITH HEALTHY, LIVING BRAIN MATTER. WE WERE TOO ***RUSHED,*** DIDN'T FOLLOW PROPER PROTOCOLS--"
WHAT HAPPENED?

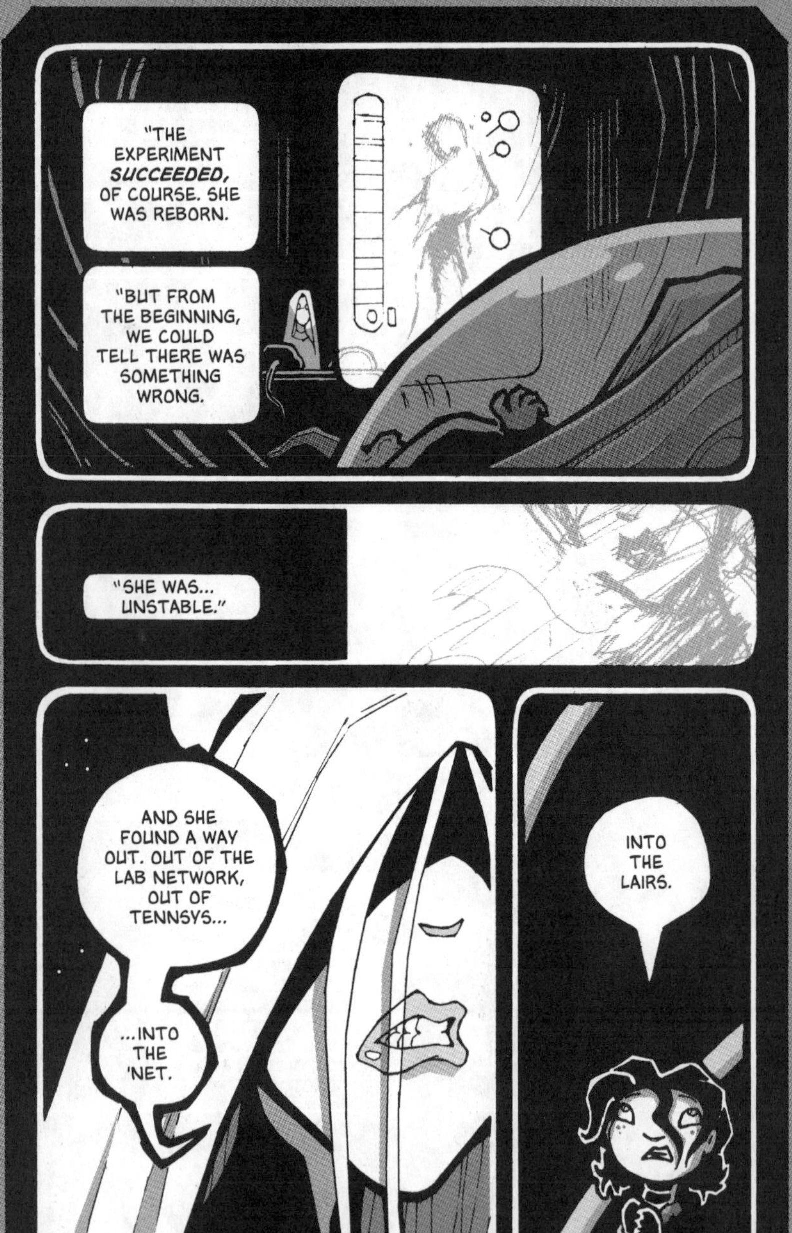
"THE EXPERIMENT *SUCCEEDED,* OF COURSE. SHE WAS REBORN.
"BUT FROM THE BEGINNING, WE COULD TELL THERE WAS SOMETHING WRONG.
"SHE WAS... UNSTABLE."
AND SHE FOUND A WAY OUT. OUT OF THE LAB NETWORK, OUT OF TENNSYS...
...INTO THE 'NET.
INTO THE LAIRS.

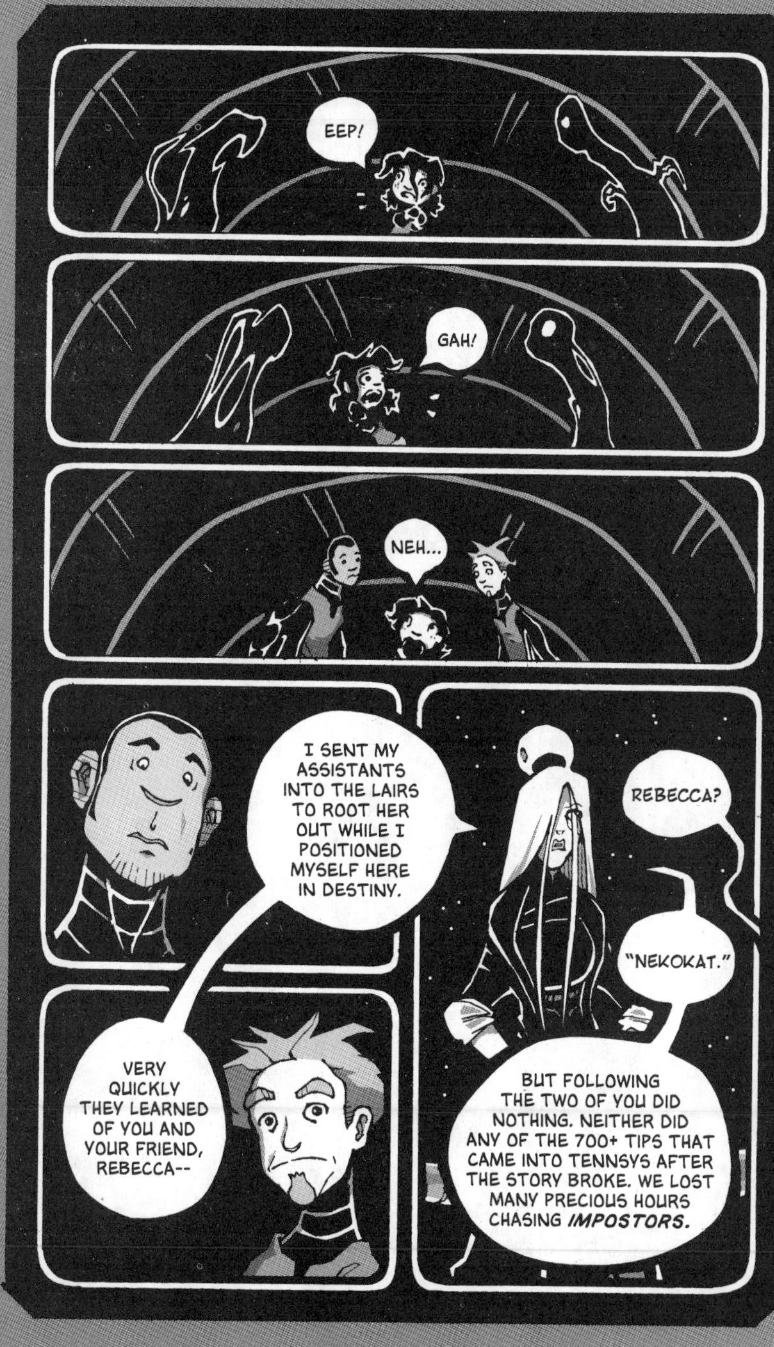
EEP!
GAH!
NEH...
I SENT MY ASSISTANTS INTO THE LAIRS TO ROOT HER OUT WHILE I POSITIONED MYSELF HERE IN DESTINY.
VERY QUICKLY THEY LEARNED OF YOU AND YOUR FRIEND, REBECCA--
REBECCA?
"NEKOKAT."
BUT FOLLOWING THE TWO OF YOU DID NOTHING. NEITHER DID ANY OF THE 700+ TIPS THAT CAME INTO TENNSYS AFTER THE STORY BROKE. WE LOST MANY PRECIOUS HOURS CHASING *IMPOSTORS.*

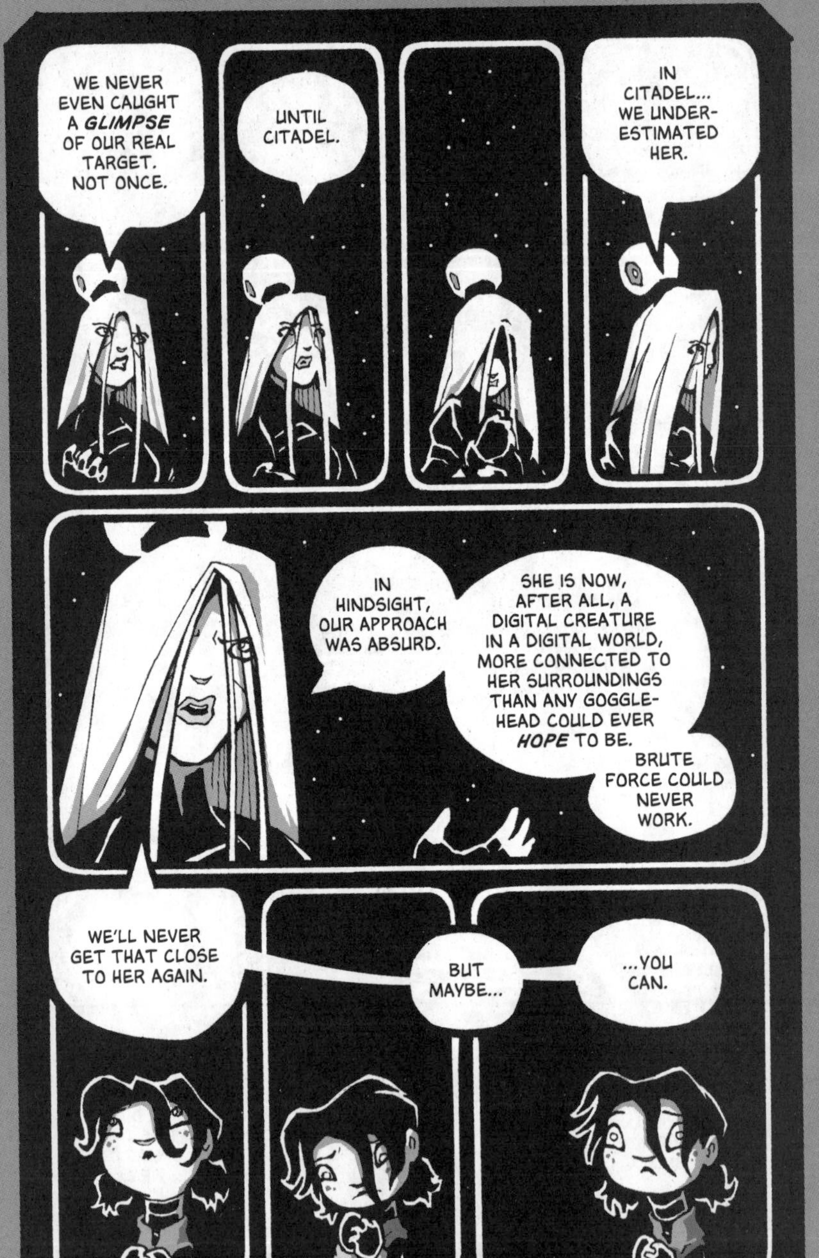
WE NEVER EVEN CAUGHT A *GLIMPSE* OF OUR REAL TARGET. NOT ONCE.
UNTIL CITADEL.
IN CITADEL... WE UNDER-ESTIMATED HER.
IN HINDSIGHT, OUR APPROACH WAS ABSURD.
SHE IS NOW, AFTER ALL, A DIGITAL CREATURE IN A DIGITAL WORLD, MORE CONNECTED TO HER SURROUNDINGS THAN ANY GOGGLE-HEAD COULD EVER *HOPE* TO BE.
BRUTE FORCE COULD NEVER WORK.
WE'LL NEVER GET THAT CLOSE TO HER AGAIN.
BUT MAYBE...
...YOU CAN.

CHAPTER FIVE

"Fallingintoit canyousee... Canyousee...
"Canyousee..."

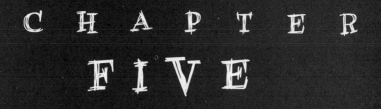

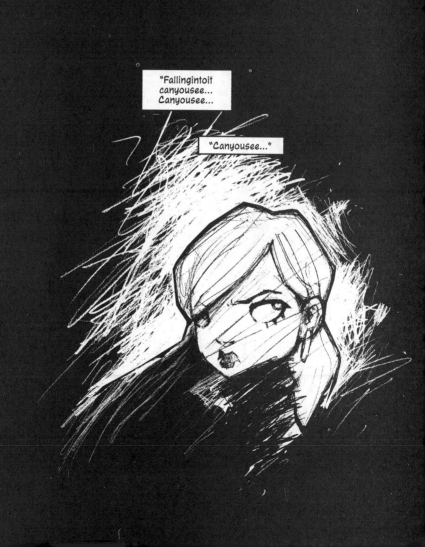

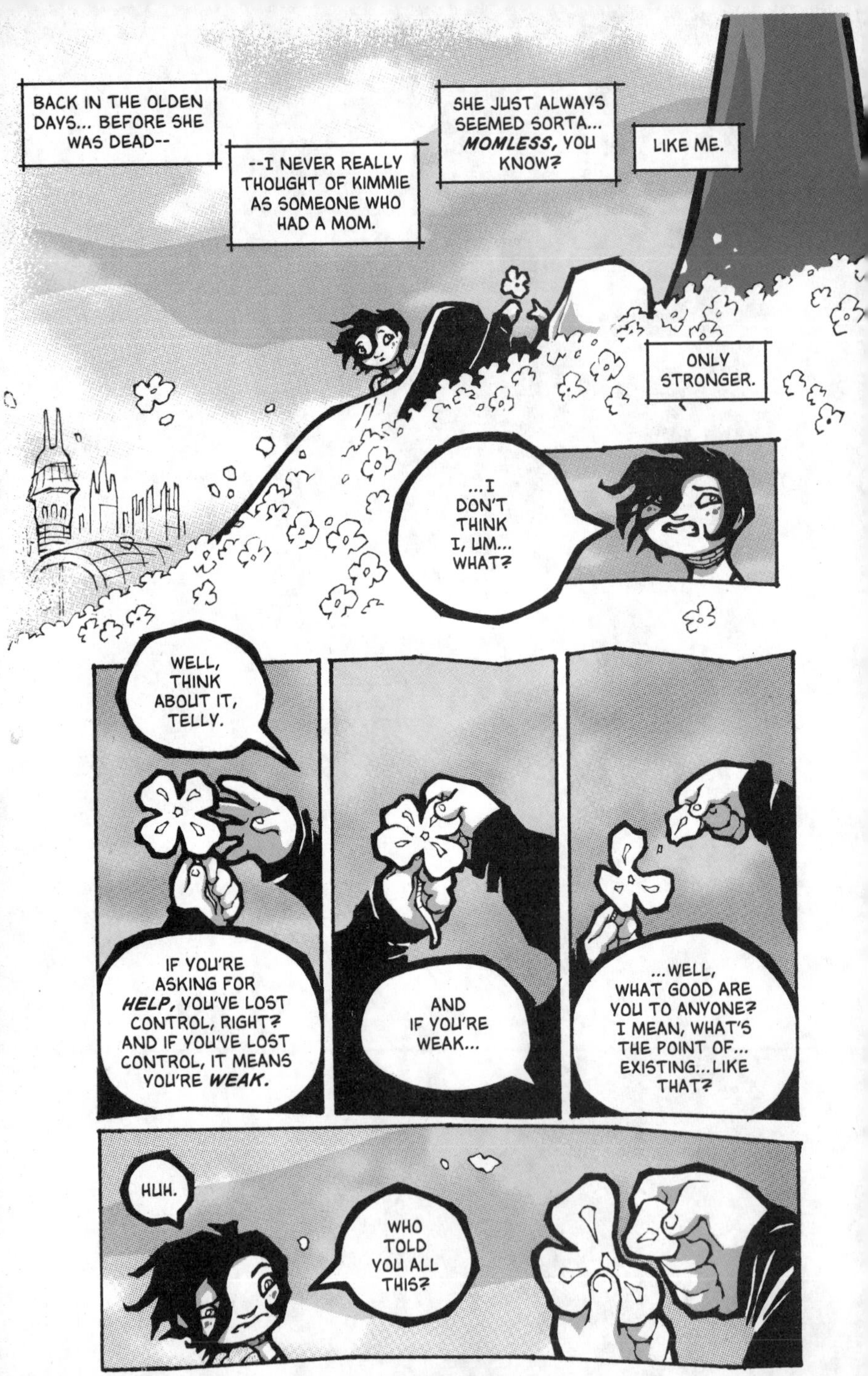

BACK IN THE OLDEN DAYS... BEFORE SHE WAS DEAD--
--I NEVER REALLY THOUGHT OF KIMMIE AS SOMEONE WHO HAD A MOM.
SHE JUST ALWAYS SEEMED SORTA... *MOMLESS,* YOU KNOW?
LIKE ME.
ONLY STRONGER.
...I DON'T THINK I, UM... WHAT?
WELL, THINK ABOUT IT, TELLY.
IF YOU'RE ASKING FOR *HELP,* YOU'VE LOST CONTROL, RIGHT? AND IF YOU'VE LOST CONTROL, IT MEANS YOU'RE *WEAK.*
AND IF YOU'RE WEAK...
...WELL, WHAT GOOD ARE YOU TO ANYONE? I MEAN, WHAT'S THE POINT OF... EXISTING...LIKE THAT?
HUH.
WHO TOLD YOU ALL THIS?

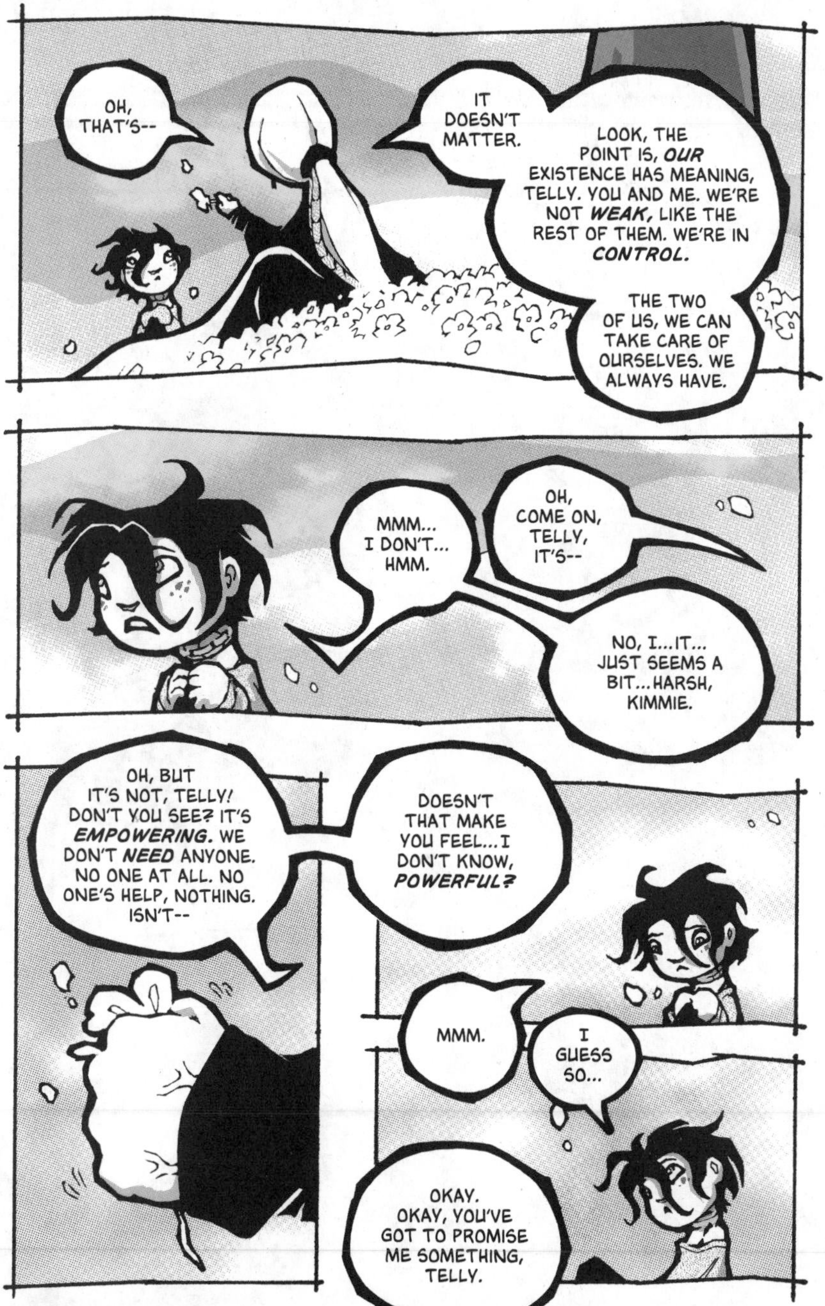
OH, THAT'S--
IT DOESN'T MATTER.
LOOK, THE POINT IS, OUR EXISTENCE HAS MEANING, TELLY. YOU AND ME. WE'RE NOT WEAK, LIKE THE REST OF THEM. WE'RE IN CONTROL.
THE TWO OF US, WE CAN TAKE CARE OF OURSELVES. WE ALWAYS HAVE.
MMM... I DON'T... HMM.
OH, COME ON, TELLY, IT'S--
NO, I...IT... JUST SEEMS A BIT...HARSH, KIMMIE.
OH, BUT IT'S NOT, TELLY! DON'T YOU SEE? IT'S EMPOWERING. WE DON'T NEED ANYONE. NO ONE AT ALL. NO ONE'S HELP, NOTHING. ISN'T--
DOESN'T THAT MAKE YOU FEEL...I DON'T KNOW, POWERFUL?
MMM.
I GUESS SO...
OKAY. OKAY, YOU'VE GOT TO PROMISE ME SOMETHING, TELLY.

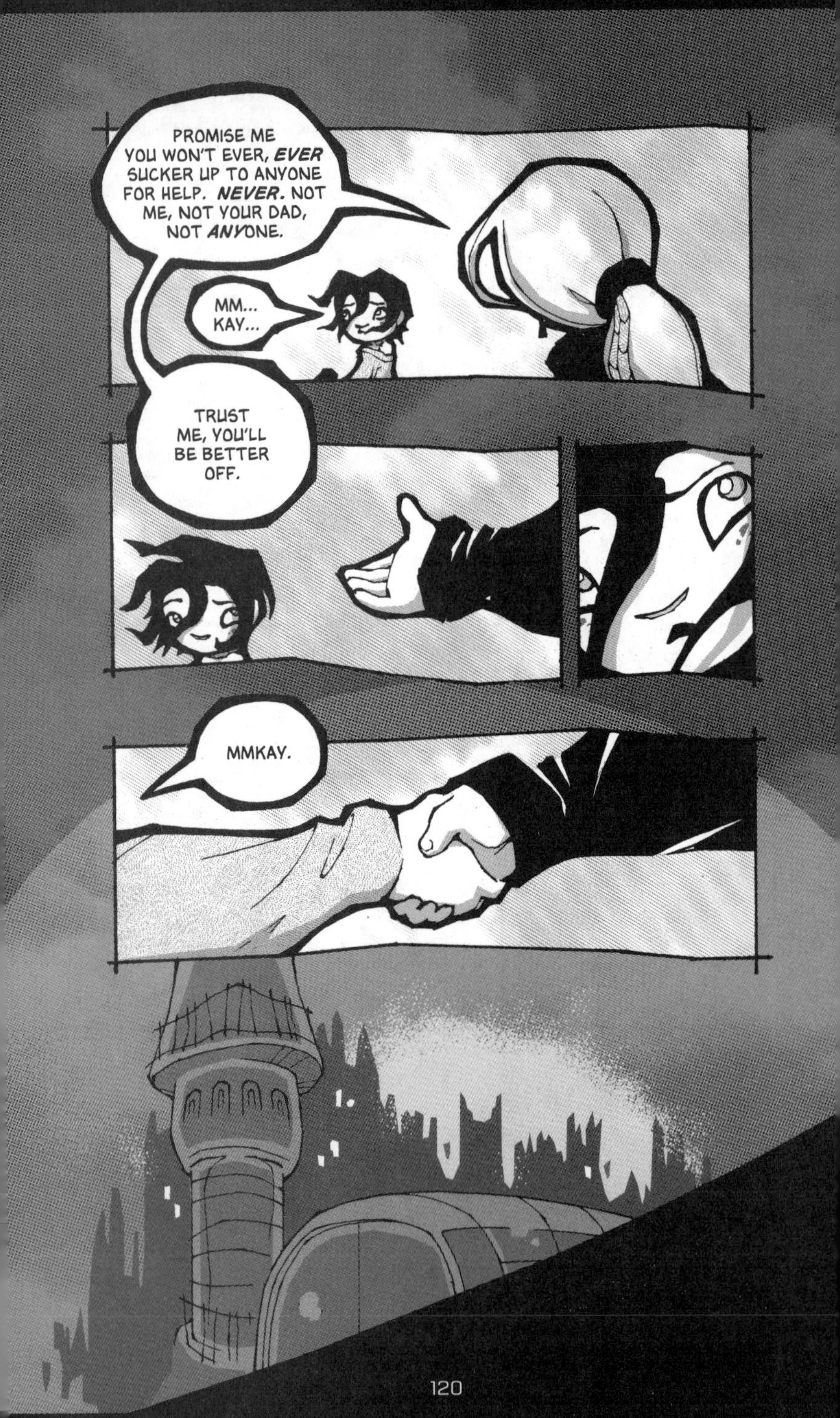
PROMISE ME YOU WON'T EVER, EVER SUCKER UP TO ANYONE FOR HELP. NEVER. NOT ME, NOT YOUR DAD, NOT ANYONE.
MM... KAY...
TRUST ME, YOU'LL BE BETTER OFF.
MMKAY.

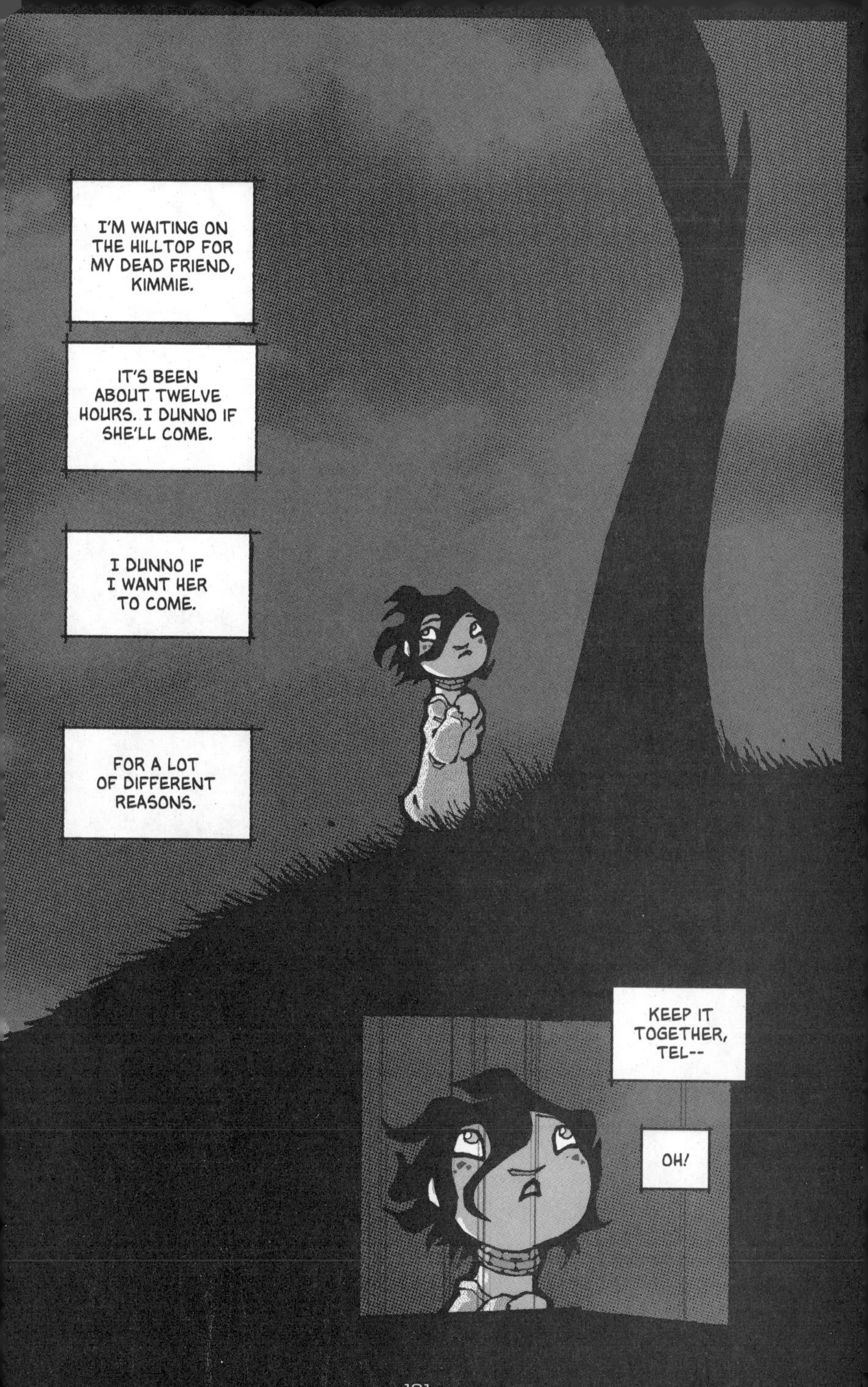
I'M WAITING ON THE HILLTOP FOR MY DEAD FRIEND, KIMMIE.
IT'S BEEN ABOUT TWELVE HOURS. I DUNNO IF SHE'LL COME.
I DUNNO IF I WANT HER TO COME.
FOR A LOT OF DIFFERENT REASONS.
KEEP IT TOGETHER, TEL--
OH!

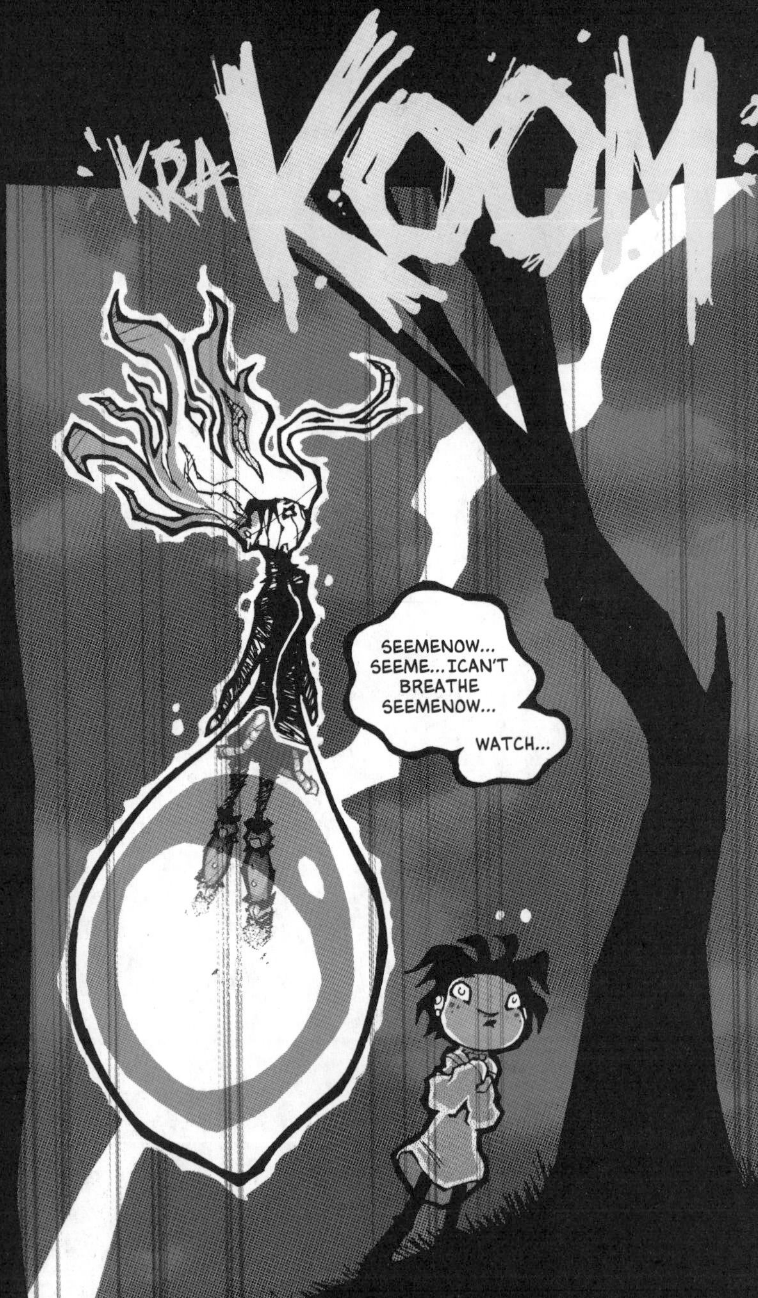
KRA KOOM
SEEMENOW... SEEME... ICAN'T BREATHE SEEMENOW...
WATCH...

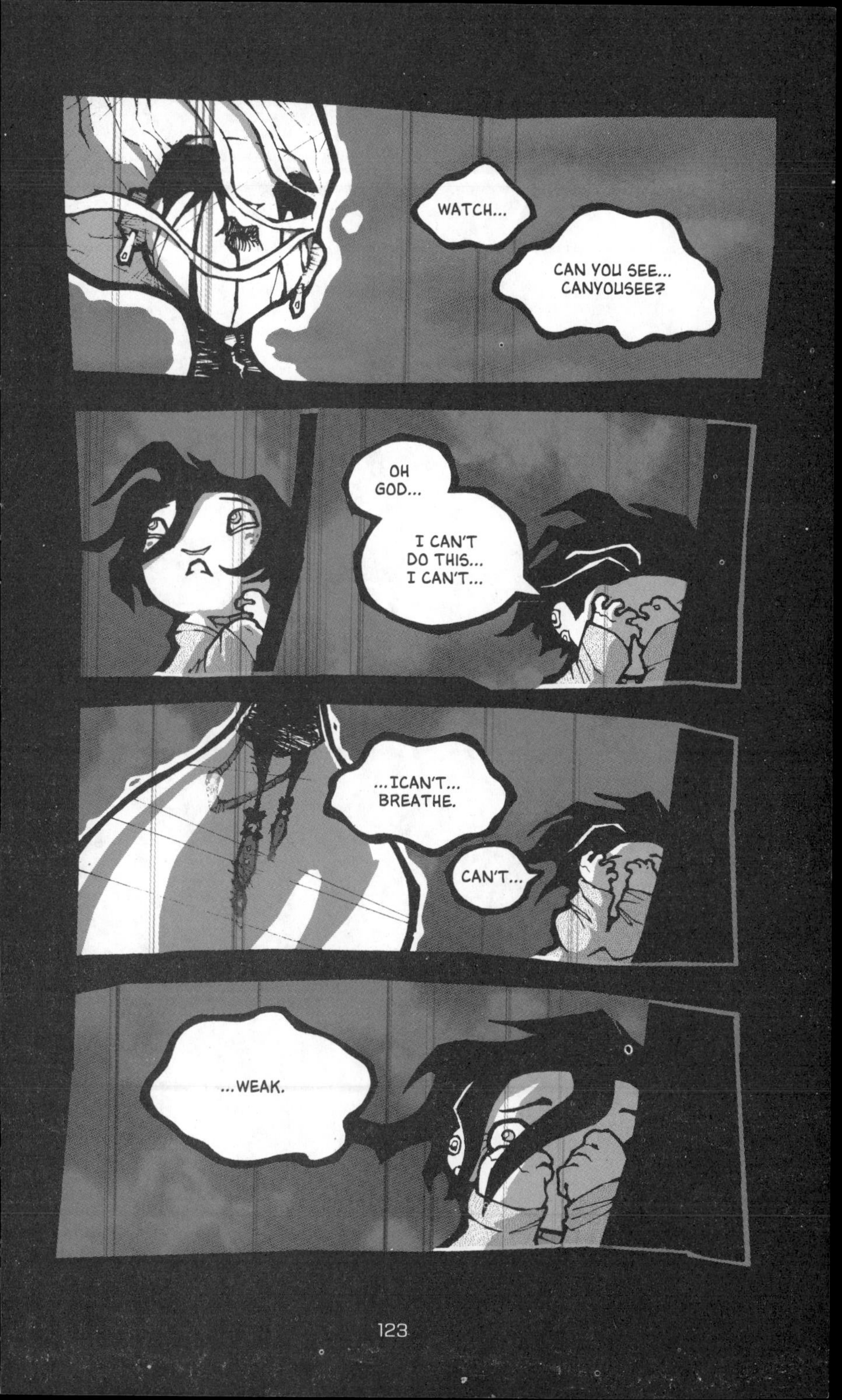
WATCH...
CAN YOU SEE... CANYOUSEE?
OH GOD...
I CAN'T DO THIS... I CAN'T...
...ICAN'T... BREATHE.
CAN'T...
...WEAK.

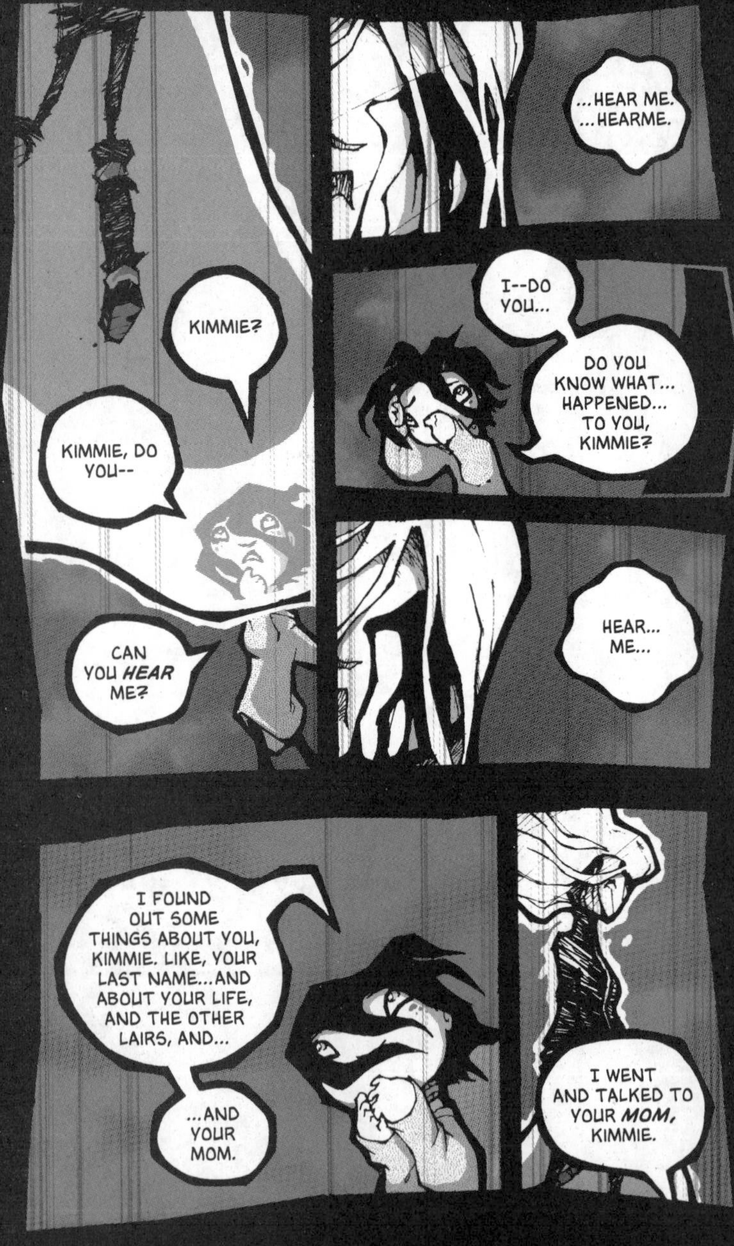
KIMMIE?
KIMMIE, DO YOU--
CAN YOU HEAR ME?
...HEAR ME. ...HEARME.
I--DO YOU...
DO YOU KNOW WHAT... HAPPENED... TO YOU, KIMMIE?
HEAR... ME...
I FOUND OUT SOME THINGS ABOUT YOU, KIMMIE. LIKE, YOUR LAST NAME...AND ABOUT YOUR LIFE, AND THE OTHER LAIRS, AND...
...AND YOUR MOM.
I WENT AND TALKED TO YOUR MOM, KIMMIE.

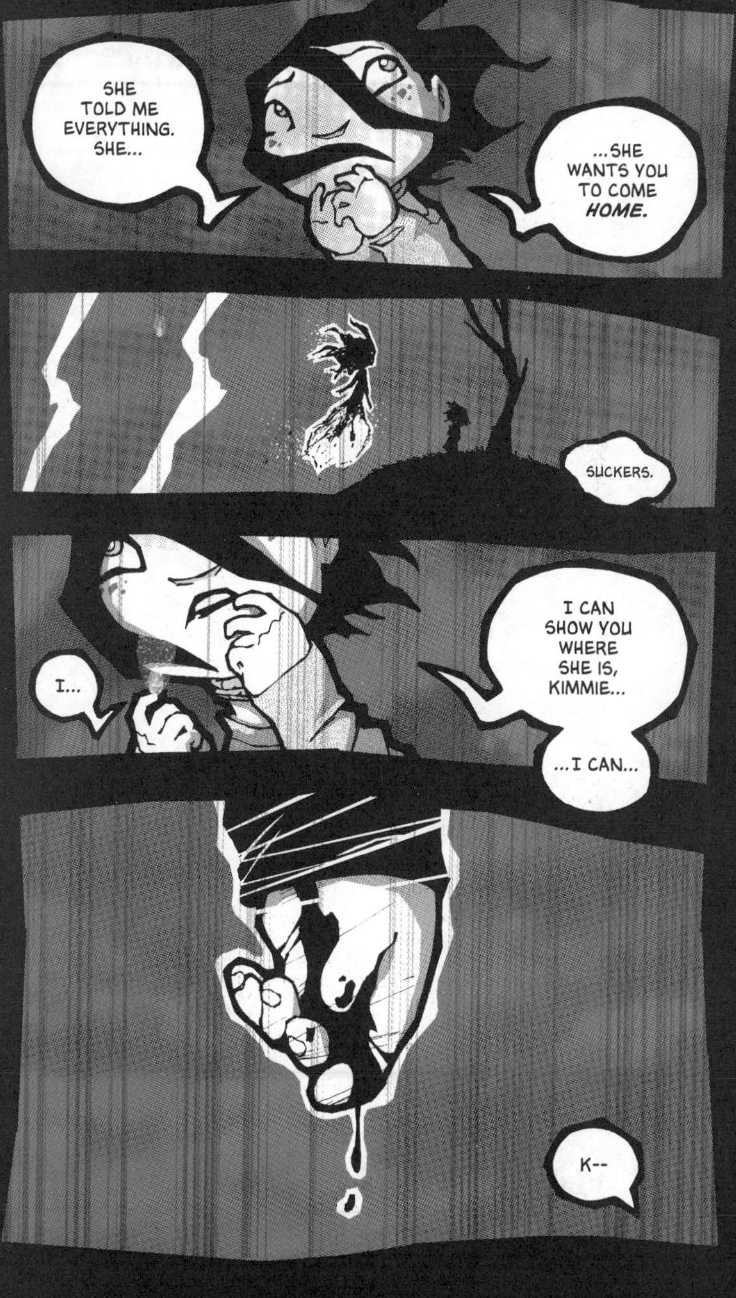
SHE TOLD ME EVERYTHING. SHE...
...SHE WANTS YOU TO COME *HOME.*
SUCKERS.
I...
I CAN SHOW YOU WHERE SHE IS, KIMMIE...
...I CAN...
K--

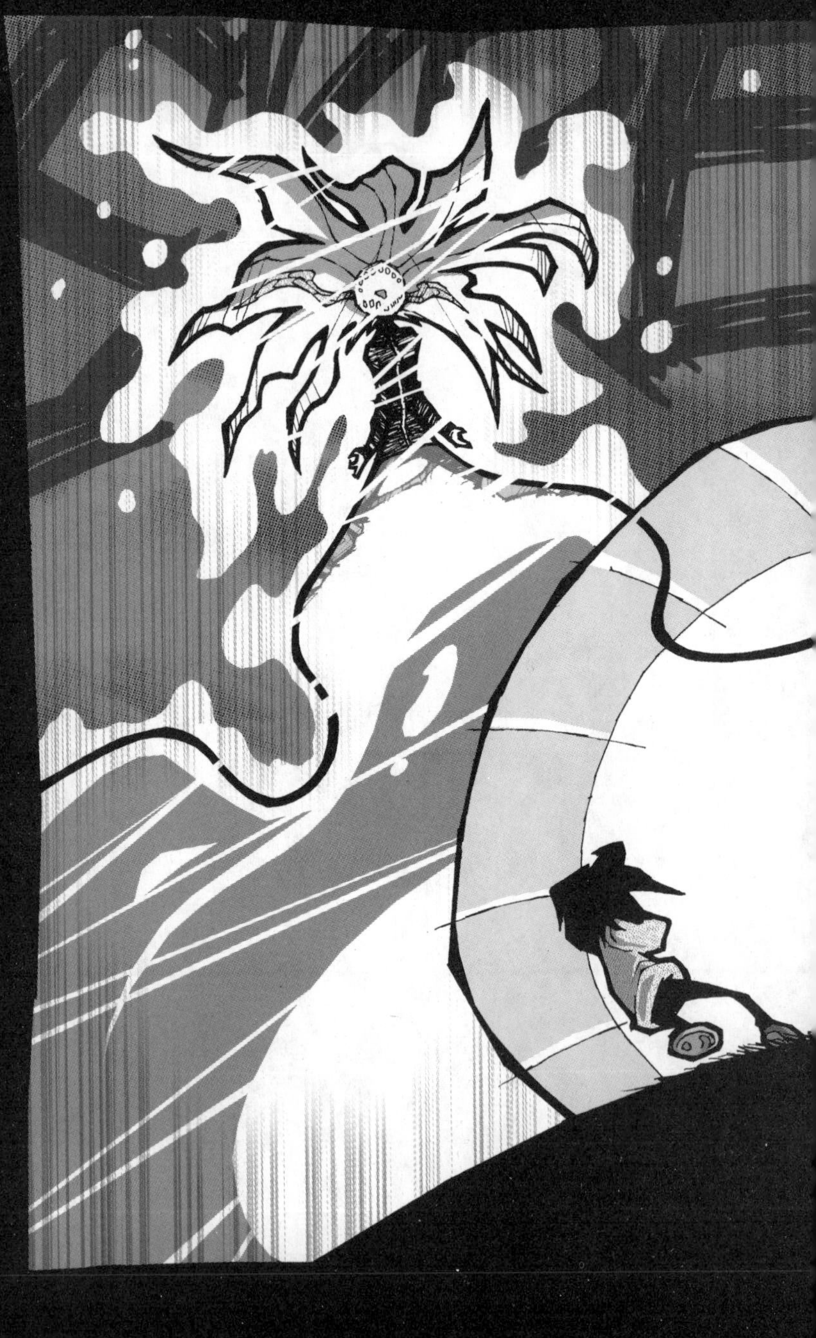

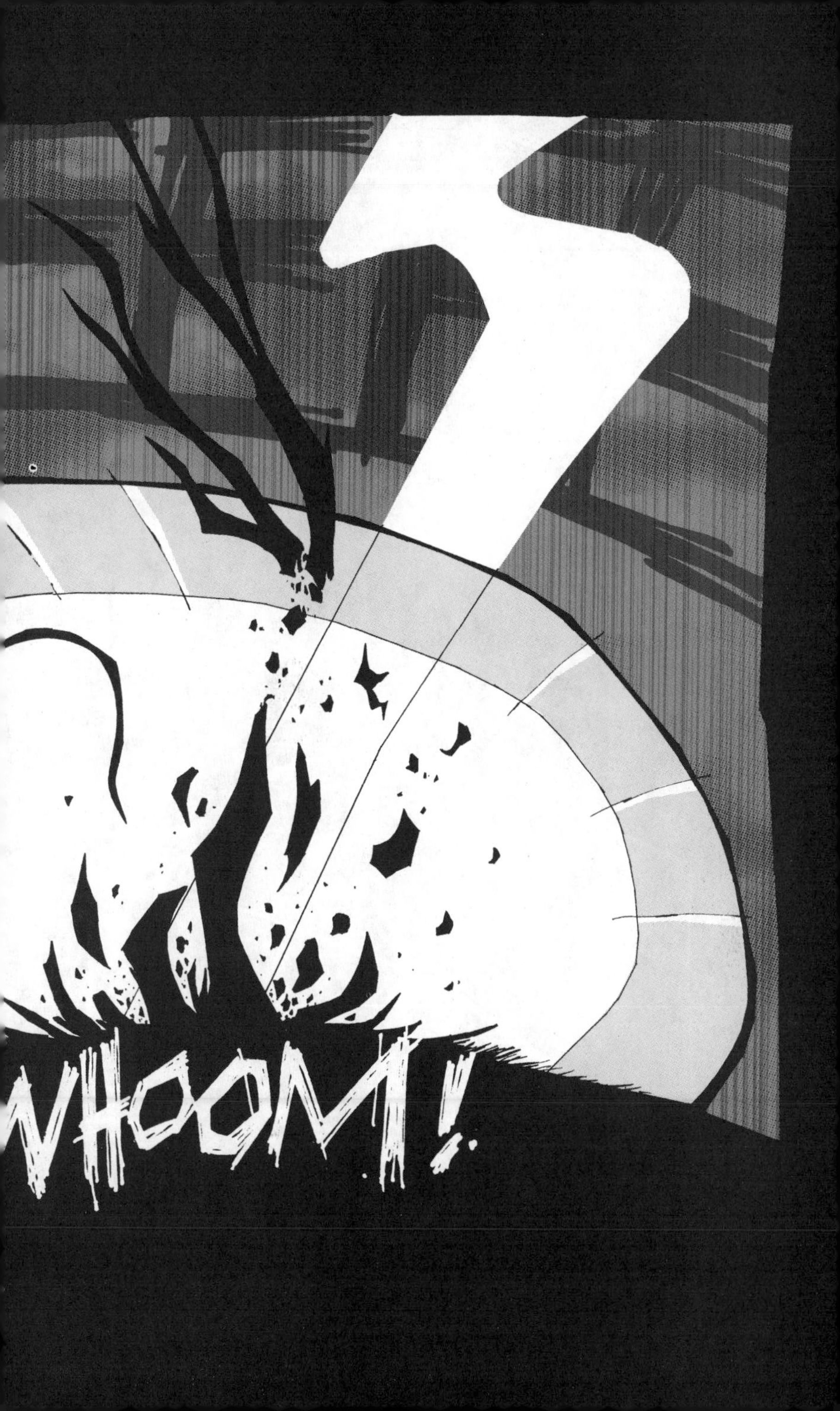
WHOOM!

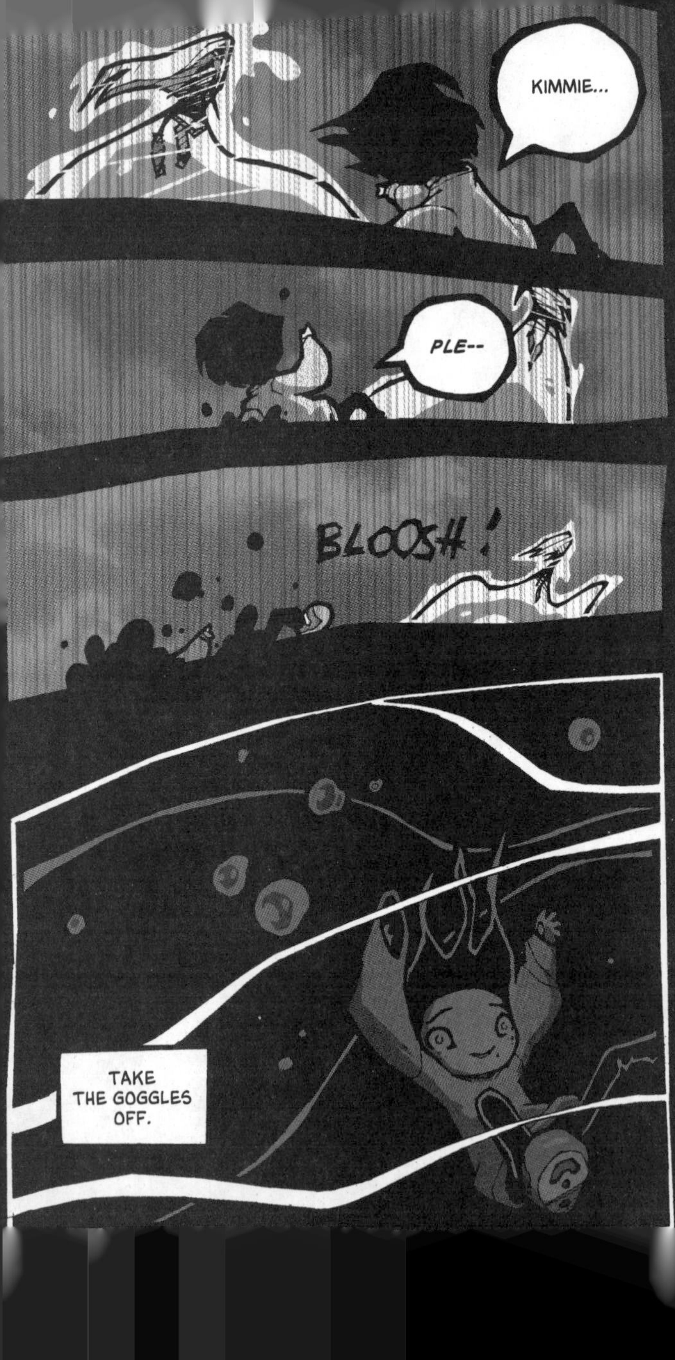
KIMMIE...
PLE--
BLOOSH!
TAKE THE GOGGLES OFF.

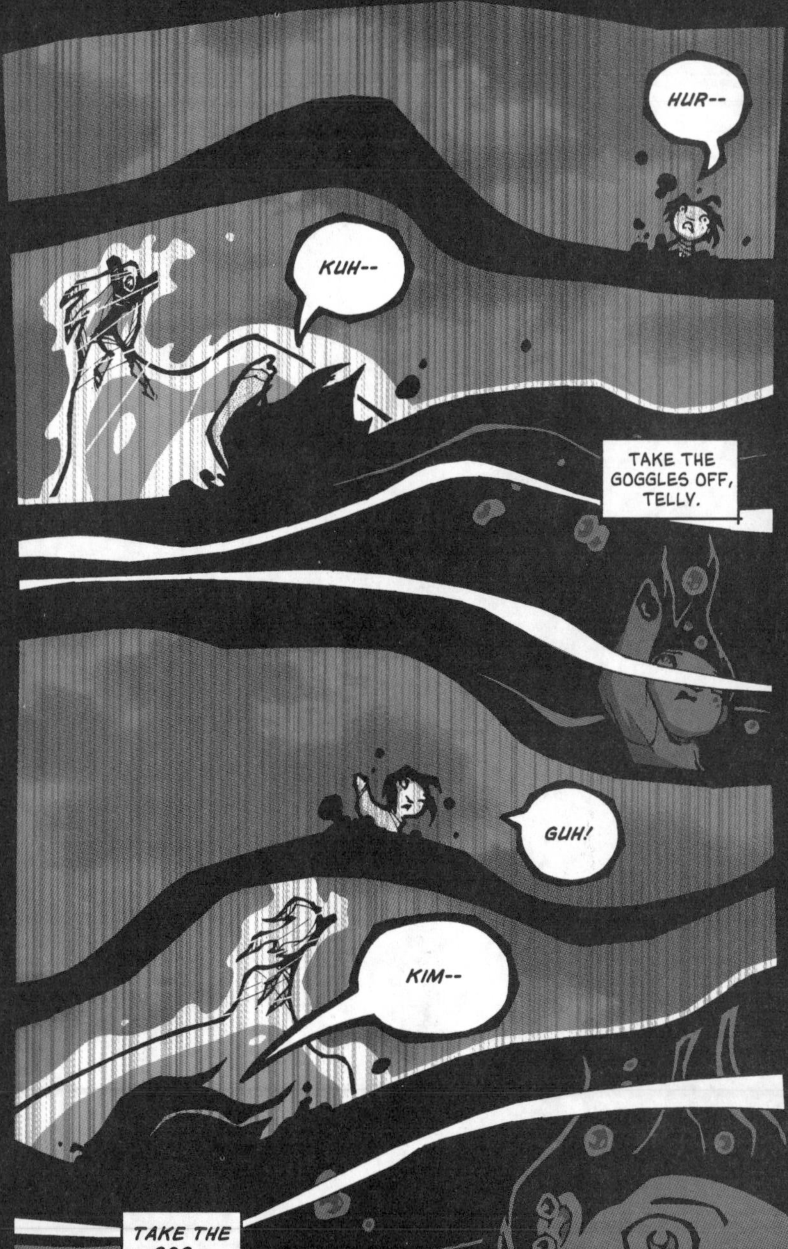
HUR--
KUH--
TAKE THE GOGGLES OFF, TELLY.
GUH!
KIM--
TAKE THE GOG--

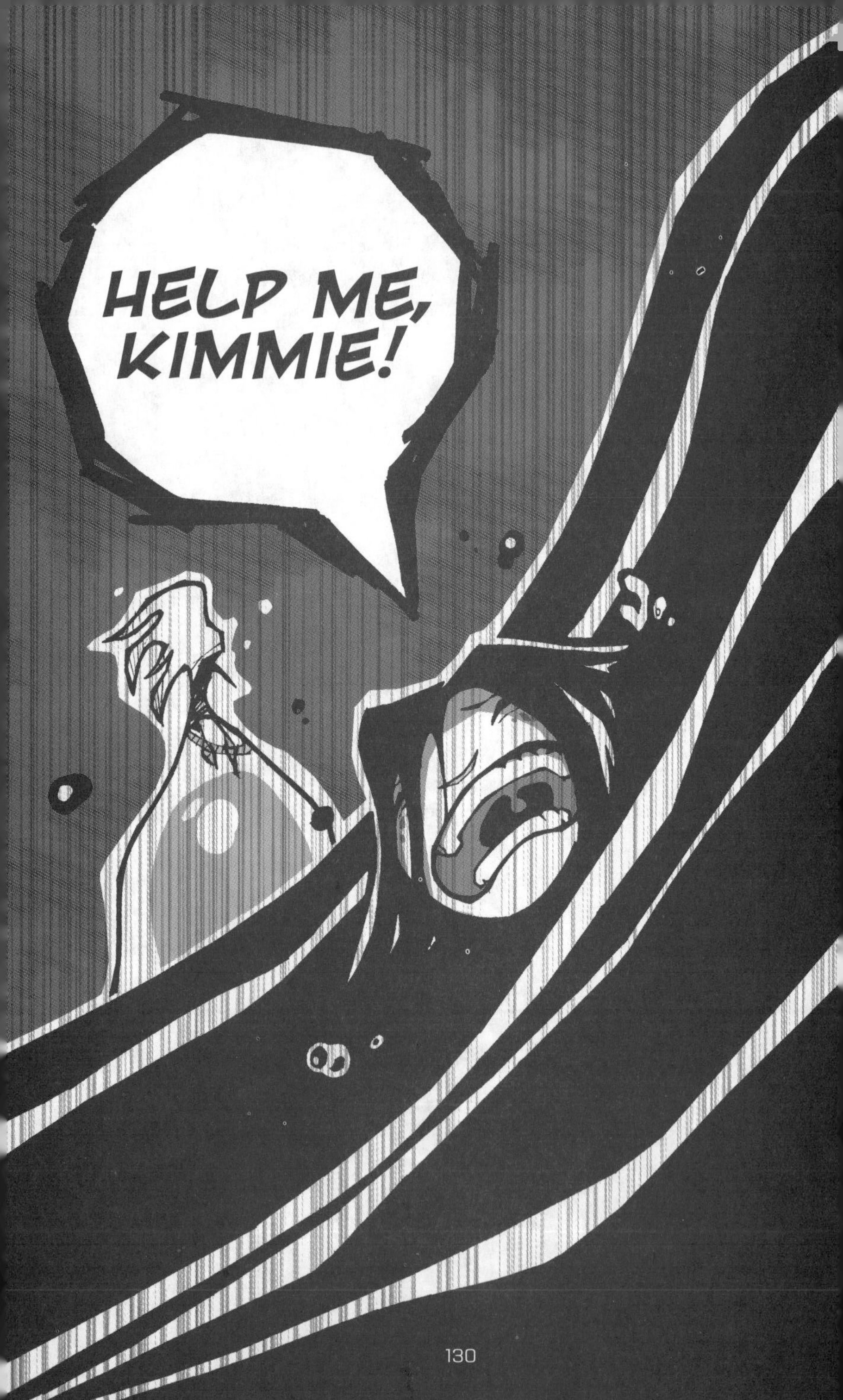
HELP ME, KIMMIE!

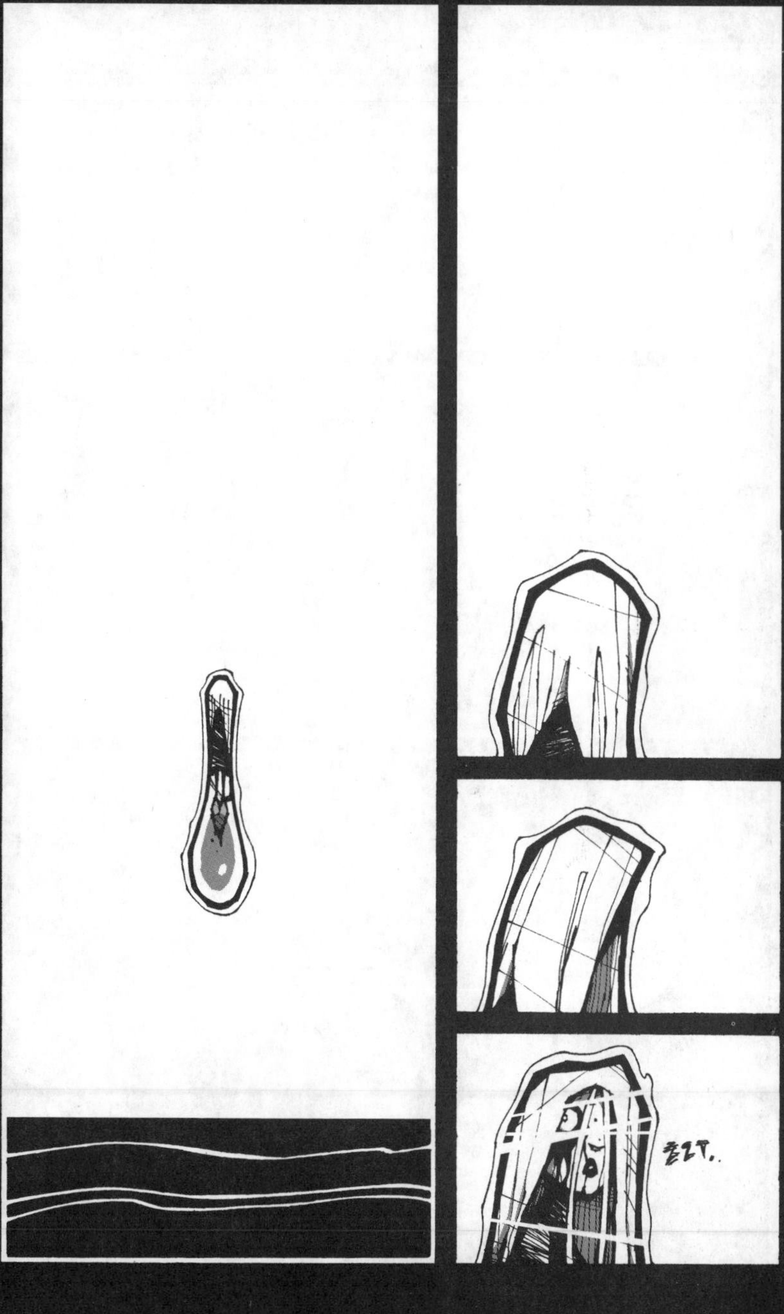
ZZT..

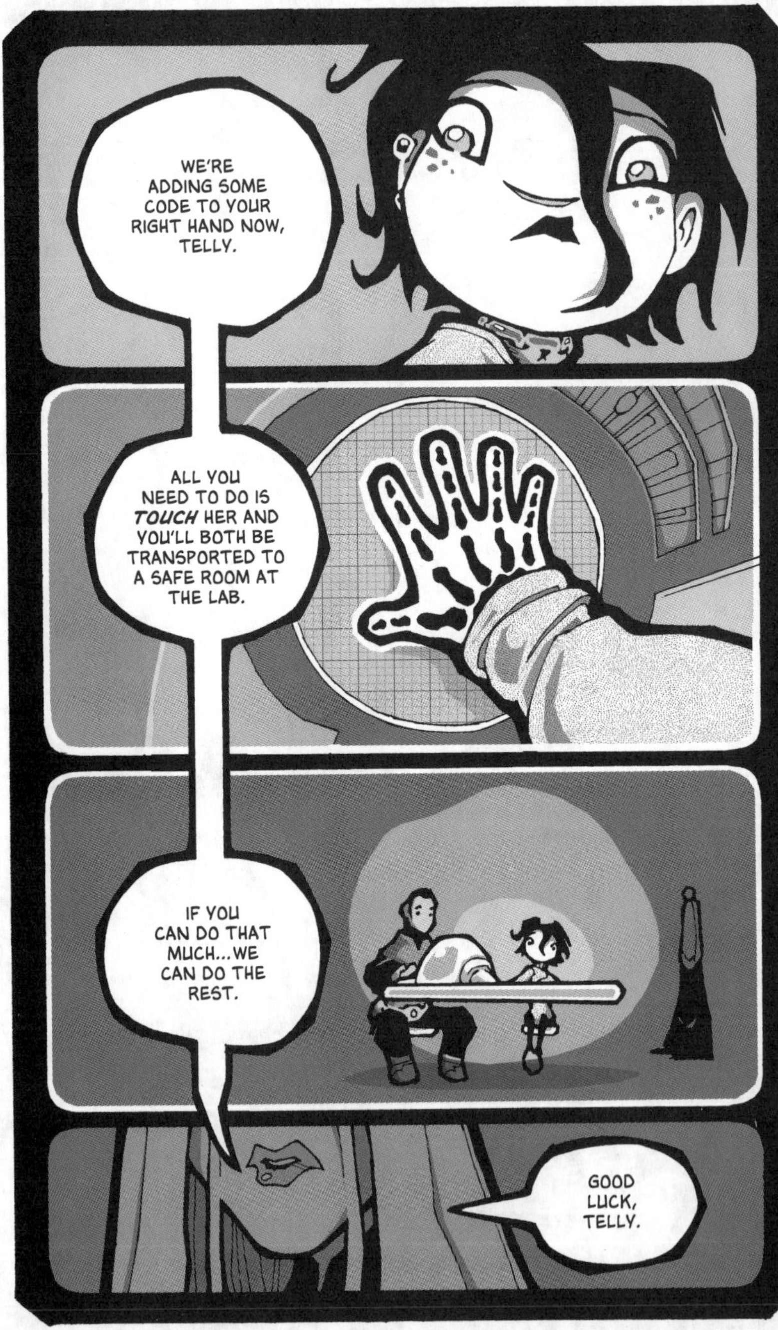
WE'RE ADDING SOME CODE TO YOUR RIGHT HAND NOW, TELLY.
ALL YOU NEED TO DO IS *TOUCH* HER AND YOU'LL BOTH BE TRANSPORTED TO A SAFE ROOM AT THE LAB.
IF YOU CAN DO THAT MUCH...WE CAN DO THE REST.
GOOD LUCK, TELLY.

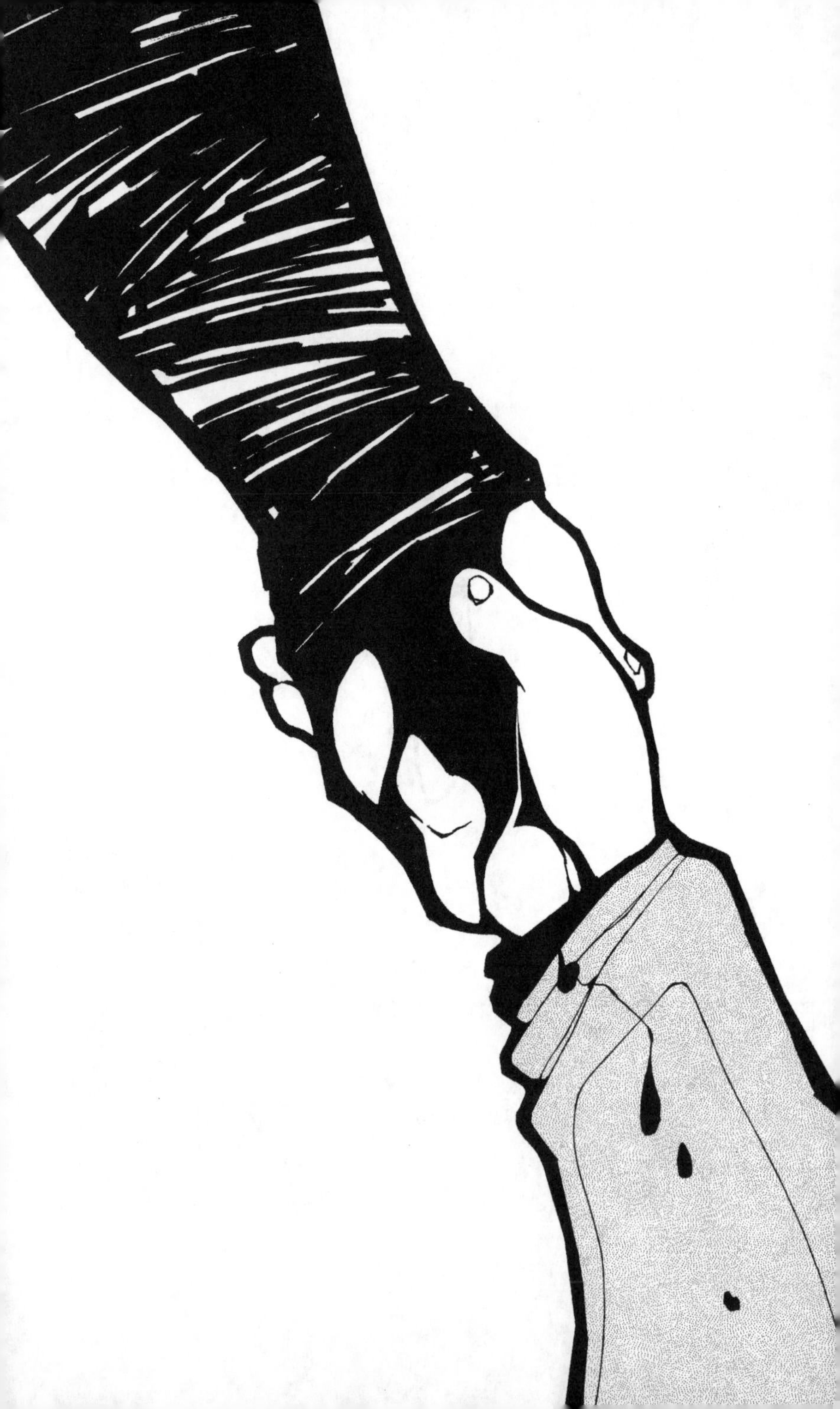

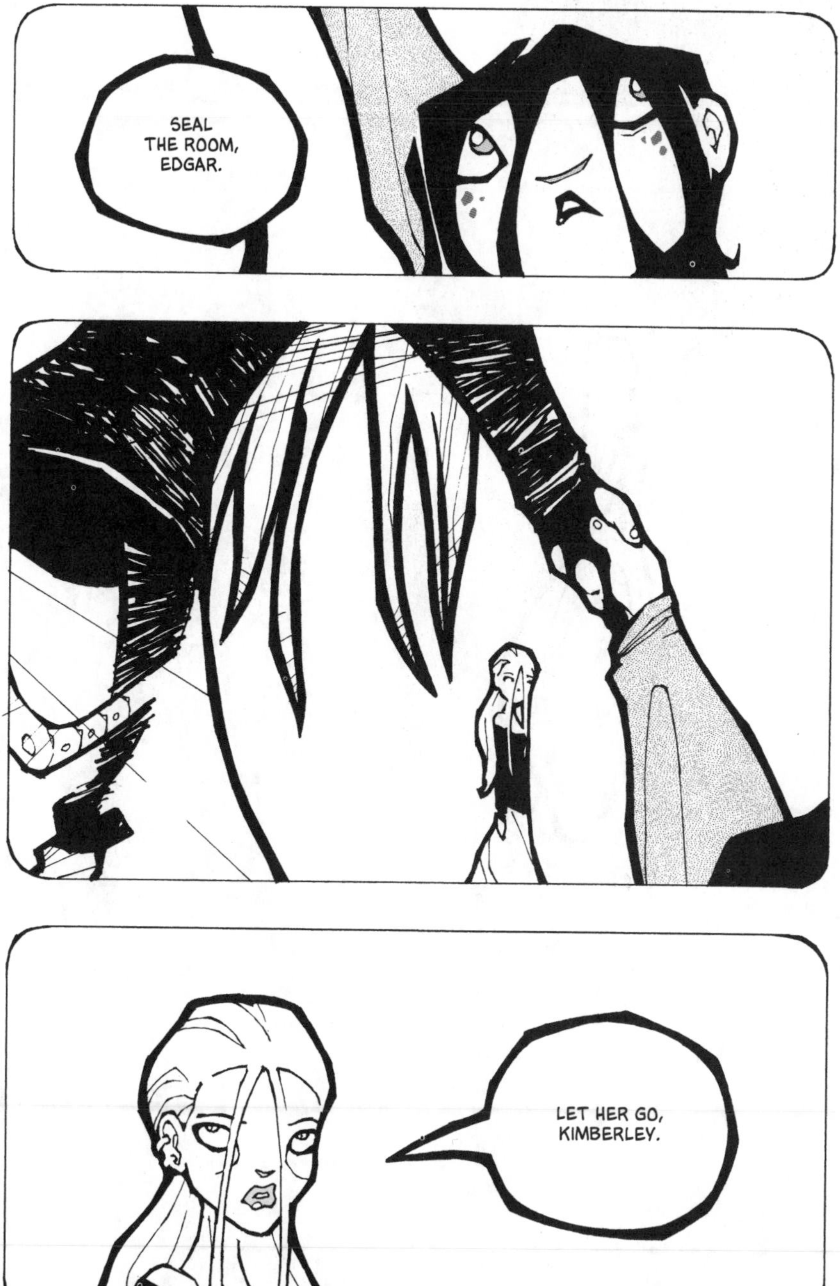
SEAL
THE ROOM,
EDGAR.
LET HER GO,
KIMBERLEY.

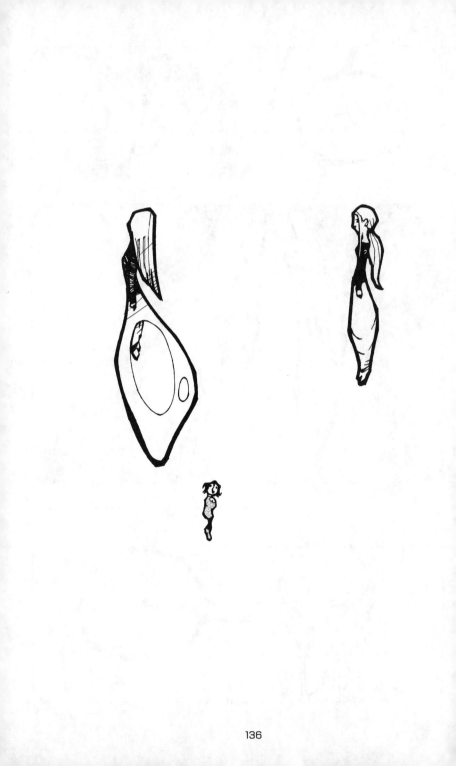

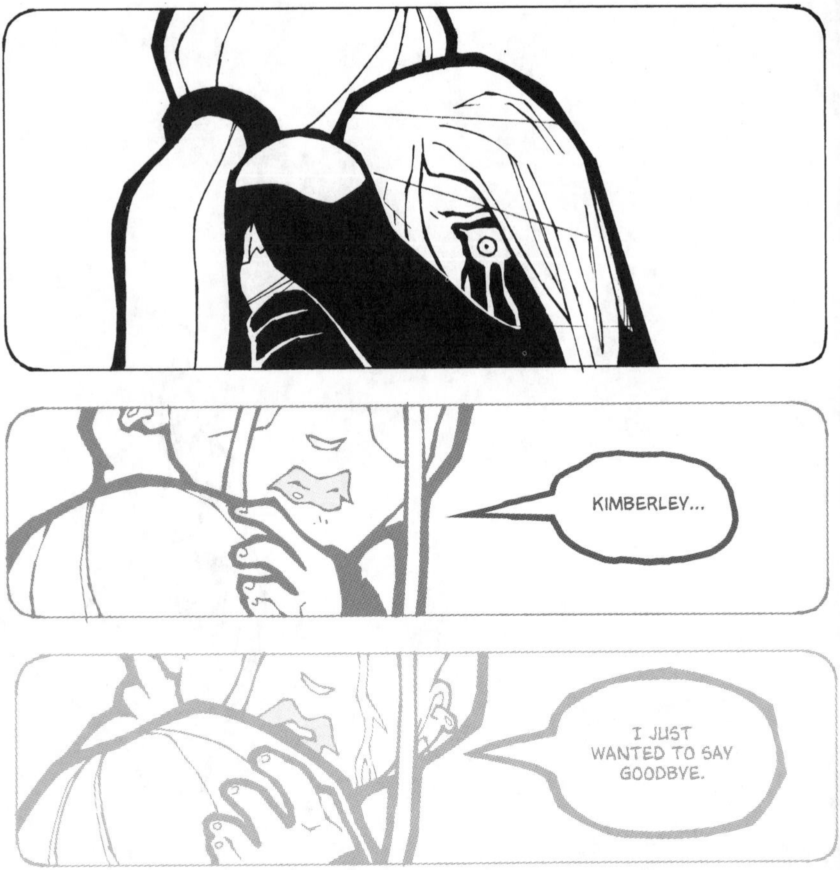
KIMBERLEY...
I JUST WANTED TO SAY GOODBYE.

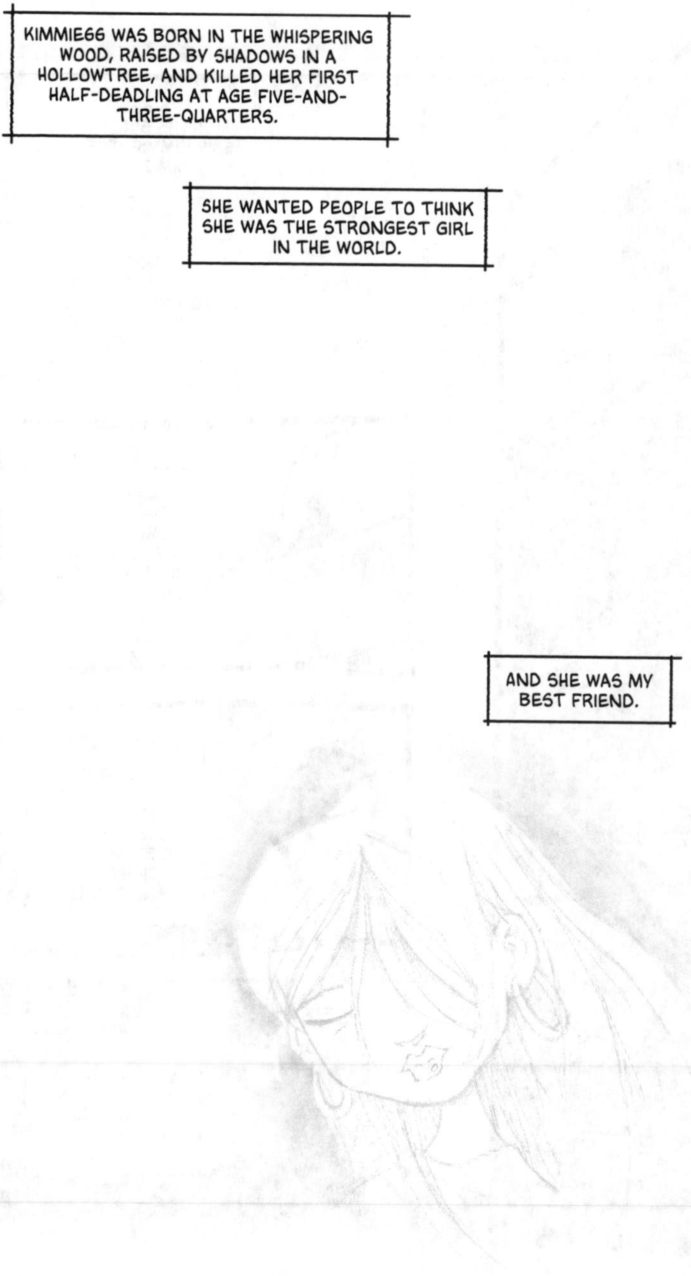
KIMMIE66 WAS BORN IN THE WHISPERING WOOD, RAISED BY SHADOWS IN A HOLLOWTREE, AND KILLED HER FIRST HALF-DEADLING AT AGE FIVE-AND-THREE-QUARTERS.
SHE WANTED PEOPLE TO THINK SHE WAS THE STRONGEST GIRL IN THE WORLD.
AND SHE WAS MY BEST FRIEND.

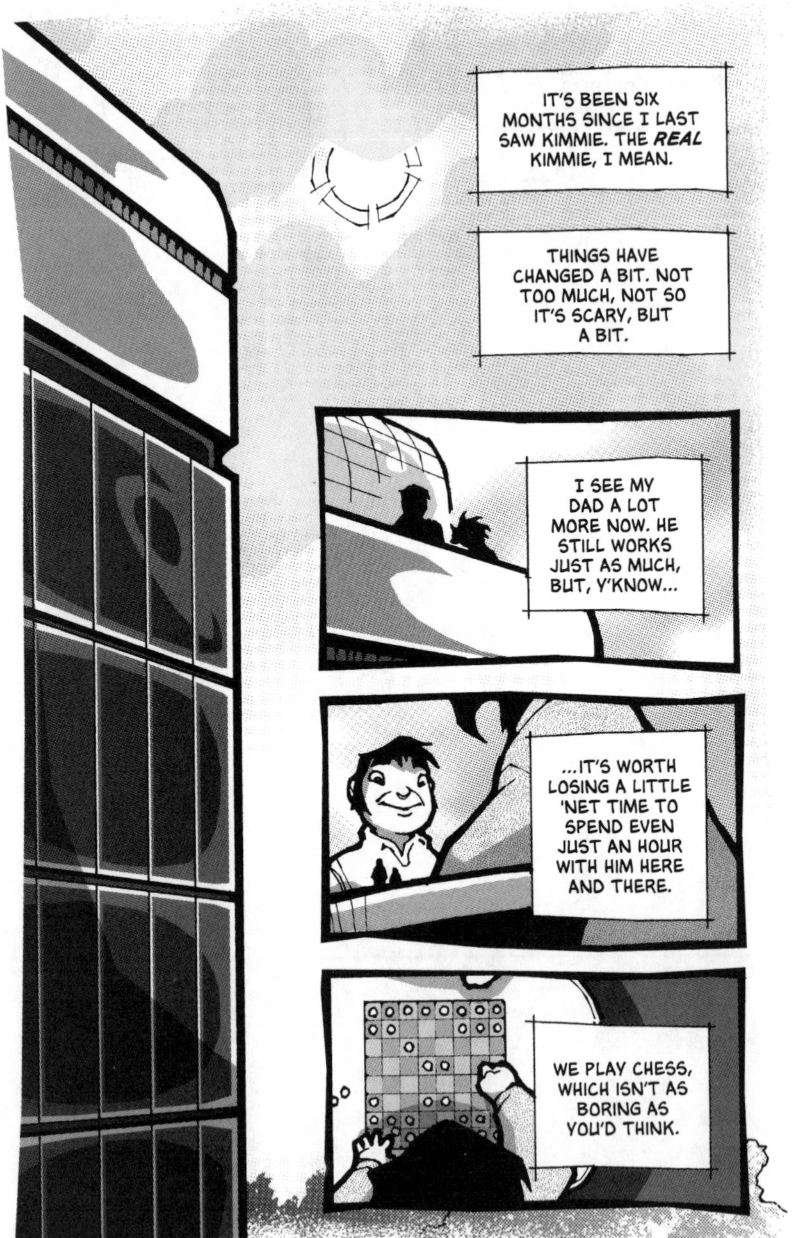
IT'S BEEN SIX MONTHS SINCE I LAST SAW KIMMIE. THE *REAL* KIMMIE, I MEAN.
THINGS HAVE CHANGED A BIT. NOT TOO MUCH, NOT SO IT'S SCARY, BUT A BIT.
I SEE MY DAD A LOT MORE NOW. HE STILL WORKS JUST AS MUCH, BUT, Y'KNOW...
...IT'S WORTH LOSING A LITTLE 'NET TIME TO SPEND EVEN JUST AN HOUR WITH HIM HERE AND THERE.
WE PLAY CHESS, WHICH ISN'T AS BORING AS YOU'D THINK.

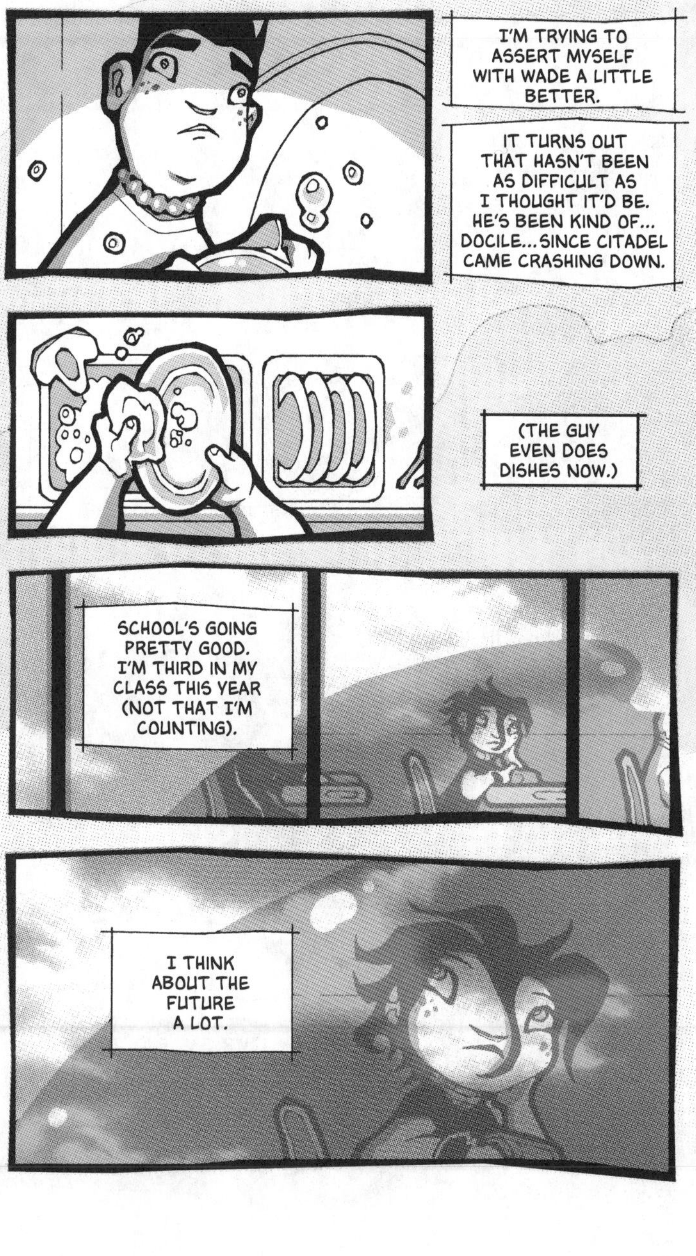
I'M TRYING TO ASSERT MYSELF WITH WADE A LITTLE BETTER.
IT TURNS OUT THAT HASN'T BEEN AS DIFFICULT AS I THOUGHT IT'D BE. HE'S BEEN KIND OF... DOCILE...SINCE CITADEL CAME CRASHING DOWN.
(THE GUY EVEN DOES DISHES NOW.)
SCHOOL'S GOING PRETTY GOOD. I'M THIRD IN MY CLASS THIS YEAR (NOT THAT I'M COUNTING).
I THINK ABOUT THE FUTURE A LOT.

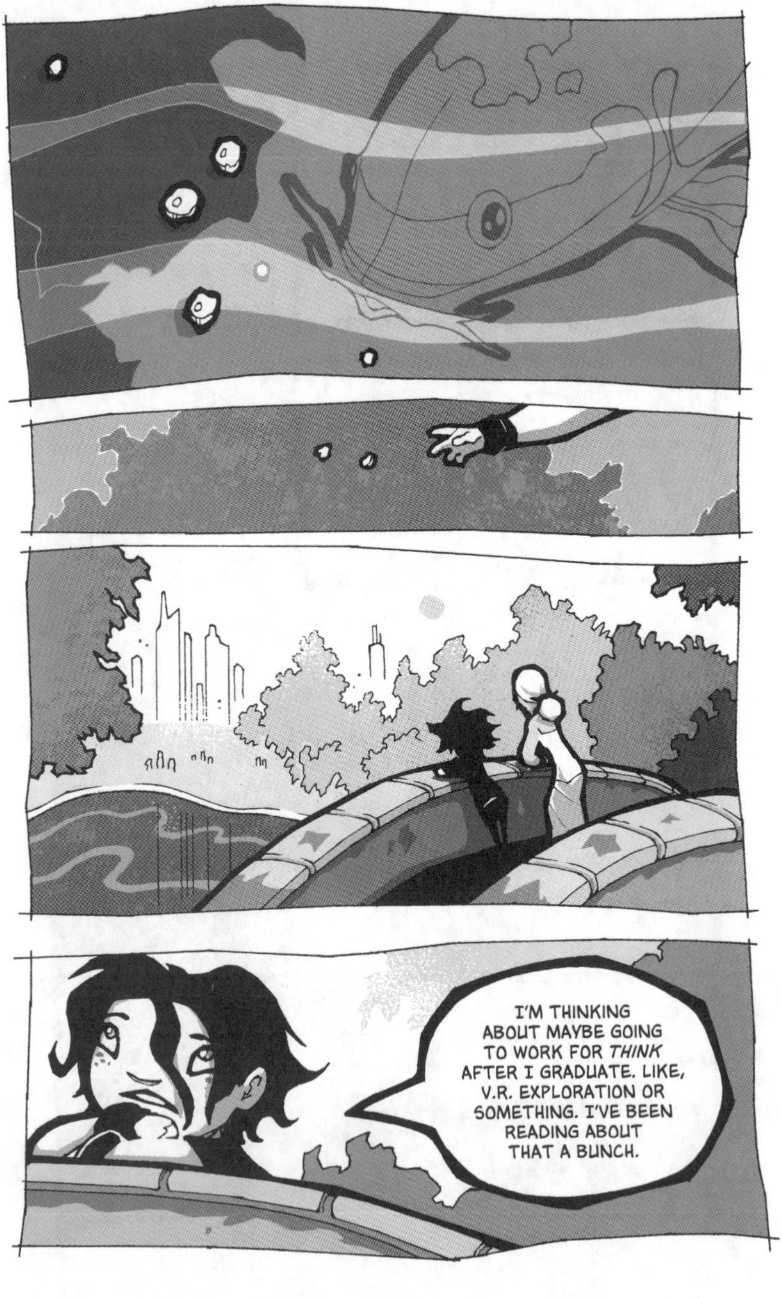
I'M THINKING ABOUT MAYBE GOING TO WORK FOR *THINK* AFTER I GRADUATE. LIKE, V.R. EXPLORATION OR SOMETHING. I'VE BEEN READING ABOUT THAT A BUNCH.

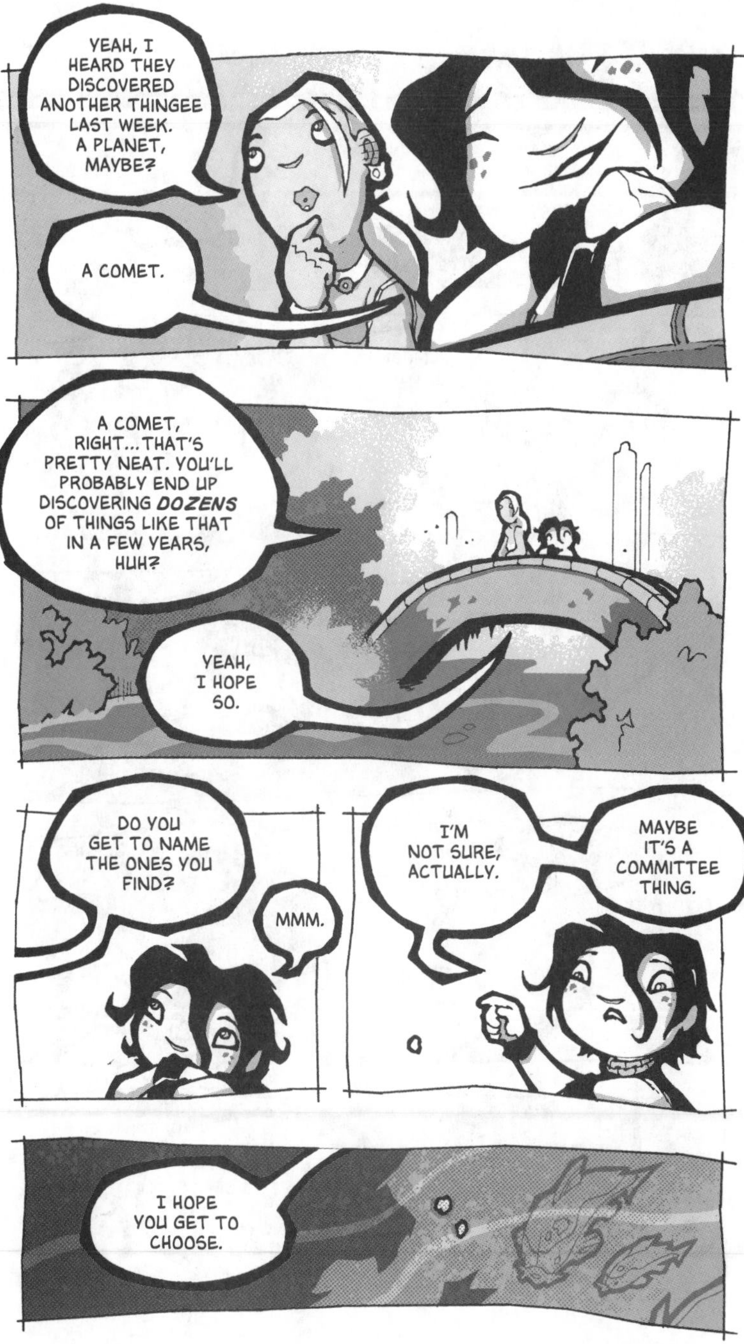
YEAH, I HEARD THEY DISCOVERED ANOTHER THINGEE LAST WEEK. A PLANET, MAYBE?
A COMET.
A COMET, RIGHT... THAT'S PRETTY NEAT. YOU'LL PROBABLY END UP DISCOVERING ***DOZENS*** OF THINGS LIKE THAT IN A FEW YEARS, HUH?
YEAH, I HOPE SO.
DO YOU GET TO NAME THE ONES YOU FIND?
MMM.
I'M NOT SURE, ACTUALLY.
MAYBE IT'S A COMMITTEE THING.
I HOPE YOU GET TO CHOOSE.

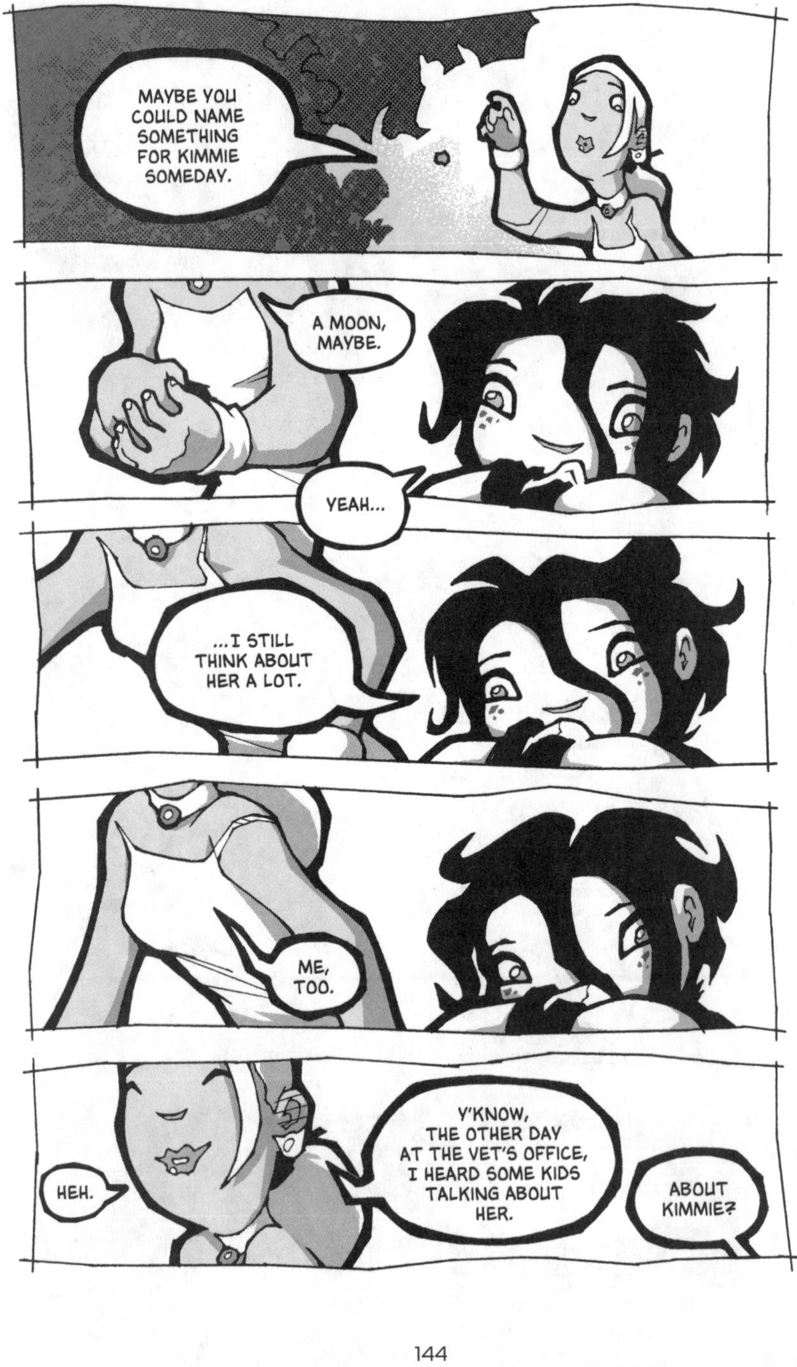
MAYBE YOU COULD NAME SOMETHING FOR KIMMIE SOMEDAY.
A MOON, MAYBE.
YEAH...
...I STILL THINK ABOUT HER A LOT.
ME, TOO.
HEH.
Y'KNOW, THE OTHER DAY AT THE VET'S OFFICE, I HEARD SOME KIDS TALKING ABOUT HER.
ABOUT KIMMIE?

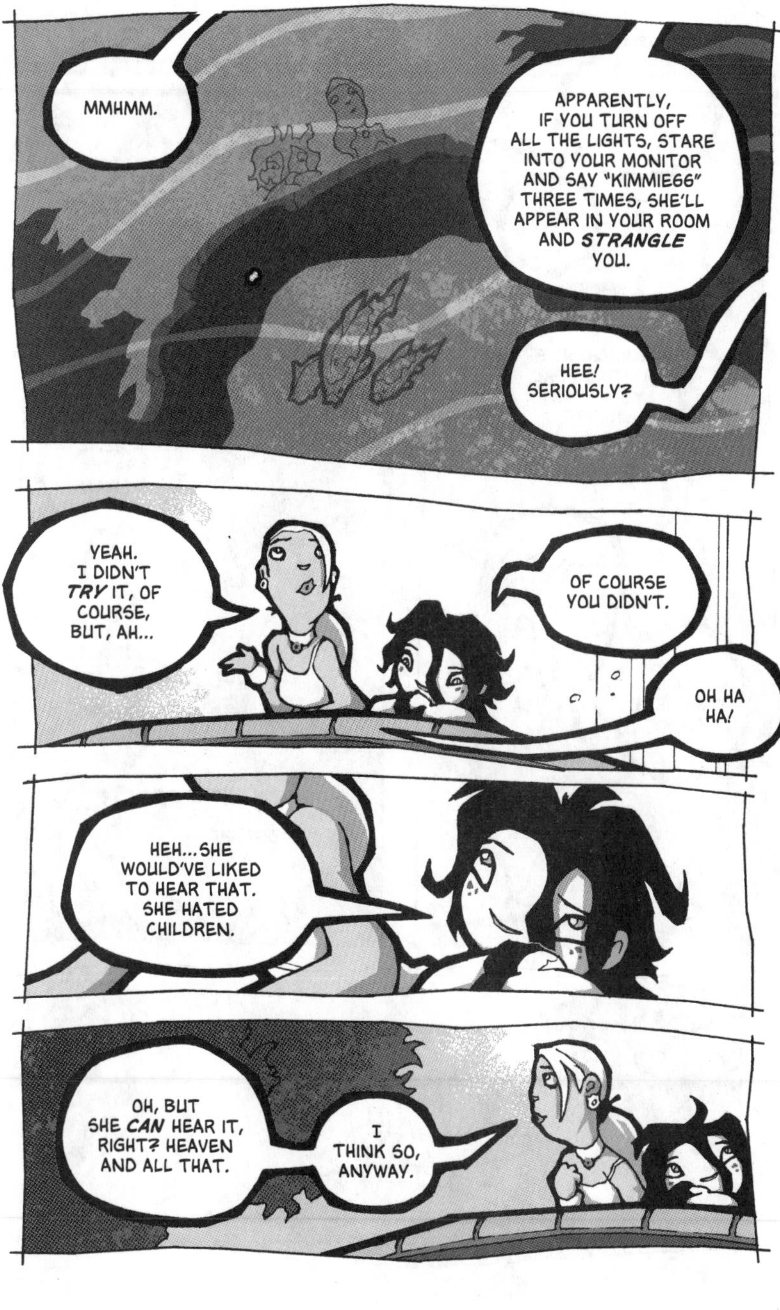
MMHMM.
APPARENTLY, IF YOU TURN OFF ALL THE LIGHTS, STARE INTO YOUR MONITOR AND SAY "KIMMIE66" THREE TIMES, SHE'LL APPEAR IN YOUR ROOM AND STRANGLE YOU.
HEE! SERIOUSLY?
YEAH. I DIDN'T TRY IT, OF COURSE, BUT, AH...
OF COURSE YOU DIDN'T.
OH HA HA!
HEH...SHE WOULD'VE LIKED TO HEAR THAT. SHE HATED CHILDREN.
OH, BUT SHE CAN HEAR IT, RIGHT? HEAVEN AND ALL THAT.
I THINK SO, ANYWAY.

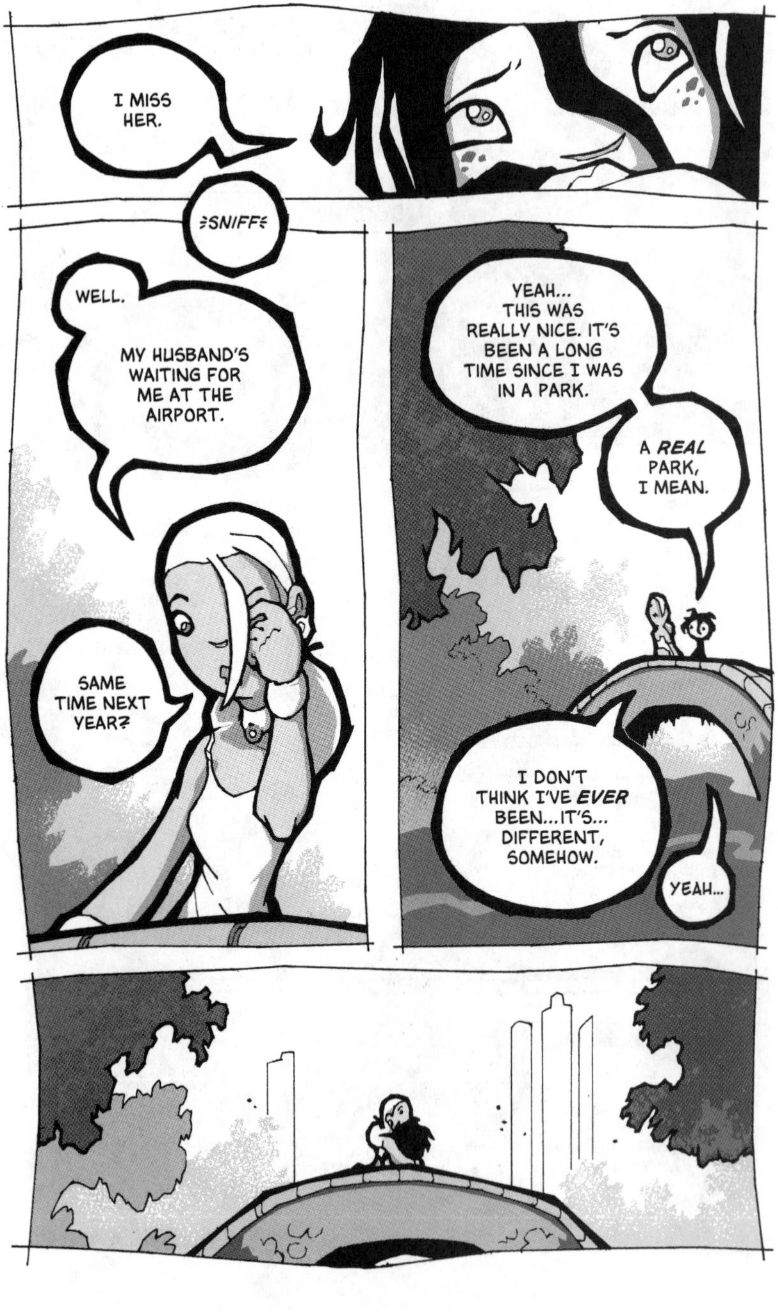

I MISS HER.
SNIFF
WELL.
MY HUSBAND'S WAITING FOR ME AT THE AIRPORT.
SAME TIME NEXT YEAR?
YEAH... THIS WAS REALLY NICE. IT'S BEEN A LONG TIME SINCE I WAS IN A PARK.
A *REAL* PARK, I MEAN.
I DON'T THINK I'VE *EVER* BEEN...IT'S... DIFFERENT, SOMEHOW.
YEAH...

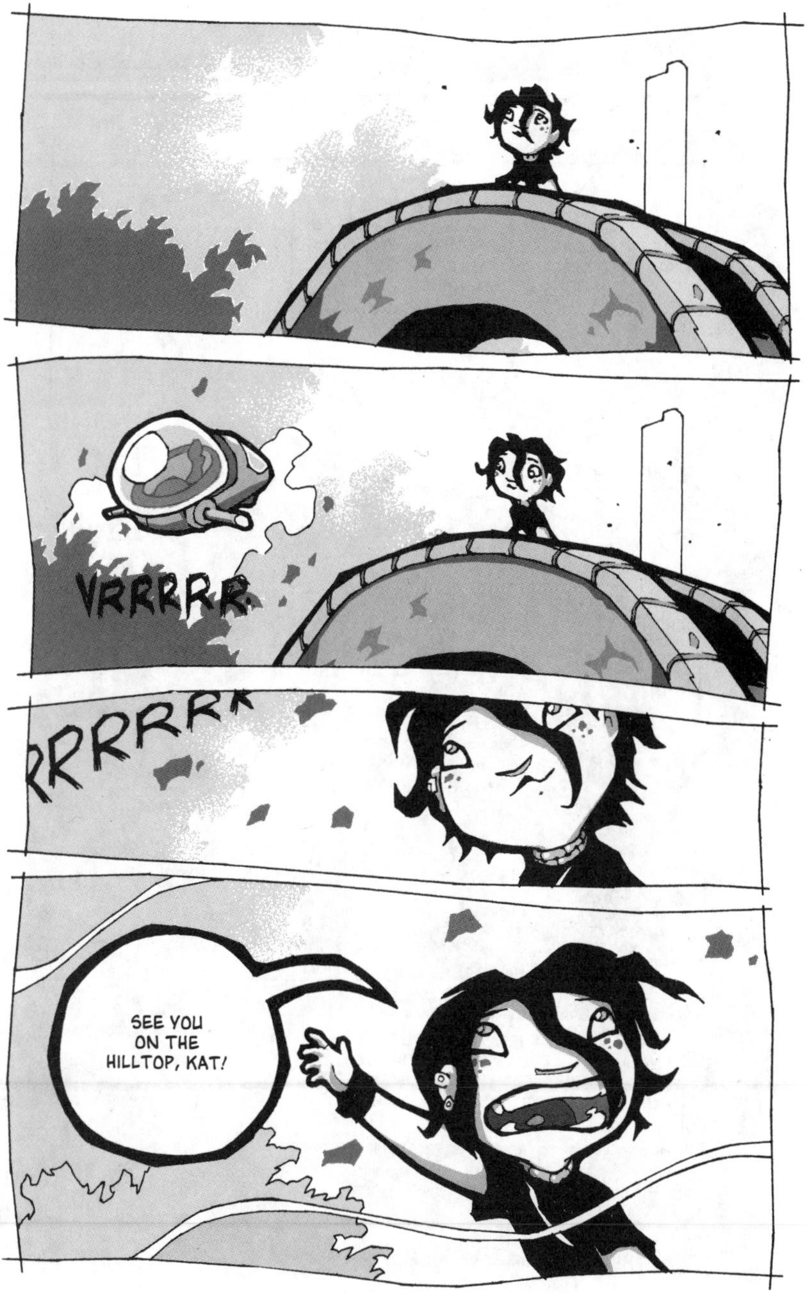
VRRRRRR
RRRRRRR
SEE YOU ON THE HILLTOP, KAT!

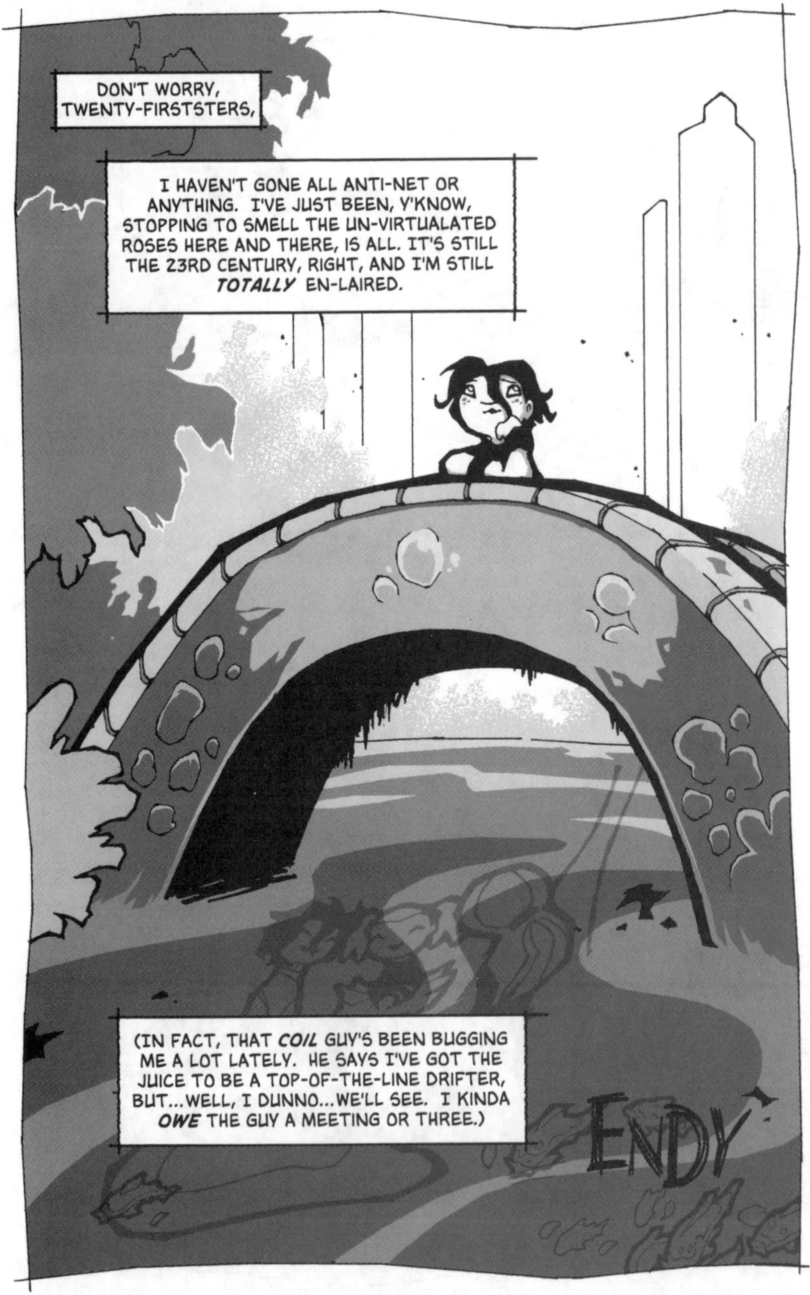
DON'T WORRY, TWENTY-FIRSTSTERS,
I HAVEN'T GONE ALL ANTI-NET OR ANYTHING. I'VE JUST BEEN, Y'KNOW, STOPPING TO SMELL THE UN-VIRTUALATED ROSES HERE AND THERE, IS ALL. IT'S STILL THE 23RD CENTURY, RIGHT, AND I'M STILL *TOTALLY* EN-LAIRED.
(IN FACT, THAT *COIL* GUY'S BEEN BUGGING ME A LOT LATELY. HE SAYS I'VE GOT THE JUICE TO BE A TOP-OF-THE-LINE DRIFTER, BUT...WELL, I DUNNO...WE'LL SEE. I KINDA *OWE* THE GUY A MEETING OR THREE.)
ENDY

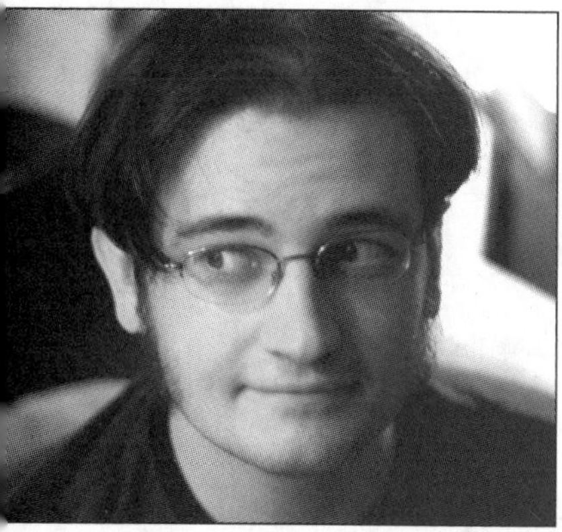

AARON ALEXOVICH

Aaron Alexovich was born in Chicago, Illinois, the year Elvis died, but currently sleeps the daylight hours away in Hillsboro, Oregon. After neglecting to graduate from the world-famous California Institute of the Arts, Mr. A. took up space in the animation industry for a little while, contributing character designs to Nickelodeon's *Invader Zim* and *Avatar: The Last Airbender*. He likes making comics way better, though. Aaron's first published work was the critically lauded "spookycute" witch tale *Serenity Rose* for Slave Labor Graphics. His website, which includes a dancing goblin, is at www.heartshapedskull.com. Bright lights make him sneeze for some reason.

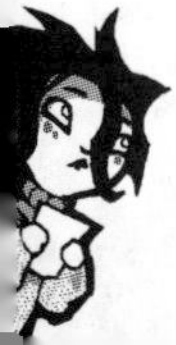

SPECIAL BACKSTAGE PASS:

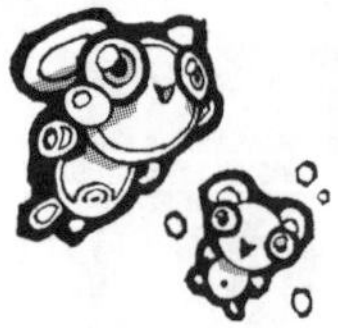

If you liked the story you've just read, fear not: Other MINX books will be available in the months to come. MINX is a line of books that's designed especially for you — someone who's a bit bored with straight fiction and ready for stories that are visually exciting beyond words — literally. In fact, we thought you might like to get in on a secret, behind-the-scenes look at a few of the new MINX titles that will aid in your escape to cool places during the long, cold winter. So hurry up and turn the page already! And be sure to check out other exclusive materal at

minxbooks.net

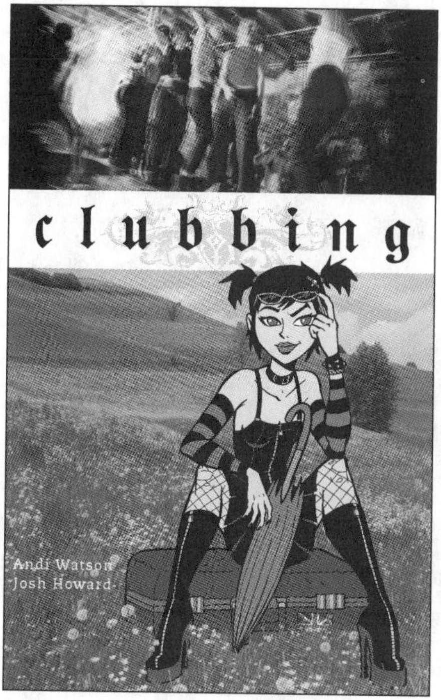
clubbing
Andi Watson
Josh Howard

A spoiled, rebellious London teenager conquers the stuffy English countryside when she solves a murder mystery on the 19th hole of her grandparents' golf course.

■ Read on.

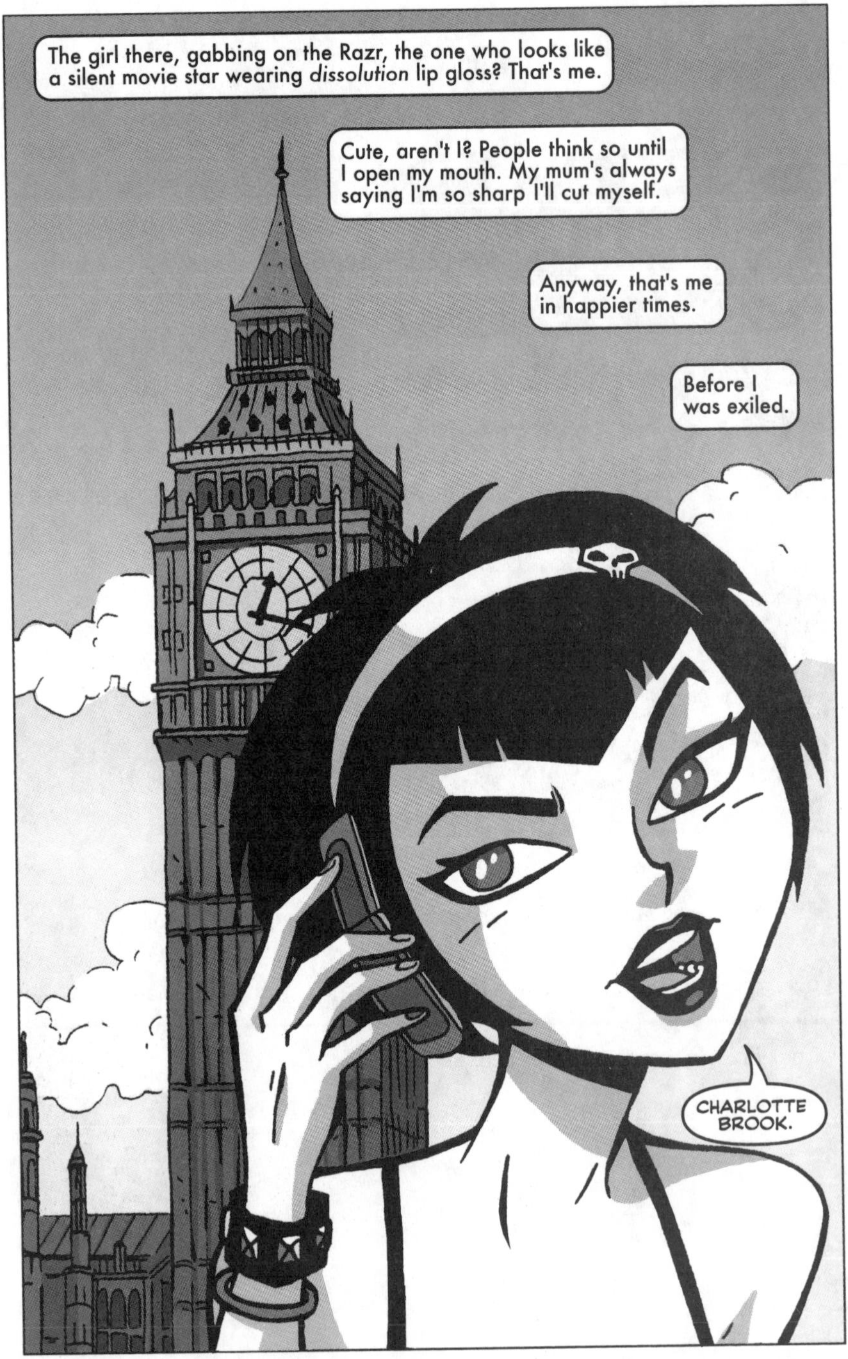
The girl there, gabbing on the Razr, the one who looks like a silent movie star wearing *dissolution* lip gloss? That's me.
Cute, aren't I? People think so until I open my mouth. My mum's always saying I'm so sharp I'll cut myself.
Anyway, that's me in happier times.
Before I was exiled.
CHARLOTTE BROOK.

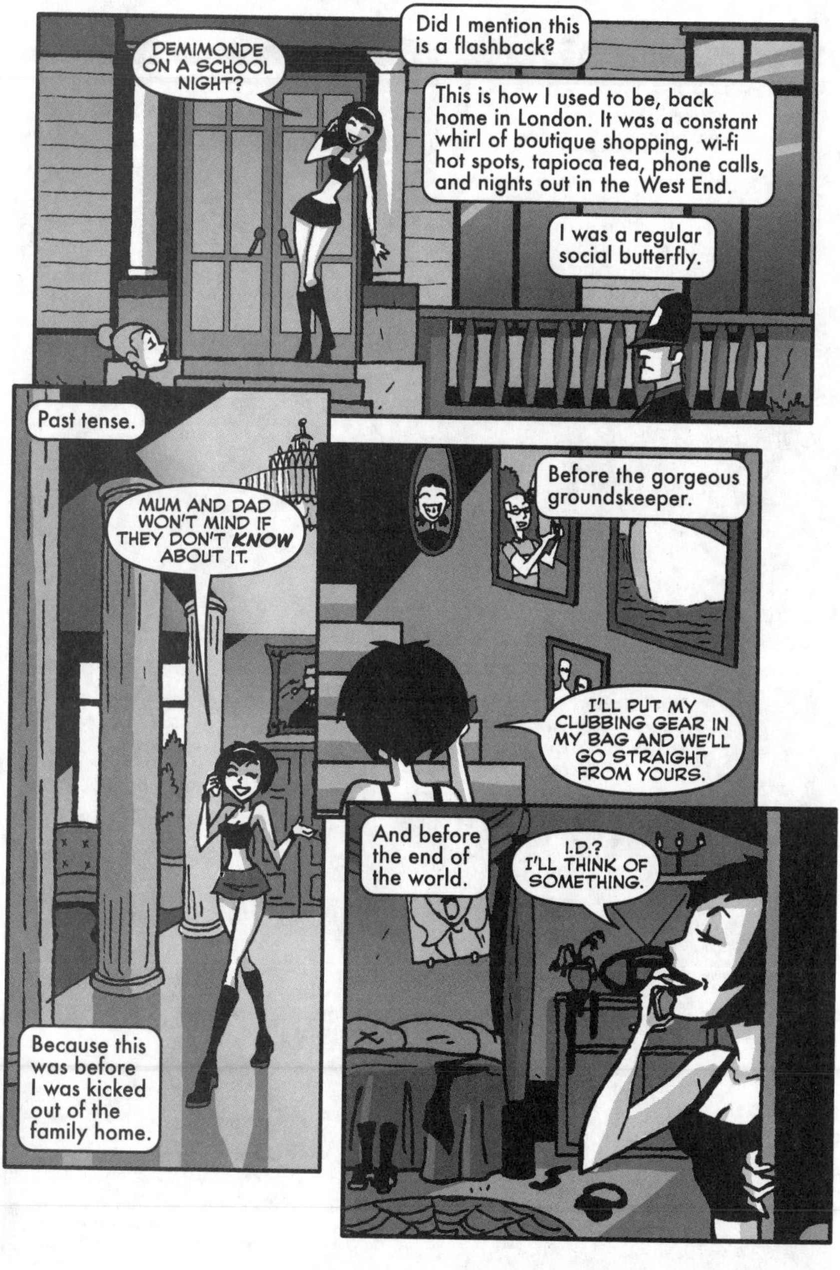
DEMIMONDE ON A SCHOOL NIGHT?
Did I mention this is a flashback?
This is how I used to be, back home in London. It was a constant whirl of boutique shopping, wi-fi hot spots, tapioca tea, phone calls, and nights out in the West End.
I was a regular social butterfly.
Past tense.
MUM AND DAD WON'T MIND IF THEY DON'T *KNOW* ABOUT IT.
Because this was before I was kicked out of the family home.
Before the gorgeous groundskeeper.
I'LL PUT MY CLUBBING GEAR IN MY BAG AND WE'LL GO STRAIGHT FROM YOURS.
And before the end of the world.
I.D.? I'LL THINK OF SOMETHING.

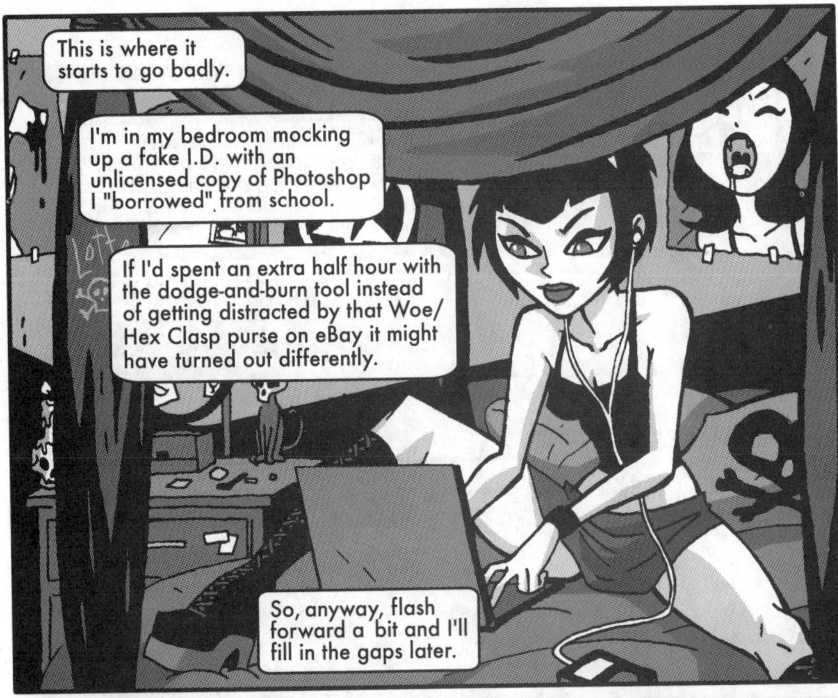
This is where it starts to go badly.
I'm in my bedroom mocking up a fake I.D. with an unlicensed copy of Photoshop I "borrowed" from school.
If I'd spent an extra half hour with the dodge-and-burn tool instead of getting distracted by that Woe/Hex Clasp purse on eBay it might have turned out differently.
So, anyway, flash forward a bit and I'll fill in the gaps later.

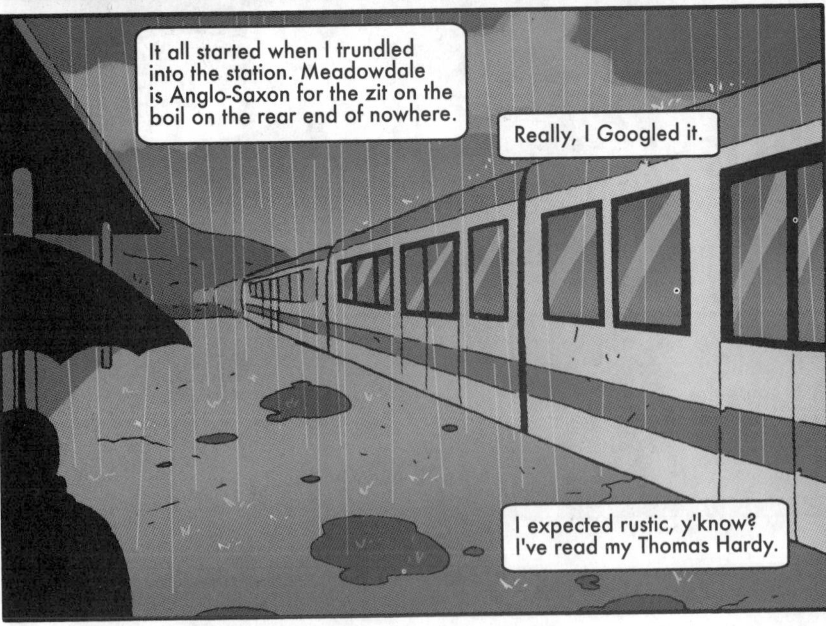
It all started when I trundled into the station. Meadowdale is Anglo-Saxon for the zit on the boil on the rear end of nowhere.
Really, I Googled it.
I expected rustic, y'know? I've read my Thomas Hardy.

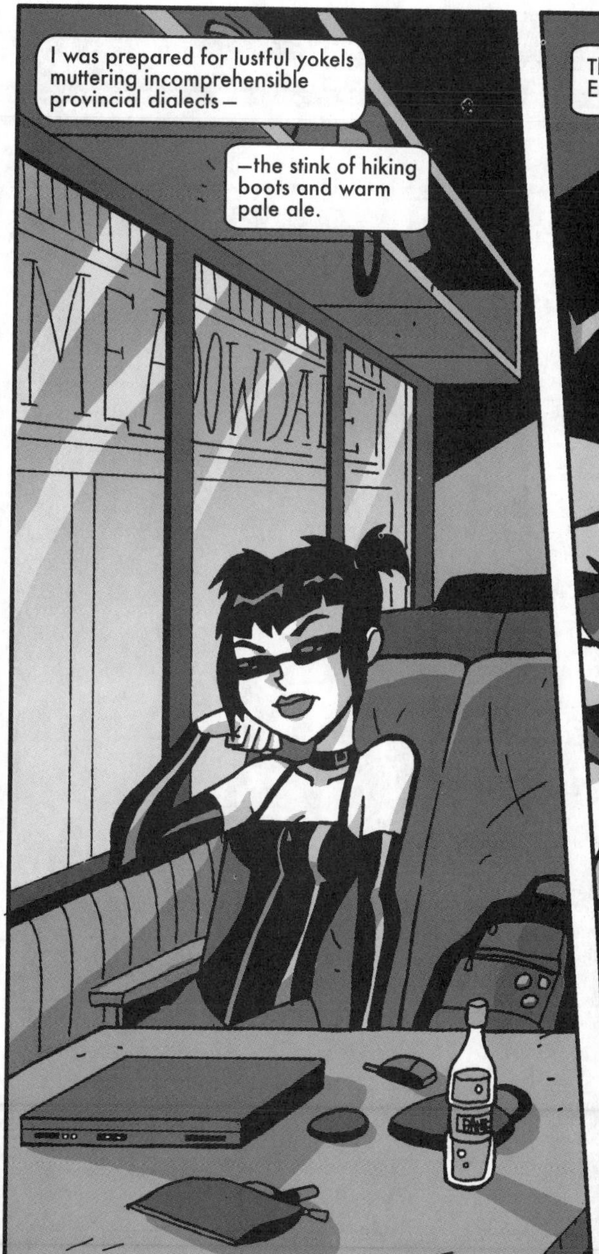
I was prepared for lustful yokels muttering incomprehensible provincial dialects—
—the stink of hiking boots and warm pale ale.
MEADOWDALE

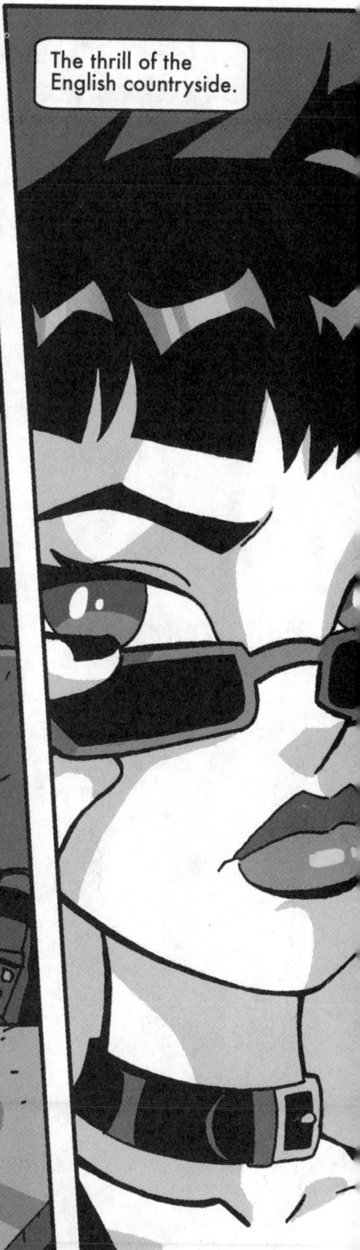
The thrill of the English countryside.

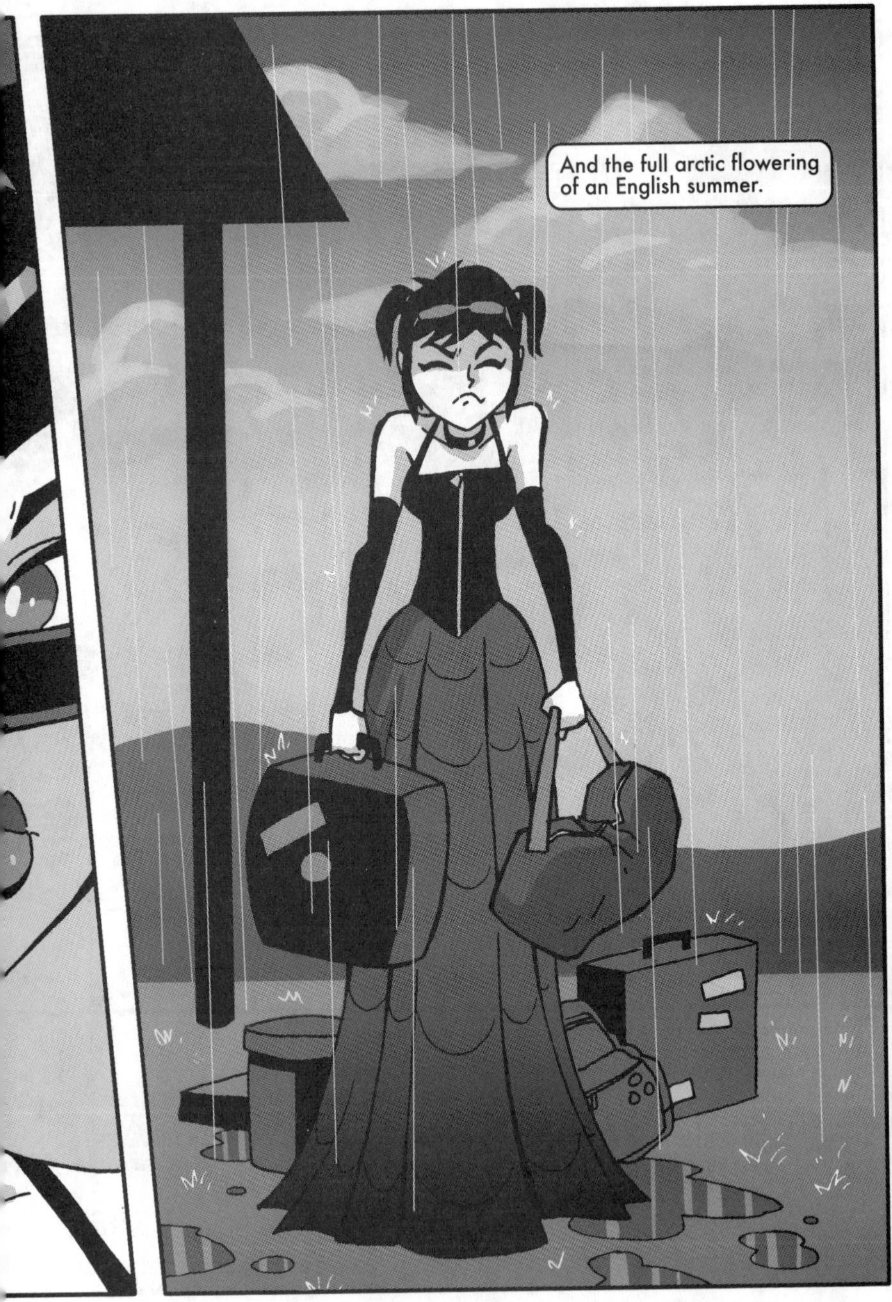
And the full arctic flowering of an English summer.

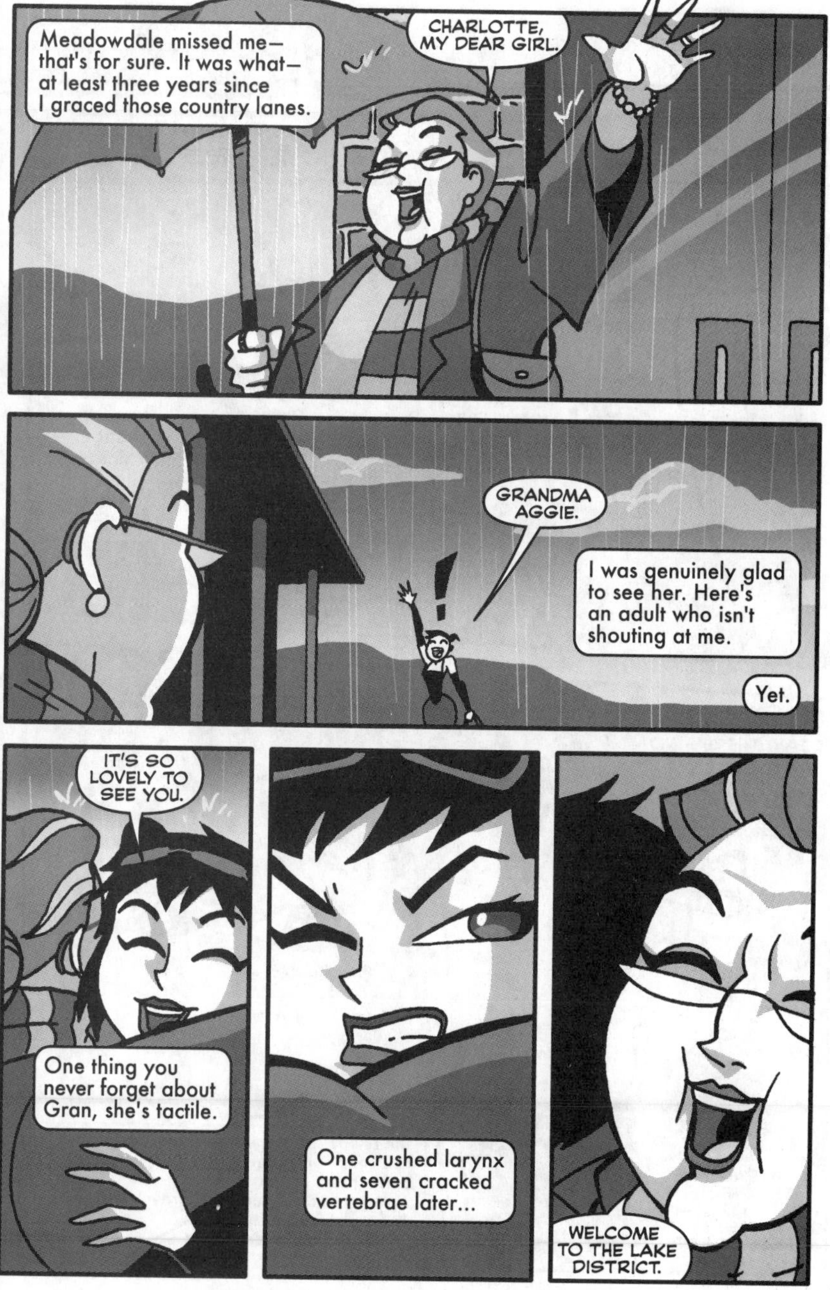
Meadowdale missed me—that's for sure. It was what—at least three years since I graced those country lanes.
CHARLOTTE, MY DEAR GIRL.
GRANDMA AGGIE.
I was genuinely glad to see her. Here's an adult who isn't shouting at me.
Yet.
IT'S SO LOVELY TO SEE YOU.
One thing you never forget about Gran, she's tactile.
One crushed larynx and seven cracked vertebrae later...
WELCOME TO THE LAKE DISTRICT.

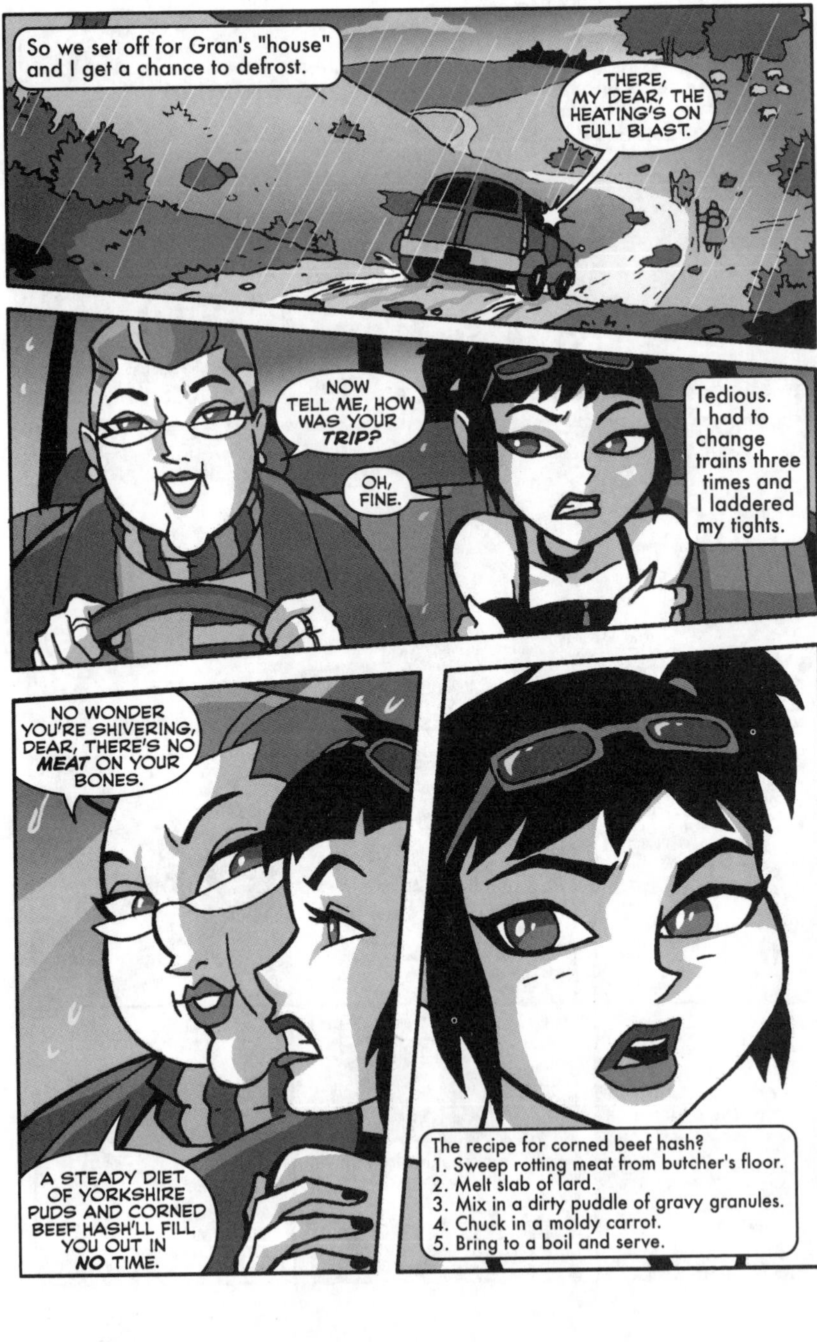
So we set off for Gran's "house" and I get a chance to defrost.
THERE, MY DEAR, THE HEATING'S ON FULL BLAST.
NOW TELL ME, HOW WAS YOUR *TRIP?*
OH, FINE.
Tedious. I had to change trains three times and I laddered my tights.
NO WONDER YOU'RE SHIVERING, DEAR, THERE'S NO *MEAT* ON YOUR BONES.
A STEADY DIET OF YORKSHIRE PUDS AND CORNED BEEF HASH'LL FILL YOU OUT IN *NO* TIME.
The recipe for corned beef hash?
1. Sweep rotting meat from butcher's floor.
2. Melt slab of lard.
3. Mix in a dirty puddle of gravy granules.
4. Chuck in a moldy carrot.
5. Bring to a boil and serve.

confessions of a
blabbermouth

MIKE CAREY   LOUISE CAREY   AARON ALEXOVICH

If there were a category in the Olympics for blabbing, Tasha Flanagan

would blab for her country. And when her mom brings home

a creepy boyfriend and his deadpan daughter, Tasha's dysfunctional

family is headed for a complete mental meltdown.

ALSO ILLUSTRATED BY AARON ALEXOVICH
■ Read on.

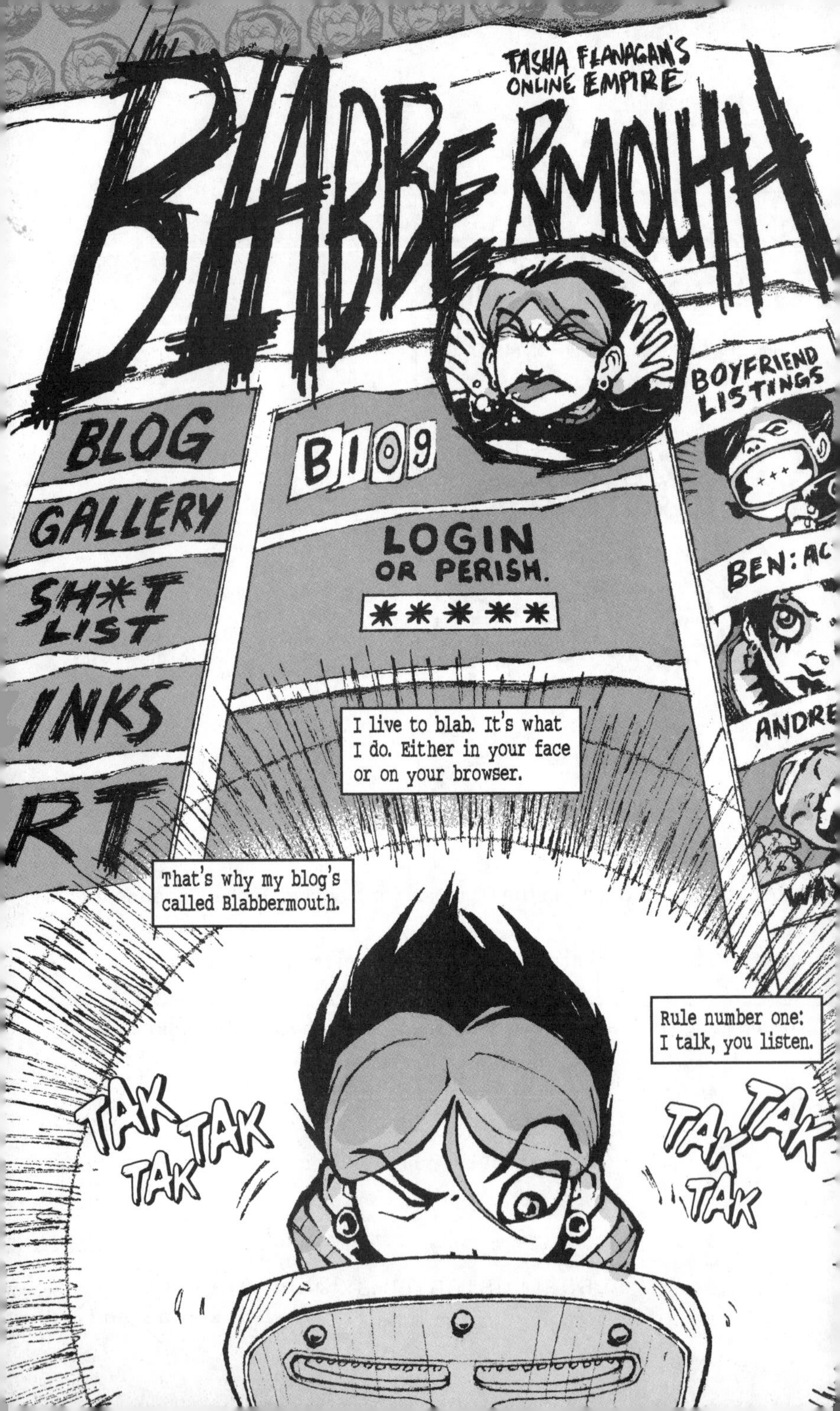
TASHA FLANAGAN'S ONLINE EMPIRE
BLABBERMOUTH
BLOG
GALLERY
SH*T LIST
INKS
RT
B109
LOGIN OR PERISH.
*****
BOYFRIEND LISTINGS
BEN: AC
ANDRE
I live to blab. It's what I do. Either in your face or on your browser.
That's why my blog's called Blabbermouth.
Rule number one: I talk, you listen.
TAK TAK TAK
TAK TAK TAK

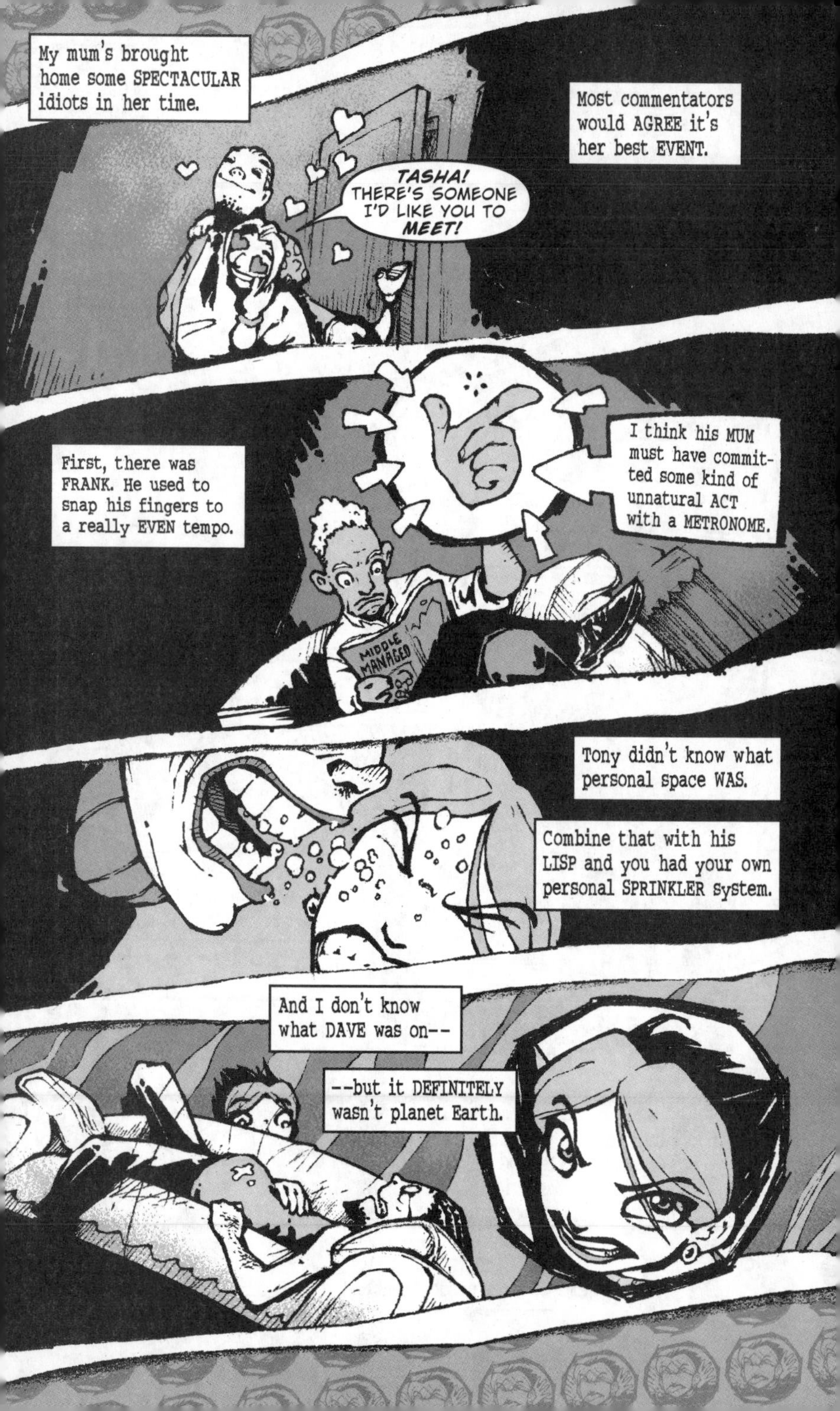
My mum's brought home some SPECTACULAR idiots in her time.
Most commentators would AGREE it's her best EVENT.
TASHA! THERE'S SOMEONE I'D LIKE YOU TO MEET!
First, there was FRANK. He used to snap his fingers to a really EVEN tempo.
I think his MUM must have commit-ted some kind of unnatural ACT with a METRONOME.
MIDDLE MANAGED
Tony didn't know what personal space WAS.
Combine that with his LISP and you had your own personal SPRINKLER system.
And I don't know what DAVE was on--
--but it DEFINITELY wasn't planet Earth.

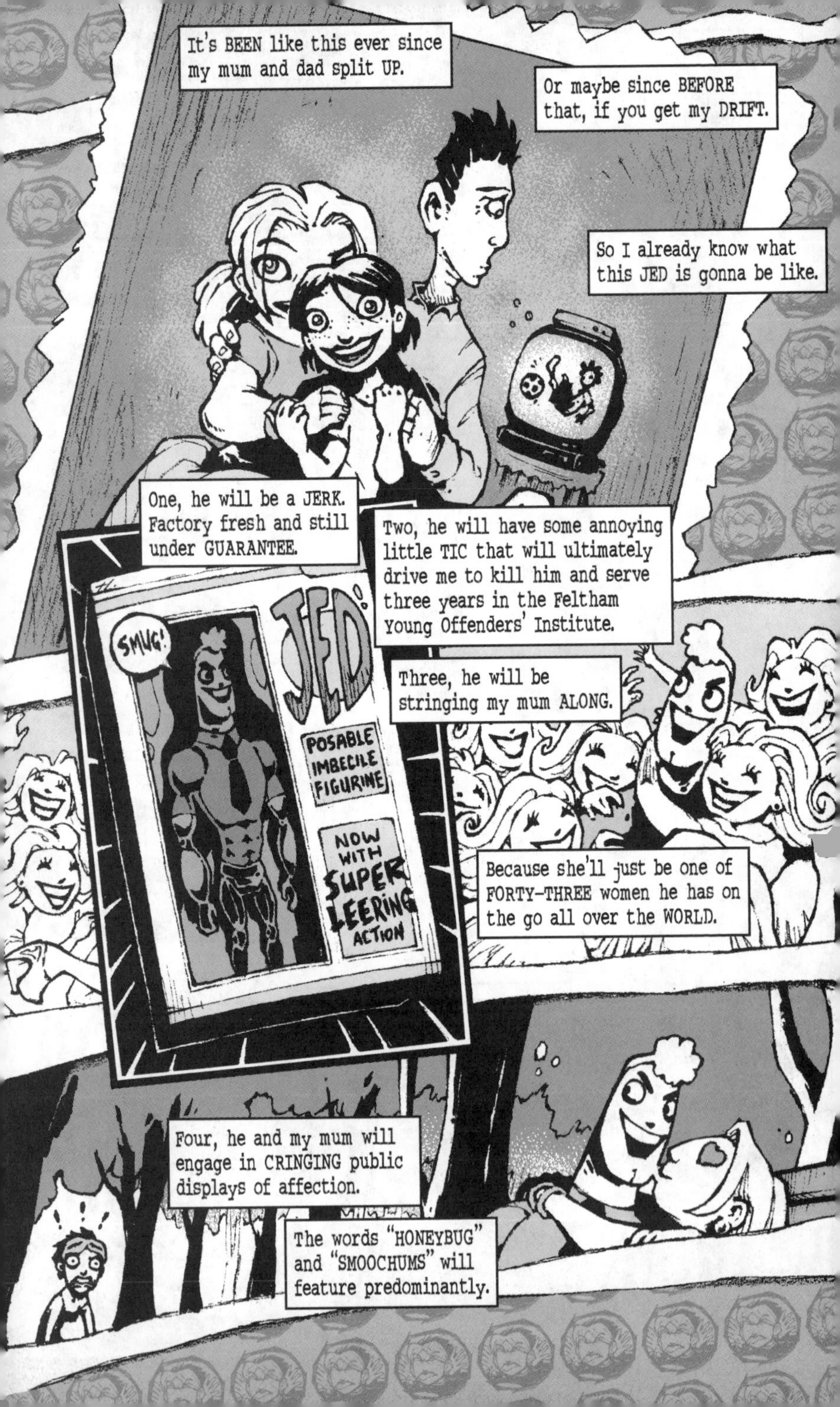
It's BEEN like this ever since my mum and dad split UP.
Or maybe since BEFORE that, if you get my DRIFT.
So I already know what this JED is gonna be like.
One, he will be a JERK. Factory fresh and still under GUARANTEE.
Two, he will have some annoying little TIC that will ultimately drive me to kill him and serve three years in the Feltham Young Offenders' Institute.
SMUG!
JED
POSABLE IMBECILE FIGURINE
NOW WITH SUPER LEERING ACTION
Three, he will be stringing my mum ALONG.
Because she'll just be one of FORTY-THREE women he has on the go all over the WORLD.
Four, he and my mum will engage in CRINGING public displays of affection.
The words "HONEYBUG" and "SMOOCHUMS" will feature predominantly.

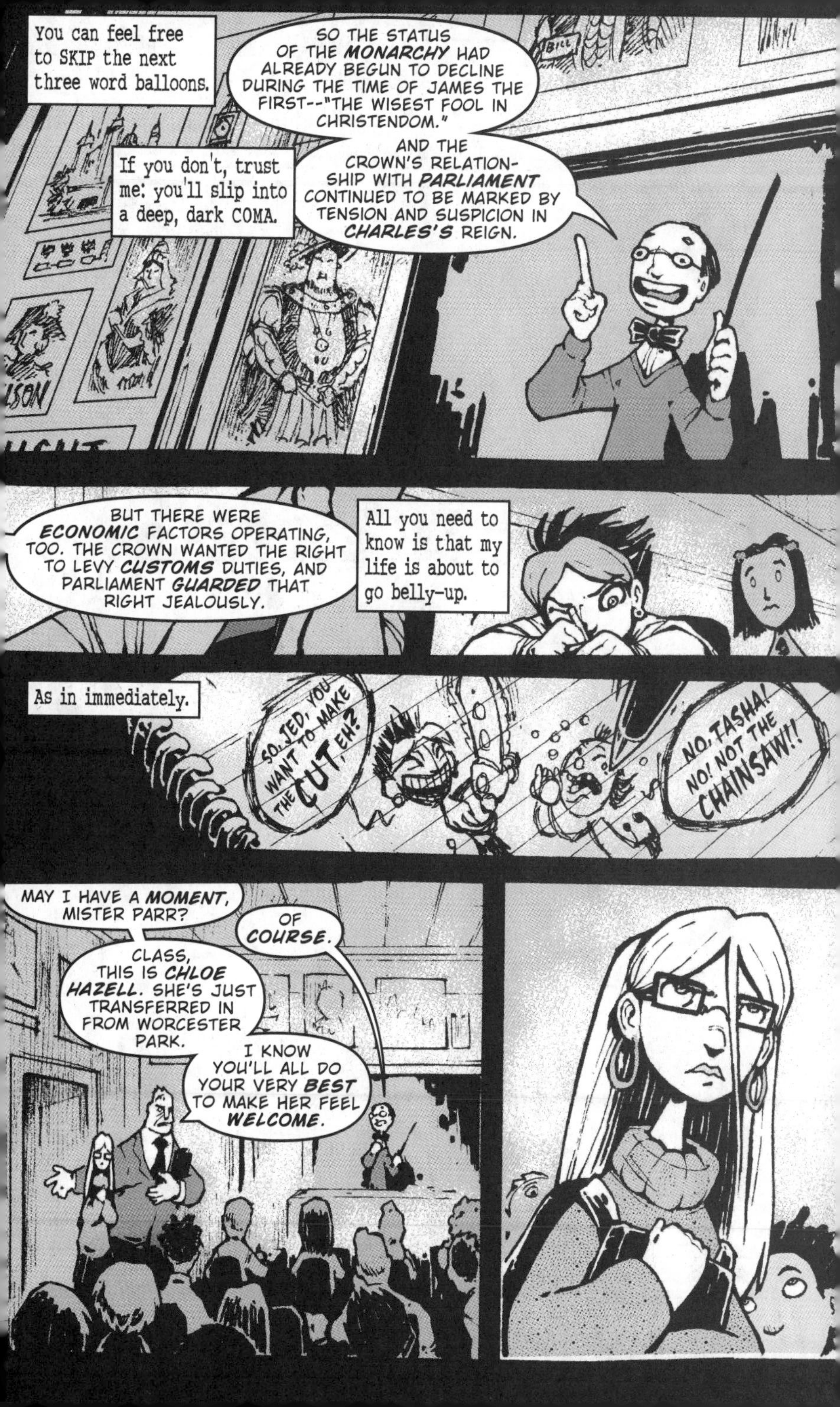

You can feel free to SKIP the next three word balloons.
SO THE STATUS OF THE MONARCHY HAD ALREADY BEGUN TO DECLINE DURING THE TIME OF JAMES THE FIRST--"THE WISEST FOOL IN CHRISTENDOM."
If you don't, trust me: you'll slip into a deep, dark COMA.
AND THE CROWN'S RELATIONSHIP WITH PARLIAMENT CONTINUED TO BE MARKED BY TENSION AND SUSPICION IN CHARLES'S REIGN.
BILL
BUT THERE WERE ECONOMIC FACTORS OPERATING, TOO. THE CROWN WANTED THE RIGHT TO LEVY CUSTOMS DUTIES, AND PARLIAMENT GUARDED THAT RIGHT JEALOUSLY.
All you need to know is that my life is about to go belly-up.
As in immediately.
SO, JED, YOU WANT TO MAKE THE CUT, EH?
NO, TASHA! NO! NOT THE CHAINSAW!!
MAY I HAVE A MOMENT, MISTER PARR?
OF COURSE.
CLASS, THIS IS CHLOE HAZELL. SHE'S JUST TRANSFERRED IN FROM WORCESTER PARK.
I KNOW YOU'LL ALL DO YOUR VERY BEST TO MAKE HER FEEL WELCOME.

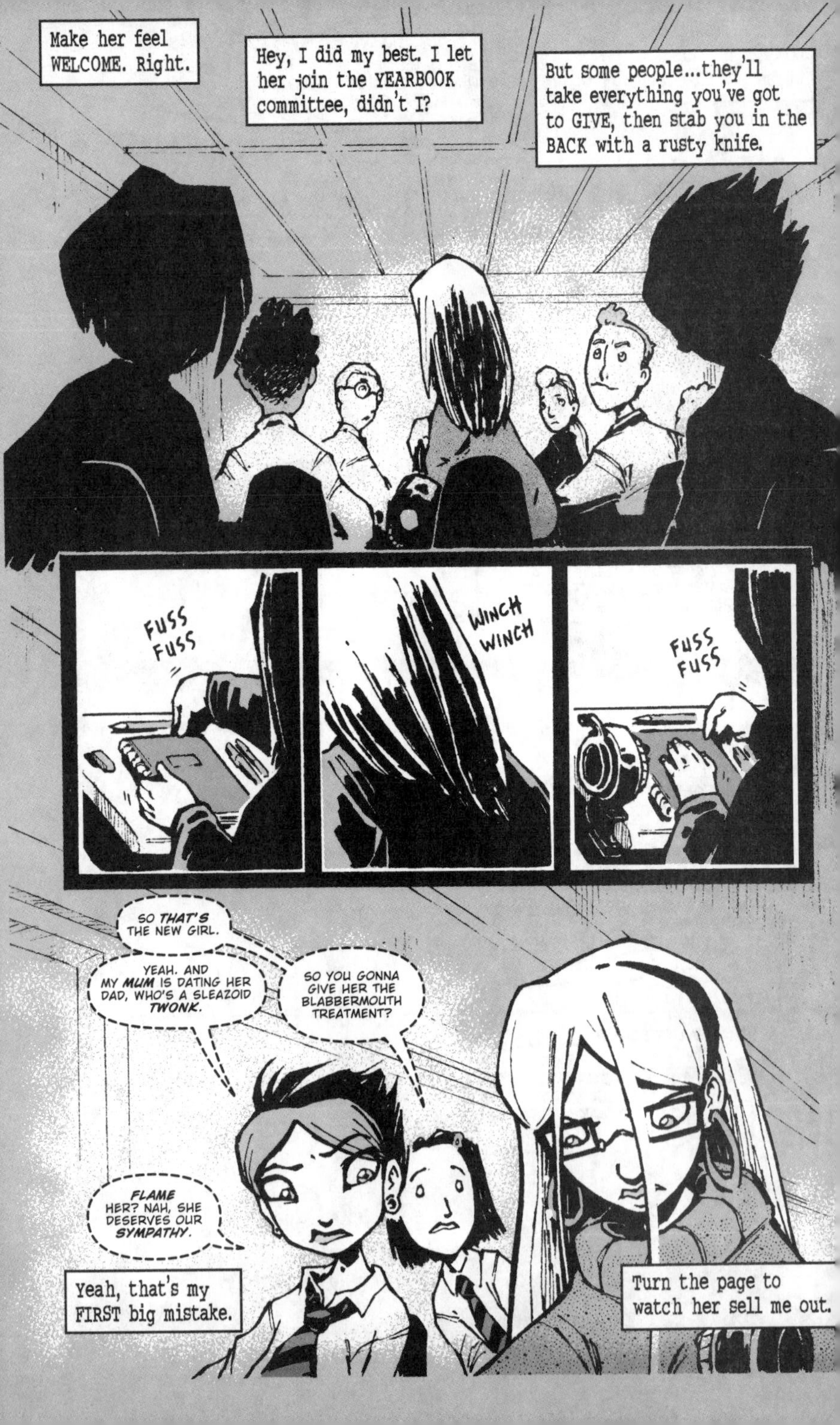

Make her feel WELCOME. Right.
Hey, I did my best. I let her join the YEARBOOK committee, didn't I?
But some people...they'll take everything you've got to GIVE, then stab you in the BACK with a rusty knife.
FUSS FUSS
WINCH WINCH
FUSS FUSS
SO *THAT'S* THE NEW GIRL.
YEAH. AND MY *MUM* IS DATING HER DAD, WHO'S A SLEAZOID *TWONK*.
SO YOU GONNA GIVE HER THE BLABBERMOUTH TREATMENT?
FLAME HER? NAH, SHE DESERVES OUR *SYMPATHY*.
Yeah, that's my FIRST big mistake.
Turn the page to watch her sell me out.

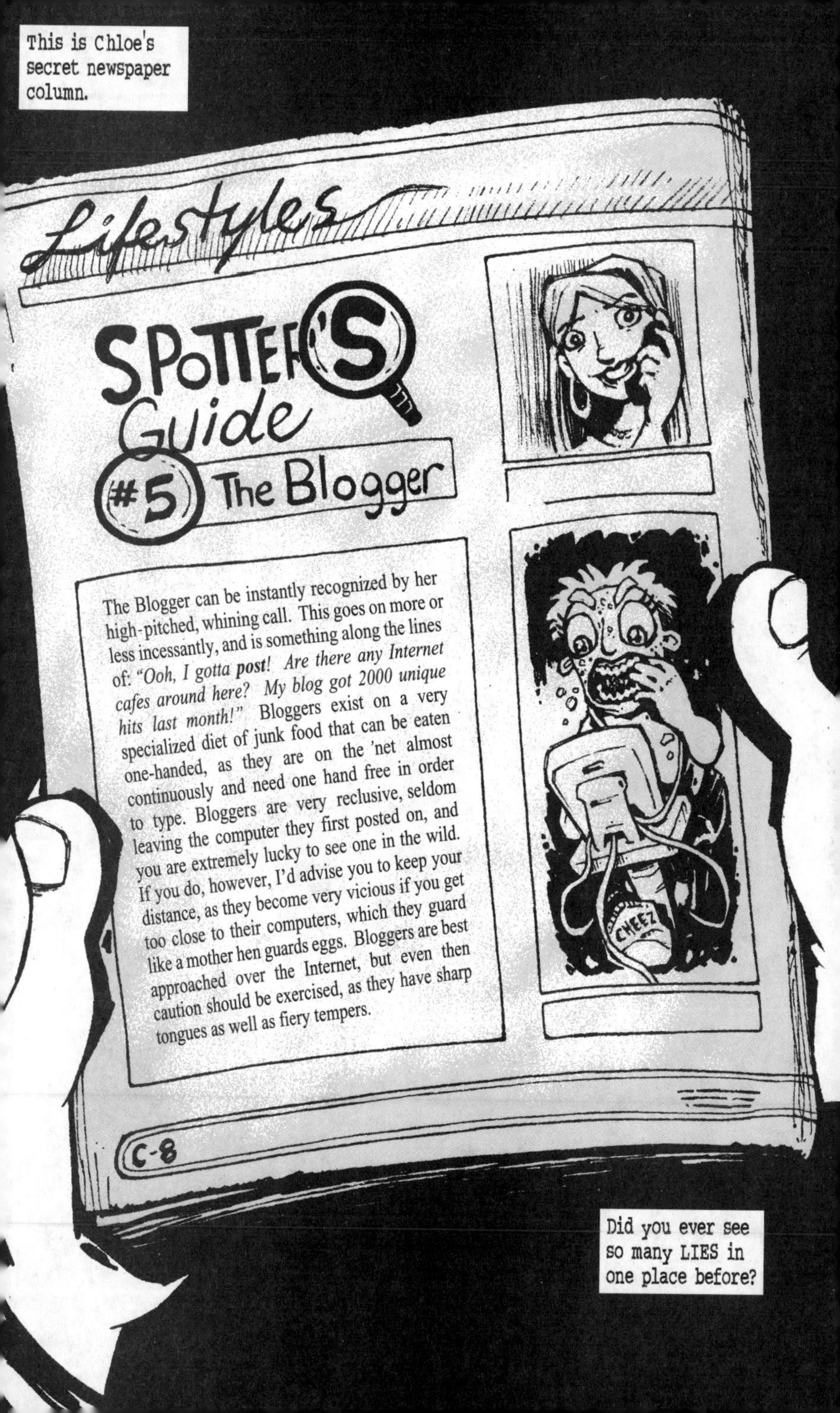
This is Chloe's secret newspaper column.
Lifestyles
SPOTTER'S Guide
#5 The Blogger
The Blogger can be instantly recognized by her high-pitched, whining call. This goes on more or less incessantly, and is something along the lines of: "Ooh, I gotta post! Are there any Internet cafes around here? My blog got 2000 unique hits last month!" Bloggers exist on a very specialized diet of junk food that can be eaten one-handed, as they are on the 'net almost continuously and need one hand free in order to type. Bloggers are very reclusive, seldom leaving the computer they first posted on, and you are extremely lucky to see one in the wild. If you do, however, I'd advise you to keep your distance, as they become very vicious if you get too close to their computers, which they guard like a mother hen guards eggs. Bloggers are best approached over the Internet, but even then caution should be exercised, as they have sharp tongues as well as fiery tempers.
CHEEZ
C-8
Did you ever see so many LIES in one place before?

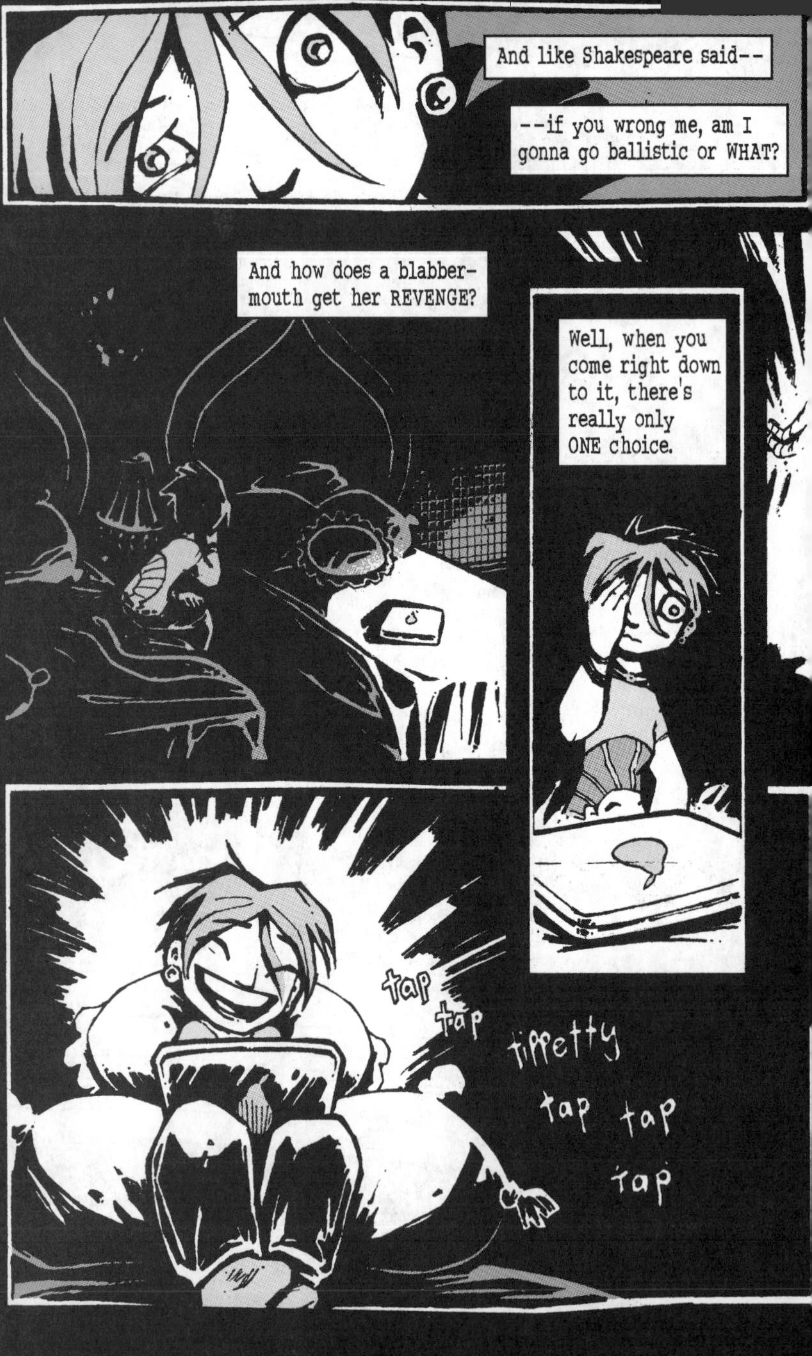
And like Shakespeare said--
--if you wrong me, am I gonna go ballistic or WHAT?
And how does a blabbermouth get her REVENGE?
Well, when you come right down to it, there's really only ONE choice.
tap
tap
tippetty
tap tap
tap

Derek Kirk Kim & Jesse Hamm

Good As Lily

What would you do if versions of yourself at ages 6, 29 and 70

suddenly show up and wreak havoc on your already

awkward existence?

■ Read on.

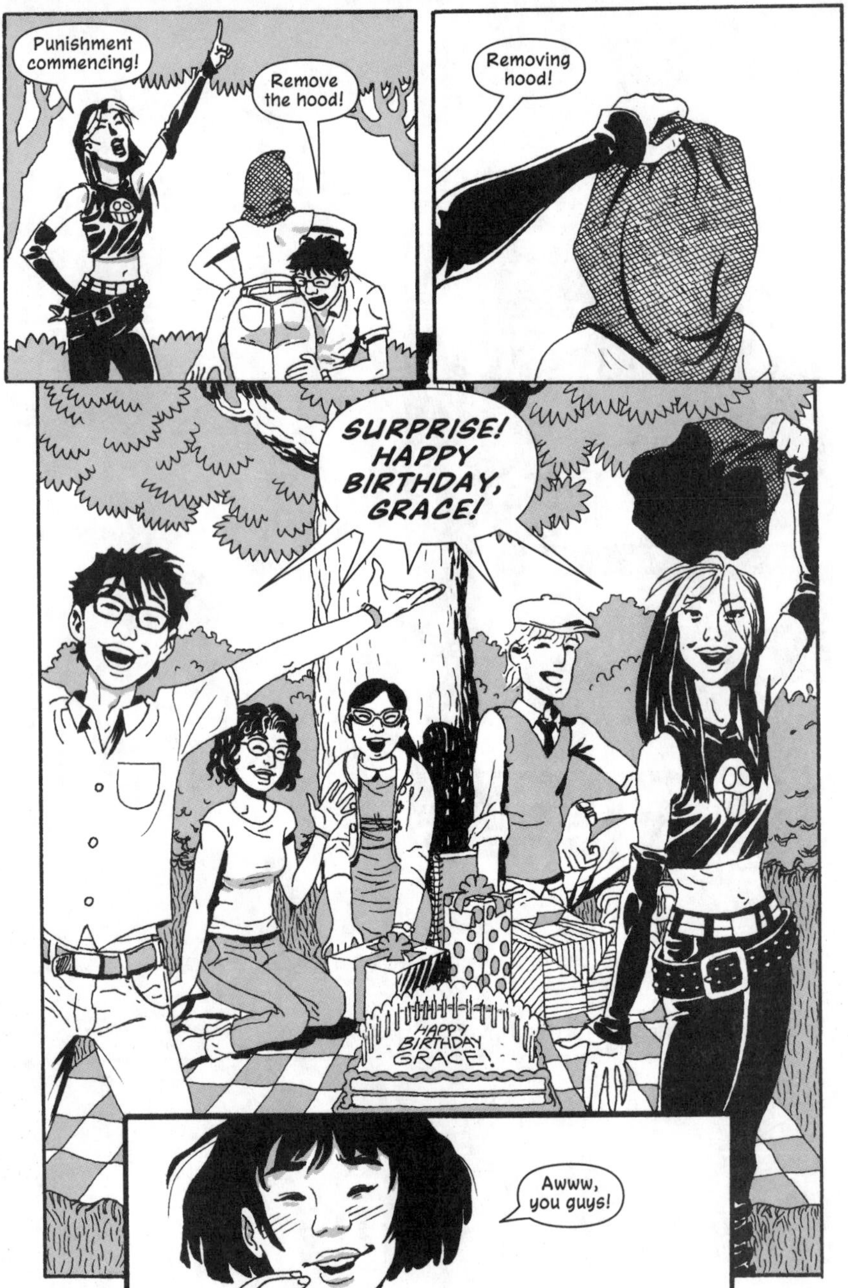
Punishment commencing!
Remove the hood!
Removing hood!
SURPRISE! HAPPY BIRTHDAY, GRACE!
HAPPY BIRTHDAY GRACE!
Awww, you guys!

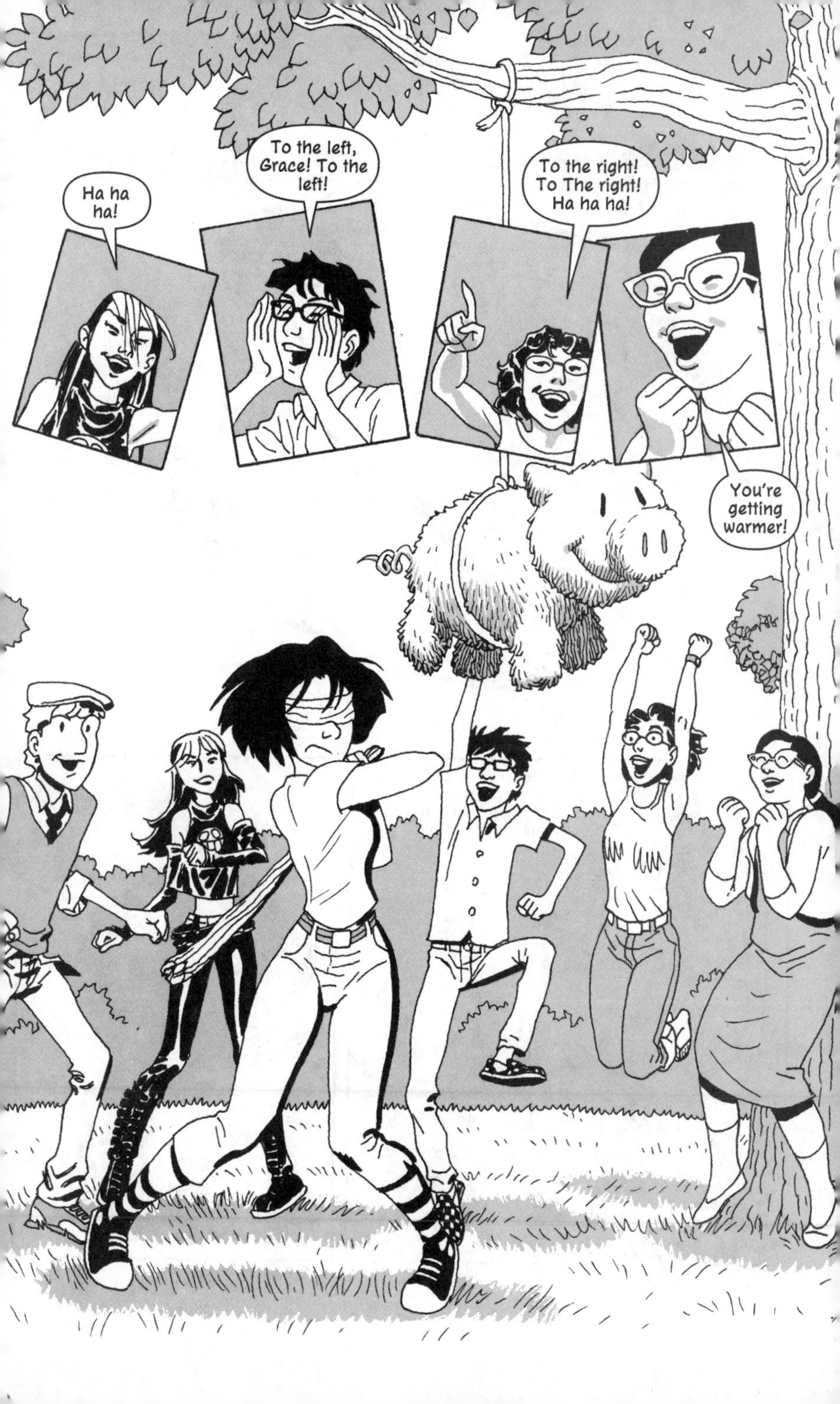
Ha ha ha!
To the left, Grace! To the left!
To the right! To The right! Ha ha ha!
You're getting warmer!

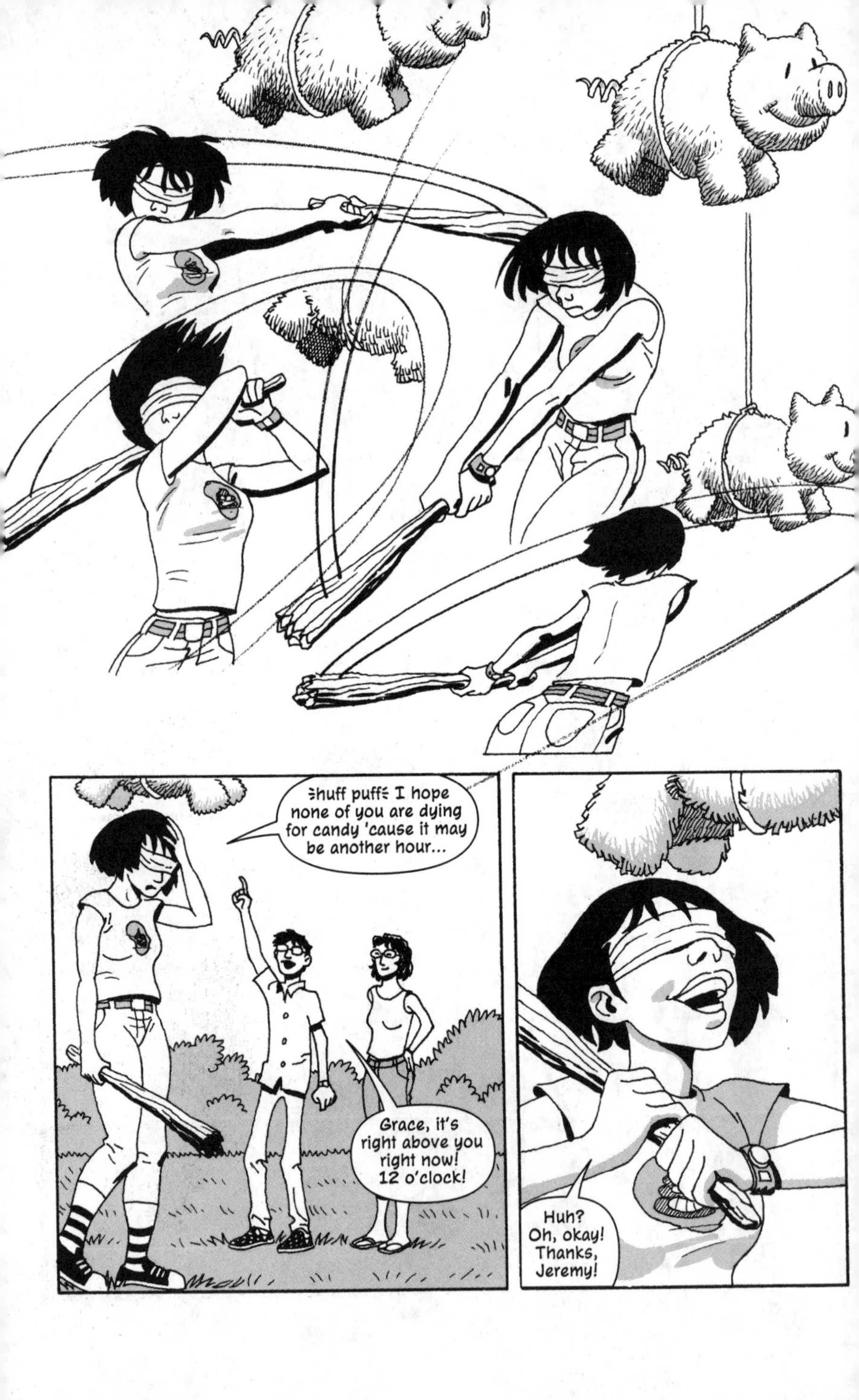

≋huff puff≋ I hope none of you are dying for candy 'cause it may be another hour...
Grace, it's right above you right now! 12 o'clock!
Huh? Oh, okay! Thanks, Jeremy!

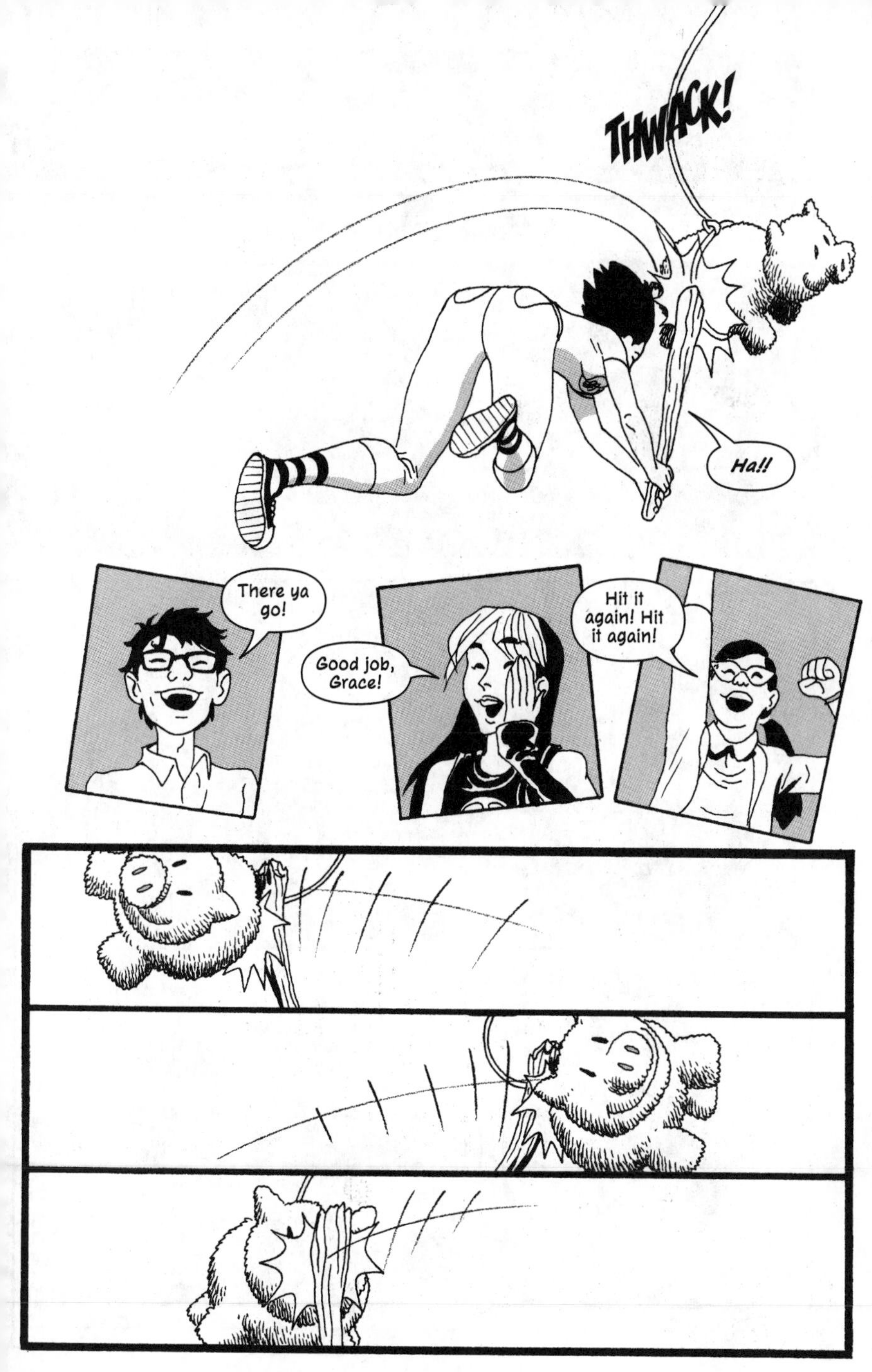
THWACK!
Ha!!
There ya go!
Good job, Grace!
Hit it again! Hit it again!

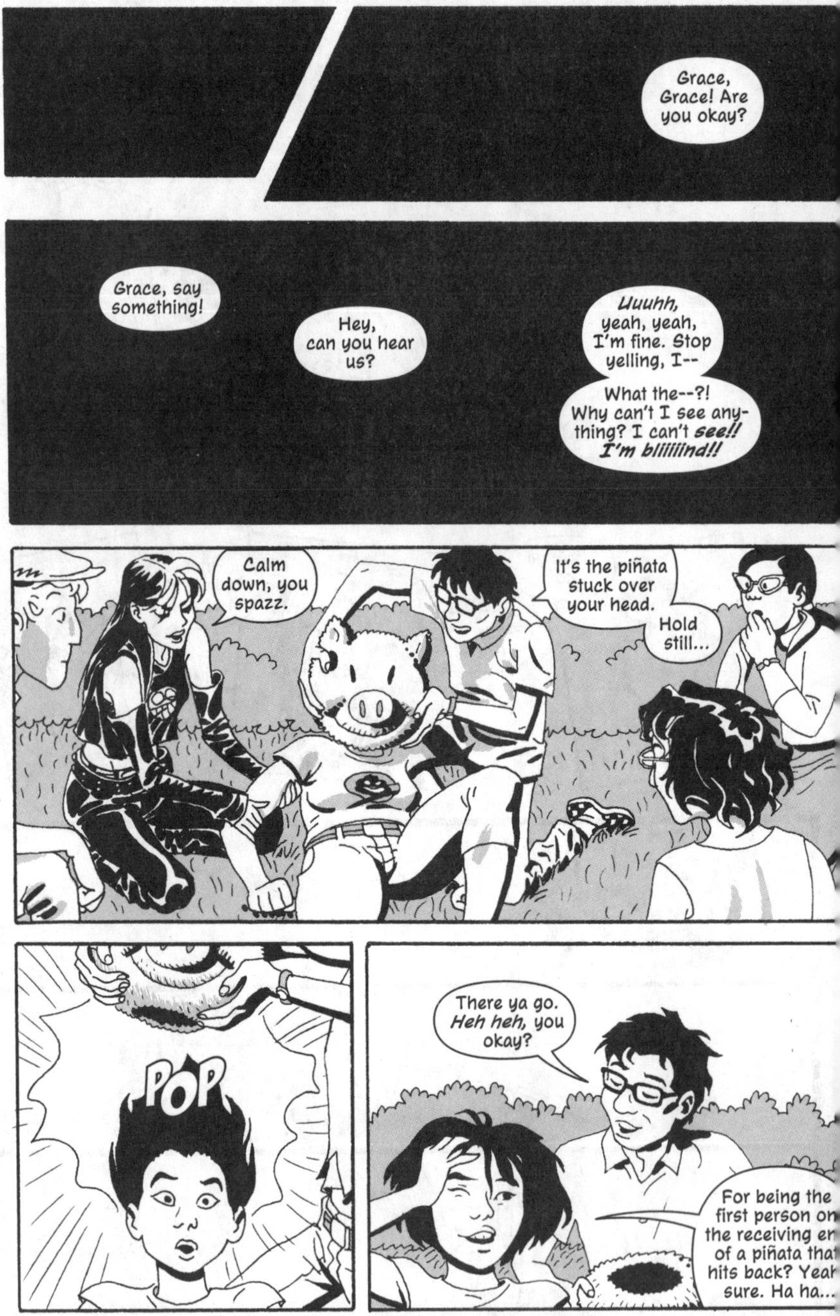

Grace, Grace! Are you okay?
Grace, say something!
Hey, can you hear us?
Uuuhh, yeah, yeah, I'm fine. Stop yelling, I--
What the--?! Why can't I see any-thing? I can't ***see!! I'm bliiiiind!!***
Calm down, you spazz.
It's the piñata stuck over your head.
Hold still...
POP
There ya go. *Heh heh,* you okay?
For being the first person on the receiving en of a piñata that hits back? Yeah sure. Ha ha...

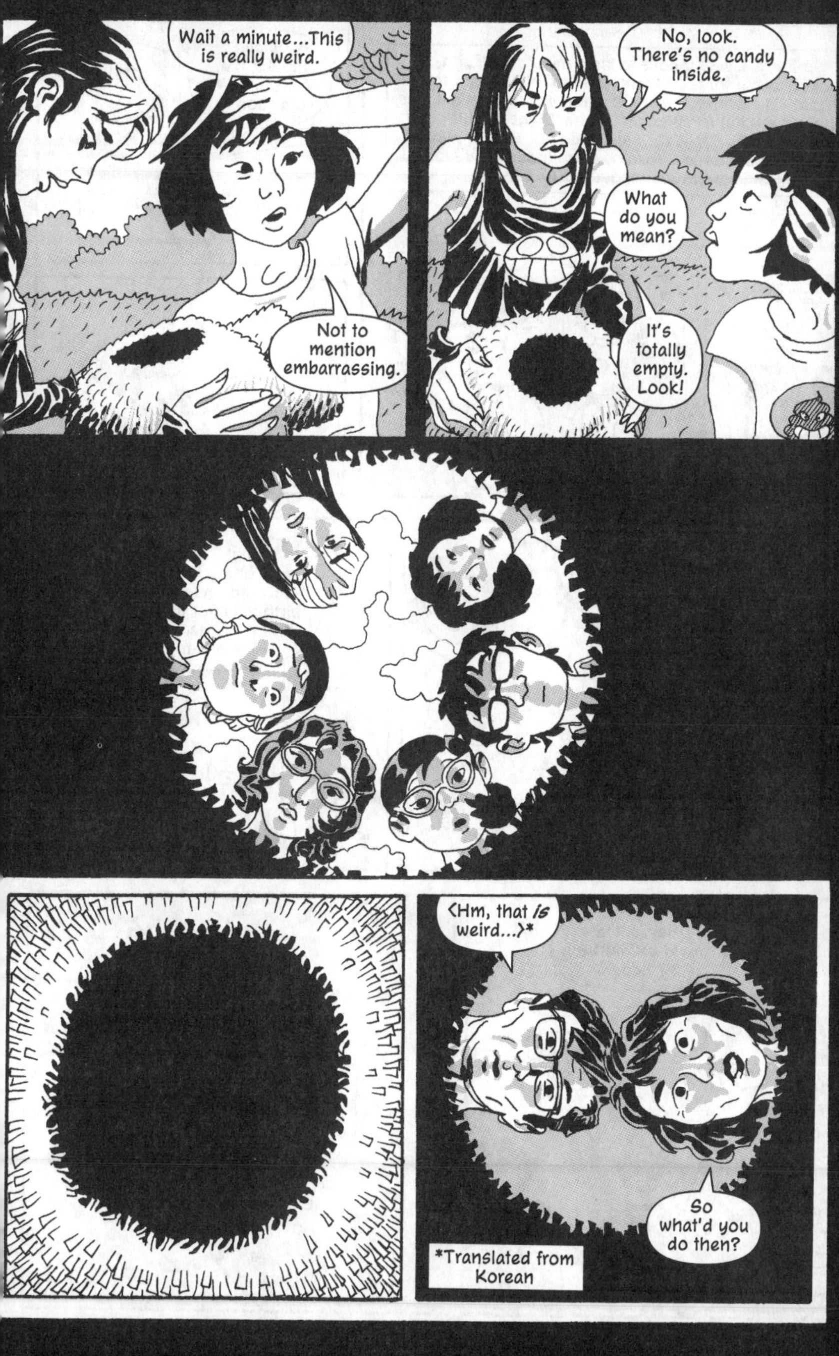

Wait a minute...This is really weird.
Not to mention embarrassing.
No, look. There's no candy inside.
What do you mean?
It's totally empty. Look!
<Hm, that *is* weird...>*
So what'd you do then?
*Translated from Korean

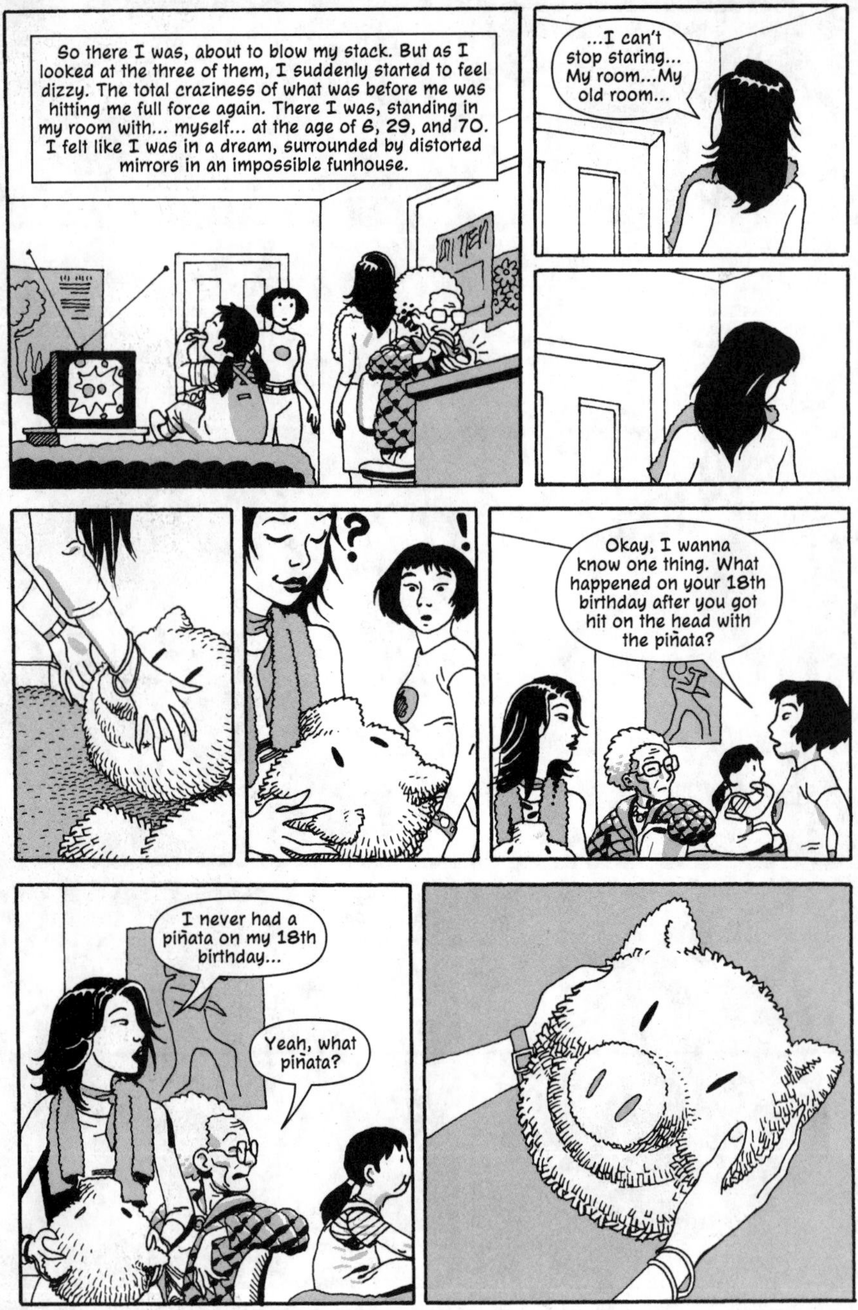
So there I was, about to blow my stack. But as I looked at the three of them, I suddenly started to feel dizzy. The total craziness of what was before me was hitting me full force again. There I was, standing in my room with... myself... at the age of 6, 29, and 70. I felt like I was in a dream, surrounded by distorted mirrors in an impossible funhouse.
...I can't stop staring... My room...My old room...
?
!
Okay, I wanna know one thing. What happened on your 18th birthday after you got hit on the head with the piñata?
I never had a piñata on my 18th birthday...
Yeah, what piñata?